Under Western Skies

Under Western Skies

. . . .

NATURE AND HISTORY IN THE AMERICAN WEST

Donald Worster

. . . .

OXFORD UNIVERSITY PRESS
New York   Oxford

Oxford University Press

Oxford New York Toronto
Delhi Bombay Calcutta Madras Karachi
Petaling Jaya Singapore Hong Kong Tokyo
Nairobi Dar es Salaam Cape Town
Melbourne Auckland

and associated companies in
Berlin Ibadan

Copyright © 1992 by Donald Worster

First published in 1992 by Oxford University Press, Inc.,
198 Madison Avenue, New York, New York 10016-4314

First issued as an Oxford University Press paperback, 1994

Oxford is a registered trademark of Oxford University Press

Library of Congress Cataloging-in-Publication Data
Worster, Donald.
Under western skies: nature and history in the
American West / Donald Worster.
p.   cm.   Includes index.
ISBN 0-19-505820-8
ISBN 0-19-508671-6 (PBK.)
1. West (U.S.) — Civilization. 2. Human ecology — West (U.S.)
3. Human geography — West (U.S.) I. Title
F591.W875 1992   978 — dc20   91-15667

10 9 8 7 6 5 4 3

Printed in the United States of America

For Wes and Dana Jackson,
and for the Land Institute
they founded

interest I have spent a lot of time reading in libraries or sitting in my study with a book in hand. But again and again my attention has wandered outdoors, as I have watched the daily history of the prairies and woods around my house write itself. Some of these essays also have a little campfire smoke in them, from a time when I was afield in the Black Hills, experiencing the place from the ground up, or in the Sierra Nevada or other places wild and tame, thinking and observing in the full, open air, as environmental historians are wont to do. Or they have some of the glare of southwestern deserts in them, or the memory of caribou walking across the summer tundra, or the sound of water coursing through an irrigation ditch in the San Joaquin Valley. The history that most excites me is like that: physical, ecological, earthy, complex as only nature can be complex. Anyone interested in the new field of environmental history, therefore, may find in these essays some likeminded fellowship, though a most imperfect, fragmentary guide to the field. There are some historians who can ignore the role of nature in our past, some who cannot. These essays are the pleasures and pains of one who cannot.

Along about the mid-1970s I found my interests as a historian swinging back west, toward the large region that begins with the Great Plains and rolls toward California. So have many others in recent years, until today the history of the American West is undergoing a thunderous reawakening, drawing attention from journalists, film-makers, novelists, and undergraduates as well as a new generation of scholars. People everywhere sense that this region is central to our nation's experience and identity, as well as unique in so many ways, and they want to know from historians why that is so and what it means. I have tried in several of these essays to engage such questions, though admittedly I have only tentative, partial answers to give. It does seem indisputably clear to me that the encounter of Americans with the western landscape has been formative and profoundly revealing. I believe too that the encounter has considerable relevance to an age that is undergoing a permanent global environmental crisis. We ride west today not so much in a traditional spirit of extravagant hopefulness or conquest but in a new, more sober awareness of the potential of tragedy and disaster we can make on this planet. These essays, therefore, represent the experience of one who has grown up in the West and has found it impossible to live too far away from it, but also one who remembers some of what we have spoiled in the West and is aware how often we have failed as a people to measure up to the place.

Some readers may wonder why I include a piece on Alaska, which by my own definition is on the periphery of the region we call the West, indeed constitutes a whole region unto itself. My justification is that I took a trip to that self-proclaimed "last frontier" while I was working on the book and could not resist the temptation to write something about that extraordinary place and its history, so little known in the Lower 48, so resonant with the western past.

I have incurred so many obligations in the course of working up these essays that I hardly know where to begin acknowledging them. All those who extended invitations to speak, who listened patiently and asked questions afterwards, who did me the honor of soliciting a contribution to some book or journal, or who gave suggestions for my work as I went along have my warmest thanks. My research assistants at Brandeis University and the University of Kansas deserve special notice and praise: Brian Donahue, Ruth Friedman, Kerstin Gorham, Lynn Hickman, and Paul Salstrom. In support of my research on many of these topics, Bea Meyerhoff and the University of Kansas have been generous and essential. I owe another pat on the back to my agent, Gerry McCauley, whose advice and friendship have done me so much good. Sheldon Meyer of Oxford University Press has been, as always, enthusiastic and supportive; and Stephanie Sakson-Ford has done a superb job of editing the manuscript. My wife Bev has, as always, been a wise critic and a generous helpmeet, patient, supportive, and astonishingly agreeable. Among the many fine colleague-teachers I have had in environmental history, I owe special debts to William Cronon, Alfred Crosby, Carolyn Merchant, Stephen Pyne, and Richard White; the exchanges we have had may not always have led to a consensus of views, but they have improved my own understanding of the field enormously. Among my associates in western history, Patricia Nelson Limerick has been an inspiring, amusing comrade-in-arms; I only wish these essays had as much of her wit in them as they do her ideas. Finally, the dedication of this book barely indicates the extent of a large personal debt I owe to some fellow Kansans, a small but wonderful group of visionaries who have made this a better state to come home to.

Rock Creek, Kansas   D.W.
November 1991

Contents

Under Western Skies

1

Beyond the Agrarian Myth

Coming down the Santa Fe Trail in the summer of 1831, a young merchant named Josiah Gregg brought a vision of the American West that must have seemed the only one there would ever be.* Raddled by years of consumption, he was rapidly restored by the bracing air and outdoor life. By the time he reached the vicinity of Council Grove, Kansas, he was able to ride a horse again, and it was about then that he was ready to raise his eyes to the surrounding countryside and contemplate its future. "All who have traversed these delightful regions," he writes in his book *The Commerce of the Prairies*, "look forward to the day when the Indian title to the land shall be extinguished and flourishing white settlements dispel the gloom which at present prevails over this uninhabited region."[1] That may seem a strange sentiment for a man whose life in the white settlements had been so sickly, but, feeling better the farther he got from home, Gregg became positively eager to forward the cause of United States expansion. Like so many other merchants and travelers of his day, all taking trails westward in search of profit or adventure, he expected to find more than the shabby little foreign town of Santa Fe lying at the end of his journey. The prospect of a bigger and broader

*Originally, this essay was given as the opening address to the conference "Trails: Toward a New Western History," Santa Fe, New Mexico, September 1989, and has recently been published in the collection, *Trails: Toward a New Western History,* edited by Patricia Nelson Limerick, Charles Rankin, and Clyde A. Milner III (Lawrence: Univ. Press of Kansas, 1991).

3

America would be there too, of a nation extending the blessings of its free institutions to the benighted Mexican and Indian peoples that it would conquer and subdue.

In his brief book on Gregg, the novelist Paul Horgan faulted him for being at time a humorless, cranky misanthrope and for showing little sympathy toward the Hispanic and Catholic civilization he encountered in the Southwest. But Horgan also admired in Gregg's narrative the grand redeeming spirit of the western frontier—the work of a "great conquest" and the expansion of personal freedom that it was supposed to make possible.[2] I, on the other hand, representing a new generation of western historians, find it harder to take such a favorable view of Gregg's vision of conquest. That almost transcendental faith in American growth seems far from being justified by the subsequent facts of history. At the same time, Gregg's misanthropy has come to seem a little more excusable with time, and I often nod in agreement at his acerbic comments on his fellow humans. In this reversal of assessment I am not alone. A growing number of citizens has become skeptical of where some of our national trails and ambitions have led.

For instance, a contemporary traveler to the West, Ian Frazier of New York City, expresses well our disenchanted mood toward the West, though he loves the places as we all do. In his recent book *Great Plains*, Frazier recalls his rambles of discovery up and down the landscape but can summon none of the firm linear confidence of Josiah Gregg. His trail jumps disjointedly from Glacier National Park in Montana to the black pioneer settlement of Nicodemus, Kansas, to the home of Lawrence Welk in North Dakota, and then to back to western Kansas and the murdered Clutter family. Along the way he is sometimes filled with joy by the region's vistas—the "still empty land beyond newsstands and malls and velvet restaurant ropes"—but it is a happiness edged with regret for the defeat of the Indian peoples, who finally for him are the lost essence of the land. The plains "are the place where Crazy Horse will always remain uncaptured. They are the lodge of Crazy Horse." And then after so many miles on the road, so many roadside markers, so many sodbusters' tales, so many fields of cattle, dust, sorghum, finding himself at last standing before an ominous MX missile site in Montana, Frazier writes what he calls the "punch line of our two hundred years on the Great Plains" (actually more of a punch paragraph):

[W]e trap out the beaver, subtract the Mandan, infect the Blackfeet and the Hidatsa and the Assiniboin, overdose the Arikara; call the land a desert and hurry across it to get to California and Oregon; suck up the buffalo, bones and

all; kill off nations of elk and wolves and cranes and prairie chickens and prairie
dogs; dig up the gold and rebury it in vaults somewhere else; ruin the Sioux and
Cheyenne and Arapaho and Crow and Kiowa and Comanche; kill Crazy Horse,
kill Sitting Bull; harvest wave after wave of immigrants' dreams and send the
wised-up dreamers on their way; plow the topsoil until it blows to the ocean;
ship out the wheat, ship out the cattle, dig up the earth itself and burn it in
power plants and send the power down the line; dismiss the small farmers,
empty the little towns; drill the oil and natural gas and pipe it away; dry up the
rivers and springs, deep-drill for irrigation water as the aquifer retreats. And
in return we condense unimaginable amounts of treasure into weapons buried
beneath the land which so much treasure came from—weapons for which our
best hope might be that we will someday take them apart and throw them away,
and for which our next-best hope certainly is that they remain humming away
under the prairie, absorbing fear and maintenance, unused, forever.[3]

And with that Frazier's trail of adventure abruptly ends: not at the
enlightened rule of peace, prosperity, reason, and liberty that Gregg envisioned but at the nightmare of institutionalized madness—the doctrine
of Mutually Assured Destruction preached by today's military strate-
gists, implanted in a West that now stands at the dead center of modern
warfare. Of course, there are other roads and destinies in this region too,
including more positive and optimistic ones; but Frazier feels compelled
to end his journey with a dark vision of a people imprisoned in their own
aggressive fear. It is a conclusion that other writers, including historians,
share and that the public is gradually coming to terms with.

A century and a half after Josiah Gregg's first exhilarating trip along a
barely rutted path, the West looks unlike anything he could have fore-
seen. In the process of becoming what it is, the region has emerged out of
the old clouds of myth and romance, and now seems for the first time honestly revealed. Today it looks a little smaller than it once did, though it
is still notable for its amplitude of space and light. Now and then it can
stir up the old indeterminate hopefulness in newcomers, but generally
what people want out of the region is more practical and limited—a job,
a home, a vacation. Liberty has turned out to be an ambiguous achievement, and in too many cases and mouths is only a hollow phrase; westerners are more aware of that fact than ever before. Clearly, the grandiose
history that white Americans once thought they were making out here in
this land beyond the Mississippi River has come apart and does not com-
pel belief as it once did. I think I know how that happened and want to
claim some small credit for historians. For this region that was once so
lost in dreams and idealization, we have been creating a new history,
clear-eyed, demythologized, and critical. We have been rewriting the story

from page one and watching it be accepted. That has been a slow, hard-won victory, and I think it is time we acknowledged the achievement.

The first bonafide revisionist, in a sense the prophet of a new western history, was Henry Nash Smith, for it was he who first told us what was wrong with the old history and dared to call it myth. That was in 1950 with the publication of *Virgin Land*. By myth Smith referred to the grand archetypal stories of heroic origins and events that all people create for themselves, a kind of folk history written by anonymous minds. Myths tell how things came to be, how they are and why they are, and if the real world does not quite correspond to them, it may come closer to the ideal as time goes on; myths can mightily affect the course of events. In later years Smith admitted he had been a little too quick to dismiss myth as simple falsehood when in truth popular belief and historical reality are joined together in a continuous dialogue, moving back and forth in a halting, jerky interplay. Still, it must be added that there is a lot of falsity in any myth, not excepting the one about the West, and such falsity can lead people into difficult, even tragic, situations.

We have had many myths about the West but the principal one was a story about a simple, rural people coming into a western country—an ordinary people moving into an extraordinary land, as Robert Athearn has put it—and creating there a peaceful, productive life.[4] In this great, good place human nature was supposed to rise out of its old turpitude and depravity to a new dignity: sturdy yeoman farmers would have here the chance to live rationally and quietly, free of all contaminating influences. By the millions they would find homes in the undeveloped vastness stretching beyond the settlements, bringing life to the land and turning it into the garden of the world. Never mind that much blood would have to be shed first to drive out the natives; the blood would all be on others' hands, and the farmers would be clean, decent folk dwelling in righteousness.

From the beginning the agrarian myth was filled with all the unresolved contradictions of innocence. Civilization was to find in this region its next, higher incarnation, and in that expectation the myth of the garden, writes Smith, "affirmed a doctrine of progress, of gigantic economic development." On the other hand, the West was supposed to offer a place to escape civilization; the myth implied "a distrust of the outcome of progress in urbanization and civilization."[5] Logic says you cannot have it both ways, physics that you cannot go forward and backward in the same moment. Yet the agrarian myth was able to hold both possibilities together because it did not follow the rules of logical discourse; instead, it was a song, a dream, a fantasy that captured all the ambivalence in a people about their past and future. Moreover, if your optimism is strong enough, you will believe that what is impossible for logic and physics is possible for you. No region settled in modern time has had so much optimism in its eyes as the West, an optimism that was all but blinding.

What people could not see was, in Smith's words, any possibility of "radical defect or principle of evil" in their garden. They knew there was plenty of evil in the world but supposed that it had all been left behind. And the people left behind were "by implication unfortunate or wicked." "This suggestion," Smith goes on,

> was strengthened by the tendency to account for any evil which threatened the garden empire by ascribing it to alien intrusion. Since evil could not conceivably originate within the walls of the garden, it must by logical necessity come from without, and the normal strategy of defense was to build the walls higher and stop the cracks in them.[6]

The perfect society growing up in the West would be free of all the problems found in the East or Europe: poverty, racial and class divisions, anger and dissent, bitter, intense conflict of the kind that had split the South from the North, that had pitted France against Germany, that had more or less been humankind's lot since the Fall in the original garden. This flawless West must be kept in precious isolation, removed from the contaminations of history and the world community.

One of Smith's most important insights was that the frontier thesis of Frederick Jackson Turner sprang directly out of the agrarian myth.[7] The first historian to undertake serious study of the westward movement, Turner believed all the way down that the old story was literally true. Returning to the wilderness men could be restored to the innocence of their youth, sloughing off the blemishes of age. He handed on his faith to his disciples, and so western history was born. From the outset it was almost an oxymoron: "western" and "history" were contradictory terms. What kind of history could be written about a people who had turned their back on time? Certainly, it could not be a history that looked anything like that of the Old World; therefore, its historians would not have to pay any attention to that irrelevant experience. They would not have to pass foreign language exams, read works from abroad, or keep up with the Paris savants. They were excused from examining radical defects in the West, for none was to be found there.

It took a detached observer from Columbia University, Richard Hofstadter, to see what it was that eventually doomed Turner and his followers to national irrelevance: Turner was not "a critic of the human scene." He often allowed his strong patriotic impulses to overrule his brain. He lacked the "intellectual passion" of a critic, sharpening his mind on the problems of his society. Gentle and humane in his personal relations, he had no capacity to see the shameful side of the westward movement: "riotous land speculation, vigilantism, the ruthless despoiling of the continent, the arrogance of American expansionism, the pathetic tale of the Indians, anti-Mexican and anti-Chinese nativism, the crudeness, even the near-savagery, to which men were reduced on some portions of the frontier."[8] Such matters did not engage Turner's intelligence, and he could not fathom why anyone would want to investigate them or would feel anguish about them. In being so evasive he was not really lying about the past as much as he was omitting whatever interfered with what he regarded as the greater truth, the genesis of a free people. The twentieth century has not dealt kindly with Turner's reputation, and the reason has more to do with the man's lack of critical acuity than of hard evidence for his theories. As Hostadter writes, "it is the blandness of his nationalism that most stands out, as it is the blandness of such social criticism as he attempted, the blandness indeed of his mind as a whole."[9]

The generation of western historians who were contemporaries of Henry Nash Smith and Richard Hofstadter, men and women who came of age in the 1950s and '60s, began to lay the foundations for a different, more academic style of regional history. They organized graduate seminars in which they trained hundreds of Ph.D.s in the field. They sent them into the archives—to the "sources," they said with solemn dignity—and taught them to collect data and make footnotes. They launched an industry of monographs. In October 1961, leaders of that generation came together in Santa Fe, New Mexico, to revive western studies in the wake of Turner's fall from authority; following that meeting they established the Western History Association and began publishing a scholarly journal, the *Western Historical Quarterly*. When those founders gathered around the banquet table, heads still bowed dutifully at the name of Frederick Jackson Turner, and a few still crossed themselves in reverence. The westward course of empire school still had its spokesmen in Ray Allen Billington and other frontier scholars. But for all those vestiges of piety historians slowly began to conceive the West in post-Turnerian terms.

For the first time the West took on a clear, concrete physical shape, essentially the area stretching from the Great Plains states to the Pacific Coast. But though they acknowledged that the West was an actual place, not that vague mythical landscape of pioneering Turner had in mind, postwar historians tended to downplay the idea that there was anything radical or distinctive about it. The story of their West was primarily the story of American economic enterprise written over and over again in new terrain—written in larger letters each time, written frequently with a heroic hand, but above all written in familiar economic language. The key words for this postwar generation remained the standard national clichés of "expansion," "development," and "growth": growth in western transportation, growth in investment, growth in population, growth in statehood, growth toward an urban civilization.[10]

Growth had indeed been a prominent idea in the settlement of the West, and that idea was, by any cool, rational analysis, incompatible with backward-looking agrarian fantasies. The postwar generation faced up to that contradiction and threw the old mythic agrarianism out the window. Far from representing an escape from history, a place for idealists and romantics, they insisted that the West was urban and progressive to its core. By all the indices of economic success, it began far behind the rest of the nation and long had to suffer as a mere colony of the East; nonetheless, it ran hard to catch up and become one with modern America. Thus, the western story appeared to be not one of pioneers turning their back on a spoiled past but one of competitive, conformist drives to be in the national mainstream.

In reaction against Turner's theme of a return to a primitive time, the postwar generation of historians, led by scholars such as Earl Pomeroy and Gerald Nash, discovered the twentieth century. The West did not suddenly end in 1890, with the passing of the frontier, they declared, but was at that point only beginning its ascent to prominence. With the passing of the brief pioneer era, it entered into a new, open-ended period of expanding technology and enterprise that had no limits in sight. Historians were impressed by millions of new migrants coming into the region, and it was their experience—their cities, work, leisure, and politics, their conflicts with and sources of capital in the East, their relations with the federal government, and especially their search for a modern affluence—that increasingly came to dominate historical research. The legendary man on horseback, fighting against a horde of menacing savages, the plowman toiling alone beneath a prodigious sky, all but faded away in this nonagrarian, professionalized, heavily footnoted, technology-centered, city-based redefinition of the region's past.

That is not to say there was no mythic element left in the postwar generation's writing. The old agrarian fantasy may have lost its hold, but there endured among many that old "doctrine of progress, of gigantic economic development" that Smith also identified as part of western mythology. We might call it the mythic world of the Chamber of Commerce, for whom the West will be an unfinished frontier until it is one with Hoboken, New Jersey, until we Americans will have written a saga of industrial conquest from sea to shining sea. Through the 1950s and '60s not a few western historians acted as though they were charter members of the Chamber, and their books and articles could almost have been introductions to company reports or state tourist brochures trumpeting the arrival of a "New West."

One may, of course, find countless things to congratulate in the region, but is it the job of the historian to shout them up, to act as the Merv Griffin of the western game show? After all, there are plenty of well-funded agencies charged with that task. What the boosters will not do, and what the historian alone is in a position to do, is to examine those radical defects of society Hofstadter talked about. For a long time, even after it had left Turner behind, the academic history of the West did not make that examination. There was little interest in dwelling on the dark, shameful aspects of the region's past. Graduate students were not expected to emerge from their seminars with a critical perspective; on the contrary, they were commonly taught to be positive and hopeful, to believe in the essential goodness of their institutions, to avoid any expressions of radical discontent, and dutifully they did so. In that moral complacency, if not in all their theories, they remained true to the Turnerian spirit, and the history they wrote remained an exercise in blandness. While the rest of the world's historians were facing up to the horrors of the Holocaust, the infamy of southern slavery, the satanic mills of global industrialization, western historians continued to wear a cheerful face. Terrible things had happened elsewhere, they knew, but on this happier side of the happy North American continent one could find only a little fraud and corruption in the land laws, only a few third-rate senators to decry, but no great evils to write about. A sense of tragedy had not yet made its way west.

One of the most important books produced by the postwar generation illustrates my point clearly: Gerald Nash's *The American West Transformed: The Impact of the Second World War.* No one before him had demonstrated so compellingly the scope and promise of twentieth-century regional history. No one had traced the emergence of the New West of urban, industrial enterprise in more enthusiastic detail. And certainly no one could disagree with many of the conclusions he reached:

The American West emerged from the Second World War as a transformed region. In 1941 many westerners had feared that the expansion of the region had come to a close. The economy was stagnant, population growth had ceased, and the colonial dependence of the region on the older East pervaded most aspects of life. But by 1945 the war had wrought a startling transformation. Westerners now had visions of unlimited growth and expansion, a newly diversified economy was booming, a vast influx of population was changing the very fabric of western society, and the region had just witnessed a growth in cultural maturity which was totally unprecedented in its history. The West emerged from the war as a path-breaking self-sufficient region with unbounded optimism for its future. World War II had precipitated that transformation, and in retrospect constituted one of the major turning points in the history of the American West.[11]

Unquestionably, those words reveal a historical imagination that has gone well beyond the old frontier, Turnerian tradition, and they come from a historian who, with others of his generation, has reenvisioned the West in a fresh light. But to my mind there are a few things missing from Nash's reinterpretation of the West, and they are serious omissions. How could one, for example, write about World War II's impact and leave out the glaring fact that this region henceforth would be dominated by the military-industrial complex, that its economic health would rise and fall with the prospects of the Pentagon and the Cold War, a fact that is obvious today from San Diego's navy yards all the way to Montana's missile silos? Or how could one leave off that list of so-called achievements the doomsday shadow of the atomic bomb—the fact that the West has been forever poisoned by nuclear fallout and, since the war, has found itself sick and dying of radiation, beset by the problems of nuclear waste disposal, living in white-knuckled fear in the vicinity of such places as Rocky Flats Arsenal, Alamagordo, Los Alamos, Hanford, and the Nevada test site? Clearly, there was more to the region than we had yet been told either by Frederick Jackson Turner or by the postwar generation of Nash and others, but it would take yet another generation to see those darker facts, to discover their roots, and to give them significance.

Around the year 1970 (the year when Dee Brown published his searing polemic against the U.S. military's aggression against Indians, *Bury My Heart at Wounded Knee*) that still untold side of the western past began to find its tellers. A younger generation, shaken by the experience of Vietnam and other national disgraces—poverty, racism, environmental degradation—could not pretend that the only story that mattered in the West was one of stagecoach lines, treasure hunts, cattle brands, and wildcatters, nor for that matter aircraft plants, opera companies, bank deposits, or middle-class whites learning how to ski. What was missing was a frank, hard look at the violent, imperialistic process by which the West was wrested from its original owners and the violence by which it had been secured against the continuing claims of minorities, women, and the forces of nature. That capacity for violence may be inherent in all people, but when it showed its ugly face among the respectable and the successful it was called "progress," "growth," "the westward movement," "the march of freedom," or a dozen other euphemisms—and it was time historians called such violence and imperialism by their true names.

During the past two decades a new western history has appeared with the express purpose of confronting and understanding those radical defects in the past. This new history has tried to put the West back into the world community, with no illusions about moral uniqueness. It has also sought to restore to memory all those unsmiling aspects that Turner wanted to leave out. As a result, we are beginning to get a history that is beyond myth, beyond the traditional consciousness of the white conquerors, beyond a primitive emotional need of heroes and heroines, beyond any public role of justifying or legitimating what had happened. Here are some of the most important arguments the new history has been making.

First, the invaded and subject peoples of the West must be given a voice in the region's history. Until very recently many western historians acted as though the West had either been empty of people prior to the coming of the white race or was quickly, if bloodily, cleared of them, once and for all, so that historians had only to deal with the white point of view. They particularly ignored the continuing presence, the intrinsic value, and the political interests of the indigenous peoples, Indians and Chicanos.

All that has dramatically changed in the last few years. Today no historian who wants to be taken seriously would dare proceed without at least acknowledging the prior presence of nonwhite groups and their persistence into the present. Some historians, white and nonwhite alike, have gone even farther to attempt to rewrite the whole story from the point of view of the conquered peoples. I do not mean to say that this is the sole achievement of scholars under the age of fifty; on the contrary, many of that immediate postwar generation have also come around to a more pluralistic point of view. Gerald Nash again may serve as an example; three of the eleven chapters in his book cited above deal specifically with the experience of blacks, Spanish-speaking Americans, Indians, and Japanese-Americans, and they are chapters filled with compassion and candor. Nonetheless, it is the younger generation appearing in the 1970s and '80s who have especially made this new multicultural perspective their own. They have discovered that minorities not only have not always shared in the rising power and affluence of the West but also have in some ways thought differently about the ends of that power and affluence. As part of that reevalution, we are increasingly asked to reexamine the process by which native peoples were dispossessed in the first place, to remind ourselves of the manner in which whites went about accumulating land and resources for themselves, and to uncover the contradictions in a majority, male-dominated culture that can in the same breath trumpet the idea of its own liberty and deny other peoples the right of self-determination. Further, we have learned to pay more attention to the substantial numbers of non-native people of color who have come into the garden of agrarian myth to live alongside the European settlers, people from Africa, the Pacific Islands, and Asia, making the West in fact a far more racially diverse place than the myth ever envisioned—more diverse indeed than either the North or South has been.

So we have arrived at an important truth that was long obscured by the old mythology: the West has not at all been a place to retreat from the human community and all its conflicts. On the contrary, it has been a place where white Americans ran smack into the broader world. It has been on the forward edge of one of modern history's most exciting endeavors, the creation, in the wake of European expansion and imperialism, of the world's first multi-racial, cosmopolitan societies. That development has obviously been a terribly difficult one, plagued by racism, ethnocentrism, brutality, misunderstanding, and rage on the part of majority and minority peoples alike, but especially marred by oppression and exploitation on the part of those holding the whiphand. All the same the invention in the West of a diverse community has gone steadily forward, until today there exists in this region the potential for an enlargement of our several cultural visions that was inconceivable in the past.

A second theme in the new western history is this: The drive for the economic development of the West was often a ruthless assault on nature, and it has left behind it much death, depletion, and ruin. Astonishing as it now seems, the old agrarian myth of Turner's day suggested that the West offered an opportunity of getting back in touch with nature, of recovering good health and a sense of harmony with the nonhuman far from the shrieking disharmonies of factories, technology, urban slums, and poverty that were making life in Europe and the East a burden to the spirit. That traditional faith in the region's natural healing power endures even now in the popular mind, which tends to think of the "real West" as a place without industry or cities, as an idyll starring Robert Redford in the role of lonely trapper wandering through an awesomely beautiful wilderness. Most of California, by that selective reasoning, is not in the West, nor are the open-pit copper mines of Arizona, or the labor union halls in Idaho, or the commuters wheezing and creeping along in a Denver freeway haze. Indeed, about the only real West we have left, according to the old mythic thinking, is the state of Montana, along with Louis L'Amour's ranch in southwestern Colorado, last, fading sanctuaries where vigorous, independent men might live in the bosom of nature.

Here again truth is breaking in, driving out myth and self-deception, as we face unblinkingly the fact that from its earliest days the fate of the western region has been one of furnishing raw materials for industrialism's development; consequently, the region was from its beginning in the forefront of America's endless economic revolution. Far from being a child of nature, the West was actually given birth by modern technology and bears all the scars of that fierce gestation, like a baby born of an addict.

Agriculture was one of the first areas where this dependency on the global industrial economy appeared. Contrary to the agrarian myth, farmers in the West were some of the first agribusinessmen on the planet, and in places like the Central Valley of California (incidentally a part of the West long ignored by historians) the results of that fact in terms of labor oppression and class conflict, as well as environmental exploitation, have been open for all to see. Supporting that drive for industrial and capitalist development has been a powerful political apparatus in Washington, D.C., whose role has largely been to promote the private accumulation of money through such public investments as water projects, mining leases, and military bases. That role is manifest all over the nation, in fact throughout the global economy, but it may be the American West that best exemplifies the modern capitalistic state at work.

Historians have more or less known this fact for a long time, but until very recently they have chosen to downplay, or even disregard, its implications. They seldom undertook to write about any of the ecological disasters and nightmares that have occurred in the West, the pillaging by oil companies and other energy and mining entrepreneurs of the public lands, the pollution of coastal waters and pristine desert air, the impact of big-scale irrigation on the quality and quantity of water, or the devastation of wildlife habitat by the hoofs and bellies of the fabled cattle kingdom.

To be sure, older historians did not completely ignore the devastation of the western environment that had gone on. Often they took a stand in favor of "conservation"—meaning the careful, rational, utilitarian conversion of natural resources into wealth. In that definition, however, the historians marginalized more radical environmentalists like John Muir, who had fought against such materialistic resource management; if he appeared at all in history texts, Muir was usually portrayed as an impractical mystic or an "ecofreak." Yet it is Muir who has turned out to be the most influential environmental reformer of his day, and it is his radical embrace of the nonhuman community that has gone out from the West to win a global audience.

Over the past decade or two the neglect of industrial capitalism's impact on the western environment has begun to be repaired, due to the fact that the study of the West, more than of other regions, has come to be allied with the emerging field of environmental history, an alliance that has encouraged doubts about the role of capitalism, industrialism, population growth, military expenditures, and aimless economic growth in the region—that questions whether they have really blazed a trail to progress.

A third argument in the new history is that the West has been ruled by concentrated power, though here, as in other places, power has often hidden itself behind beguiling masks. The old "frontier school" liked to believe that the West did not have much of an internal problem with power and hierarchy. Power lay in the hands of easterners, while the West was a simple democratic place, unfortunately at the mercy of those outsiders but fortunately far removed from them physically. The postwar historians continued that fantasy by somehow writing about technology, growth, and urbanization without talking much about the knot of power gathering in the West. Now we can be more frank. The West has in fact been a scene of intense struggles over power and hierarchy, not only between the races but also between classes, genders, and other groups within the white majority. The outcome of those struggles has a few distinctive features found nowhere else in America—power elites that don't quite look like those in other parts, particularly located at points of intersection between the federal land management agencies and their client groups: for example, the Bureau of Land Management and the various livestock associations, or the Bureau of Reclamation and western irrigation districts.

Though distinctive, the western elites have followed the old familiar tendency of power to become corrupt, exploitative, and cynical toward those whom it dominates. Power can also degrade itself, as it degrades others and the land, yet it commonly tries to conceal that fact by laying claim to the dominant myths and symbols of its time—in the case of the American West, by putting on cowboy boots and snap-button shirts, waving the American flag, and calling a toxic dump the land of freedom.

Perhaps the single most important, most distinguishing characteristic of the new western history is its determination not to offer cover for the powers that be—not to become subservient to them, by silence or consent. A rising generation of historians insists that it is their responsibility to

stand apart from power and think critically about it, as it is to think critically about western society as a whole, about its ideals and drives, about
the contradictions it has created, about its prospects for new identities,
goals, and values.

This may be the hardest pill of all for more traditional historians to
swallow. They may go so far as to agree that it is now time to talk seriously
about admitting nonwhites to the conversation; perhaps it is even okay to
use such hard but honest phrases as capitalism, conquest, imperialism,
and environmental destruction to talk about the West. But for Pete's
sake, they add, don't talk critically (which is to say, hostilely) about those
in power, for after all they are the great, necessary agents of progress and
development. They make possible our universities, our salaries, our
libraries, and our history and art museums. Don't knock them, and don't
get the image of being a knocker. And if you must talk critically about
power, or generally take a critical look at your society's past, don't show
much passion or bite. Don't reveal that there may be important ideals
that have been violated or argue that there are new ones we must discover;
if you do, you will be considered romantic, naive, biased, polemical, or
ungrateful. You may even become "an ideologue" (a dreaded label which
often is applied to any historian who doesn't take the dominant or official
ideology for granted). In other words, keep western history, and the West
itself, safe from controversy or radical challenge. Be sure to write in a style
that is intellectually timid, long on footnotes and bibliography but short
on original ideas, especially short on uncommon or unconventional ideas.
If you have any such ideas, keep them to yourself or cover them over with
a camouflage of dull gray prose so that no one will take them seriously.

History, insist many traditional western historians, is supposed to be
an "objective science," intent only on collecting the pure, distilled, empir-
ical truth. Nothing could be more misleading than that notion. The history of this region, if it wants to be vital and listened to, cannot be kept
isolated from public controversy, struggles over power, the search for new
moral standards, or the ongoing human debate over fundamental principles and values. Rather than claiming to be some detached laboratory
technician, the historian ought to be unabashedly and self-confidently an
intellectual whose express purpose and primary justification for being is
that he or she lives to question all received opinions, to take alternative
ideas seriously, to think as rationally as possible about them, and constantly work to demythologize the past. When historians fail to see themselves as critical intellectuals, as I believe historians of the West have
done, they become ideological in the most dangerous sense: they become
prisoners of ideology rather than masters of it.

The new western history insists that scholars must perform deliberately and thoughtfully the role of cultural analyst, even to the point of presuming now and then to be a self-appointed moral conscience of their society. While accepting membership in that society, and being sympathetic to its needs and interested in its fate, historians must also be free to act like outsiders, as all intellectuals do, free to transcend the common pieties of their region and explore freely the larger world of ideas.

In order to perform effectively this complex role and be true to their role as intellectuals, western historians must study and learn from other peoples, trying, for example, to look at the past through the eyes of an American Indian. Even more radically, they must try to examine human behavior from a nonhuman perspective—to look, as it were, through the eyes of the rest of nature. That is often an unpopular stance to take, for the public does not find it easy to tolerate what may seem to be a betrayal of its interests. White intellectuals seem especially disloyal when they take the side of nonwhite minorities, minorities who can be as outraged as the majority by any criticism. Most minority history is still where Frederick Jackson Turner's history was in 1893; it is a celebration of "my people," a record of what "we" have accomplished, a lament for how "we" have been neglected or oppressed or unappreciated. Eventually, one supposes, that will change, as it has in the case of the dominant white majority, and Hispanic and Indian and Asian-American communities will find themselves confronting their own intellectual dissidents. Meanwhile, the white majority of the American West has reached the point where it ought to be secure enough in its power and wealth that it can expect something from historians besides that subservient role of cheerleader or defender. I believe we have indeed arrived at that point, and that is precisely why a new generation of western historians has arrived on the scene, gaining national and international attention for the region, a generation indebted to the work of all their predecessors but ready to perform a very different role in society.

Here then, as I see it, is the program of the new western history:

- To find ourselves prefigured in our ancestors and find in them the origin of the problems and questions that plague us today;
- To achieve a more complete, honest, penetrating view of those ancestors as well as ourselves, including the flaws and ironies in their achievements; to question their and our successes, to explore other points of view and discover new values;
- To free ourselves from unthinking acceptance of official and unofficial myths and explanations;

2

New West, True West

I say to my colleague in Chinese studies that I teach western history. "Doesn't almost everyone in this department," he complains.* "The history of England, Germany, France, Italy—it is all western history in our courses. Nobody here knows or cares anything about the East." I cut him short to explain that what I mean by the West is not Europe, not the whole of western civilization. My West is the *American* West: that fabled land where the restless pioneer moves ever forward, settling one frontier after another; where the American character becomes self-reliant, democratic, and endlessly eager for the new; where we strip off the garments of civilization and don a rude buckskin shirt; where millions of dejected immigrants gather from around the world to be rejuvenated as Americans, sounding together a manly, wild, barbaric yawp of freedom. That is my West: precisely that and nothing more. "Oh," my colleague ventures, more perplexed now than cantankerous, "you mean 'the West'—the frontier, Indians, Clint Eastwood?" I nod vaguely and sidle off. It is all so hard to convey over a single, polite glass of academic sherry.

For a field that has been around so long, western American history can be frustratingly difficult to pin down. Soon it will be a full century old. Often, with such advanced age comes a clarity of purpose as well as a rec-

*This essay was first published in the *Western Historical Quarterly* XVIII, April 1987.

ord of achievement. Not so in this case. The record is impressive enough: the field now has several excellent journals, regularly holds good scholarly conferences, and boasts an immense bibliography that no one could read in a lifetime. But as for clarity of purpose, the field is still groping about in adolescence. It doesn't quite know who it is or what it wants to be when it grows up. What are its boundaries? Where is "West" and where is not? There is still no settled, mature answer.

There is, to be sure, an established body of writing about the history of the West, and usually it would be to such a body that we would turn for resolving what the field of study is or ought to be. In this case, however, the traditional literature is more a cause of confusion than a remedy. For it reveals that the West is just about anything that anyone has ever wanted it to be. That it has been located anywhere and everywhere.

My own private confusions of place may, in their ordinariness, illustrate that wonderful ambiguity we sense about the field. I was born in the Mohave Desert of southern California, an area the books say is indubitably part of the West. I grew up on the Great Plains, and again the books tell me that that is West too. But when I moved some years ago to Hawaii, was I still in the West or was I out of it? For an answer I might consult the *Western Historical Quarterly,* which reassures me in its index to recent articles in the field that the islands do indeed belong. The Hawaiian monarchs, resplendent in their feather caps and fed on taro, mullet, and the milk of coconuts, are to be understood (whatever their personal views of the matter) as having lived in the American West alongside Chief Sitting Bull and Geronimo; while Captain James Cook of Yorkshire was as much a western adventurer as Meriwether Lewis or John Charles Fremont. Now then, go to the other geographical extreme of the country. Move, as I have recently done, five thousand miles from Honolulu to the small Massachusetts town of Concord, founded in 1635 as the first inland settlement of the Bay colony. You will learn that it too, is, or has been, in the realm of the West! The authorities have it so. For example, that grand and indispensable reference work, *The Reader's Encyclopedia of the American West,* includes an entry on the settlement of Massachusetts, and it is a longer entry than the one on the Oregon Trail.[1] Thus, you may go west or east, young man or woman, and you will always in fact be going west.

As defined by its historians, the West has been nothing less than all of America, or all that we have conquered. For further evidence of how the part has swallowed the whole, consider the last work of the Harvard historian Frederick Merk, *A History of the Westward Movement,* published in 1978, one year after his death. He might as well have called it the story of the nation. There are chapters on Indian culture, cotton growing in the South, the Dred Scott decision, the industrialization of the Great Lakes, the Tennessee Valley Authority, and farm policy in the Kennedy-Johnson years. After more than six hundred pages of tracking American development, Professor Merk, in his moving peroration, expands even further his notion of the West as an "open frontier" to sweep in all of science and technology, all human control over the environment, all "the relations of man to his fellow man." "This is the frontier," he concludes, "now challenging the national energies."[2] If we follow his reasoning, the West is to be found wherever there is optimism, a love of freedom and democracy, an indomitable will to overcome all obstacles, a determination to make things better for the future. That is, I will grant you, the state of Oregon he is describing, but it also might be Australia or Hong Kong.

But hold: there is still more to the West than we have yet fathomed. Long before there was Merk's cotton gin, long before there was a colony planted on the cold Massachusetts shore in the seventeenth century, long before America was even discovered and named, the historians tell us of an even more ancient, shadowy West. On its existence we have, for example, the magisterial authority of the man who, until his death in 1981, was regarded by many as the dominant name in western history: Ray Allen Billington, senior research associate at the Huntington Library. His textbook, *Westward Expansion: A History of the American Frontier,* may be taken as one of the most authoritative delineations of the field. According to this book (4th ed., 1974), the American West was merely "the last stage in a mighty movement of peoples that began in the twelfth century when feudal Europe began pushing back the barbaric hordes" pressing in on Christendom. The Crusaders, off to do battle with the Moslems, were the first pioneers, and Jerusalem was their frontier. They did not prevail, but after them came the more triumphant Marco Polo, Christopher Columbus, and Ponce de Leon—came a whole multitude pushing the domain of the West out to the remote corners of the earth. In Billington's account the great saga rolls for eight centuries, until it reaches the American Populists defending themselves against "ruthless exploitation of eastern interests." If I have the story right, there is an undeniable grandeur to it, stretching as it does from the armies of Richard the Lionhearted to those of old Sockless Jerry Simpson in droughty, dusty Kansas. My grandfather, himself a raggletaggle populist with tobacco juice streaming from his mouth, would have loved it. But then, just as we are ready to spring with Billington into the future, the grandeur abruptly fades away. With the defeat of the Populists in 1896, he declares in one of his last chapters, the West came to a sad death. It will have no more history to make in the twentieth century. Once the West was going everywhere, now it is gone.[3]

To discover where the American West is supposed to be, I have been consulting major books published within the last ten or twelve years, books by scholars of stature from whom we have learned much. But having read them, I could not put my finger on the map and say, "There is the West." The books have attached too abstract a meaning to the word, so abstract in fact that it has become bewildering. The West is "movement," "expansion," the "frontier," they all say, and apparently any kind of movement, any expansion, any frontier will do.

The primal source of this abstractness, this elusiveness of subject, must be located in the mind of the scholar who has gotten so much praise for imagining the field in the first place: Frederick Jackson Turner. He started historians down a muddy, slippery road that ultimately leads to a swamp. That destination was not apparent for a long while. The route signs Turner put up had a deceptively concrete promise to them. In a letter written in the 1920s, he pointed out that "the 'West' with which I dealt, was a *process* rather than a fixed geographical region."[4] Earlier, he had made the same distinction in the notes of his Harvard course on the West: it was described as "a study of selected topics in the history of the West considered as a process rather than an area." That process, he explained in an unpublished essay, included:

1. the spread of settlement steadily westward, and
2. all the economic, social, and political changes involved in the existence of a belt of free land at the edge of settlement;
3. the continual settling of successive belts of land;
4. the evolution of these successive areas of settlement through various stages of backwoods life, ranching, pioneer farming, scientific farming, and manufacturing life.[5]

In short, Turner's "process" was really four of them, or rather, was a tangled web of many processes, all going on at once and including the whole development of American agriculture and industry, the history of population growth and movement, the creation of national institutions, and, somewhere in the tangle, the making of an American personality type. No wonder western history has ever after had trouble staying on track.

When you are lost, the most sensible strategy is to go back to the point of departure, back where Mr. Turner once stood pointing the way, and look for another road. Ignore the signs saying, "This way to process," and look instead for the one reading, "To a fixed geographical region." Or better yet, look for the specific processes that went on in the specific region. We may grope and argue a lot along that way too, but we won't end up back in Massachusetts befuddled by Puritan theology or back with the Crusaders defeated and dead.

My strategy of diverging from Turner and his frontier theme is hardly original. It was implictly recommended almost thirty years ago, in a 1957 article published in *Harper's Magazine*, by a man then described as "the West's leading historian," Walter Prescott Webb. The article was entitled "The American West: Perpetual Mirage." Had it been taken more fully to heart, it might have started the field off in a more promising direction. There was absolutely nothing in it of Turner's vaporous notion of the West as frontier advance. On the contrary, Webb gave the West a set of firm coordinates on the North American landscape. In his second paragraph he declared,

> Fortunately, the West is no longer a shifting frontier, but a region that can be marked off on a map, traveled to, and seen. Everybody knows when he gets there. It starts in the second tier of states west of the Big River.[6]

The West, in other words, begins with the Dakotas, Nebraska, Kansas, Oklahoma, and Texas. So defined, the West would become, along with the North and the South, one of the three great geographical regions of the coterminous United States.

In Webb's view, what sets this western region off from the other two major regions is the lack of enough rainfall to sustain traditional, European-derived agriculture. In that second tier of states the average yearly precipitation falls below the twenty-inch minimum needed to grow crops in the accustomed way. From there to the California coast the region is mainly dry: in its extremes it is a desert, elsewhere it is a subhumid environment. Admittedly, within it are some anomalies and further diversities—the Pacific Northwest Coast outstanding among them—which, for the sake of analysis, Webb had to ignore. Every region is, after all, only a generalization and is subject to exceptions.

This more mappable West, as everyone in the field knows, was an idea Webb took from the nineteenth-century explorer John Wesley Powell, whose *Report on the Lands of the Arid Region of the United States*, published in 1878 as a House of Representatives document, identified the 100th meridian as the line roughly dividing a humid from a subhumid America.[7] Webb nudged the line eastward a couple of degrees so it lay right outside Austin, Texas, where he lived. And he boldly declared that Powell's arid region was one and the same as the American West. For the post-World War II generation, he sensed, the two regions had merged completely, and historians had better acknowledge the fact and stop harking back to Turner.

I know in my bones, if not always through my education, that Webb was right. His notion of the West as the arid region of the country fits completely my own experience and understanding. Born eighty years to the day after Frederick Jackson Turner—on the 14th of November, 1941 (Turner was born on the 14th of November, 1861)—I have never been able to think of the West as Turner did, as some process in motion. Instead, I think of it as a distinct place inhabited by distinct people: people like my parents, driven out of western Kansas by dust storms to an even hotter, drier life in Needles, California, working along the way in flyblown cafes, fruit orchards, and on railroad gangs, always feeling dwarfed by the bigness of the land and by the economic power accumulated there. In my West, there are no coonskin caps, nor many river boats, axes, or log cabins. Those things all belong to another time, another place—to an eastern land where nature offered an abundance of survival resources near at hand. My West is, by contrast, the story of men and women trying to wrest a living from a condition of severe natural scarcity and, paradoxically, of trying to survive in the midst of entrenched wealth.

This picture of the West, I submit, is closer to the one most western historians carry around in their heads today. When pushed hard to make a stand, we usually line up with Webb and Powell, not Turner. For instance, on the first page or so of the introduction to his book *Historians and the American West,* Michael Malone grants that he means by the West more or less what Webb meant: "the entire region lying west of the 98th meridian, the line of diminishing rainfall which runs from the eastern Dakotas on the north through central Texas on the south."[8] But having admitted that much to ourselves, we often resist the logical implications in what we have done. We still feel obliged to keep feeding Turner's ghost at the table. We may accept the modern view that the West is a settled region distinct unto itself, but we are not always steadfast, clearminded regionalists in writing its history.

The main questions I now want to raise are these: What is regional history and what is it not? And what strategies should we employ for analyzing this West as region, as opposed to the West as frontier? For the sake of intellectual and moral vitality, regional history should be as inclusive as possible, dealing with anything and everything that has happened to anyone in its territory; it should be total history. Clarifying its purpose should never mean imposing a rigid, doctrinaire formula, especially on so wonderfully diverse a place as the West. But some things are more significant than others in the making of a region. The region has its core influences, just as it has peripheral ones. What we must do is determine what is in that core and what is not.

Begin with what is not. Regional history is not, in the strictest sense, merely the history of the American nation replicating itself, politically, economically, or culturally. Any regional historian must proceed from the assumption that his region is, in some important way, a *unique* part of that greater whole. To find nothing but sameness in it would make his entire enterprise useless. Felix Frankfurter once wrote, "Regionalism is a recognition of the intractable diversities among men, diversities partly shaped by nature but no less derived from the different reactions of men to nature."[9] I will come back to the complicated role of nature in a moment, but for now let us concentrate on that word diversity. The regional historian must be out looking earnestly for it, even when it's hard to find or define, even when it's hard to feel good about when located. But do we do this? Not systematically enough. In fact, one school of thought denies that there has been anything unique or innovative about the West to discover.

Such was the position taken by Earl Pomeroy in 1955, when, in another heroic effort to free us from the influence of Turner, he wrote that "the Westerner has been fundamentally imitator rather than innovator."[10] By example after example, ranging from architecture to territorial government, Pomeroy showed how people in the West drew on the East for their ideas and institutions. To a point he was right, and the argument long overdue. But carry his argument too far and the objection must be raised, why then study the West at all? Why bother with uncovering more and more examples—mere copies of the original? Better to examine the original itself. If we insist too strenuously that the West has been merely a borrower from the East, it becomes not a region but a province, a dull little backwater of conformists and copycats, all looking to some eastern capital for their inspiration. Nothing would be more tiresome to an active mind than to dwell year after year in such a place. The more ambitious would quickly go elsewhere. Pomeroy certainly did not want that to happen; indeed, he warned the field against slipping into intellectual mediocrity. Yet too much emphasis on the West as continuity would certainly lead us straight to mediocrity and boredom.

Pomeroy properly admonished us against the excesses of exceptionalism. It can lead to extravagant claims of originality, a bumptious chauvinism, a sagebrush rebellion against "outside interference." It can conceal the crucial formative role the federal government has played in the region, particularly through its evolving territorial system, as both Pomeroy and Lamar have shown.[11] But, finally, regionalism is about telling differences or it has nothing to tell.

Nor should regional history be confused, as it sometimes is, with the history of ethnic groups migrating into a place and taking up residence. In fact, I will venture to say that ethnic history and regional history are often conflicting endeavors. In America, ethnic history commonly deals with those "intractable diversities" that have been introduced into this country from abroad and their struggle to survive in the face of pressures to assimilate. Whereas in Europe an ethnic group usually had a regional base—that is, was rooted in a specific geographical place—in the United States it became a movable identity: a language, some music, holidays and foods, religion, all journeying through space, to a steel town, the prairie, suburbia, yet marvelously remaining intact. Many ethnic groups have come to live in the American West, of course, but the fact of their being in the West is not necessarily the same as their being *of* the West. The ethnic group becomes central to the region's history when and where and to the extent it becomes altered by that region, or develops an active voice in defining the region's "intractable diversity."[12]

Quite different from ethnic history, and presenting an even more intricate problem of fit, is the history of the indigenous peoples who have been invaded and conquered, in this case the Indians and, more ambiguously, the Hispanics. To a greater extent than anyone else, by the fact of their much longer occupation and engagement with the environment, they belong. They are not immigrants, they are natives. But for all that, they are not to be readily or casually absorbed into the study of region. They are sovereign nations that have been unwillingly regionalized—made a part of the "West" (also of the "South" and "Northeast," but especially of the "West") as they have been made by force a part of America. The regionalist who does not begin with their story, their interaction with the place, continues the injustice of their expropriation. But inclusion alone will not do; it is not adequate now merely to make them regional Americans.

Finally, in a mood of rigorous clarification, we must caution that regional history is not quite the same thing as the history of the American or world economic system and their hierarchies of superior and subordinate parts. The western terrain has again and again come under the thumb of some eastern entrepreneur. As William Robbins has recently argued, we need to develop "a broad theoretical formulation that examines the West in the context of its national and international relations" in order to understand that outside exploitation.[13] Quite so, and we ought to ask where all the region's coal, gold, uranium, and timber have gone, and who has profited from them, ask how they have helped build a system of industrial capitalism. But one must be careful not to simply substitute that investigation of outside exploitation for a more complex inquiry into regionalism and its tensions.

The region, the nation, the world: all three are terms in this historical equation, all interacting through time, continually shifting in weight and value, and the regional historian, though committed mainly to understanding the first of them, must not ignore the others. His special task is to understand how those outside economic and political forces, empire and capital, have entered the West and dealt with its regional peculiarities, either by trying to stamp them out or by becoming themselves transformed into new, more indigenous forms.

Those are some of the things, it seems to me, that lie on the periphery, or pose as potential traps, to regional history. What then lies in that core history of the West? What forces and events are to be found there? Recurring to Frankfurter's words, it is the story of the West as one of those intractable diversities which have been "partly shaped by nature but not less derived from the different reactions of men to nature." In other words, the history of the region is first and foremost one of an evolving human ecology. A region emerges as people try to make a living from a particular part of the earth, as they adapt themselves to its limits and possibilities. What the regional historian should first want to know is how a people or peoples acquired a place and, then, how they perceived and tried to make use of it. He will identify the survival techniques they adopted, their patterns of work and economy, and their social relationships.

Put more modishly, the region derives its identity primarily from its ecologically adapted modes of production—or more simply, from its ecological modes.[14] If those modes are precisely the same as those existing elsewhere in the country or world, then we have not got much of a region to study. On the other hand, if the modes are too radically different, we may not have a region at all but rather a foreign civilization. Somewhere between those poles of conformity and differentiation lies the region.

So, leave aside as a related but separate kind of inquiry Merk's wide-open frontier, and Turner's process of settlement, and Pomeroy's insistence on continuities. Forget for a while the broader tides of imperialism and Christendom and urbanization and the marketplace. We want to concentrate our attention first on how people have tried to wrest their food, their energy, their income from the specific land in question and what influence that effort has had on the shaping of the West's society and culture.

In our oldest and most distinctive region, the American South, there has been only one dominant ecological mode over most of its history, the plantation system of agriculture in which tobacco and cotton were cultivated by African slave labor. That mode has given the South an enduring identity, a fate that, even now, it has not escaped. More than a hundred years after its defeat in the Civil War, the South can still read its past mode of living in the present conditions of its soils, its long backward economic status, and its still troubled racial relations.

In the West, however, we have to deal with not one, but two, primary ecological modes under white occupation. The first of these modes is the life of the cowboy and sheepherder. The second is the life of the irrigator and water engineer. Call these the *pastoral West* and the *hydraulic West*. Neither is found anywhere else in the United States; they are unique to the lands lying beyond Webb and Powell's line of demarcation. What we must understand is how they have evolved side by side, what social impact each has had, where and how they have been in competition with each other, how they have coexisted into our own time, and what cultural values are embedded in each.

All the world knows that the American West is fundamentally a land of cowboys. It is not a myth, however much the fact may have been mythologized in fiction and movies. When the cowboy arrived and commenced punching cows, the West ceased to be a vague frontier of exploration and began, over broad reaches of its territory, in every state from the Great Plains to the Pacific, to take shape as an articulated region.[15]

This West did not develop the way Turner had anticipated. For in his West as process, as social evolution, the pastoral life is supposed to be only a passing stage of settlement and soon must give way to the farmer and the manufacturer. Beyond the 100th meridian such was not to be the case.

The fur trapper, the miner, and the dirt farmer came to the West, as they did elsewhere on the continent; so too did the missionary and the Indian fighter. All of them had important roles, but none was distinctive to the region, with the possible exception of the hardrock miner. The cowboy, on the other hand, came to stay and built a special way of life.[16] By the early twentieth century that life was firmly rooted in place and being depicted in such works as Wister's *The Virginian* (1902) and Adams' *The Log of a Cowboy* (1903). Even now, in this last quarter of the twentieth century, the pastoral life thrives as well as it ever did. The techniques of range and herd management may have changed, but the basic ecological mode has remained intact. So also endures the cult of self-reliant individualism that has grown up around this mode. We are not in any danger of losing the way of life, nor of missing its historical significance. But even were it to disappear abruptly, it would leave as lasting a mark on the West as the cotton plantation has left on the South.

The hydraulic West, on the other hand, has been much less noticed by western historians.[17] It has taken us by surprise, and we have still not fully comprehended its meaning. This is so for several reasons. The hydraulic West came of age only after World War II, while western historians have, until late, been preoccupied with the nineteenth century. It is a more technically abstruse and more organizationally complex mode then ranching, and therefore requires more effort to penetrate. And, although it has inspired a few songs, movies, and novels, there is too little romance about it to attract much popular attention. It is, in fact, too faceless, anonymous, impersonal, even at times too sinister, to be celebrated and loved. This West has been created by irrigation ditches, siphons, canals, and storage dams. In it daily existence depends on the intensive management of that scarce, elusive, and absolutely vital natural resource, water.

The hydraulic mode of living is much older than the grazier's, going back as it does hundreds of years to the Hohokam Indians of Arizona and other native societies.[18] In the modern era of white dominion, the mode first appears in 1847 among the Mormons in their state of Deseret and, soon thereafter, in the Greeley vicinity of Colorado and in California's Central Valley. California would eventually become the principal center of hydraulic development, radiating an influence all the way to Montana and Texas. By 1978, the Census of Agriculture reported 43,668,834 irrigated acres in the seventeen western states: one-tenth of the world's total. California counted 8.6 million acres; Texas, 7 million; Nebraska, 5.7 million; and Idaho and Colorado, 3.5 million each. The market sales from those lands amounted to one-fourth of the nation's total, or $26 billion. Taken by counties, all but one of the top ten agricultural producers in the nation are in the hydraulic West, and eight of them are in California alone.[19]

This water empire is a purely western invention. To be sure, a lot of capital and technology has been invested on farms all over the United States, in the form of machinery, pesticides, fertilizer, and the like; looked at as merely another form of technology, the hydraulic West may appear to be nothing more than an advanced version of modern agribusiness. However, the regional distinctiveness lies in the fact that the typical irrigator is not merely trying to enhance his production by buying a little water now and then. He is critically dependent on that single resource and, to survive, must have it delivered on a steady, reliable basis. There is no room for marketplace competition in his life, no freedom to buy or do without, no substitute available. The western farmer does not have any real choice in the matter; he lives or dies by the level of water in his ditches. This stark fact of utter dependence on an indispensable resource creates a special mode of production.

Given such dependency, the regional historian wants to know what social changes the hydraulic West has worked. How are people organized in this mode? What are their relationships with one another? What qualities of mind and thought appear or take on new emphasis? In what ways does the irrigation infrastructure make this West different from the East or, for that matter, from the pastoral West?

Oddly enough, though he did not think of the West as a region, Frederick Jackson Turner was among the first to discern the peculiar characteristics of this hydraulic life. In an *Atlantic Monthly* article of 1903, he noted that in the preceding fifteen years western settlement had reached the Great Plains, where "new physical conditions have . . . accelerated the social tendency of Western democracy." The conquest of that country would be impossible, he went on, "by the old individual pioneer methods." The new region required "expensive irrigation works," "cooperative activity," and "capital beyond the reach of the small farmer." The condition of water scarcity, he wrote, "decreed that the destiny of this new frontier should be social rather than individual." He compared it to the changes in social structure going on elsewhere in America: this West would be from the outset an "industrial" order, giving rise to "captains of industry," home-grown or imported versions of men like Andrew Carnegie, who were taking charge of the country generally. The task of settling the arid West, like that of creating an industrial society, was too monumental for ordinary people using ordinary skills to carry out; they must therefore "combine under the leadership of the strongest." They would also be forced to rely on the federal government to build for them huge dams and canals as well as show them "what and when and how to plant." "The pioneer of the arid regions," Turner concluded, "must be both a capitalist and the protégé of the government."[20] That these were fundamental differences from the requirements of raising flood and fiber in the East, Turner clearly understood, yet strangely he assumed that his vaunted frontier democracy would be unaffected by them. To see matters otherwise would have shattered the hopeful, nationalistic pride he felt in the westward movement. We, on the other hand, can put realistic names to the social conditions emerging in this West: hierarchy, concentration of wealth and power, rule by expertise, dependency on government and bureaucracy. The American deserts could be made to grow some crops all right, but among them would be the crop of oligarchy.

That fact was already faintly discernible eighty-three years ago. By the late 1930s, John Steinbeck could confirm them in his novel *The Grapes of Wrath*, which portrays the hydraulic West through the eyes of the Joads of Oklahoma. Forced to migrate west, the Joads become members of a permanent underclass of stoop-and-pick laborers, an underclass that had access neither to the land nor the water needed to make it flourish. Steinbeck sensed that there was no simple alternative to that undemocratic outcome, not so long as the West wanted or needed a hydraulic system and wanted it to grow more and more elaborate. Some form of power elite, whether possessing capital, or expertise, or both, would be required to carry out that ambition. It need not be a capitalistic elite that would rise to command. Government could intervene in the outcome, not only to develop more water but also to distribute it into more hands. But in doing so, the government would itself become a form of concentrated power, threatening to dominate people's lives to an often intolerable degree. Quite simply, the domination of nature in the water empire must lead to the domination of some people by others.[21]

Another outcome of the hydraulic mode, likewise unanticipated at the beginning and even now not commonly realized, is an intensification and concentration of urban growth. Cities need water too; and in a region of scarcity, where water sources are few and far between, the city must reach out over great distances to fill that necessity. The bigger the city, the more power it has to wield over its rivals. In this competition, the small community is at a disadvantage, short as it is of both capital and technical virtuosity. Inevitably, it loses out or it becomes a dependent on the metropolis, as the Owens Valley of California has done in its struggle with Los Angeles. Webb noted the outcome of this unequal competition: "The West is today virtually an oasis civilization."[22] Despite an abundance of space, people have found themselves being driven to a few isolated oases where they live packed closely together, while all around them the land stretches away like a great, wild void.

Finally, the hydraulic West has touched and shaped people's imaginations in ways we have hardly yet understood. Old ideas have been reborn there, or they have been applied in new ways. For example, the Americans who came into the region brought with them a deeply rooted drive for mastery over the natural world. They did not come to contemplate the land, nor would they easily tolerate any deprivations it imposed on them. We will make a stand here in this awesome canyon, westerners began to say, and hold back with our common force the full might of the Columbia, the Snake, the Missouri, the Platte, the Rio Grande, the Colorado. No individual or small knot of people among us can achieve that triumph. It will require all of us working as one, all of us united in the pursuit of power. In contrast to the pastoral West, with its glorification of rugged individualism, this hydraulic mode has promoted the cultish idea of the collective domination of nature.[23]

There are many resemblances between this hydraulic West and the modern technological society, as found today in Moscow, New York, or Tokyo. But they are not quite the same thing—not yet anyway. The technological society believes it has escaped all environmental restraint, overcome all limits, and at last stands free of nature. But in today's West such a boast would be ludicrous. The region obviously has not yet learned how to manufacture a single molecule of water, let alone water in unlimited quantities, nor even to find a single substitute for it. Water remains a severely limited resource, yet it is irreplaceable. Until the West discovers how to produce this resource in unstinting abundance, it must continue to obey nature's demands. And in that obedience the West remains a region set apart from other regions.[24]

Through this recapitulation of the two major western modes, I have been indicating a strategy of analysis that, if followed, would take us to the true West at last. Walter Prescott Webb told us where we might find it some time ago, but then he himself got discouraged and turned back. There was not enough intellectual substance along the way, he feared, to satisfy the historian. "Western history," he wrote in his 1957 essay, "is brief and it is bizarre. It is brief because the time is so short and its material deficient. Western history is bizarre because of the nature of what it has got." Having spent some time in England as a visiting professor, having traveled widely around the East and South, he had come home to the West in the fifties with a heightened sense of it as a place "full of negatives and short on positives." Above all, the region's lack of water seemed to him responsible somehow for its failure to achieve a larger cultural significance.

> What is the biographer going to do for a region that has so few men of distinction? What is the historian going to do with a country almost without chronology or important battles or great victories or places where armies have surrendered or dead soldiers were buried? How can he make a thick history out of such thin material?[25]

We have heard such laments before. It is the old, piteous cry of the provincial who has lost confidence in himself and his ability to find complex meaning in his surroundings. Perhaps, to avoid such doubt, the western historian ought to stay away from places like Oxford. Or if he insists on visting them, he ought to remind himself that, looked at up close, their old kings and warriors were not any better than the new ones; that, anyway, battles and armies are not the only stuff of history. He ought to read and reread as often as possible what Ortega y Gasset once wrote, that arid lands do not necessarily make arid minds.[26] But Webb forgot all that. Late in his life he seems to have lost enthusiasm for the West as region and instead began denigrating it. Now it falls to a later generation—our generation—to push ahead toward a deeper, fuller, and more intellectually complex regionalism.

If Clifford Geertz can find large meanings in the cockfights of Bali and Emmanuel Le Roy Ladurie in the peasants of Languedoc, the western historian need not despair of the West.[27] For those with imagination to find it, there is plenty of thick history to be written about this region. Within its spacious boundaries and across its sparse, dry expanses, through what is now more than two hundred years of European settlement and many thousand of Indian life, this region offers for study all the greed, violence, beauty, ambition, and variety anyone could use. Given enough time and effort, it may someday also offer a story of careful, lasting adaptation of people to the land.

We are beginning to know where the true West is, what it has been, what it might have been, what it might still be. We are beginning to know the place for the first time.

3 •••••••••••••••••••••••••

Cowboy Ecology

Ask almost any group of people the world over, from Peoria to Perth, and they will say that the American West is about the cowboy and his life of chasing cows on the range.* They may add, without much encouragement, that the West has come to symbolize the whole national identity of the United States. Instead of seeing in that response a measure of truth, historians have tended to dismiss it as popular myth-making, a fashion of mass culture, essentially false and insignificant. Those who write the history of the nation have more or less ignored the life on the range (as they have life in the Trans-Mississippi West generally). A survey of fourteen popular American history textbooks shows that the range industry, cowboy, and ranch receive, on the average, less than two pages' worth of attention out of almost a thousand pages of text.[1] The historians say one thing about what is important in our past, popular intuition says another. In this case, I believe, popular intuition is worth heeding, though not for all the popular reasons.

One prominent exception to the academic trend to scant the West is Daniel Boorstin, who opens the third volume of his survey of the Ameri-

*An early version of this essay was given as a paper at the American Historical Association annual meeting, San Francisco, December 1989; and a revised version was delivered as the annual Charles L. Wood Lecture in Agricultural History, Texas Tech University, Lubbock, February 1991.

can experience with a celebration of the "go-getters," a generation of entrepreneurs who, in the aftermath of the Civil War, "went in search of what others had never imagined was there to get," men who "made something out of nothing." Prominent among them were cowboys in the broad sense of the term: western cattle drovers like Charles Goodnight and cattle shippers like Joseph McCoy, two among many who saw the possibility of extracting meat out of the unlikely environment of the "desert."[2] Boorstin regards such men as the archetypes of a new America that refuses to be constrained by traditional, rigid morality but plunges ahead into modern ambiguity, making up rules as it goes. Others, less persuaded that free enterprise has made old morals obsolete, have called those cowboy entrepreneurs a generation of thugs and rustlers. Most academic historians have to come to regard the whole saga of cowpunchers, cattlemen, and the beef and wool industry with some boredom, if not distaste, and deny its relevance to the mainstream of social change and conflict.

The status of ranching history, and with it western history, seems especially low when compared with the status of the plantation history of the American South. Even at this late point in the twentieth century, after so much urbanization and economic growth, the plantation still stands at the very center of southern studies. Moreover, unlike the ranch, it occupies a prominent place in the textbooks. Yet the ranch and the plantation were alike spawned by the capitalist revolution in agriculture. Each institution has been a powerful determinant of a regional identity. The critical difference between them lies, of course, in the fact that the plantation practiced an especially heinous form of labor exploitation, which has left an enduring mark on race relations, not only in the United States but in a number of other societies, mainly in the warmer latitudes where Europeans came to force nonwhites to raise exotic food and fiber for them on a large scale. The plantation has been a cruel instrument in the European conquest of people of color, and historians seeking to understand that long story of racial conquest, exploitation, and injustice have rightly given it careful attention.

But out on the western range human relations have always seemed a lot more open, sunny, nonrepressive, and therefore forgettable. True, every ranch required, somewhere in the past, a dispossession of native peoples. And on the typical ranch there was a poorly paid work crew and it was partly nonwhite: Indian, Mexican, African-American, and if one includes the Hawaiian Islands, even Asian and Polynesian. The European languages spoken out west included Spanish, German, Danish, and the Gaelic dialects; far more often than the southern plantation, the range was a microcosmic league of nations under white hegemony. We have tended, through the influence of too many John Wayne movies, to assume otherwise; the full history of the diverse racial and ethnic relations on the range has yet to be written. All the same, compared with chattel slavery, the work relationships there seem to be rather ordinary and even benign, more egalitarian than exploitative. The system was one of wage laborers selling their services freely, sometimes for only a season or two, then moving on. With the job necessarily went a lot of autonomy. Since chasing after steers often took one far away from the scrutiny of a foreman, since in fact the work demanded a great deal of self-directedness and initiative, and since the hired men were allowed to ride big horses and carry big guns across a big space, there was relatively more personal freedom for workers in the ranching industry than in, say, the textile factory or the cotton field. Consequently, the idea of a "cowboy proletariat" is a seed that has been sown a few times by historians but always fallen on stony ground.[3]

However, if labor and racial exploitation did not occur on the range to the same terrible degree they did on the plantation, there is another aspect that stands out as distinctive, compelling, and historically significant. This is an issue that is absolutely crucial to the course of western American development, one that has much to teach the rest of the nation. And, above all, it is an issue that is vital to much of today's world, particularly the developing nations of Asia, Africa, and Latin America. I mean the question of how we are to get a living from a fragile, vulnerable earth without destroying it—or, put otherwise, how we are to lead a sustainable life that does not deplete the natural environment nor communities that depend on it. For this issue the West, because so much of it is ecologically marginal for many human purposes, has represented one of the preeminent laboratories on the planet. It is, as Walter Prescott Webb once noted, a semi-desert with a desert at its heart.[4] Compared with the North and South, the western environment did not yield easily to agriculture or urban growth, and only in recent decades, with the aid of modern, sophisticated technology to pump the water and cool the air, has the region acquired much population. Such is also the condition of much of the Third World: they too face the challenge of marginal lands—lands that are too hot, too cold, too dry, too mountainous by the standards of modern agriculture; lands that defy human ambitions, but lands that today, under the pressure of explosive population growth, are being brought under cultivation or husbandry and are being settled.

Compounding those environmental challenges is the question of what form of tenure or property rights will best assure a sustainable agricultural future: individual or communal, entrepreneurial or bureaucratic? Here again, the history of ranching in the American West offers a relevant experience, for it has been wracked from its earliest days by debate over the question.

But in order to be useful in these ways cowboy history has to be presented more forcefully than it has in terms of comparative human ecology, emphasizing the relation of people to other animals, of animals to vegetation, and of vegetation to patterns of tenure. In the rest of this essay I want to sketch that alternative, comparative approach and suggest lines of research that can bring the region's significance home to scholars all over the world. We ought to begin by getting outside our regional provincialisms, overcoming our insistence on American uniqueness, and trying to situate the cowboy and his ranch in the broad panorama of human adaptation to the earth.

Except in California, where everything is a ranch—out there they have diet ranches, avocado ranches, golf and tennis ranches, suburban ranchettes, and retired President ranches—a ranch is an extensive farm that specializes in raising cows, sheep, goats, or horses. But it is also a modern reworking of an ancient pastoral way of life, and we need to understand what it replaced in order to comprehend fully what it has been and what it is becoming.

Pastoralism, an adaptation emphasizing the herding of livestock, seems to have begun as a simplification of agriculture, with its mixed economy of plants and animals. Possibly it appeared in response to the pressure of a growing population on a limited space; some people may have been excluded from farming and forced to find a living in more marginal lands—that is, they were forced out of river valleys onto broad uplands or into high mountains or out on the steppes where only scrubby brush grew and the rainfall was scanty and erratic. There they had to abandon much of their old life, limiting their subsistence base to various ruminants. Apparently, the earliest people to be thrown out into the wasteland were the nomads of the Middle East, the children of Ishmael, who took to roaming the deserts with their camels, goats, and sheep, though maintaining a mutualistic relationship with the agrarian settlements, now trading with them, now raiding them, maintaining that interdependent relationship well down into recent times.

The anthropologist Brian Spooner has identified six broad cultural regions emerging from this ancient history of nomadic pastoralism: sub-Saharan Africa, where people's livelihood came to be based on herding cattle; the vast desert belt that stretches from the Sahara across Arabia to India, a zone where the camel has been the key animal; the mountain plateaus of Iberia, Italy, Greece, Turkey, and Afghanistan, based mainly on sheep; the Central Asian Steppe, also sheep-based; and the circumpolar region from Norway to the Bering Sea, where the reindeer has long been the principal herd animal, the chief source of clothing and food.[5]

Perhaps the most important inquiry for a modern historian of the West to make of that long nomadic tradition is how all those peoples, living closely with animals in so many different places, managed to sustain their way of life. In east Africa, for example, tribes followed flocks and herds for 10,000 years; though, in the accounts of some authorities, they had a profound effect on the flora of the continent, they nonetheless managed to achieve a state of fluctuating equilibrium, at least until very recently.[6] Whatever damages to nature they did, whatever tragedies they may have experienced over those ten millennia, they survived down to the days of note-taking anthropologists. How did they do it? How did they regulate their impact on the land to keep it producing? How successful were they in conserving the graze or browse on which their stock depended? What kind of land degradation could one find among pastoral peoples and how severe was it?

There are as many answers to those questions as there were traditional nomadic pastoral societies. In some cases, particularly in severely dry areas, the herding life produced a highly independent folk who relied on constant mobility to preserve their ecological base. It was a regular thing to squabble amongst themselves and make war against rival tribes. Among the Qashga'i of southwestern Iran, for instance, each extended household traditionally kept its herds separate from others in the tribe, grazed them on pasture allocated by the headmen, and got along with few social rules. Each household tried to build its herds as large as it could, keeping a steady pressure on the range, demanding more room from the headmen when they enjoyed a surplus of animals. The tribe in turn asserted control over as much land as it could and defended it against competitors. A rough—and sometimes it got very rough—balance of power among area tribes determined who had winter and summer pasture access. Within each tribe there was a hierarchy based on livestock wealth, though private property in land was unknown.

Traditional nomads showed little interest in resource conservation or pasture improvement, though they were incredibly knowledgeable about the lands they exploited. (I use the past tense because true nomadism today has virtually disappeared.) They had to know where there would be grass in the months ahead, how many head of animals it would support, where there would be waterholes, when to expect drought. As they depleted their supplies locally, they went looking for more, sometimes entering into the territory of others where they used diplomacy if they could, but took by force of arms if they must, to gain access. Eventually, when their overgrazed pastures had recovered, they brought their stock back to chew it all up again. So long as their human numbers remained limited by war and disease, and their herds were regularly culled by drought, hunger, predation, theft, or infertility, they managed to stay within the carrying capacity of their range, the vegetation evolving toward resilience and tenacity.[7]

In other cases, however, the history of pastoralism took an altogether different direction. The strategy of survival was not one of wandering impermanently from one site to another, in an endless cycle of nomadism, but of learning to stay in one place and adjusting to its limits. The circumalpine environment of Europe furnishes many examples of this more intensive, sedentary form of pastoralism. There the herders traditionally spent a part of the year grazing their animals in nearby alpine meadows— practicing a kind of vertical and partial nomadism called transhumance. At summer's end they trailed their stock down to established villages, where they fed them through the winter on stored hay; thus, they lived much of the year like other farmers, but harvested milk and cheese rather than grain. The high summer pastures of this region have been used since Neolithic times, and since the Middle Ages there has "gradually evolved what would appear to be the most stable and finely balanced form of peasant society and culture in the European area."[8] Similar patterns of settled village life, limited pastoral movement, and cautious environmental control can be found in the Andean region of South America and in the Himalayas.[9]

The classic ecological study of mountain pastoralism is Robert Netting's *Balancing on an Alp*, which examines the still-thriving Swiss community of Törbel, located above the Rhone Valley toward Zermatt and the Italian border. For at least seven centuries daily life there has been hedged about with precise written rules and regulations that no desert nomad would find tolerable; the earliest of them, an ancient scrap of parchment written in Latin, dates as far back as 1224 A.D. Mainly, the regulations deal with land use. They specify, for example, exactly who in the village has the right to graze livestock, who in effect owns a share in this community pasture. So strict is the observance of the rules that no outsiders have ever been allowed to break into that closed circle.[10] Each family is also limited to the number of cattle they can winter over on their individual hay crop, which is raised on their private landholdings; there are 5000 such parcels in the community, and a family may own as many as a hundred of them, scattered among everyone else's, along with a share in the many large storage barns. It is a close-knit, egalitarian community where there are neither rich nor poor. The feudal ages never disrupted the socio-ecological order, nor has the modern capitalist economy succeeded so far in breaking it down. It strikes a balance between communal and individual ownership. It defines needs locally and firmly limits them. Above all, the pastoral life in Törbel is based on a strong, persistent, widely shared sense of natural limits; otherwise, the regulations would cease to be acceptable. As Netting puts it "The centuries-long survival and continued productivity of both alp and forest testify to the effectiveness of communal management, the wisdom of conservation measures, and the continued enforcement of rules against overgrazing and indiscriminate timber cutting."[11]

One could travel around the world examining the variety of pastoral ways of life. My point in making only a quick discursus is to suggest that the student of the American West has a vast history to become at least passingly familiar with and a wealth of possibilities for comparative analysis. The cowboy belongs to this greater world of human ecology, not merely to Wyoming.

The North American ranch began to emerge as an institution in the southern part of Texas during the 1860s, and its story belongs completely to the post–Civil War era of the nation. Though it adopted terms, tools, and animal lore going back into the dim past of Iberian and Celtic antecedents, the ranch was unmistakably a modern capitalist institution. It took form in the marginal environments of the New World, where heretofore there had been only a few domesticated animals. It specialized in raising exotic cattle and other animals to sell in the marketplace, furnishing meat, hides, and wool to the growing metropolises of the East and to Europe. Livestock became a form of capital in this innovative system, capital that was made to earn a profit and increase itself many times over, without limit. But the animals were only one part of the capital—a mere mechanism for processing the more essential capital, the western grasslands, into a form suitable for human consumption. The cattle carried the grass, as it were, to the Chicago or Kansas City stockyards, where they were slaughtered by the millions and carved into beefsteak.[12] From the earliest period in the United States the scale of this industry was continental, growing up as it did with the national railroad lines; then, following the invention of the refrigerated ship in 1879, it became transoceanic and global.[13]

Following the Swiss and Maasai cowherd, the Berber and Baluchistan shepherd, the Peruvian llama- and Yemeni camel-tender, the North American cowboy steps forth, a brand-new figure in the long tradition. But like his predecessors, he must confront the old fundamental questions: What is his relationship to the land to be, and how long can he sustain himself in comparison with the others?

The first quarter-century of American livestock ranching, lasting from about 1865 to 1890, was, according to every historian who has written on the subject, an unmitigated disaster—colorful, exciting, fabulous, yes, but a disaster all the same. From Texas north to the Canadian plains and all the way westward to the Pacific, thousands of entrepreneurs assembled their herds and drove them onto the public lands, millions of acres lying open to private enterprise. They had no tribal headmen to guide them, no ancient parchments to spell out their rights and responsibilities, little or no knowledge of the landscapes they were invading, and no willingness to wait for any of these to appear. The range belonged to no one, they claimed; therefore, it belonged to everyone. The first individuals to arrive simply appropriated what they wanted and, without legal title, began to take off the grass. Others soon arrived and claimed the same right. Then there was a multitude, some of them individuals, some of them corporations, not a few of them "cowboys" living in Edinburgh or London. Let one of the most prominent of these newfangled pastoralists, Granville Stuart, describe the frenzied scene in Montana in the boom years:

> In 1880, the country was practically uninhabited. One could travel for miles without seeing so much as a traveler's bivouac. Thousands of buffalo darkened the rolling plains. There were deer, elk, wolves and coyotes on every hill and in every ravine and thicket. . . . In the fall of 1883, there was not a buffalo remaining on the range, and the antelope, elk, and deer were indeed scarce. In 1880 no one had heard tell of a cowboy in "this niche of the woods" and Charlie Russell [the famous cowboy artist of Montana] had made no pictures of them; but in the fall of 1883, there were 600,000 head of cattle on the range. The cowboy . . . had become an institution.[14]

But, he might have added, a mere five years later, in 1888, much of the western ranching industry was lying in ruins, the victim of severe overgrazing and desperately cold winters. Many thousands of animals were lying dead all over the range, starved and frozen; the survivors were riding in boxcars to the stockyards for rapid liquidation by their owners. Even faster than it had boomed, the new American pastoralism busted. It would take decades for it fully to recover.[15]

That collapse of what we might call the "the laissez-faire commons" was one of the greatest, as measured in the loss of animal life, in the entire history of pastoralism. It has been told many times in western history courses, and probably forgotten as often, for Americans do not like to remember that they once failed abysmally in a form of husbandry where illiterate African tribesmen had succeeded. My purpose in recalling it here is not merely to emphasize the failure of our early cowboy capitalists but rather to draw attention to the predicament it created. We had acquired a vast public domain, a large part of which would never be suitable for agriculture; it was as marginal as they come. What it offered was a pasture of considerable potential for livestock, one covering several hundred million acres. But who would own it? Who would manage it? Was there any safe, humane, permanent way to turn that grass and the poor, dumb, hoofed animals living on it into modern dreams of unlimited personal wealth?

Over most of the present century there have been two competing answers to that set of questions, and neither has so far managed to make its case convincing enough to settle the matter once and for all. Some have said the public range should be given or sold to private interests. Others have said the range ought to remain federal property. I should add that neither preference has much continuity with that long tradition of Old World pastoralism; indeed, they are both based on a rejection of tradition, on a confidence in the new, and perhaps it is that fact which had made neither of them quite an adequate or acceptable solution.

One of the recommendations that came quickly out of the debacle of the 1880s was predictable in a nation devoted to the principles of free enterprise: turn the whole public domain over to the ranchers as their private property and let them manage it without hindrance. If farmers could get free homesteads of 160 acres, why should the stockmen not get free ranches of 1600 or 16,000 acres, get whatever they needed to raise their herds and flocks? In the eyes of many it was a matter of fairness for those who lived by herding instead of cropping. But when the claim of a right to a freehold of 16,000 acres did not seem to get much recognition, other, more compelling arguments emerged, based on economics and ecology. Privatizing the range, it was argued, would give the western grazier a real incentive to manage the land better and avoid the kind of irresponsible free-for-all of the 1880s. With a fee simple title in hand, he would be more likely to invest in long-term improvements, especially fencing. The fences were all-important, for a set of fences, it was said, would allow the stockman to bring in a better grade of animal, free of the fear that they would breed indiscriminately with lesser stock. Fences would also make possible a system of pasture rotations, confining the animals to areas where the vegetation was in good shape, keeping them off areas that needed to recover. There would be less erosion, depletion, and weedy invasion. Under a program of privatization the range would yield a higher economic return while simultaneously remaining a more healthy and productive environment.[16]

Such was the answer that began to be heard in congressional hearings from the first part of the twentieth century on to the present, an answer one can follow among individual stockmen, their lobbying groups (the National Livestock Association, the National Wool Growers Association, the various state versions of the same), their senators and representatives, and a number of resource economists. In 1929 President Herbert Hoover, impressed by this collective din, proposed to turn over the remaining public domain, after forest and park withdrawals, to the western states, which they could then dispose of to individuals or corporations. The measure failed when it was learned that he did not mean to include mineral rights with the grass. More recently, between 1979 and 1981, a number of western states, beginning with Nevada, tried to claim federal lands within their borders with the idea of putting them into the hands of stockmen and miners; this was the so-called "Sagebrush Rebellion," but eventually it too fizzled out.[17]

An opposing solution came from conservationists and government officials, along with a number of scientists. The great western pastures, it was argued, had been acquired at the price of considerable blood and money by the federal government on behalf of all the American people, and they should stay public. Since almost everything else had been disposed of into private hands, these lands were all that was left of a public heritage. Here again there was a moral dimension to the argument, an appeal to social democratic ideals of equality and commonwealth. There was also an effort to refute the claim that only privatization could produce the greatest economic return; on the contrary, it was insisted, public ownership would insure the greatest return to the greatest number of people. But perhaps the most effective part of the argument, though it was seldom put very bluntly, was that the private entrepreneur simply could not be trusted to look out for the long-term ecological health of the range resource. He would tend to exploit rather than conserve it; making the pastures private would not be a reliable way to protect them for posterity. A much better solution would be to create a centralized bureaucracy of disinterested, scientifically trained professionals to oversee the public range.

In 1934 Congress, leaning toward this second proposal, passed the Taylor Grazing Act, which for the first time established a significant measure of control over the unappropriated public domain. The purpose of the Act was "to stop injury to the public grazing lands by preventing overgrazing and soil deterioration, to provide for their orderly use, improvement, and development, [and] to stablize the livestock industry dependent upon the public range."[18] The legislation set up a National Grazing Service to carry out those purposes through a system of leasing public lands for a fee; together with the Forest Service, which administers grazing leases within the national forest system, the Grazing Service (later the Bureau of Land Management) would supervise ranchers over a domain encompassing by far the largest part of the rural West. Some stockmen would have their entire ranch on the public lands, but the average lessee would mix private holdings with public leases in about a 4:6 ratio. The leases were almost, but not quite, a rancher's private property. They could be traded in the market, could serve as bank collateral, and could be fenced. But always, in the corner of the rancher's eye, there would be the specter of a federal bureaucrat armed with a mandate to protect the public's interest in the land. During the 1960s and '70s, after a long era of pusillanimous neglect and under rising pressure from conservationists, the bureaucrats began to assert their mandate in modest but galling ways. They contended that, since many leases were badly overgrazed, a lot of stock would have to be removed or lessees would lose their leases.[19] In the eyes of many rancher-lessees that newly assertive bureaucracy had come to be an unacceptable infringement on their freedom and a threat to the security of their tenure.[20]

The long contest between these two rivals in modern American-style pastoralism has given much of the West a peculiar set of property and managerial arrangement: a hybrid of capitalist and bureaucratic regimes, each assuming it knows what is best for the nation's pocketbook and for nature. The significance of the struggle is immense. On a planet where land has everywhere been put under more and more intensive use, the West speaks directly to the question of where we can find the ideal manager. Is it the man or woman dressed in Stetson hat and boots, claiming to belong to the land and to know it intimately, but speaking the language of private property, business, and profit maximization? Or is it the government official, also likely to be dressed in traditional western garb, as much a local resident as the other but trained in the discourse of biology and range management? Does the self-interest of the capitalist really lead to rational land use, as many claim, or is it destructive of self, society, and the land? Can those who have no immediate economic stake in the land be trusted to make better decisions about its use? Has either the modern capitalist or bureaucrat the ability to surpass Old World pastoralists in supporting human life out on the margins of the good earth? The West offers millions of acres and decades of experience in which to find answers for those questions.

So far we have seen shelves and shelves of books written on the western range, but very little of that literature has systematically addressed the big questions of tenure, environment, and managerial strategies. What is needed is a new history of the West that will compare the condition of the range under private and public (or quasi-public) ownership, that will explore the impact of rangeland science on management, that will test the claims made by the rival parties and help resolve the old debate. And we need a history that will put the West more fully into the global picture of people, animals, and arid lands.[21]

We do not yet have that more probing, critical history but we do have enough evidence to suggest some tentative conclusions, and I want to review some of it now. Overall, it lends support to the view that ranching has, on the whole, had a degrading effect on the environment of the American West. Most of that effect has come through turning pastoralism into a capitalistic enterprise, but ranching under supervision by the federal government has often not mitigated that impact and, in some ways, has made it worse.

The least-studied impact has been on the native fauna of the West. When and if we think about it, we realize that the invasion by millions of head of exogenous horses, cattle, sheep, and goats in the span of a few decades must have come with the explosive, shattering effect of all-out war. As Robin Doughty writes about Texas: "Efforts to introduce and establish novel, potentially valuable animals and plants . . . created an agricultural landscape that massively disrupted and restructured native fauna and flora."[22] The wildlife reeled and died before the onslaught. They lost their habitats to the invaders; they fell before the guns of the invaders' owners. What we need to do as historians is document that destruction and discover its magnitude. So far rather little of that sort of work has been done; much effort has gone into calculating the collapse of the native human populations under the European invasion, but almost none into the precipitous decline of the many nations of wild animals. How many bighorn sheep were there before longhorns and Herefords came onto the range? When and how did they disappear? How many ground-nesting birds like scaled quail and prairie chickens did the region once support? What effect did alien cattle hooves have on riparian environments—desert water holes, high-mountain lakes, streams and rivers—and the fish, insects, reptiles, birds, and mammals that lived in them? The chief exception to our general ignorance is the fate of the bison, whose near-extermination we have documented in some detail; Tom McHugh, for example, estimates there were once 32 million of these animals on the grasslands, with another two million living in wooded areas bordering the plains, while Ernest Thompson Seton set the original North American total at 75 million.[23] Today, the combined populations of bison, bighorn sheep, elk, and pronghorn antelopes in seventeen western states does not amount to 1 percent of what they once were.[24]

Aside from the wholesale replacement of the large wild herbivores by domesticated stock, we have good records on the death of the West's predator and rodent species, mainly because the principal record-keeper, the federal government, did most of the killing. Wyoming may be taken as representative of that destruction. After decades of unorganized killing by cattle and sheepmen there, the Bureau of Biological Survey took over so-called "pest control" in 1915. Subsequently, ten to twelve government hunters, using guns and poison baits furnished by Congress, went out each year to "clean up" the unwanted wildlife and make the range safe for livestock. By the late 1920s there were no more than five wolves left in Wyoming, and mountain lions had been nearly wiped out. Taken together, the federal agents, the hunters hired by the state, and those of the various grazing associations killed a total of 63,145 animals from 1916 to 1928. The body count was as follows: 169 bears, 1,524 bobcats, 36,242 coyotes, 18 mountain lions, 31 lynxes, 706 wolves, and 1,828 embryos of all the above. Badgers, beavers, civet cats, blackfooted ferrets, foxes, martens, minks, muskrats, opossums, raccoons, skunks, weasels, porcupines, rattlesnakes, prairie dogs, ground squirrels, pocket gophers, jack rabbits, eagles, and magpies also died in great numbers because of the threat they posed to the range industry.[25] Multiply those numbers by all the western range states over a period of a century and a quarter, coming right down to the 1990s, and you can begin to grasp the enormous scale of faunal change that the cowboy brought to the countryside.

We know a great deal more about the impact of cattle and sheep on the vegetation, for vegetation to a grazier is "forage" and forage is money. The first comprehensive effort to write up that impact came in 1936, after Senator Frank Norris of Nebraska pushed through a resolution instructing the Department of Agriculture to collect information on "the original and present condition of the range resource, the factors which have lead to the present condition, and the social and economic importance of the range and its conservation to the West and to the entire United States." Since its founding in 1905 the Forest Service, through its various experiment stations, had accumulated data on range conditions; then, starting in 1932, a time of national depression and the beginnings of severe drought conditions in the West, the Service undertook a more extensive survey, which the Norris resolution brought to print. More than a hundred Forest Service officials examined vegetation on over 20,000 plots, some of them relict samples of the native vegetation growing along railroad tracks or in cemeteries, others areas that had been heavily grazed by livestock, and sent in their observations on how plant species had changed in number and distribution. They combed through reports by early explorers, travelers, and naturalists to supplement those measurements and push back their understanding of the land's history into the nineteenth century. The survey divided the range into ten major types, including short grass, sagebrush-grass, salt-desert shrub, and woodland-chaparral, covering an area of 728 million acres, or nearly 40 percent of the total land area of the continental United States. Even now the 1936 survey is the most thorough ecological accounting we have of the first half-century of western pastoralism, from the first days of the cattle kingdom to the Dust Bowl years. It provides an important benchmark for later federal surveys.[26]

The Forest Service found that overall the range had been depleted by 52 percent from its virgin condition: that is, a range once capable of supporting a hundred grazing animals could now support only 48. Put another way, from an original capacity to feed 22.5 million animal units the range had declined until it could carry only 10.8 million.[27] "The plant cover in every range type," according to the report, "is depleted to an alarming degree. Palatable plants are being replaced by unpalatable ones. Worthless and obnoxious weeds from foreign countries are invading every type. And throughout the entire western range the vegetation has been thinned out until even the conservative estimates place the forage value at less than half of what it was a century ago." Admitting that there had never been a state of perfectly stable or uniform abundance on the range, the report nonetheless argued that the white man had disturbed the ecological equilibrium radically, raddling the plant cover by overstocking, allowing the soil to erode, and making natural regeneration more difficult for many native species. Overall, 13 percent of the West had suffered "moderate depletion" (0–25 percent loss of forage value), 34 percent "material depletion" (26–50 percent loss), 37 percent "severe depletion" (50–75 percent), and over 16 percent "extreme depletion" (76–100 percent). The short-grass country of west Texas, for example, was mainly placed in the severe category. Even worse were the Dust Bowl area of the southern plains, the western slope of Colorado, much of the Great Basin, and the Big Horn valley of Wyoming, all naturally scanty lands where grama and buffalo grass, sagebrush and winterfat, galleta and greasewood grew. Drought could explain some of this appalling loss of plant life, but officials placed most of the blame on "the apparent indifference of those controlling the use of the land."[28] "There is perhaps no darker chapter nor greater tragedy in the history of land occupancy and use in the United States," they wrote, "than the story of the western range."[29]

Who was responsible for the ecological degradation? In 1936 about half of the western range was in private hands (376 million acres), the rest in federal, state, and Indian ownership. The Forest Service wanted to know not only what was growing on all those acres but also how the type of ownership affected their condition. Clearly, the worst lands were those in the public domain—lands no one had wanted for homesteading, lands left over from the pioneer era, lands now freely grazed by ranchers who did not own them. That acreage showed an average of 67 percent depletion from pre-invasion conditions. To be sure, the public domain consisted mainly of the most marginal lands for livestock—much of it was nothing but desert anyway. Still, they had deteriorated from a low but stable level of productivity due to unrestrained stocking by men who had no one to answer to, apparently not even their children. Here was a continuation of the nineteenth-century tragedy of the laissez-faire commons.

But for anyone who insisted that such lands be sold to the lessees to allow more incentive to protect them, the report had disturbing news. Private landowners were not doing very well on their own property either, on land which they had bought and fenced and might have hoped to hand on to their descendents. Generally, the private rangelands had been the best property the West had to offer, lands along the river bottoms or wherever there had once been attractive stands of grass. "Very surprisingly," the report states, "fee-simple private ownership has been so little of an incentive to the preservation of the range resource that depletion stands at 51 percent." The pressures of mortgages, or overinvestment, of good old human acquisitiveness had led private ranchers throughout the West to pack their acres with animals to a self-destructive level. In a chapter specifically on private ownership the report concluded that many ranchers had taken the short-term view that land is a temporary source of income, a form of capital to be quickly liquidated if something better was offered somewhere else. "The concept of stewardship," they lamented, "has been largely undeveloped."[30]

In much better condition than both the unsupervised public domain and the private rangelands were the national forests, which showed a decline of only 30 percent from virgin conditions. Maybe that was not an unpredictable finding in a Forest Service report. Critics have argued that the agency was too eager to make itself look good in hopes of getting more land transferred into its hands. All of its ecologists and experiment station personnel supposedly twisted the facts their way—sent in faked reports, somehow found plant cover growing on agency lands that wasn't really there, on the other hand failed to see plant cover on the private range that *was* there. Without access to the many individual reports or any independent verification of them, we will never know for sure just how much the Service distorted to make everyone else look worse than they. But in defense of the report's trustworthiness, we can say that every survey of the western range made since the 1930s has tended to the same conclusion: the combination of scientifically trained, disinterested supervisors and public land tenure provides better protection for the range environment, on the whole, than simple private ownership.

Much has happened on the range since the thirties. In 1979 one of the leading experts on their condition, Thadis Box of Utah State University, declared: "On the whole, the rangelands of this country have improved over the last few decades and will continue to improve in the future."[31] The basis for his optimism was the growth of range management as a science and the application of that science to both public and private, but especially public, lands since the thirties. Box could point to several recent surveys for support. A 1969 study done by an independent group, Pacific Consultants, for the Public Land Law Review Commission found that almost 20 percent of the public domain could now be categorized as excellent in terms of vegetation, compared with only 1.5 percent in the mid-1930s. The standard used by government scientists to evaluate range condition has varied over time and from agency to agency in number of categories and in techniques of evaluation, but overall the criterion used has remained fairly consistent: the degree to which the vegetation departs from the natural potential (or climax state) for the site. In 1974 Congress passed the Forest and Rangeland Resources Planning Act, which requires the Department of Agriculture to make a general assessment periodically of forest and range resources under all forms of ownership. The last major assessment, published in 1981, found 46 percent of the rangelands in the contiguous 48 states to be in fair to good condition.[32] Hardly, to be sure, an impressive number. After more than a hundred years of ranching, more than half the lands devoted to it are still in poor or very poor condition. And that despite the fact that we have trained thousands of professionals, have seen published thousands of expert journal articles, have turned out hundreds of Ph.D.s in the field of range management, and have accumulated lots of grassroots experience,. For all that learning much of the region is still, in Edward Abbey's phrase, "a cow-burnt wasteland."[33] It has been torched, chained, plowed, herbicided, desertified, and eaten down to the roots. After much expensive manipulation to get better cover established on it, millions of acres are covered with worthless cheatgrass, along with mesquite, sagebrush, Russian thistle, and prickly pear. All the same, Thaddis Box is probably right: ever so slowly, the picture is improving, and it is doing so fastest on the lands held by the federal government. More than 60 percent of Nevada, a state almost wholly owned by the feds, is now in fair or better condition.[34]

Understandably, in these days of strong conservative political sentiment in the western states, which rejects the whole idea of government competence, the federal agencies have been more reticent about their record compared with that of private landowners than officials were in the New Deal era. But at least one independent study of comparative stewardship suggests that the contrast in conservation between the best federal managers and that of private owners found in the 1930s still prevails. Two scientists, Michael Loring and John Workman, compared range conditions on private and public land in a northeastern county of Utah, where the ecosystem is dominated by sagebrush and bunchgrass. Thirteen percent of Forest Service acres, they discovered, were in excellent condition (i.e., three-fourths of more of the "natural" or climax vegetation was still growing on them), compared with 4 percent of the Bureau of Land Management Lands, and only 2 percent of private and state lands. At the other end of the scale, 29 percent of non-federal lands had to be classified as poor, compared with only 14 percent of U.S. Forest Service Lands and 16 percent of Bureau of Land Management lands. The private-property owners are still not performing as well as many privatizing theorists say they should. So striking is the difference in stewardship that the authors of this study warn: "Any transfer of [federal grazing land] to private ownership might bring a decline in range condition."[35]

Of course, these materials do not constitute a full ecological history of the western range. A local study here, a survey back then—precious little evidence, I confess, from which to draw any grand conclusions. There are many questions for which we don't have thorough, or even adequate, answers. Has that experience of a single Utah county been replicated elsewhere, in the privately held Sand Hills of Nebraska, for example, or in the national forests of New Mexico, or on the deserts of southern California? Is the Bureau of Land Management, after being so ineffective as a land steward for so long, becoming today as conservation-minded as the Forest Service? Did either agency continue to make progress on reducing overgrazing by their lessees during the Reagan and Bush administrations? Have there been some enlightened private landowners who have done a better job preserving the native fauna and flora of the West than the federal government, or at least have not diminished the forage value of the range, and if so, how did they do it? Are we, as a nation, moving at last toward a sustainable life on the range? Or are we failing, and is it time to get all the cattle and sheep and goats off all the public's land—all the money-making, land-abusing animals that Abbey called "these ugly, clumsy, stupid, bawling, stinking, fly-covered, shit-smeared, disease-spreading brutes"?[36] And even if it is, will that decision be made soon? The historian answers, probably not. Ranching is going to remain a part of the West, on public and private land alike, for as far into the future as we can see. Likely, we will continue looking for the best way to raise our meat and wool on the land without degrading it. To do that, we need a full ecological history of American range management, one that goes beyond the narrow matters that most range technicians seem to know and care about, one that is alert to all the effects of various tenure systems and to all the socio-ecological regulatory systems of other cultures.

One conclusion, however, seems inescapable from what we know about the pastoral past, in this country and abroad. The safest strategy over the long run appears to be one that opens decisions about using the range to as many people as possible. The most stable systems of grazing have been those in which the experience, knowledge, and moral pressure of a whole community guided the individual grazier. In a traditional Swiss village that community may have been comprised of peasants, while in today's United States it may include range ecologists, environmentalists, private owners and lessees, and bureaucrats, all cooperating to get the best fit between livestock and the land. The completely laissez-faire economy, the system in which private property is regarded as a moral absolute and individual greed is allowed to go unchecked, has amply demonstrated its destructive energies.

I am aware the most folks, when they think of cowboys and the West, do not have in mind all that I have touched on here, and therefore they may resist this new kind of pastoral history. Many still idealize the cowboy as living a life of total freedom in an open country, living in a West beyond restraint. Pastoralism has always had that effect on people toiling in fields and cities; though they may see that the herders are often poor, primitive, and uncouth, they nonetheless admire them for their freedom to roam the high mountains, the distant savannahs, the deserts, to possess all the untrammeled freedom of space. In America we have added to that old set of pastoral idealizations some up-to-date ones: our cowboy-rancher somehow has come to stand for the ideal of free enterprise and for the institution of private property. Historians need to take all those images and ideals seriously—more seriously than they have—but histo-

4 •

Hydraulic Society in California

No region on earth has had more to do with shaping the twentieth century than California.* That is as true of agricultural history as it is of mass culture, sexuality, urbanization, atomic bombs, and the shift from bourbon to wine. Put a historian down anywhere in the state, and he or she will find something profound to say about modernity. My own choice is to be deposited by the side of a concrete-lined irrigation canal in Kern County, by a stream that is not a stream, where no willows are allowed to grow or herons or blackbirds nest. That intensely managed piece of nature tells us a great deal about contemporary rural life and land use, some of it profound, some of it disturbing, all of it indicative of a world-wide momentum. The factual history of that canal and the agriculture dependent on it is rather well known in particulars. What is needed now is a theoretical and interpretative framework for those facts, a task this essay undertakes, though only in the most preliminary fashion.

In 1939 two books appeared on the emerging character of California agriculture. They each had a galvanic impact on public thinking, and more than forty years later they are both still in print, still capable of jolting us out of moral torpor. The first was John Steinbeck's *The Grapes of*

*This essay was first published in *Agricultural History* 56, July 1982.

Wrath, the second, Carey McWilliam's *Factories in the Field.*[1] Together they framed a compelling interpretation of that rural order which to date has not been persuasively challenged. A succession of able historians has filled out and updated the original accounts, but no one has yet changed the fundamental terms of discussion.[2] Forty years covers a long span in the modern history of ideas, however, and we may be ready today to try another angle of vision.

The human consequences of industrialization and the making of a new rural proletariat were the themes that superseded all others for Steinbeck and McWilliams. Describing California, they echoed eighteenth- and nineteenth-century protests (from writers like Oliver Goldsmith and William Cobbett) against the enclosure acts in England, and they reminded readers too of the cities of Depression America, where millions were made helpless by the failing of industrial capitalism. Karl Marx was an obvious if remote influence, particularly on McWilliams, who tried hard to argue in 1930s Marxian socialist terms that California agriculture had evolved out of a feudal state shaped by Spanish land barons. Capitalist entrepreneurs had taken over from them to build an industrial empire, which rested on the backs of stoop-and-pick workers recruited from all over the world. The eventual outcome of that history, he predicted, would be an uprising of the exploited undergroup—collectivizing the factory farms so that their productivity would become available for the common welfare. Class conflict, in other words, was what the California story in agriculture was all about.[3]

Altogether missing from that interpretation—and again it is McWilliams I have in mind especially—was the peculiar ecological situation in California: the interaction of men and women there with the land, which is after all at the heart of any farming system. It will be my own argument that a new ecologically oriented inquiry will not only give us a fuller account of the state's agricultural evolution but also, and this may be the most surprising result, will establish a more satisfactory framework than old-fashioned, generic Marxism for making sense of that history of class exploitation. It will do so by showing that nature's fate is humanity's as well.

At no point in his novel did Steinbeck so much as mention the fact that the vineyards of California, its orange groves and cottonfields and vast tomato patches, were supported by an elaborate irrigation regime.[4] McWilliams noted the fact only in passing. The contemporary ecology-based agricultural historian, in contrast, finds in irrigation a key formative element, an underlying infrastructure out of which social relations grew. What is exemplified in the state is not only "factory farming," as

McWilliams and Steinbeck made us aware, but more specifically a modern *hydraulic society*—a social order founded on the intensive management of water. That regime did not evolve in isolation from the industrial system, of course, but all the same it was a distinctive emergent, reflecting the geography and arid climate of the state. We ought to be scrutinizing, therefore, not only historical analogies like Cobbett's England but also those desert landscapes of the world where large-scale irrigated agriculture has flourished as it has in California.

The phrase "hydraulic society" comes from two students of ancient cultures, Julian Steward and Karl Wittfogel.[5] They maintained that in the great river valleys of Mesopotamia, Egypt, India, and China a striking cultural convergence took place during the 3000 years before Christ. In each of those places it became necessary, under the pressure of population growth, to plug all the rivers with storage dams, diverting the water into elaborate networks of canals and ditches to irrigate the peasants' fields. Construction and maintenance of those massive public works required the marshaling of vast corvées—faceless armies of laborers—for at least a part of every year. And where workers were brought together in this regimented fashion for the conquest of nature, there had to be organizers. A remarkably similar power elite emerged, consequently, in all those irrigated systems. It included scientists and engineers who achieved sophisticated ability to manipulate the natural riverine environment, an expertise they willingly put to the service of even more powerful authorities. There were priests who gave spiritual legitimacy to the regime. And there was an overclass of agro-managerial bureaucrats who took charge of directing that knowledge and spirituality, of directing the peasants, and of directing the rivers; it could not have been otherwise, given the need to maximize agricultural production. Carried far enough, the process of intensifying environmental management stripped the peasant and his small-scale community of much of their autonomy, their competence, concentrating hegemony in fewer and fewer hands, until at some late point in this intensification an imperial despot appeared, who personified in his exalted rule the new human power over nature. The fabled Assyrian ruler, Queen Semiramis, was reputed to have inscribed on her tomb what may stand as the ecological creed, and the hubris, of the advanced hydraulic civilizations: "I constrained the mighty river to flow according to my will and let its water to fertilize lands that had before been barren and without inhabitants."[6]

The engineered waters of the Tigris, the Euphrates, and the Nile were then, according to the theory of hydraulic society, the environmental basis for the first authoritarian, complexly hierarchical civilizations. I take this to be the essence of the hydraulic thesis: the domination of nature is an ambition that first appears stark and unchecked in the archaic desert empires, and thereafter the ambition, wherever and whenever it recurs as a compelling cultural idea, is always associated with the domination of some people by other people.[7] This is a grand, imposing argument, defying a narrow, reductive, "scientific" formulation (domination being necessarily a difficult concept to quantify), and undoubtedly open at numerous points to challenge and skepticism. Wittfogel in particular can be justly criticized for reading into the past the totalitarian tendencies of our own era, while at the same time he failed to see how closely parallel in many ways are the modern capitalist-based irrigation societies and the ancient hydraulic power complexes. We will do well to keep such caveats and reservations in mind while, nonetheless, realizing that it is precisely such high-wire acts, such big ideas, as this one we must follow if that Kern County irrigation canal is going to be understood for what it truly is.

In California and the West has emerged the most elaborate hydraulic system in world history, overshadowing even the grandiose works of the Sassanians and the Pharaohs. In 1976 the federal Bureau of Reclamation alone operated 320 water-storage reservoirs, 344 diversion dams, 14,400 miles of canals, 900 miles of pipelines, 205 miles of tunnels, 34,620 miles of laterals, 145 pumping plants, 50 power plants, and 16,240 circuit miles of transmission lines.[8] That technology has remade completely the western river landscape. The Colorado has not reached the sea for twenty years, while the Columbia, the Snake, the Missouri, the Platte, the Brazos, and the Rio Grande, over much of their length, are descending staircases of man-made tanks.[9] Water sparkling in a Beverly Hills swimming pool may have fallen as rain in the Rockies or in the Sierra. En route to its final consumptive use, it may have generated electricity for a neon cowboy in Las Vegas or lapped against the bow of a sailboat on Lake Mead. Large-scale irrigation from this same triumphant engineering has helped make California the most powerful agricultural region on the planet—the home base for what has become an international agribusiness empire. It is time we examined this modern regime in the light of the Wittfogel-Steward thesis. To what extent do we find similarities in social organization between the two hydraulic eras, and just as important, what are their differences? Further, what does that comparison tell us about the ecological basis of social power—the relationships between resource use, technological upscaling, and democratic control?

The theme of irrigation is a familiar one in western American history.[10] Though it has never fed popular fantasies as cattle drives and fur trapper rendezvous have, it has had more permanent consequences than almost any other aspect of what is speciously referred to as "the winning of the West." In 1878 John Wesley Powell predicted with considerable foresight that irrigation would bring about a new phase in American civilization. It would domesticate the West for settlement, opening, he hoped, a wide field of opportunity for a nation that was elsewhere drifting toward industrial monopoly. It would also, he promised, establish the foundations for a powerful new economic order, based on cooperation and brotherhood rather than on competitive individualism.[11] Another early enthusiast, William Smythe of Nebraska and San Diego, declared in 1905: "The essence of the industrial life which springs from irrigation is its democracy."[12] The transition from such high initial hopes to the 1930s despair of John Steinbeck's Okies is one of the most dramatic turnabouts in our history. How can we explain it? In this fashion, I submit: irrigation in California and the West did in fact mark a new phase, but past a critical threshold of development it became demonstrable that irrigation would do little to promote democracy, that instead it was capable of creating Leviathan in the desert.

The origins of California irrigation under American auspices date not long after the 1849 gold rush, when miners sought to grow foodstuffs around their diggings. The next century and a quarter of intensification followed a clearly structured pattern. First, the process of diverting river water ran at least twice into a dead end, temporarily exhausting the possibilities for rearranging the natural ecosystem for human gain and enforcing a kind of equilibrium state or even regression. We can call this experience a *diversion plateau*. Second, lifting the agricultural economy above such a plateau required innovation, that is, creating new forms of social organization that could design and put into play a more complex hydraulic machinery. Always that gathering of social force involved a certain loss of autonomy as decision-making moved to a higher level—a process we can refer to as the *centralization and capture of power*. In the American case such centralization was often the work of government, while it was private economic interests that captured the apparatus and exercised the domination it allowed. The third part of the pattern was an overall tendency toward involution, wherein the ever-more-complicated apparatus became a straitjacket that prevented a genuine choice among alternative futures. The innovations I have mentioned were increasingly required to prop up the system, to overcome self-generated problems, and to prevent the unthinkable catastrophe of total collapse. That is a fate endured by other irrigation societies in history—which I will term *infrastructure trap*. Let us review briefly how these three processes operated.

The rivers of California, particularly those that flow out of the Sierra Nevada and down the Great Central Valley, are in season raging torrents of energy. For thousands of years they defied their own channels every spring, flooding the sloughs, the soddy meadows, and what John Muir called "the bee pastures of heaven."[13] Aboriginal farmers accepted in most cases that tumultuous authority: when the floods relented, they rushed to plant corn and beans in the mud, hoping to harvest them before the soil dried out. Only in a few places in what would become California were diversion ditches—really shallow furrows—dug. The early Spanish and American invaders, on the other hand, made more and bigger furrows, and midstream on the smaller tributaries they threw up brush dams to force a steady stream into their gardens.[14] That scale of intervention made little ecological disturbance, but it allowed a satisfactory living for a pioneer family wanting nothing more than self-sufficiency. Few of the Americans who began farming in California, however, were interested in pursuing a self-sufficient life. They brought ideas about markets and profitability along with plow and seed to the western river valleys. Most of the rich agricultural soil, they soon discovered, lay on the larger floodplains, where simple dams of brush and rocks were feeble constraints, completely inadequate to tame a San Joaquin carrying melted snow from some of the highest peaks on the continent. Even the joining together of two or three settlers' efforts could not constitute enough human force to manage the major rivers. By the early 1870s California had reached its first diversion plateau. It could go no farther toward market development without inventing a larger, more potent harness—a yoke that would unite many people's energies. But who would hold the reins?

The parallel with ancient hydraulic societies would seem to hold true to this point. California, growing in numbers of farmers every year, was forced to expand into more intractable lands, just as the hill husbandmen were forced by demographic pressure to come down to the edges of the Euphrates. But there was already apparent an important distinction between the ancient and the emerging modern regimes. Mainly that difference was created by the marketplace economy, which would not be restricted for long to any plateau of development. From its earliest point California irrigation intensification was driven essentially by production for profit, not profit for use, values. A potential market for irrigated produce lay in the goldrush camps, then in coastal cites, in eastern states, in Europe, and as some visionaries early saw, in Asia.[15] Profit in this place quickly proved to be a sharper goad than population pressure and hunger had been in ancient times, propelling California in a matter of decades through a process of elaboration that had taken other cultures hundreds and even thousands of years to complete.

The marketplace then was the most powerful determinant of the course taken by the American irrigated agro-ecosystem. It soon produced one of the key institutional devices that Californians used to climb off their first plateau: the private corporation. The San Joaquin and King's River Canal and Irrigation Company was incorporated in 1871, with headquarters in San Francisco where most of its shareholders lived, to construct a large new irrigation system. When this system was completed two years later, it ran almost forty miles and watered 16,000 acres a year. "The farmers and settlers in the San Joaquin Valley," the company's promotion brochure read, "are too poor to carry out the necessary canals and ditches by themselves, and require the cooperation of capitalists."[16] Water now became a commodity to be mass-produced and mass-consumed. Powerful entrepreneurs like Isaac Friedlander, Henry Miller, and James Haggin undertook to abstract water from its natural milieu and create a demand for its use. A pamphleteer of the day saw in this new phase of corporate irrigation enterprise America's answer to the lush gardens of Babylon, "and a wealth, imperial in its luxuriance."[17]

Paradoxically, California irrigation, in its reorganization on the Great Valley floor, seemed at first to be tending toward a more decentralized, democratic rural economy. Immense wheat farms, some as large as 50,000 acres, were broken up for sale to individuals or to colonies of cultivators.[18] A forty- or eighty-acre orchard under the ditch was about all a single man or woman could handle, and it afforded a substantial enough income for a while. The state that had once been described as "the rich man's paradise, and the poor man's hell" now began to resemble, in the eyes of some observers, "the land of the common people," a rural eden of "small estates, of small enterprises, of small fortunes."[19] But here was the rub: title to land without title to water meant little in a dry country. So long as small farmers had to buy water from a distant corporation, they had obtained a new prosperity at the cost of a substantial portion of their independence,.[20]

In addition to corporate capitalism, there was a second ladder devised to climb from the lower to a higher level of diversion. It was called the irrigation district, and it was a unique product of the arid region. The 1887 Wright Act authorized California farmers to organize quasi-governmental entities that could build common irrigation works and tax local residents to pay for them. The district was, in other words, a public corporation brought into being by a majority vote of landowners and often coercing a recalcitrant minority to share the expense. It was a means of getting more income out of a river without surrendering to urban capitalists. By 1920 there were 71 irrigation districts in the state, most of them put together in the boom years of 1915 to 1920.[21] The largest, covering over half a million acres, was in Imperial Valley, land of broiling sun, rich green crops, and recurring violence between growers and their hired laborers. Imperial had been carved out of the desert by high-risk capitalists who had tapped the Colorado River bonanza, but even after its reorganization along nominally more democratic, locally managed lines, the district could not shake off its origins. Being competitive in marketplace America meant here, as in other districts, adopting to a large extent the private corporation's top-down pattern of internal authority. To survive and prosper, they were compelled to take the advice given to districts by Frederick Newell, one-time head of the U.S. Reclamation Services:

> There must be a strong central organization headed by a manager who is removed from the danger of being influenced by individual water users, and who has enough assistants, responsible directly to him, to enable him to carry out effectively the general plans and policies. . . . The most efficient manager of an irrigation system is usually one who has had experience in large corporations and who has had training in handling large affairs.[22]

That person, ideally, was an engineer like Newell himself, especially an engineer who could offer both technical expertise and business acumen. It was such men who would effectively hold the reins in districts like Imperial.

A long training in forming irrigation districts, in conforming to unified water plans, and in submitting to strong leaders helps greatly to explain why California eventually became the most powerful agricultural region in the United States. While farmers elsewhere were more apt to cling to precommercial values, to family-centered operations, and to their vernacular farming ways, the western irrigated grower threw all that encumbrance off, submitting instead to a new professionalism. The shift enabled him to keep pace with the corporate industrial economy. "Cooperation helps to make farming profitable," a university dean of agriculture and a farm editor pointed out; it was a lesson that California farmers learned from water control and went on to apply to marketing, beginning in 1895 with the formation of the Fruit Growers' Exchange.[23] In the 1920s these marketing cooperatives were so effective that they prospered even in the midst of agricultural depression, as grocery stores across the country increasingly featured their nationally advertised name brands—Sunkist, Sunmaid, Sunsweet, Mistmaid, Diamond Brand, Blue Diamond, Blue Ribbon.[24] Irrigating farmers also had unrivaled access to credit, to the capital needed for maximizing their technological efficiency, and they gained political leverage to protect their position even in a highly urban state. Most important, they secured on their own terms a labor pool large enough to harvest their produce cheaply, and, through collective employer strength, they kept those laborers firmly under control decade after decade: first the Chinese, then the Japanese, the Filipinos, the blacks, the Okies, and the Mexicans—California's polygot, wage-based version of the Egyptian corvées.[25]

Thus flourished the second phase of the hydraulic society's life cycle, lasting from the 1870s to the 1930s. Then once again a plateau was reached, threatening stagnation or worse, sudden economic decline. There was not enough pure water to support a constantly expanding irrigation demand. Every drop that could be economically taken directly from the rivers was taken, and farmers began to mine their underground supplies at breakneck speed. The more they pumped and the deeper they pumped, the more saline became the water spreading over their crops, poisoning the roots and raising the specter of irreversible damage to the land.[26] Walker Young, the Bureau of Reclamation's regional construction engineer, explained the prospect in these dark terms in 1937:

> More than a million acres face an acute irrigation crisis . . . Between 40,000 and 50,000 acres of producing lands have been abandoned, and 200,000 acres are in the process of gradual reversion to desert. Another 400,000 acres in the fertile Sacramento—San Joaquin Delta are menaced by intrusion of salt water from San Francisco Bay.[27]

Salvation from this nemesis, it became clear, demanded a level of engineering, organization, and money that no private corporation or local district could possibly summon. Retrenchment or innovation were, as before, the only routes open.

California farmers were, naturally enough, not prepared to give up the markets they had won, the technology they had invested in, or the social order they had built on irrigation. But getting to the next, higher plateau necessarily involved an appeal to the state or federal government for aid. In the midst of the Depression, when state coffers were overdrawn, California water interests chose, reluctantly it must be said, the federal government to do the bailing out. With an influx of federal cash—the hundreds of millions of dollars needed to bring new water into the state's irrigated economy—would come, so the more farsighted realized, the next step in centralization of power. Decision would no longer be made exclusively within California by farmers, districts, San Francisco investors, or even by the state engineer. Washington would have to be wooed and consulted. Out of desperation as much as deliberate thought, farmers plunged ahead, and the New Deal quickly said yes to their entreaties. In the late thirties federal engineers began planning the intricate Central Valley Project, the first stage of which was completed over the next decade, propping up the factories in the field with subsidies from the national treasury.[28]

Every western state, over the past forty years, has felt compelled to take a similar course; indeed, most states, lacking California's size and wealth, have gone much farther toward federalization, placing their destiny irretrievably in the hands of government water experts who speak a recondite language few dirt farmers can understand. Now and then those experts have attempted to impose an unwelcome social philosophy on local irrigation districts, creating as they have most recently the hotly controversial acreage limitation issue over who is eligible for federal water subsidies.[29] But for the most part the superintending bureaucracy has only halfheartedly and sporadically tried to achieve social reform—for a period in the 1940s and again in the late 1970s. The reason is clear enough: the technocrats are in reality only subordinate members of the ruling elite, constrained to design and administer a hydraulic agriculture that will be competitive in an increasingly international marketplace. And there again we see that important difference between our own modern irrigation society and its ancient counterparts: the first operates under unrelenting world and national capitalist pressures, which are impersonal, anonymous, and identified with "iron laws of economic necessity"; while the second were self-contained, bureaucratic command economies that took the personal word of the emperor as the word of God.[30]

Since California farmers agree with, and are the only means to realize, the ruling commercial values of modern hydraulic society, it is improbable that federal centralization will mean any upheaval in local structures of wealth. In fact the story of California irrigation in this latest, post-thirties phase has been the story of the establishment of concentrated private hegemony, at once economic and ideological, over publicly developed engineering works. But make no mistake about this: considerable autonomy has been delivered to remote, outside forces, to a collusion of bureaucratic and marketplace power centers. The individual farmer and the small community have become less than ever masters of their fate.

The most likely prospect for major historical change at this point comes not from government, not from a shrinking number of workers, not from California irrigators themselves, but directly and indirectly from nature. Most ancient hydraulic empires collapsed at the point when there were mounting ecological difficulties and a lag or breakdown in the managerial skill needed to meet them. In the middle of the thirteenth century invading Mongol horsemen came upon a scene of devastation in what is today Iraq. A once populous country was now empty of people and lying in ruins. Old decrepit canals were dry and choked with silt, while a whitish alkaline residue lay everywhere on the soil. The scene told of a society that had fallen into the infrastructure trap, building a bigger and bigger water system until they could no longer keep pace with the ecological backlash they were creating.[31] The state of California, some recent evidence indicates, may be approaching a similar alkalinity fate, as even the casual traveler can see along Interstate 5 in the southern San Joaquin Valley. All the environmental problems encountered in the 1930s have resurfaced, along with several unprecedented ones; meanwhile, the remedies are becoming more expensive and complicated to apply.[32] For the moment these complex problems may still seem solvable, but add to them the newer threats of inflating energy costs and pests resistant to pesticides, and the future becomes even more insecure, more unpredictable. It seems unlikely, in any case, that a massive, intricate irrigated agriculture, especially one tied to an expansionary marketplace engine, can save itself forever from self-destruction, though it may be that the trap's closing will be evaded for a long while yet.

We have been telling, someone may say, a parable of modern life. And the idea of hydraulic society might be applied, metaphorically if not exactly, to technological culture's relationship everywhere with the earth. Lewis Mumford, in *Technics and Human Development,* has made precisely that case, arguing as he does that the Age of Pyramids has returned in spirit and ethos, bent as before on establishing "absolute centralized control over both nature and man."[33] Megamachine is the name he gives to that restoration. He might have been thinking of California agriculture, but he wrote about the Pentagon and moon shots. Take California's agricultural history as only a small part of the larger whole. Take it as indicative rather than absolutely distinctive. But see it also as the peculiar convergence of a special geography and a familiar culture. In the vast arid spaces of California and the West, I have been suggesting, the universal modern predicament appears with a stark, uncluttered honesty not always found in other landscapes. Here we are able to see etched in sharpest detail the interplay between humans and nature and to track the social consequences it has produced—to discover the process by which, in the remaking of nature, we remake ourselves.

Hoover Dam:
A Study in Domination

The highway takes one northwest out of Kingman, Arizona, past the turnoff to Chloride, and runs along the Black Mountains, heading, it seems, farther into desolation.* Then it bursts through an opening in a rock wall, and there it sits—Hoover Dam—gleaming white in the hot desert sun, hurting one's eyes with its stark brilliance. Taking the highway across the dam, the traveler pulls up in a narrow parking lot and scrambles out to see this engineering wonder of the modern world, this answer to the pyramids and the ancient Colossus of Rhodes. When it was completed in 1935, Hoover Dam was the most massive structure of its kind in the world. It introduced a new era of building high-rise dams in country after country, remaking the face of the earth and altering the distribution of social and economic power on it. Among the leading symbols of twentieth-century technology Hoover Dam stands tall—near if not at the very top of the list of revealing "expressions of the age." Even now, more than fifty years after it was dedicated, in a time when many symbols and ideals of modernity have become discredited, Hoover still has the capacity to stir admiration and renew people's faith in the conquest of nature.

*This essay is a revised version of one published with the same title in *The Social and Environmental Effects of Large Dams*. Vol. 2 *Case Studies*, Edward Goldsmith and Nicholas Hildyard, eds. (Camelford, Cornwall, U.K.: Wadebridge Ecological Centre, 1986).

On a busy day thousands of tourists en route to enjoy the neon thrills of Las Vegas or the crowded, dusty campgrounds of the Grand Canyon pause to marvel at the dam. It has become one of the most popular travel attractions in the West—a ritualistic experience of "doing the West" and celebrating what its history has been. And what precisely do these tourists see when they stand on the dam's crest, looking down on Lake Mead, the man-made body of water created by the dam, flooding the Black Canyon of the Colorado River and over a hundred miles of upstream watershed? Is it the success of the westward movement or the defeat of wild nature they see and marvel at? Does there run through their minds a worry about the precariousness of human control, about its costs and dangers, or a rush of pride in the triumph of solid concrete over rambunctious river?

An elevator carries sightseers down into the bowels of the dam where immense turbines whir away, unceasingly generating electricity for cities like Los Angeles and Las Vegas, making the river pay for its own imprisonment. What do the visitors hear in that humming? The soft sound of money piling up, or the din of an anarchic, mindless acquisitive force let loose in American society? If the Bureau of Reclamation, the government agency conducting the tours and operating the dam, has its way, what people will see and hear will be completely reassuring. The official Hoover Dam story is supposed to convey a message of serene, benevolent order to travelers passing from one part of this unpredictable, irrational life to another. At least in this corner of the southwestern desert, nature is supposed to be under our firm control, working hard to make us all rich; and we can go on our way confident that responsible, competent people are in charge, assured that nature is no longer much of a threat to our welfare and that we are the very lords of life.

One long-dead traveler who will never see Hoover Dam but who might have had something less reassuring to say about its meaning was Henry Adams. When he was alive, the Black Canyon of the Colorado was still a remote, hidden country, all but inaccessible to civilization. Adams, therefore, had to go the Chicago and the great World's Fair of 1893, and from there to the Paris Exposition of 1900, to find his symbols of modernity. What he found in both places was a display of dynamos, or electric turbines, humming away as they still do inside the power plant of the dam. His reflections on those industrial displays, published in his autobiography, *The Education of Henry Adams,* might still be a provocative accompaniment to any Hoover Dam visit today. "The dynamo," he wrote, "became a symbol of infinity." It stood for a vast new power unleashed in human life, quite unlike anything before it, a mechanical power that acknowledged no limits and would seek to remake the whole world in its own image. "Before the end, one began to pray to it; inherited instinct taught the natural expression of man before silent and infinite force." The modern dynamo had come to be a religious-like symbol, driving out all the previous symbols of divine power that had ruled over human life for so long: nature, spirit, God, the Virgin Mary. What Adams also saw was that this cultural power of the dynamo represented a new king of rationality, one that did not deal with ultimate values and ends as the old religions had, but was focused instead on means, on instrumental effectiveness. The result of that shift was that the new, divine-like power, impressive and irresistible though it was, lacked any deep, carefully considered purpose or sense of direction. To those who sat down by such a machine and thought long and hard about its significance, as Adams did, the message was simply one of "more"—more profit, more comfort, more power for the sake of power.

In addition to the moral vacuum at the center of the coming technological society, Adams discerned another meaning: the power that was generated came to rest in fewer and fewer hands as centralized, bureaucratized structures of wealth and authority took command. "Once admitted that the machine must be efficient," Adams wrote, "society might dispute in what social interest it should be run, but in any case it must work concentration."[1]

The dynamo was, by itself, perhaps too technical and abstract a symbol of twentieth-century modernity to convey to ordinary minds all that Adams found in it. But put that machine inside the concrete wall of Hoover Dam rising 726 feet from bedrock, a dam three city blocks thick at its base, containing over three million cubic yards of cement, and the message becomes more visible. Put that concrete plug smack in the path of one of the most spectacular rivers on the planet, the Rio Colorado, which has carved the awesome Grand Canyon on its way to the sea, and the message gets harder yet to overlook. Surround that dam and river with an immense arid landscape, use the water and energy from them to conquer that landscape and create a urban civilization, an agribusiness empire, and you have the makings for an unrivaled study in the modern domination of nature and its consequences.

The Colorado River, though known to the Indians for tens of thousands of years, was not discovered by European civilization until 1540, when the Spanish naval commander Hernando de Alarcon sailed up the Gulf of California to the river's delta. Three hundred twenty-nine years later John Wesley Powell and a party of nine men put in at the headwaters of the river in Wyoming and raced off in the current, fetching up several months later, minus three of the men, at Grand Wash Cliffs, not far from the site of the future dam. Fifty years after that courageous exploring expedition, in the year 1922, several western American states signed a compact dividing the river among themselves, opening it for development. Then in 1928 the Boulder Canyon Act was passed by Congress, authorizing the construction of a dam that would be the first major step in controlling the river.[2]

Those five centuries of learning about the Colorado (actually most of the learning was concentrated in about five decades) seem almost never to have raised in people's minds a simple question: What changes in society would be required to master the Colorado's flow? Only Powell gave the matter much consideration; he recommended that both big government and big business stay away from the river, that ordinary settlers be encouraged to organize themselves into "cooperative commonwealths" and set about in their own way to make use of the watershed. Had his suggestion been followed, development would have been confined to the smaller side streams and upcountry valleys, for the main river was too strong for any local group of settlers, with limited capital and expertise, to harness.[3]

The Colorado runs for almost two thousand miles and drains an area of 244,000 square miles. Its volume is not great—far less than, say, the Mississippi or Congo or Amazon; even the Nile, another desert river to which the Colorado has often been compared, has a bigger average flow, discharging as it does 100,000 cubic feet per second at its mouth, whereas the Colorado, in its natural state before it was dammed and diverted, discharged one-fourth that amount. But the grandeur of the Colorado, its ability to defy human intervention, lay in the inexhaustible force it exhibited in its thrust to the sea. Over its course it drops from an elevation of 14,000 feet, generating in the process millions of horsepower of energy. From a time well before there were humans living on this planet, the river used that energy to grind its way seaward through the Colorado Plateau, a rising massif of sandstone and shale that makes the Hoover Dam impediment look like the merest pebble. Over the last thirteen million years the river has washed away more than a quadrillion tons of rock, sand, and gravel from that plateau, leaving behind it the most spectacular canyons found anywhere. It has wound its way deeper and deeper through that resistance, cutting meanders as much as a mile down, for hundreds upon hundreds of miles. All rivers are indefatigable workers, but this one has had a fanatic's determination in its industry. It would accept no compromises, make no detours, in the pursuit of its end but would push on night and day forever, until the plateau was gone, until there was no more work to be done, until it died of its own labors.[4]

Debouching from its multihued canyons, the Colorado carried one of the heaviest silt loads of all the world's rivers. The suspended sediment floating past the modern-day site of Yuma, Arizona, amounted to 160 million tons a year, more than all the railroad cars ever made could carry. For months at a time the river would run low, a slack, sluggish ooze to the gulf; but with the spring thawing of the mountain snowpack or with a torrential summer storm the sediment would become a mighty avalanche; great boulders would tumble along in the churning water. Overloaded by rock, dirt, and water, the current would slop over its banks onto the surrounding floodplain, where it would deposit some of its burden. The deeper the river sawed into that plateau upstream, the higher its bed rose above the lowlands downstream. Eventually the lower Colorado ran along a self-made ridge, well above the desert floor. In its struggle for equilibrium, tearing down to build up, the river was setting the terms for its conquest. All of it would have to be mastered, or none of it could be. And that comprehensiveness of control would necessitate a new social organization, a new set of instrumentalities, that would prove Henry Adams absolutely right.

A demand to bring the Colorado under human domination led in the late 1920s, as noted, to the scheme of building a gargantuan storage dam and reservoir. There were at least three distinguishable voices making that demand. The first of them was the collective clamoring of a westward-moving population, seeking new homes on the warm, dry California coast. That pressure, it should be emphasized, did not come from within the river basin itself. In the twenties the only sizable cluster of people living near the river and the Hoover Dam site was located up in Las Vegas, some thirty miles away, and they amounted to a minuscule 7000 inhabitants. Far more important was the pressure coming from outside the basin. In the last quarter of the nineteenth century Los Angeles grew from an adobe outpost of 10,000 people to a city of 200,000, with ambitions to bring in many, many more. After tapping the Owens Valley lying off to its northeast, draining it nearly dry, the city leaders began looking to the Colorado to slake their thirst. Yet theirs was mainly a contrived pressure. It was not so much a spontaneous demand from a mounting indigenous population as it was the deliberate strategy of a group of urban entrepreneurs to *induce* a migration boom. Their salesmen fanned out to midwestern and eastern states, promoting among Iowa farmers and New Jersey factory workers, often in the most extravagant style, the promise of a new life in the sun. Those who bought the pitch would most certainly need water where they were going, but the primary, decisive "need" was one hatched in the imagination of West Coast urban promoters. As William Mulholland, the chief water planner for Los Angeles, declared in 1907, "If we don't get the water, we won't need it. We have got to have water or quit growing."[5]

A second set of demands came from agricultural capitalists down in California's Imperial Valley, just north of the Mexican border. In 1901 they had begun to move into that area, which was one of the hottest, most sterile in the West. Soon they had farms, some of them over 3000 acres large; they had the beginnings of an army of Chicano laborers to plant and harvest their crops, and they had railway links to urban markets for shipping whatever they wanted to raise. What they did not have was a secure grip on the Colorado River, their only source of irrigation water. In 1905–7 the river left its high course and raged down into their valley, threatening to wipe out their entire investment. Then came dry years when there was not enough water to fill their ditches and canals. What they wanted, what they thought they "needed" to make money, was a steady flow and a bigger one—and that would require a great deal of skilled hydraulic engineering.[6] In the popular novel of 1911, *The Winning of Barbara Worth*, which is set in this valley, the characters are completely forthright about their motives toward the desert and the river. One of the community's leaders, a banker, says to an agriculturist: "We all want to make what we can in this new country; that's what we came in for."[7] In the pursuit of that economic ambition, they supported the construction of Hoover Dam, for it would stop the dangerous floods and enhance the flow from year to year.

A third group of voices came from within the federal bureaucracy, mainly from government engineers who wanted to exercise their technical expertise on the Colorado River. They were part of the Bureau of Reclamation, which had been established in 1902 with the assignment of developing irrigation projects in the American West. After a couple of decades of smallish, marginally successful undertakings, the Bureau was itching to get its hands on something big, something monumental. From 1914 to 1923 the director of that agency was Arthur Powell Davis, a nephew of the explorer John Wesley Powell; and more than any other single individual, it was Davis who conceived and pushed through the Hoover Dam idea. "I . . . considered problems in all of the Western States," he wrote, but there was "none which . . . excited my interest and imagination so much as the development of the Colorado River basin."[8] Early on he had envisioned placing the river under a single centralized control (that of his own agency, of course) in order to develop thousands of new irrigated farms for landless city people. Another federal engineer who shared Davis's passion for technological conquest was Francis Crowe, who joined the agency in 1904 and rose to become general superintendent of construction. He helped make the first rough surveys of the Hoover site, later recalling, "I was wild to build this dam." For Crowe the project in the Black Canyon meant a "wonderful climax—the biggest dam ever built by anyone any-where."[9] In 1925 he resigned his government position to join the Utah Construction Company, which subsequently became one of the Six Com-panies, the private consortium that undertook to build the dam—and it was Crowe who directed the work.[10]

Those were the principal voices urging that the Colorado be taken in hand and taken apart. Disparate though their motives may have been, they had one thing in common: all wanted, with a desire that knew no bounds, to dominate nature. Only a river as wild and full of life as the Colorado could satisfy their desire. All of the voices spoke in terms of cool, calculating reason—of scientific planning, of market strategies, of hydraulic principles—but always under the rational surface there was an unfathomable layer of irrationality, a vague, unspecified longing, a will to power. If the river had a fanatical zeal about it, the men who came to con-trol it were fanatics too, fanatics in George Santayana's definition of the term: men who redouble their efforts as they lose sight of their aim. They would not be satisfied until the river was under their total domination, from its headwater to its mouth—or, in other words, until the river was dead.

Hoover Dam was followed in 1938 by Parker Dam, located 150 miles downstream and furnishing water for the California Aqueduct, which supplied the city of Los Angeles. Then came the building of Imperial Dam and the All-American Canal to supply the agribusiness interests farther south on the Mexican border. Then Davis Dam began to go up in 1946, and soon after, Morelos Dam in Mexico. Also, there were Laguna Dam, Palo Verde Diversion Dam, and Headgate Rock Diversion Dam. And on the upper river there was Navajo Dam, finished in 1962, an earth structure containing 27 million cubic yards of material, followed by Flaming Gorge Dam in Wyoming—and then Seedskadee, Savery-Pot Hook, Meeks Cabin, Vernal, Bonneville, Rifle Gap, Joes Valley, Paonia, Blue Mesa, Morrow Point, Crystal, Soap Park, Crawford, Silver Jack, Lemon, Frying Pan–Arkansas. The names proliferated endlessly, all of them echoing a lost, colorful frontier past, all of them in fact denoting a technological sameness and emerging industrial era. Last and most impressive in the Colorado control system was the immense monolith at Glen Canyon, a full 710 feet high, only a shade less than Hoover. More schemes remained on the drawing boards, but these were enough to make the dream of domination a reality at last. Blocked, trapped, stilled, and siphoned off, the Colorado finally ceased in normal seasons to reach the sea.

During the very period of Colorado river construction the German social philosopher Max Horkheimer argued that the conquest of the natural world has become the ruling passion of modern society. In terms strongly reminiscent of Henry Adams, he pointed out that such a passion has led us into a moral chaos. We know more and more about *how* to do things, less and less about *what it is that is worth doing.* Horkheimer called that state of affairs "the eclipse of reason." The work of reason ceases to be the discovery of the ultimate aims of life; it is reduced to the job of reducing whatever it encounters to the status of a mere tool. Nature becomes, at the hands of that instrumentalized reason, a mere miscellany of raw materials waiting to be worked up into something "useful." It ceases to have its own logic, order, or intrinsic value. Although Horkheimer was living as a refugee from fascism on the outskirts of Los Angeles when he wrote those thoughts, he never applied them directly to the case of Hoover Dam and the Colorado. And he might well have, for nowhere is there a clearer expression of what he was talking about than here.[11]

The social consequences of an instrumentalized river are the same as those of an instrumentalized nature everywhere. According to Horkheimer, "The human being, in the process of his emancipation [technology appears to offer a means of human freedom], shares the fate of the rest of his world. Domination of nature involves domination of man."[12] In other words, when the tourist looks into the flat water backing up behind a dam like Hoover, he is in fact seeing his own life reflected. What has been done to the Colorado has been done to him as well; he too has, in a sense, been conquered and manipulated, made to run here and there, made to serve as an instrument of production.

That human outcome becomes unmistakably clear when one asks, who gained power in the construction of the Colorado control complex and toward what purposes have they put that power? To ask those questions is not precisely to ask who has received some material benefits from the hydraulic control apparatus. Unquestionably, a lot of people have in some measure. Of course, most of the benefits have tended to collect in a few hands. But even if that were not true, even if the benefits had been distributed more equally than they have, that fact would not, as Henry Adams noted, alter the separate, equally important fact that power and authority have become increasingly concentrated in the pursuit of greater instrumental efficiency. The tourist may loll in the water as long as he or she likes, may bathe in it, drink it, ride a boat through it; may eat the fruit and vegetables it produces, may consume the electricity it generates— and do all those things without sharing in any real way the power that makes those benefits possible.

Among those who have gained considerable economic and social power through controlling the Colorado River have been the agribusinessmen of Imperial Valley. Even before Hoover and the other structures began to go up, they were a force to be reckoned with, thanks to building their own, early water works. The very name "Imperial," chosen deliberately to attract investors, spoke of their intentions: they were unabashedly imperialists, seeking power. Each increment they made in river control was a step closer to achieving that ambition of power. Today, there are fewer than 700 farm owners in the valley, and a mere 72 of them own more than half of the land, amounting to more than 300,000 acres. Those owners employ 12,000 people in their fields, the vast majority of them Mexican nationals, many of whom cross the border to work each day, or they are largely Americans of Mexican ancestry. By the standards of a modern urban, industrial society they are not well paid, which explains why this area, though one of the four leading agricultural producers among the nation's counties, has a low average standard of living. The farm owners, in contrast, have all risen to a state of rural grandeur, thanks to the federal guarantee of river water, and in some cases they have risen to the status of international food marketers. "Bud Antle," for instance, is no longer merely a single farmer but a large corporation, harvesting 20,000 acres of lettuce and celery in California and Arizona as well as in Africa. Without the managed Colorado River, Bud Antle, Inc., would soon be covered with desert dust.[13]

Another of the emergent powers in the Colorado River basin is the federal Bureau of Reclamation. In the twenties it was still a feeble organization, with a mere trickle of funds coming to it from the rural settlers on its projects. It was in some danger of being wiped out. The building of Hoover Dam saved it from that fate and helped make it the most famous and accomplished desert conqueror in world history. Eventually its name would be blazoned not only up and down the full 2000-mile length of the Colorado, the Bureau's own property as it were, but also along the San Joaquin, Sacramento, Rio Grande, Missouri, and Columbia, along virtually every stream in the American West. Congressmen and senators would come to seek its advice. Its engineers would be wooed and fêted in a thousand little towns and big cities. It would have immense quantities of electrical energy to sell, and in that role as engineer-supplier-manager would have much to say about the urbanization and industrialization of the West.

When it began to run out of construction sites to carry on its mission, when it was threatened with declining into a dull caretaker's job, the Bureau began to extend its reach in new directions—toward planning "attractive, healthful, and inspirational environments," as one of its publicists put it, toward building nuclear power plants, toward coal mining, toward pollution control, toward a coast-to-coast national role if possible.[14] The Bureau also eventually went abroad in search of work in Asia, Africa, and South America, encouraged by the fact that, as one of its commissioners, Michael Straus, pointed out, "the American concept of comprehensive river basin development ... has seized the world imagination."[15] In all those ways the Bureau tried hard to be the indispensable service bureaucracy, and as it succeeded it was rewarded with a large share of power. After all, power in a society dedicated to the absolute conquest of nature does not belong to those who try to think rationally and systematically about the ends of domination or who challenge the unexamined, unspoken ends. Nor is it the exclusive possession of those who profit most by environmental domination, whether they be agribusinessmen, industrialists, or urban merchants. Power also comes to those who offer the means of conquest; it comes to all the principal agents and spokesmen of instrumentalism.

The chief political lesson of Hoover Dam then is that a new concentration of economic, social, and political power is the outcome of the domination of nature. And how could it be otherwise? Is it conceivable that a loose gathering of simple farmers could carry out such an engineering triumph? Or that a hundred little villages could achieve as much as the single, focused energies of a Los Angeles elite? Yet, strange to say, that obvious political lesson of the dam at Black Canyon and its companion structures has escaped observer after observer. Here, for example, is J. Kip Finch, late dean emeritus of Columbia University's engineering college, hailing the western hydraulic feats as evidence of "the increasing mastery of man over nature which has made possible our continuing progress toward a better life." "Nature," he goes on, "has been harnessed to meet man's needs on a scale that not so long ago would have been regarded as completely visionary and impossible."[16] There is not a word in that exuberant outburst about the fact that it is not "man" who has achieved mastery over western American rivers, but *some men*, while the rest of us have looked on in passive wonder. Or about the fact that the "progress toward a better life" of which the dean spoke so confidently has turned out to have been a gradual slide into what Horkheimer and his associate Theodor Adorno called "the world of the administered life," in which the average citizen has most of his or her life planned and administered by powerful external forces.[17]

The principal historian of Hoover Dam, Joseph Stevens, has fallen into the same mental trap as the dean of engineering. In the final pages of his work, he resorts to an almost hagiographical language that drives out all analysis or critical awareness, and leaves the most interesting and significant historical questions about the dam unasked. "In the shadow of Hoover Dam," he writes, "one feels that the future is limitless, that no obstacle is insurmountable, that we have in our grasp the power to achieve anything if we can but summon the will." Nowhere does Stevens try to define who that "we" is or ask what that "anything" ought to be. The feelings he expresses are in a sense religious, and the religion he calls us to follow is one of the domination of nature by instrumental reason. "Some try to suppress this feeling," he admits, "thinking that it is naive to be enthralled by an engineering marvel, dangerous to be seduced by twentieth-century technology, which cynics say is untrustworthy, exploitative, and destructive of the environment and the human spirit." But go stand in the presence of Hoover Dam, he admonishes, and all that doubting will disappear; you too will become a believer. A believer in what? In the destiny of the next generation, he vaguely replies; in "the romance of the engineer" and "the courage of the construction worker."[18] To doubt any of that romance, or to ask questions about the uses of courage, or even to wonder what kind of society Hoover Dam has helped us get in the West, is apparently not permitted; only "cynics" would ask such questions. Stevens is hardly unique in writing the history of water control in this reverential spirit, the spirit of a true believer espousing a cause that has no name but only a few empty slogans. But such history writing has always been dangerous. It tends to subordinate a full, critical, free exercise of human reasons, a reason looking for worthy ends, and lead readers into the worshipful, authoritarian zeal of fanaticism. The American West has a well-established tradition of such attitudes.

For a long while it looked as though the concentration of power along the Colorado was invulnerable to any challenge. Most historians were certainly not going to raise any hard questions. The workers had been paid off, their strikes busted, their jobs ended, and they were not around any more to challenge the project. And there was no one else in sight to mount that challenge. So warned Henry Adams and Max Horkheimer earlier, as they cast about for some escape from an unquestioning drive to "modernity" or for some "revolutionary" group that could seize control and disperse power. Every possibility of protest that came to their minds had one of two flaws: either it would be too ineffectual to mount a genuine challenge, or it would be too ready to set itself up as a substitute authority, rather than search for a radical alternative. But in the 1970s and '80s a new possibility for change appeared on the western river scene, though it was not necessarily a benign or happy one. Nature, it now appeared, might be pushed and pushed to the point where it refused to function any longer—where it might, that is, collapse ecologically and carry down with it the whole panoply of human instrumental control. Rather unexpectedly, after so long a period of human confidence in technology or of fatalistic acceptance before its advance, that prospect began to seem more and more plausible on the Colorado River as elsewhere.

The primary environmental threat on the river today, and it is now a very serious one, is from salinity buildup. In its undeveloped state the Colorado always carried lots of dissolved salts to the sea, mainly washed from exposed saline shale formations or drained from springs and seeps in the upper basin. Those natural sources of "salt loading" are estimated to have once produced over six million tons of salt per year.[19] From the beginning then the muddy red water was rather alkaline, enough so to corrode teakettles and damage more sensitive crops, but not enough so to make the water poisonous to all forms of life. Now, however, the technological domination of the river has increased significantly that alkalinity to the point that the water is becoming unfit to use, in cities and on farms alike.

The problem originates in part in the agricultural fields in the states of Colorado, Wyoming, and Utah. As farmers there withdraw water for irrigation, they leach salts out of their soils and put them into the hydraulic cycle. A typical irrigated acre in the Grand Valley of Colorado for example, adds eight tons of salt to the river each year. The resulting polluted water will be used again and again farther downstream, each use adding to the mineral load. Large storage reservoirs make the condition worse, for as their contents evaporate in the intense sun—the average rate of evaporation is 10 percent of the water per year—the salt becomes increasingly concentrated. Two thousand miles of river use, storage, more use, more storage, still more use and storage, and you have a sure recipe for the utter degradation of water quality.

The salinity problem first began to reach ominous levels in the 1950s. Then in late 1961 Mexico made a formal protest to the United States government that a water treaty between the two countries was being violated by the Americans; the Colorado River, which furnishes Mexican farmers with irrigation supplies too, had become so salty it could not be put on their fields. The immediate cause of the decline in quality was a Bureau of Reclamation project on the tributary Gila River in Arizona, the Wellton-Mohawk Irrigation and Drainage District, which was dumping its heavily polluted water across the border. As a consequence Mexico's salinity average jumped from 850 to nearly 1500 parts per million (ppm). The outcome of their protest was that the United States agreed to spend several hundred million dollars erecting and operating a desalinization plant for Mexican farmers. That was, however, only the beginning of the search for a solution to a problem that has steadily worsened year by year.[20]

At Lee's Ferry, the traditional dividing point between upper and lower basins, the average natural level of salinity would be 250 ppm, or roughly 5.1 million tons of dissolved salts in an annual flow of fifteen million acre feet of water. By 1969 the level had gone up to 655 ppm. By the end of this century, according to one estimate, the level will have reached 780 ppm, or three times the natural concentration. Downstream the problem gets, of course, much more severe. By the late 1960s the salt level at Imperial Dam was 850 ppm, and by the year 2000 it is projected to reach 1,210 ppm.[21] What that has meant, and will mean, for the agribusinessmen of Imperial Valley is heavy, unprofitable expenses. From 1929 to 1972 the Imperial Irrigation District was forced to spend $67 million on tile drains and on linings for their ditches and canals to relieve the salinity nemesis. Every few years and at considerable cost those drains must be cleaned. Each increase in lower Colorado salinity requires still more remedial measures from the district. By century's end, therefore, the increased annual expense may be as high as $40 million. Since this is a cost that farmers in areas with abundant rainfall do not have to pay, the Imperial growers must eventually find themselves at a serious disadvantage in the marketplace.[22]

The most popular panacea along the Colorado is to find a way of passing the clean-up cost on to American taxpayers across the nation. During the governorship of Ronald Reagan, the Colorado River Board of California (made up of his appointees) proposed that the Bureau of Reclamation be given the job and expense of controlling upper basin salt sources, that it undertake weather modification to increase streamflow to dilute the salt, and that it be authorized to bring fresh water to the watershed from California's northern coast and even from the Columbia River.[23] The first part of that advice was acted on by Congress when it passed, in 1974, the Colorado River Basin Salinity Control Act. How much farther American taxpayers will be willing to go to alleviate the salt problem will be a study in not only political power but public gullibility. At some point in their

generosity toward the western water empire taxpayers may begin to realize that salinity is not a mere "side-effect" of a wonderful achievement
but is an inevitable accompaniment of any large-scale river control
scheme in an arid environment; that it is a systemic problem which can
never be truly solved, one that has plagued every major irrigation system
in history and destroyed many.[24] At some point too Americans may realize that there are cheaper ways to get food than this and that there are
more sensible places to put cities than in the desert. At that point they
may shake loose from their passive, administered life, and the Colorado
pyramid of power may begin to crumble.

Nature has a way of undermining the most entrenched elites in history,
especially when they have overreached themselves and, in their
unbounded eagerness for more, made themselves ecologically vulnerable.
The salt buildup in the Colorado plumbing works has the potential of
doing just that. Otherwise, it is hard to see what else would be likely,
within the next few decades, to have any revolutionary effect.

What began with Hoover Dam in the 1930s is now virtually complete:
a work of environmental mastery that, for clarity, thoroughness and
drama, is hardly equaled anywhere on earth. We are now in a better position to see the consequences, both social and ecological, of that work, to
ask what the costs have been and whether they were worth paying, and to
consider whether we would pay them again someplace else were we given
the chance. Unfortunately, however, the casual tourist passing by the
dam, eager to get on to the brightly lit casinos and an air-conditioned
motel room, seldom takes advantage of that chance for enlightenment. He
or she may, for a quick moment, lean out nervously over the dam's crest,
peering down the steep, curving face to the water below, and in that
moment gain a brief glimpse of human mortality; but he or she is unlikely,
in a typical tourist visit, to wonder about the deeper meaning of the structure itself. That is, unless he or she happens to stop and contemplate at
length the dark brown andesite breccia walls of the canyon on either side
of the dam, asking what its history has been.

Running water, soft and yielding though it is in the human hand and
so easily stopped by a concrete wall, is a power we do not have enough
experience to appreciate. Before our species was born that water cut down
through that brown rock for almost a thousand feet. Think on that fact
for a while, and all the rhetoric of the Bureau of Reclamation, all the technology worship of many engineers and historians, begins to seem a little
hollow. What an utter foolishness it is to believe that any lasting mastery
over nature has really been won. Even at this very moment the Colorado
River is busy preparing to saw through the Hoover Dam, laying down its

Freedom and Want:
The Western Paradox

We Americans are supposed to be a practical, level-headed people with a firm grip on reality, but it is not quite true.* We are also a nation of dreamers. Our imaginations are easily captured by a whiff of myth or romance, our feelings are quick to rush after a promise, and some of our dreams are more extravagant than those of any hallucinating jungle tribe. It takes all the disciplined effort we can muster simply to bring our tangled yearnings to the surface of discussion, never mind being able to identify their ambiguities and confront their contradictions.

Nowhere is this tendency more pronounced than when we talk about one of our favorite dreams, the American West. Say the word "West" and, immediately, vistas of mustangs galloping across wide-open spaces under immense, unclouded skies fill our imaginations, and sober reason has to come panting after. Say the word and we are off living in a dream, experiencing its old powerful emotions but as ever finding it difficult to say how the dream ends. As a people, we are quick to invent fantasies but slower to find plausible, realistic endings for them.

The most famous novel ever written about the Old West, the cowboy West, illustrates the tendency well. I mean, of course, *The Virginian*, pub-

*This essay was first given as the opening plenary address to the conference on "The Wyoming Vision: Images of Self and Place," sponsored by the Wyoming Association for the Advancement of the Humanities, Cody and Powell, Wyoming, April 1987.

lished in 1902 by the Philadelphia socialite and Harvard graduate Owen Wister. It is a book that has stirred the imaginations of millions, but it does not succeed in giving those imaginations a rational course to follow. In the end the book is plagued by a serious paradox, of which the author seems unaware. To the extent that it expresses what we as a people have felt about the West, it reveals that we have been chasing after conflicting ends, which we have not carefully sorted out or reconciled, and therefore we stand naively divided against ourselves.

Wister's story is about the discovery of a new kind of man the West is supposed to have produced. One day, it goes, the narrator, getting off a train in Medicine Bow, Wyoming, is met by a paragon of manly youth and goodness. The paragon is called simply "the Virginian," though at the age of 14 he abruptly abandoned his native home, parents, and siblings—lit out for the territories, like a taller, cleaner Huck Finn—and ever since has supported himself by his own abilities. Apparently he has eaten well, for he has grown up to physical perfection. None of the privations or the hard knocks or the bad companions along the way has managed to leave a blemish on either his physique or character. Though working as a mere hired hand on the Sunk Creek Ranch, he stands tall beside his companions: a 24-year-old demigod, free-spirited and independent, uncompromising in his integrity, exhibiting an utter confidence in himself, ranking as a true gentleman in all but outward circumstances. And, withal, he is completely unassuming. Wister portrays him as a natural nobleman, formed not by civilization and its institutions but by the spontaneous influence of the land working on an innate goodness. Here in the West, Wister believes, he has discovered a finer type of American growing up than can be found back east in Pennsylvania or Massachusetts.

Then comes the difficulty of knowing what to do with a man so nicely formed outside civilization: How is he to find a living, make a marriage, take a hand in the running of society? For the marriage part, Wister manages, after a tediously long mating dance, to hitch his Virginian to a blue-blooded New England schoolmarm, Molly Stark Wood, and they go for their honeymoon to a high mountain meadow, skinny-dipping together and broiling trout. But solving the career part gives Wister a little more trouble. Part way through the book he tells us that the hero has for years been carefully saving his wages, indicating that he does not intend to remain a cowhand all his life; however, Wister is far too enthralled by this cowboy's simple ways to want to see him actually put those savings to work. Not until page 502 in my edition does the author throw together a hasty sketch of the Virginian's eventual worldly success. This hired man at last rises to become a partner with his boss, the distinguished Judge

Henry. With all those savings, he buys a spread of his own and lays out modern improvements, fencing the range and stocking it with improved breeds of cattle. And that is not all: "When I took up my land," the Virginian explains, "I chose a place where there is coal. It will not be long before the new railroad needs that." Sure enough, the railroad soon lays tracks to his door and carries away fuel for its locomotives. Eventually, we are told in the last paragraph, the simple man of the saddle becomes "an important man, with a strong grip on many various enterprises, and able to give his wife all and more than she asked or desired." So ends the saga of a man of nature, now elevated wonderfully to the rank of industrial capitalist, his adoring wife becoming in the end an indulged child of the consumer culture.[1]

By holding it off so long and then leaving it so sketchy, Wister appears not to have had his whole heart in that ending. He intended to recreate nostalgically a frontier world that was passing away, and all the while he was worrying whether in the future we would be able to find such men again. Probably most readers have shared Wister's nostalgia—and liked the Virginian less the more he rises. Not one in ten who knows the story remembers or cares much about that ending. The vision we hold of the West, the vision we most want to hold onto, lies in some shadowy, receding realm of nature, as it did for Wister, and we would rather not think too hard about endings.

Yet to put matters thus is too simple. We *do* care, or say we care, as Wister cared and said he cared, about the future West too. And many among us believe, as he did, that building railroads, digging coal, and bringing the industrial revolution to this region is a noble act; many still believe that such a technological future is one worth saving and working for. And come to that, we too (most of us anyway) want to loll around with Mrs. Virginian in a cornucopia of purchased things—furniture, clothing, and everything else that we could ask for or desire. There can be no denying that the ending, short and flat as it may be, has behind it as powerful a dream as any that has animated America or the West.

Two dreams then are tugging at our feelings: one of a life in nature, the other with machines; one of a life in the past, the other in the future. Nature makes us what we are, we still like to think, makes us good and decent; but it is technology that makes us better. If the West has any spiritual claim to uniqueness, I believe it lies in its intensity of devotion to those opposing dreams. Call it then, without too much risk of distortion, the "Western Paradox." Without quite being able to acknowledge the fact consciously or intellectually, we know that our hopes for this region do not quite hang together, that there is no easy, smooth progression from one dream to another, as Wister's novel pretends, that at some point we may even have to choose between them.

The western paradox exists in large part because the landscape has encouraged it. Here nature wears a face that is at once powerfully attractive and powerfully repellant, leading westerners both to embrace and repudiate it. The West is, by national standards, terribly dry. Its average precipitation is less than 20 inches a year, less than half that of the East Coast or Europe. The most obvious effect of so low a rainfall is the kind of vegetation that naturally grows here: the sporadic, bunchy grasses and forbs, the scattering of greasewood and sagebrush, the relative paucity of forests. A second effect is that the West can count only a very few rivers, all well distanced from one another and many of them drying up by summer's end. For all its scenic grandeur, for all its abundance of rock and minerals, this region's landscape says, at least in biological terms, that this is a place of scarcity. Sometimes it says the word scarcity in a whisper, hinting faintly and uncertainly of droughts to come; then again it says it in a hard, dry rasp that only the deafest can fail to hear. Water, or rather its absence, is at the very heart of the western paradox.

John Wesley Powell was the first person to define the West as the "arid region" of the country. That was in 1878, and a number of historians have since pondered the implications of his concept. What impact, they have wondered, has scarcity in a vital natural resource like water had on the habits, institutions, modes of producing a living, values and identities of the people who have taken possession of this land? Have they accommodated themselves to that scarcity? Has it set them free? Or have they sought to overcome it? Have they sought even to the point of forging a new kind of servitude for themselves? Have they sought to the point of regret?

One side of the western paradox, I have suggested, is the dream of growing up happily in a state of nature. It is basically a dream of achieving unlimited personal freedom. An ancient dream, it was active long before there was an America and was brought to this continent in the heads of millions of immigrants. But the eastern part of the United States was not the ideal landscape, at least not to the degree the West was, for stirring up such hopes of a free life in nature. The East astonished immigrants with its spontaneous abundance, but not with its openness or ease of movement. While still at sea and approaching the land, the first European travelers marveled at the aromatic, organic smell of plenty wafting out to them. Once ashore, they could not talk enough about the wild grapes festooning the trees, for all the grapes they had seen back home had been carefully cultivated, pruned, and staked in vineyards. They were impressed by the richness of the land, the wealth of wood for building and fuel; here in the New World they could have bigger farms, bigger farmhouses, bigger fires in those farmhouses than they had had in the Old World, and the poor could have them as readily as the well-to-do. But this easy abundance of the eastern American environment could be an obstacle as much as a blessing. Men still had to hack their way through it, chop it down, bring it under control. Only when they had done all that could they at last talk about how free they were. And the places they could not penetrate and clear—the Great Dismal Swamp of Virginia, the dark, twisty bayous of Louisiana, teeming with bird life, crawfish, cypresses, and tattered draperies of gray-green Spanish moss—never came to be associated in the American mind with liberation, unless it was in the mind of a runaway slave.

Come into the western country, however, and the reactions of travelers were unanimous: here at last was the true promise of American freedom. Here in a landscape generally free of trees, where no forests crowded in and impinged on the view, all physical restraint seemed to be removed. Among the earliest white men to experience that openness were the two explorers whom President Thomas Jefferson sent out in the summer of 1804, Captains Meriwether Lewis and William Clark. As they were pushing their pirogues up the Platte River, they decided one morning to scramble up the bank and walk for a short distance into the interior. Clark wrote in his journal this description of what they saw:

> This Prarie is Covered with Grass of 10 or 12 inches in hight, Soil of good quality & at the Distance of about a mile still further back the Countery rises about 80 or 90 feet higher, and is one Continued Plain as fur as Can be seen, from the Bluff on the 2nd rise imediately above our Camp, the most butifull prospect of the River up & Down and the Countery Opsd. prosented it Self which I ever beheld.[2]

Clark gives no indication that any deeper thoughts occupied his mind at this moment; but if he did not feel a sense of utter release, of total liberation from duty, authority, responsibility, and work, then he should have stayed on the boat and washed the skillet. Many of us who have read the Lewis and Clark journals have no doubt what *we* would have felt had *we* been fortunate enough to have been there at that historic moment, and the feeling would have been freedom—freedom not available to people living in the East, freedom made possible only by the dry air, the short grass, and the horizon running off to infinity.

Similar versions of encountering the pristine West occur again and again in the literature of both fact and fiction. For an example from fiction we could turn to that marvelous evocation of the Rocky Mountain fur

trade, A. B. Guthrie, Jr.'s *The Big Sky.* In an early scene Uncle Zeb Cal-
loway, a trapper of many years, returns from the mountains to visit his
Kentucky kin and, with his tales of mountains and plains, lights up the
eyes of a young boy named Boone Caudill: "He spoke in a big voice and
waved his arms and talked about being free like it was something you
could heft."[3] It is not long after that Boone himself leaves Kentucky to
find his future in the West.

For an example from nonfiction we could turn to the autobiographical
sketch of a twentieth-century man, Richard Erdoes, author of *Lame Deer,
Seeker of Visions.* In the epilogue of that book Erdoes explains that he
grew up in Vienna in a mixed Jewish-Catholic-Protestant family, and
when faced with Nazi repression, he felt compelled to flee to America. He
entered the region in 1940:

> My first encounter with the American West was a strangely emotional experi-
> ence. Naturally, it took place in South Dakota. We had been driving all day
> through corn country, flat and rather monotonous—widely spaced farms with
> white picket fences, each house surrounded by enormous cornfields. We
> crossed the Missouri and the old highway began to undulate, dip and rise, dip
> and rise, roller-coaster fashion. We drove over one dip and suddenly found our-
> selves in a different world. Except for the road there was no sign of man. Before
> me stretched an endless ocean of hills, covered with sage and prairie grass in
> shades of silver, subtle browns and ochers, pale yellows and oranges. Above all
> this stretched the most enormous sky I had ever seen. Nothing in my previous
> life had prepared me for this scene of utter emptiness which had come upon me
> without warning. I stopped the car and we all got out. There was emptiness of
> sound, too. The calls of a few unseen birds only accentuated it. I found myself
> overwhelmed by a tremendous, surging sensation of freedom, of liberation from
> space. I experienced a moment of complete happiness.[4]

Erdoes was writing about South Dakota, but he might just as well have
been encountering Nevada, Wyoming, eastern Oregon, or Alberta. All
those places have their open spaces too, and all of them have had the effect
of setting people free. Even a stay-at-home like Henry David Thoreau,
who never saw any of those spaces, who got no farther west than the Sioux
Agency in Redwood, Minnesota, could easily imagine and put into enduring words the experience so many others would have: "Eastward I go only
by force," he wrote, "but westward I go free."[5]

Free of what, we might ask? For many, the bondage has been the expectations of others, their importunings and demands, their dependency,
their entrapments, emotional and economic. Men have gone west to get
away from women, women to get away from men. Children have left the
confinement or authority of their parents, and parents have left their chil-

dren behind. The novelist Owen Wister came to escape the pressures of an imperious, snobbish mother and her social class in Philadelphia. Another famous refugee, Theodore Roosevelt, came to North Dakota in 1885 to forget the painful and near-simultaneous loss of his wife and mother and, after a string of career failures, to get a new start for himself.[6] Others have fled bills or mortgage holders or jobs. Or pollen. Or bureaucracy. Or noise. Or, in the case of Erdoes, the threat of being placed in a concentration camp. Praiseworthy or ignoble, trivial or profound, the reasons for seeking freedom are less important to us here than the fact the West has served them all. Its dessicated, unobstructed land has cleaned out many consciences, given many people comfort, and renewed much self-confidence.

Not only have Americans of European ancestry been served by the West in this way. For thousands of years the native people also came and went, celebrating *their* freedom on the land. The peculiarity of the European newcomers lay in their tendency to attach an intensely private meaning to freedom. They came with a strongly developed sense of selfhood, of individuality, conceiving of themselves as more solitary than collective. They assumed, along with the French philosopher Jean-Jacques Rousseau, that before there was a "society" there was a "me," and that "me" was, on the whole and more often than not, a "good me." The white freedom-seekers came repeating to themselves, "I need more space than I am getting. Give me enough room, give me the whole wide West, and I will put myself right."

So individual following individual, family following family, we white Americans have come into this land of scarcity, of natural deprivation, and gloried in it. We dispossessed the native race that was holding and using it, and ever since we have been taking great gulps of free air. We have found a vast space in which to be natural again, to be unencumbered except by the encumbrances we freely choose and then only as long as we choose them. But here is the rub: If this vision of liberation is to endure, this western space must *stay open*, which is to say, it must *stay dry*. Freedom in our western vision requires aridity. It depends on a brillance of light, an openness of terrain, a clean spaciousness that gives us plenty of room to spread out and look around, to get some distance from the crowd, to deal with our private selves, to renew hope. It requires the West as it naturally was and is. A little more water might spoil it all.

That has been one of our western dreams then. But there is the other and opposing one, the dream of putting technology to work making the West over into something else. The arid West may offer a kind of freedom to the individual spirit, but it may also suggest the deadly specter of poverty. You cannot eat freedom, the cynic says. What will you do for food in such a land? How will you grow crops without water? Can you get along without property and fences, and if not, where will you get wood for those fences? Where is your fuel? Where are your housing materials? Where are your grapes garlanding the trees, ready to be plucked? Will you have to buy all those things from people in the East, and if so, where will you get enough cash to pay for them? Can you get much a living here without bringing in more water?

Like Owen Wister's novel, this western region has had some difficulty figuring out how it can achieve material success and yet maintain the landscape of freedom. And that is where it gets snared in the coils of paradox.

For a long time now scarcity has not been an appealing prospect in the white American, or in the white European, mind. We have reorganized our whole way of life, our institutions and laws, to triumph over it. I maintain, in fact, that the drive to overcome the fear of scarcity has been one of the greatest forces pushing us toward the modern world. That fear orginated in early modern Europe. As their populations began to press against the land and their resource base to decline, the European people heaved themselves up to make a mighty cultural revolution. They determined they would never again be denied anything. A dream began to take form of endless plenty delivered through the benevolent agency of science and technology.

Among the first to express that dream of unlimited abundance were the early capitalistic entrepreneurs of England, France, Germany, and Italy. Everything with them came to be regarded as potential merchandise, everything existed to be made to yield greater and greater quantities of wealth. Save your capital, they urged their fellows, and invest it in technology. Learn to grow two blades of grass where one grew before. Search the globe over for unexploited raw materials to feed into your industrial apparatus. Work twice as hard as the man next to you to get those raw materials and the apparatus into your possession. Let everyone drive himself exactly in this way, accumulating as much private wealth as he can, and eventually we will all be as rich as kings and never have to suffer privation again.

This fear of scarcity and this determination to escape its hold once and for all animated not only early merchants and entrepreneurs, not only those innovating capitalists who gave the world modern industrialism with all its factories and wage slaves, but it also animated the socialists. In the view of Karl Marx, for instance, humankind will never achieve its full measure of self-realization until there is an abundance of goods provided for every man, woman, and child on earth. For the socialists as well as for the capitalists, technology has been the only true source of that abundance; such wealth does not come spontaneously from nature. The two groups of ideologues may argue endlessly over who can do a better job of producing and distributing that contrived abundance, but they do not disagree on one fundamental belief—on the necessity of banishing all material scarcity from the earth. They are both devoted to the maximum production of commodities.

This profound cultural revolution has drastically changed our species' relationship to the rest of nature. It has made man the measure of all things, elevated him to be the end and goal of history, set him up as the master of the planet. It could hardly be otherwise. To banish all conceivable scarcity requires our total domination of nature. With the rise of bourgeois society, Karl Marx wrote approvingly in his book, the *Grundrisse,*

> nature becomes purely an object for humankind, purely a matter of utility; ceases to be recognized as a power for itself; and the theoretical discovery of its autonomous laws appears merely as a ruse so as to subjugate it under human needs, whether as an object of consumption or as a means of production.[7]

What this social observer did not go on to say is just as important as what he said. When nature becomes purely a matter of utility, a thing inviting its domination by technology, it dies for us. It ceases to be significant in our lives, except as we can turn it to use. Henceforth we live alienated from it.

I have made this short digression into abstract and general ideas, the ideological underpinnings of modern technological civilization, because I believe there is no understanding of life in the American West in isolation from the broader currents of history. This West has never been a wholly self-defining society. It has taken its leading ideas from larger circles of thought, including the intellectual history of capitalism and socialism, of Adam Smith and Karl Marx, and has participated in what is now the worldwide dream of controlling nature. Here as elsewhere, that dream has been the most powerful force for change around. It has carried all of us along, as it has the earth, in its train. The dream has come into our heads, into all our heads to some degree, simply as a function of being alive at this time, and any future that will be invented here in the West must come to terms with it.

More than that, the people who have settled this western region of the United States have shown themselves to be especially receptive to the vision of a technologically dominated environment. If the fear of scarcity drove Europeans, living in one of the most moderate climates, to under-take a cultural revolution, consider what such a fear must do to those coming into a desert of near-desert. Then the fear would tend to concentrate the mind even more. It would still the voices of critics and doubters. We must find more water, settlers would say to themselves; we must use every possible technology to extract as much of it as we can out of this place. We must not rest until we have achieved control over every molecule of moisture. Each river we come to must be turned into a commodity and consumed entirely. The West must be redeemed everywhere by hard work and unflagging dedication until it has lost all semblance of naturalness, until it is a luxuriant oasis of ease and delight.

An early expression of that spirit of conquest appears in a 1906 issue of the *North American Review,* which grandly predicted that one day irrigation would redeem one hundred million acres of the West and put them to productive use. As that happened, the West of emigrant trains and free-roaming cowboys would disappear forever. Already, the article continues,

> The old cabins and dugouts are [being] replaced by modern dwellings. The great ranges are fast passing into orderly farms, where cultivated crops take the place of wild grasses. Steadily is man's rational selection directing the selection of nature. Even the cowboy, the essential creation of Western conditions, is rapidly passing away. Like the buffalo, he has had his place in the drama of civilization. The Indian of the plain must yield to civilization or pass away. Custer, Cody, Bridger, and Carson did their work and passed on. Pioneers of the old school are giving place to a young and vigorous group of men of intellect, will and ceaseless activity, who are turning the light of scientific discovery on plain and mountain. . . . [A] nation of two hundred millions of freeman, living under American Common and Statute law, stretching from the Atlantic to the Pacific, fifty millions of whom occupy the arid region of the continent, where the word "desert" is unknown, will soon be a mighty reality.[8]

Such confidence would prove, over the ensuing years, to be a little too grandiose. But all the same much of the prediction would come true.

But the drive for technological control does not involve simply commanding every river to flow where we want it to go. In dry farming, ranching, mining, and manufacturing, there have been manifestations of the same drive to conquer. And once again, the West is not alone in its quest for unlimited abundance; it is merely striving to stay abreast of a competitive world intent everywhere on intensifying production and consumption, with no end in sight.

To be sure, the dream of abolishing scarcity through technology has not yet been fully achieved, not when half a billion of the world's people are still living on the edge of starvation and the world's population is set to double in the next four decades. Not when thousands in every western American state want, but have no access to, a middle-class standard of living. Not when the wealthiest classes still maintain that they do not yet have enough—do not yet "have it all." After several centuries of techno-logical wizardry, including all the damming and siphoning and diverting of water that has been done here in the West, the old pinch of scarcity is felt as sharply as ever. Will we ever have enough water to slake our thirst? Will we ever have enough to sell? Will we ever be in paradise?

The elusiveness of success is not the only problem becoming apparent in this drive to control nature. Another is that the control we achieve, as it is pushed to higher and higher levels of intensity, turns out to be self-defeating. The water we command becomes increasingly degraded in quality. Instead of becoming more useful to more people, it becomes less so. The silt carried in the dammed-up rivers coagulates behind the dams, until finally it forms great brown tubs of mud drying in the sun and the days of water control are finished. Western towns and industries that have built their fortunes on hydraulic engineering may, if present trends continue, someday end in collapse. What we once thought was so per-manent comes to seem increasingly a passing and even self-destructive relationship with the place.

There is also the consequence that a nature intensely controlled is no longer a nature capable of offering a sense of freedom. Increasingly, we find ourselves trapped in the very technology we have devised to master the world around us. For example, the irrigating farmer learns, as he rushes about from headgate to headgate, turning so many acre feet a day into his beans or alfalfa, just how demanding his life has become. He has to regiment himself in order to regiment the river. And that may be only the first loss of freedom the individual experiences in such a situation. To get more water from farther away, he or she may be compelled to join a formal irrigation district, hire technical experts, and submit to the lead-ership of a privileged local elite. The tables of organization governing the irrigating rancher or farmer get more and more complicated year by year. He or she may have to consult regularly with a state authority or with a federal reclamation bureaucracy, strung out all the way to Denver or Washington, holding the vital capital and knowledge that the man on the land needs. Government officials, engineers, bankers, water lawyers, labor organizers, equipment manufacturers, all enter into the individual water user's life, all of them demanding, clamoring, legislating, all of them furnishing something the irrigator can no longer furnish for himself. It is a plain fact that only the simplest kinds of scarcity can be overcome with-out some loss of personal freedom. You cannot maximize technological abundance without setting up powerful government agencies, corporations, and other chains of command, other hierarchies of authority, and these endanger democracy and independence as they grow. You cannot have it both ways. And thus we are once more in the realm of paradox.

If I *had* to choose between the freedom of that dry, wild, open West of yesterday and some vision of a totally managed regime of advanced water engineering, I would take the freedom. But the problem with this paradox is that it won't let you choose so extreme a way out. We are forced to admit that both dreams have something attractive to offer, and therefore we must struggle with all the wisdom and intelligence we can muster to reconcile them. We must do so fully aware that there can be no perfect reconcillation nor any that will suit for all time. This is a struggle that will go on as long as there are people wanting to dwell in this place.

To date the West has hardly acknowledged that it has created any contradiction at all. It has simply built more dams, made more money, packed in as many people as it could, ignored the costs to the environment and society that had to be paid, and told itself all the while it was the freest place around. Now that will no longer do. We have arrived at the age of complexity in this region, when it is clear that neither a simple-minded nature fantasy nor a simple-minded greed will give us a future worth living.

The best way to deal with any paradox is to find a way to transcend it. Find some new vision for this region that will, in a thoughtful way, incorporate what was most noble in its old visions, leaving out the base excesses. Achieving a greater degree of personal freedom is a noble dream, but only if it includes a sense of responsibility and discipline. Getting an easier living from the land is also a fine ideal, but only if that living is not wasteful, corrupt, or extravagant. An alternative vision ought to suggest how we might live free *and* live well for the longest period of time—all of us, men and women, white and nonwhite, natives and immigrants alike. It ought to suggest how we can occupy this place without consuming it or letting it consume us. That is going to take us a while to figure out.

I believe that such a vision will begin to appear when and as, and only when and as, the people of the West begin to care deeply about their communities, especially their smaller communities where the relationships among people are the most direct and intense. Those communities may not in every case be models of decency or intelligence or tolerance, but it is only through caring about them that we can begin to learn to be at home in this place. They are what we all need in order to feel secure enough about ourselves to care about the broader world. They are what we need to learn how to care for the land that is now in our possession.

Those smaller, vulnerable communities can be found wherever we live, in cities as well as in the remote backcountry. But the ones that most concern me are those that are tied directly to the land in some essential economic way. They stand at the intersection of the human and the natural order, and if they are free to decide their own destiny, if they are secure and healthy, if they are intent on surviving for a long, long time, then we have some reason to think that the West may be on its way to resolving its paradox.

Perhaps such a devotion to preserving community is already beginning to appear in this region, but I think it has a way to go. Individual survival and advancement are still the main measure of success here as in other parts of the nation. We continue to approach nature as isolated, almost antisocial, individuals, either seeking total release from all entanglements with others or insisting on an unlimited right to acquire as much private wealth as we can. Either way, we relate to the natural world as individuals far more readily than we do as communities. This has long been the American style. It has made us both ardent backpackers and stripmine operators, but it has not encouraged us to think about how we can live harmoniously with the land as social groups, as collectivities, over periods of time that far exceed any individual's lifetime. Until we learn to think in the latter way, I suspect we will never be more than transients passing through this place.

At the heart of the western paradox, I have said, is water: water as a scarce, vital resource that all living things, all communities, require to survive. In struggling toward some admittedly imperfect resolution of that paradox, the critical questions become these: What is a good use of this water and where is there a technology appropriate to that use? How much water should be diverted to grow crops for international export as opposed to local consumption? How much should go to support traditional communities of ranchers and farmers, and how much to attract new industrial and urban consumers? How much water can a community drink before it begins to drown? How much water should be turned into money, and how much left for other, nonconsumptive uses? How much flow should be left in the rivers to keep them in a state of ecological health and beauty? Can we have strong communities while we heedlessly deplete our water supplies? Can we have strong communities where people have lost any awareness of limits?

One major reason why the West has created a paradox for itself is that it has not yet sought or developed a strategy of water use that will allow its communities to endure as permanent homes for the human spirit. The West has dreamed wonderful, colorful, extravagant dreams. It has tasted the dream of freedom from all restraint and, having done so, cannot forget what it was like. It has developed means for extracting immense wealth out of its rivers and lands, even to the point of compromising that freedom. Those have been the visions of the past. But the West has not yet succeeded in the hardest challenge of all: finding a relationship with aridity and water that will help Americans *stay in this place.* Successfully meeting that challenge requires developing a new kind of creative imagination for the future.

7

Grassland Follies: Agricultural Capitalism on the Plains

"The history of any land begins with nature, and all histories must end with nature," J. Frank Dobie once wrote.[1]* He was eloquently right, but until very recently such a view was not regarded seriously by academic historians, who commonly took nature for granted, beginning and ending their studies with an air of human omnipotence. That attitude, however, is becoming harder to maintain in innocence, as a group of ecologically informed historians challenge it. It is now more acceptable to say, with Dobie, that nature has played a stage-center role in the making of history—the making of its setbacks and tragedies as well as its progress and triumphs. Whether defined as climate, as vegetation, as the presence or absence of water, as soil and topography, or more compositely as ecosystem and biosphere, nature has been a force to be reckoned with in social evolution. Many geographers and anthropologists have long acknowledged that fact. And now historical thinking, if it wants to be taken seriously, must to some extent also become ecological.[2]

There have been some important exceptions to the historians' neglect of environmental perspectives. Strikingly, those exceptions have come mainly out of the Great Plains. Dobie was a well-known son of this region, growing up and teaching here. So was his University of Texas associate,

*This essay was originally published in the *Great Plains Quarterly* 6, Spring 1986.

Walter Prescott Webb, who stitched history and environment together in his writings.[3] And so was the man who, more than any other, anticipated the emerging ecological synthesis in history: James Malin of the University of Kansas. As far back as 1950 Malin was envisioning history as a process of "ecological adaptation" and was promoting the grasslands as an ideal laboratory for tracking that process.[4] These scholars, particularly Webb and Malin, were not always clear about what they meant by adaptation—whether it was a process of yielding to natural exigencies or of surmounting them by means of technology—but they were all convinced of the profound importance of the human dialogue with nature.

The Great Plains have uniquely had an impact on the historical imagination because conditions of settlement there have presented so stark a contrast with those in more humid American environments. But in the case of Malin there was another, more specific influence at work, riveting his attention on the earth. During the 1930s he found himself directly in the midst of the Dust Bowl, as dramatic an example of *maladaption* as any in human ecological experience. Anyone who lived through the "dirty thirties" or the subsequent echoes of it, as he did, could hardly fail to be impressed by the relevance of environmental health to human welfare and happiness. The Dust Bowl made emphatically clear the consequences nature can have for people, the surprises she can bring to those who leave her out of their calculations.

In the traumatic years of the Dust Bowl, the Great Plains offered at once a stimulus to the rise of an ecologically oriented history and a compelling subject for historians to grapple with. My main purpose here is to move toward a cultural explanation for this disaster, one that will, when complete, be adequate to its significance and alert to its complexity. Such an explanation cannot be the work of any single individual, for it demands what no individual alone can achieve: first, a detailed, interdisciplinary investigation of the special environmental conditions of the Plains— their cycles of weather and climate, of drought and rainfall, their grassland ecosystems as a force for moderating and buffering those cycles— and, second, a probing interpretation of the cultural elements introduced here. Of course, the rubric of culture in that account will encompass the tools, the agricultural techniques, devised to make a living from nature, but more basically it must be seen to refer to the values, world views, classes, and institutions active on the Plains. Those social and mental structures have created the tools and determined how they have been used. Finally, it is in the swirling interaction of all these agencies that an adequate explanation of the Dust Bowl is to be found. Ecological history is not monocausal. It assigns neither to nature nor to culture a sole, exclusive authority over the past, its rhythms and events.[5]

James Malin, an early advocate of the field of ecological history, attempted an explanation of the Dust Bowl experience. Or rather, he suggested a couple of explanations, both of them fragmentary and not entirely compatible with each other. Part of their weakness as history comes from Malin's bias and provinciality, which prevented him from taking a detached view of the culture he was seeking to understand. Their value, on the other hand, is that they make any simplistic alternative impossible to sustain. Though I will argue that his explanations do not satisfy the tests of evidence or logic, whether taken singly or in tandem, they still have their supporters and so require some attention.

In the first place, Malin argued that the Dust Bowl was essentially the work of nature, being caused by conditions of severe drought; that therefore it was an inevitable disaster and the plains people its victims, not its perpetrators. In 1946 he published in the *Kansas Historical Quarterly* a series of three articles arguing that dust storms "are a part of the economy of nature and are not in themselves necessarily abnormal."[6] Painstakingly, he tried to show that, long before there was white settlement and plowing of the native sod, dust storms had blown across the region. Some of the dust storms in his examples may in fact have been due to drought and others to prairie fires, both events being capable of destroying natural vegetation and freeing the soil to move. Severe, prolonged drought can ruthlessly destroy the grassland ecosystem; it certainly did so in the distant past, might have done so to some degree in the thirties, and undoubtedly will do so again in the future. Unfortunately, however, Malin could not, from his travelers' reports and newspaper notes, establish conclusively that drought had been the sole and sufficient cause of the pre–Dust Bowl storms. Nor could he demonstrate that any of the earlier storms matched those of the 1930s in intensity or scope, though he did make it incontestable, if anyone doubted the point, that not every puff of dust had a human origin. In arguing that case, he must grant the critical point that dust storms are evidence of ecological disturbance and disequilibrium, whatever the cause. The difficulty he faced was how to assign all, or even most, of that disturbance to natural factors—and he could not, as a historian working with archival evidence, surmount it.

Scientists, climatologists and ecologists in particular, may one day be able to tell the historian why droughts happen. They may eventually be prepared to trace their contribution to wind erosion acre by acre, square mile by square mile, county by county. But neither in the thirties nor in the decade or two after was science able to give a clear, reliable answer as to whether humans or nature was responsible for the Dust Bowl. More recently, however, photographs taken from orbiting earth satellites have begun to supply the kind of data that Malin lacked—and it has not been strong for his case against nature. In the late winter of 1977, when the Plains were roiled again by high winds and dirt, when Oklahoma was stunned by its worst dust storm in twenty years, the meteorologist Edward Kessler demonstrated precisely, with the aid of the new high-level cameras, that the source of the dust was west Texas farms, plowed and planted to seed, while neighboring New Mexico lands left in grass remained stable.[7] The dust could actually be seen picking up from one side of a fence, the plowed side, and streaming eastward. Aerial cameras have documented that it was not the ragged, pervasive specter of drought but the human mind and its ill-considered land practices–a mind marking its presence by straight fence lines—that was the main culprit in the 1970s; and the cameras show persuasively that the same was probably true in the 1930s. There can hardly be any doubt now that the destruction by plow of the grass cover on vulnerable lands—semiarid lands where the soil is loose and the horizon flat and open to winds—has been the leading reason for the devastating scale of dust storms in the twentieth century.

Malin seems to have realized, even as he was writing, the inadequacy of blaming nature for the Dust Bowl. There was clearly something more at work—in the culture of plains people and the nation. Here is what he wrote at the end of his dust storm series:

> The worst manifestations of soil blowing as related to agricultural operations occurred during the pioneering process. The country was new, the population was not settled-in on a firm and stabilized foundation in harmony with the new environment. . . . The older and better established communities usually kept their soil fairly well under control. In recent times, because of the technological revolution in agriculture and as the result of the initial exploitive stage of power farming, the period of the late 1920s was analogous in a sense to pioneering. In the light of that experience and well-considered conservation measures, the worst features of those eras need not be repeated. There is no reason to assume that dust storms can be prevented altogether, because without question they were frequent and severe prior to white settlement and the plowing of the sod, but the damage incident to agricultural operations should and can be minimized by careful soil management.[8]

This conclusion took most of the wind, and much of the dust, out of his earlier argument. It was an almost backhanded way of admitting that there had been, after all, significant cultural forces at work creating the Dust Bowl disaster.

Malin's second thesis, when closely examined, had problems of its own. It began with the claim that ecological disequilibrium on the Plains and the dust storms it generated was due, not merely to nature, but to the culture of a "pioneer" people. The settlement of the region was going through a youthful phase when the land was still unfamiliar to its new inhabitants. As newcomers, they did not understand what their environmental limits were nor have the techniques to overcome them. Added to their lack of knowledge was an instability in their social organization; things generally, the soil included, were out of their control. That primitive phase would give way, Malin was sure, to one of "better established communities," when the population would stay put, when farm turnover would come to an end, when generation would begin to follow generation on the same piece of land. Then erosion (except for what was natural and inescapable) would come to an end. In later writings, Malin would do path-breaking work on the phenomenon of frontier instability; in 1946 he associated such instability with the land destruction of the thirties. But there was some uncertainty in his reasoning; he was not at all sure what he meant by "pioneering." Modern power farming in the form of the tractor and the mechanized harvester had appeared on the Plains, he pointed out, immediately before the major dust storms—a state of affairs hardly found on the archetypal American frontier or in classic pioneer life. He described the plainsmen as going through an early "exploitive stage" with that technology; their culture in the late 1920s was only "analogous in a sense to pioneering."[9] With this sentence Malin shifted the terms of his indictment. Advanced technology now became the culprit, undermining at least temporarily the good judgment embedded in a traditional agronomy. But the tractor was not forever to be a bad influence, for once the revolution was assimilated a new plateau of civilization would be reached. Thus no matter what he meant by pioneering, whether he had in mind the entering of a new land or the adoption of a new technology, Malin remained optimistic. The Dust Bowl episode was a brief spot of darkness and chaos on the road to order, and nothing like it would happen again.

In the passage quoted above, conservation appears as a normal activity of a culturally mature region. It is defined not as the preservation of grassland ecosystems but as a regime of "careful management" of the soil, and it will arrive, Malin asserts, with time, with affluence, with more (not less) technology, with population equilibrium. The confidence behind these assurances resembles closely that of the so-called Progressive conservationists, as described by Samuel Hays.[10] Like Malin, they maintained that environmental destruction was a result of a pioneering culture—of poor, ignorant, unsettled people—and that it would disappear with progress. But unlike the Progressive conservationists, for whom the state was the proper agency to assume active command and move the society beyond its pioneering crudities, Malin denied that government was needed to enforce conservation. Careful management would come about inevitably with further development of the private economy.

Was Malin right in this confidence? Was the Dust Bowl merely a passing stage in the plains region's cultural maturing? And is environmental adaptation a product of progress and prosperity? The answer to all those questions must be a qualified no. The dirty thirties were largely the outcome of a well-established, long-maturing economic culture, that of agricultural capitalism. Moreover, its recent apotheosis as agribusiness has not made it a more adaptive or stable culture, nor more preservation-minded. To be sure, in the aftermath of the thirties it has been placed under some restraint by other, countervailing forces in American culture; nonetheless, agricultural capitalism remains the dominant agency on the plains today, and the prospect is less reassuring than Malin wanted us to believe.

Any attempt to understand the cultural roots of the Dust Bowl must begin with a scrutiny of Great Plains rural society in the late 1910s and the 1920s. Before that time there were, of course, forays by farmers into the fragile shortgrass country, the lands lying beyond the hundredth meridian; there was precedent for both agricultural settlement and widespread ecological disruption. And there was a recurrent pattern of crop disaster and farm failure, of retreating to ground representing less risk. But in the teens and twenties there occurred the critical assault on the grasslands that some have called "the Great Plow-up." A brief summary of the history of those years will tell us much about how and why there was a Dust Bowl.

World War I put the American wheat farmer into a happy dither. As the Turks cut off shipments of grain from Russia, the largest producer and exporter of wheat in the world, Europeans turned to the United States, to the Great Plains, for their food supply. Wheat, it was said in Washington and in the western provinces, would help win the war by feeding the Allies and toughening their resolve. When the war ended, Europe for a while still needed food imports, and by 1919 America, under government-set goals, harvested 74 million acres of wheat—yielding 952 million bushels in all, a 38 percent increase over the 1909–13 average, and providing 330 million bushels for shipment abroad. Most of this gain came in winter wheat, the standard variety grown over most of the southern Plains, which was planted in the fall and cut in the following midsummer. From 1914 to 1919 Kansas, Colorado, Nebraska, Oklahoma, and Texas had expanded their wheatlands by 13.5 million acres, mainly by plowing up 11 million acres of native grass.[12]

The Great Plow-up, initially provoked by the wartime mobilization of the national economy, might have been expected to pass with victory. Such was not to be the case. The war integrated the plains farmers more thoroughly than ever before into the national economy—into its network of banks, railroads, mills, implement manufacturers, energy companies—and, moreover, integrated them into an international market system. When the war was over, none of that integration loosened; on the contrary, plains farmers in the 1920s found themselves more enmeshed than ever, as they competed fiercely with each other to pay off their loans and keep intact what they had achieved. By the mid-twenties that integration did begin to pay off; having squeezed through the postwar depression, many plains farmers began to rake in substantial fortunes. There was, for instance, Ida Watkins, the "wheat queen" of Haskell County, Kansas, farming two thousand acres; in 1926, she made a profit on her wheat of $76,000, more than President Coolidge's salary. Down in the Texas panhandle the movie mogul Hickman Price set about to show plainsmen what modern commercial farming could really do, how it could apply the large-scale business methods of Henry Ford to the mass production of wheat. His factory farm stretched over fifty-four square miles and required twenty-five combines at harvest time. In every part of the Plains there were pacesetters like this man and woman who fervently believed in capitalistic enterprise and sought to apply it to the unproductive grasslands. These two were among the largest and most successful entrepreneurs; the less aggressive were forced by the competitive marketplace to follow their lead.[13]

The mobility of Malin's machines not only allowed these large-scale enterprises to develop but also encouraged widely dispersed holdings. It was now possible to drive one's equipment to another county or even to another state, plant wheat, return home in a few weeks, and wait until the next spring before visiting the land again—in other words, to become a "suitcase farmer." This was particularly attractive to wheat speculators, many of whom were city bankers, druggists, or teachers; they put in their seed, went back to their regular work, and waited to see what would happen to the Chicago grain futures. In a year of high prices they might make a killing, paying for an entire farm with one crop, then selling the land at a tidy sum to another fast-buck chaser. Not all suitcase farmers were looking for such quick returns; some of them were more concerned about their investment's long-range security.[14] But the machine made possible, as it made common, an exploitative relationship with the earth—a bond predominately commercial—so that the land became little more than a form of capital that must be made to pay as much as possible.

All across the flat open spaces the tractors steadily plowed away, especially in the second half of the twenties and up until the very eve of the dust storms. Occasionally they even worked at night, their headlights moving like fireflies in the grass. Near Perryton, Texas, H. B. Urban, an altogether typical wheat farmer of the day, arrived in 1929 and cranked up his two International tractors; each day he and his hired man broke out twenty acres of native prairie, until virtually his whole section of land was stripped of its grama and buffalo grass. In thirteen southwestern Kansas counties, where there had been two million crop acres in 1925, there were three million in 1930. Altogether in that period farmers tore up the vegetation on 5,260,000 acres in the southern Plains—an area nearly seven times as large as Rhode Island. Most of the freshly plowed ground went into wheat, so that over the decade of the twenties the production of that cereal jumped 300 percent, creating a severe glut by 1931. That, in sum, was the environmental history immediately preceding the dirty thirties. When the black blizzards began to roll across the region in 1935, one-third of the Dust Bowl region—33 million acres—lay naked, ungrassed, and vulnerable to the winds.[15]

This Great Plow-up was not dictated by Malthusian population pressures, which in many parts of the world have been responsible for decisions to put marginal land into food production. Nor was it exclusively or primarily drought that disrupted the ecological system of the Plains; it was humans and the economic culture pushing them ahead. Nor was their push carried out in ignorance or inexperience. For over a century men had been coming into the shortgrass country, observing it, and writing about its risks. For half a century before the Dust Bowl, cattlemen had trailed their animals to railheads there, and farmers had repeatedly tried breaking the sod to make houses and crops, leaving a record of devastating reverses as well as some years of bounty. Furthermore, by the second and third decades of the twentieth century the region could by no means be labeled an intellectual frontier; an extensive scientific literature was available on it, and the hard realities of the country had permeated widely into common consciousness.[16] All of this information was almost studiously disregarded in the 1920s plow-up. To describe those who did that disregarding as backward, primitive folk, as a hard-living rabble of frontiersmen, simply will not do. On the contrary, they were, especially the leaders among them, people with access to capital and expertise; some of them were in fact men and women of education and broad sophistication. The historical problem to be solved is why such people used their capital as they did, why they demanded and quickly deployed the new machinery, why they chose to hear what they did from the past and present, shutting out what did not appeal to them—what, in other words, they were after and why. If we call them hungry, then we must be careful to specify what they were hungry for. If we call them pioneers, then we must go further to distinguish them from other pioneers in national and world history.

Essentially, the Great Plow-up was the work of a generation of aggressive entrepreneurs, embued with the values and world view of American agricultural capitalism. They smelled an opportunity to create a profit on the Plains and, in the classic way of entrepreneurs, they charged out to create that profit—to derive from the land both personal wealth and status. No matter that others had failed or that the risks were high; these entrepreneurs were convinced they would succeed, as indeed they did in the short run. For a few years at least they made the region say money instead of grass. Throughout the twenties a scattering of reporters came to watch them succeed, writing up their achievements in glowing prose for newspapers and magazines. Many of these farmers had once been lowly clodhoppers; now they were making their mark on the world, were getting celebrated as "kings" and "queens" of wheat. And justly so, for the food that poured from the erstwhile grasslands was, if the environmental costs are disregarded, a positive gain for the nation and the world as well as for the entrepreneurs. They heard little criticism. Standing behind them all the way, trumpeting their contribution to humanity repeatedly so that it was not lost on the American public or on the farmers, was a vast chorus of bankers, millers, railroad executives, and government officials, all of them looking forward themselves to sharing in the abundance being created. It is, of course, the nature of entrepreneurs, in agriculture as in industry, to disregard the voices of caution and criticism, to show themselves venturesome where others have been ruined, and to court disaster.

Entrepreneurialism was not a new cultural innovation on the Plains. It had been around, gathering force, seeking territory for its expression, for several centuries—indeed it had been the animating ethos of the economic culture of capitalism since its rise to hegemony.[17] Out of that imported cultural heritage we can single out several influential ideas about nature and farming, all of them endlessly reiterated and repeatedly acted on by Europeans and Americans long before anyone had contemplated plowing the high Plains. Each of these would be an idea with bleak consequences in the 1930s.

First, the agricultural entrepreneur stood for the idea that the land's true and only end was to become a commodity—something to be used, bought, and sold, for human gain. The land itself, divided into property

and made an object of speculation, was the first part of nature to be com-
modified by this culture, then came its products. That drive toward com-
modification was never uncontested or universally accepted. On the
Plains there were, as there had been elsewhere, many rival cultural values
present; often these had been brought over from Old World farming or
religious traditions, or from some obscurely intertwined, peasant-
grounded combination of the two.[18] These rivals for moral authority
found their way into much of the literature and art of the region; into, for
example, the novels of Willa Cather, who spoke often of the mysterious
spiritual power of the Plains—of an indwelling presence in nature there,
one particularly accessible to many women and to recent immigrants.[19]
But it is safe to say that the typical wheat entrepreneur did not read
Cather or put much stock in peasant modes of thought. None of that, he
was quick to insist, was rationally compatible with his drive to dominate
and commodify.

Second, entrepreneurialism was part and parcel of the social ideal of
economic individualism. It deliberately made, with no end of paradox, the
pursuit of private wealth into a social ethic. The implications in that individualism for the ecological communities of the Plains were predictable:
farmers would not be expected to accommodate their ambitions to the
whole of nature, or recognize and use those ecological interdependencies
for their own survival. Likewise, they would, and did, reject any restraint
on their economic freedom to get what they could from the Plains in their
own terms now, in their own generation. All others, future and present,
must look out for themselves. Here again Malin was simply wrong; it was
the entrepreneurial culture, not frontier life, that was destructive to communal bondedness and social stability.[20]

Third, risk was treated in this economic culture almost as a positive
value, as a needed spur to success. Without risk, there could be no gain.
This idea has been emphasized earlier; what should be added now is the
insistent search by the bearers of entrepreneurial culture to find ways to
pass the risks on to someone else. Since they saw themselves as taking
chances that, if profitable, would enrich the entire society, entrepreneurs
hoped that others would pay some of their costs. In the case of the Dust
Bowl those costs included the damage that the dust storms did to health
and property and the rehabilitation they necessitated. More than $2 bil-
lion was spent by New Deal agencies in the thirties to keep the farmers of
the plains region in business.[21] As risk-spreaders, these federal programs
signified the maturation of the national capitalist economy: the coming
of a new era when entrepreneurial drives need not entail such severe pen-
alties for failure. Back in the 1890s, when little outside assistance had

existed, the plains settler had learned that he had either to adapt to nature or leave. The generation that came to plow in the twenties and ate their own dust in the thirties successfully evaded much of that disciplining. They lived in a more humane and protective age that allowed them considerable economic freedom while removing some of the old anxiety and the bitterness of defeat.

Bring these ideas, this economic culture, into a volatile environment where intermittent drought was a fact of life—and the outcome could hardly be anything different from the dirty thirties. That such an outcome would seem to be unavoidable is clear in the famous government report, *The Future of the Great Plains* (1936). Its chief author, the economist Lewis Cecil Gray of the Resettlement Administration, one of the country's leading agricultural historians, made an analysis of the cultural roots of the Dust Bowl similar to the one suggested here, of "the attitudes of mind" inherent in an expansionary, entrepreneurial society.[22] The evidence was clear to Gray that the disaster could not be wholly laid at the door of nature, of imperfect technique, of inadequate knowledge, or of "frontier society." As in the case of that other great tragedy of the decade, the Depression, the Dust Bowl was a crisis made and delivered by socially destructive forces in modern American culture.

In 1946 James Malin vigorously rejected Gray's cultural analysis of the plains debacle, and he was not alone. His was a common response in the region, somewhat so in the thirties and unabashedly so by the time he wrote. A resurgent national economy, a new war raging in Europe, the success of the federal relief programs in helping people hang on until better times—all these elements made deeper critical inquiry unpopular. Most important of all, nature contributed to the renewal of self-assurance. The return of rains, accompanied by bumper wheat crops in the early 1940s, demonstrated that the environmental damage had not been permanent— and, indeed, it has been difficult until the present nuclear age for humans anywhere to inflict irreversible destruction on the earth and its fabric of life. Nature has extraordinary powers of recuperation, a fact that has been proved many, many times in the long geological history of the Great Plains. When the healing comes, it is easy and altogether human to suppress the memory of misjudgment and loss; to revert to old, familiar ways and deny responsibility. That was precisely what Malin hoped would happen: a renewal of faith in the culture of entrepreneurial farming. Any effort to find a different path for the Plains he harshly identified with "totalitarianism."[23]

Despite assurances that the Plains would achieve a mature agricultural capitalism in the post–World War II period; that the land and society would come under firm, enlightened control; that no radical reform in the culture would be necessary, the region's recent ecological history has seen some disturbing chapters. High crop prices and great profit expectations have again and again produced waves of profit-seeking enterprise when grasslands have been destroyed to make more crops. In the aftermath of each of those waves have come new cycles of dust storms, some of them as grueling as anything in the thirties. Then, so the familiar pattern goes, the blowing dust brings in its train warnings from federal soil scientists, larger budget requests from federal agencies, and talk of new state and national laws to reform the culture. Perhaps these frequent replays of the thirties have produced a cumulative reform of the culture. One might argue, though not precisely in the terms Malin did, that the capitalistic agriculture has in fact been substantially altered since the 1930s; that it no longer enjoys the power and influence it once held in the region; that today it is strictly hedged about with governmental authority; and that these reforms, these countervailing pressures, have successfully prevented another Dust Bowl from occurring.[24] It will take a few serious, prolonged droughts to test thoroughly the accuracy of such an argument. Very recent evidence, however, indicates that the entrepreneur is still around, still sitting tall in the tractor seat—and the old danger is not over.

In the late spring and early summer of 1983 the national news again announced the impending threat of western wind erosion. For example, *Time* reported that wheat operators had torn up the sod on 6.4 million acres of marginal grasslands in Montana and Colorado. Depressed livestock prices and favorable federal wheat support programs were responsible for this frenzy. "I want to make a buck," was the way one Montanan expressed his motives to *Time*. He and his neighbors had broken 250,000 acres of grazing land over the preceding decade. "We face the possibility of another Dust Bowl," said the executive vice president of the Montana association of conservation districts. So serious was the threat that the conservative senator from Colorado, William Armstrong, with backing from the Reagan administration and the Montana Stockgrowers Association, introduced a "sod-buster" bill that would deny federal payments of any kind for crops grown on highly erodible land. And a Colorado county began contemplating the issuing of permits by its commissioners before any more sod could be plowed up.[25] Unmistakably, leaders of the region were being forced to admit that they did not yet have sufficient public authority to restrain risk-taking entrepreneurs, nor could they depend on capitalistic maturity to achieve soil conservation. Whether they now had the will to establish that authority remained to be decided.

The ecological history of the future Great Plains is still to be accomplished, still to find its historians. When they come to write it, they will have a subject of international significance, for these days the dry lands of the earth are everywhere under pressure and scrutiny. In that future history, as in past accounts, we may expect the key issue to be the fit of the Plain's economic culture to its environment. And we can predict that historians will return often to the dirty thirties to understand what that culture has been and what it is in the process of becoming.

The Black Hills:
Sacred or Profane?

You have been creeping across an endless plain, one foot wearily falling in front of another, a plain that blinds you with its light and resists all your domesticating instincts, when you glimpse at last a dark line of mountains rising on the horizon, and you begin to hope again. Ahead lies water, fuelwood, green forests, a plenitude of game, the reassurance of bounded space. For most travelers it has been the long vista of the Rockies that has offered that epiphany, that moment of revelation and renewal. But lying off to the north and east is another chain of mountains offering an anticipation of the Rocky Mountain experience. They loom four thousand feet above the surrounding terrain, reaching at their highest point, Harney Peak, a height of 7,242 feet. Scores of other mountains, including Sugarloaf, Flag Mountain, Signal Hill, Seth Bullock Peak, Beechers Rock, and Mount Rushmore, each over a mile high, make up the full range, an elliptical uplift area of about 4500 square miles, along with the outlying Bear Butte just north of the main range and Devil's Tower over in Wyoming. Their slopes are covered with ponderosa pine, juniper, northern spruce, and fir, giving them from a distance a darkish hue. The Indians have called them Paha Sapa, a name the whites translated as the Black Hills.

A tourist approaching the Hills today is soon lost in a scraggly thicket of billboards that at once exaggerate and diminish the old sense of coming into a promised land. "Wall Drug," many of them read, "World's Largest." "Black Hills Gold—Pan Your Own." Visit Reptile Gardens." "Have Fun with the Flintstones in Bed-Rock Village." "See Mount Rushmore, Shrine of Democracy." "See the Black Hills Passion Play: A Modern Miracle. The Last Supper. The Garden of Gethsemane. The Road to Golgatha." "See Wind Cave National Park." "Enjoy America's Foremost Vacation Spot." Out of this dizzying array of the exotic and mundane, the pious and ludicrous, emerges a billboard image of the western past filled with legendary figures, most of whom apparently lived lives of violence: "See the grave of Wild Bill Hickok, master gunman of the Old West." "See the grave of Calamity Jane." (They're buried near one another in Deadwood, South Dakota, like an old married couple of gunslingers.) See Crazy Horse Mountain, where the great chief is being reincarnated on the face of granite. Walk where Sitting Bull walked. Ride with General George Armstrong Custer and the fighting Seventh Cavalry. They were all here, caught up in a drama none of them could fully understand or control, all reduced today to a single jumbled pantheon of our heroes and heroines, peopling the half-truth history of the celebratory mind. A deeper, more informed understanding of the western past is as elusive in the Black Hills as anywhere else. It does not appear on any billboards or in the handouts of the local tourist offices or even in the books written by many academic scholars. But it is beginning to emerge from the writings of a newer, more critical generation of writers, journalists, and historians—a story that has all the grandeur, beauty, complexity, and dark ambiguity of the Black Hills themselves.

There is one group of people in particular who have not been lulled into a genial complacency about the past. They too can be highly romantic, like all Americans, and they have their own version of what has happened in these parts, a version with its own colorful violence, its own self-flattering legends, but a version that ends in the Raw Deal. I refer, of course, to the Indians of the area, specifically, the Lakota, or western Sioux.[1] For them the Black Hills are still contested ground, and they are still waging a desperate campaign to defend themselves against the invading whites. Today's Hills, with all their billboards, national parks and forests, gas stations, and curio shops, can symbolize their persistent status as victims of the westward movement. The "Indian Wars" are not, in their view, over. The Lakota may have lost again and again, but they remain determined to go on struggling, with whatever means they have, until the whites yield a little and the battle turns. And for Indians all over the United States, the Lakota have made these mountains the most visible and significant, as they are physically the largest, battleground in the struggle for land possession between the races on this continent. Who owns the Black Hills? We do, the whites assume as they drive down the highways looking for a motel. We do, counter the Lakota, in a moral if not legal sense, and we will persist in that claim until the history books tell the western story our way.

In the early morning of the fourth of April, 1981, some fifty Indians drove into the Black Hills National Forest and, twelve miles from the out-skirts of Rapid City, took possession of a valley. One of their leaders, Bill Means, proclaimed it was their land according to the terms of the 1868 Treaty of Laramie, the 1978 Indian Freedom of Religion Act, and an obscure 1897 law that allowed schools and churches to build quarters in the forest preserves. Their object was to make a settlement around a school that would teach the traditional Lakota way of life. The name they gave the camp was Yellow Thunder, in honor of the memory of an Indian man who had died after being kidnapped, beaten, and paraded nude before an American Legion gathering in Gordon, Nebraska, a death the occupiers believed was the result of white racism and had been inade-quately punished. Two days after the occupation began, Chief Frank Fools Crow, 93 years old, visited the site and declared to reporters: "The Black Hills belong to me. This is a church in itself. This is the foundation of Indian religion." His words may serve to define the mixed purposes of the occupation—part political, part spiritual.[2]

Most of the occupiers were young males, including many members of the militant American Indian Movement (AIM), which had been founded by Dennis Banks and Bill Means's brother, Russell. Earlier, in 1973, AIM had seized control of the tiny settlement of Wounded Knee on the Pine Ridge Indian Reservation, the scene of a pitiless massacre of Lakota men, women, and children by the U.S. Army in 1890. In belated retaliation for that tragedy, 200 modern Indians, armed with rifles, their long hair wrapped in red windbands, took eleven white hostages, barricaded them-selves in a trading post, several houses, and a church, and held off a small army of FBI agents, Pentagon advisors, and federal marshals for more than a month, before finally surrendering to the superior force. Two of their number died by the white man's guns, and their leaders were led off to face charges of murder, arson, kidnapping, and insurrection.[3] But, in contrast, up in the Black Hills the occupation was more relaxed and peaceful. Beyond a defiant roadblock the occupiers lived quietly in tepees and trailer houses; they erected a holy sweat lodge which they entered naked to pray. Through the summer and, defying all predictions by state and federal officials, through the next winter they stayed on. In fact they continued in the valley until 1988. Angry forest rangers hung around the camp's perimeter, carrying guns, binoculars, and walkie-talkies, insisting that the Indians had no right to be there; the valley had already been leased to a white lumberman who wanted to harvest its trees and quarry gravel for roads from the very place where Camp Yellow Thunder sat. But officials did not force their way in or summon heavy firepower. And this time there was no shoot-out, no graves to be dug.

In further contrast to the violent scene at Wounded Knee, the occupiers filed for a special-use permit, asking permission to establish an 800-acre permanent settlement in the valley. The Forest Service refused. Over the preceding five and a half years the Service had issued 58 such permits to public and private groups, including church groups; it had denied only four applications, three of them to Indian groups. The Indians wanted too much land and for too long a period, said the Service; they asked for more than the regulation limit of eighty acres and for a tenure of more than thirty years. The Forest Service officials did not indicate they would welcome any sort of applications from any one in the occupation group. In Washington, D.C., a coalition of 38 congressmen and women, representing 29 states, asked the Service to grant the application anyway, but the congressman from South Dakota, Tom Daschle, disagreed, arguing that there was little public support in his state for the Indian presence. On 22 November 1982 the Service took the occupiers to court, seeking their eviction. The trial soon bogged down in lengthy delays and recriminations. A new charge appeared against Russell Means and his other brother, Ted, of illegally cutting down some green trees to build a sun dance ceremonial site. They were acquitted of that charge. The eviction trial went on. In January 1987 a district judge in Sioux City ruled that the Forest Service must allow AIM to establish a religious settlement in the Black Hills. But in September 1988 the Eighth Circuit Court of Appeals overturned the ruling, denying that the First Amendment right of freedom of religion would be violated by an eviction. In June 1989 the Supreme Court refused to hear an appeal from Camp Yellow Thunder, and the occupation came to an end. Unless they followed strict procedures in making their application, and perhaps even if they did so, the Indians would not be allowed back into the valley to worship, as Protestants were already doing elsewhere in the Black Hills.

In addition to AIM, support for the occupation came from the Black Hills Alliance, an environmental group formed in 1979 to forestall the invasion of the mountains and nearby plains by some of the nation's largest energy and mining companies. The Alliance found members among traditional Indian men and women, white ranchers and farmers, and environmental and anti-nuclear activists—the first time many of them had crossed racial lines to fight a common threat. The most immediate threat they faced was that of 27 corporations, including Union Carbide, Exxon, Kerr-McGee, Westinghouse, Gulf, Mobil, and the Tennessee Valley Authority, who were after uranium ore deposits. TVA, for example, owned mineral rights to more than 100,000 acres in the region, where it was busily looking for fuel to feed a string of nuclear reactors, existing and projected, in the South. In fact during the very period that Indians were fighting in the courts for the right to a permanent site in the Hills, those companies were exploring over 5,000 mining claims they had staked. North and west of the Black Hills other corporations were intent on digging up vast coal deposits and burning the coal in thirteen electric generating plants, each producing 10,000 megawatts, sending the power to urban consumers in the Midwest. All those enterprises needed water, lots of water, and the most likely sources were the Missouri River and the aquifer underlying the Hills. Indeed, the state declared and the companies agreed, the Black Hills aquifer would have to be "dewatered" (i.e., pumped dry) in order to prevent its contamination by radioactive wastes. Those were signs that a massive invasion of the land and resources was imminent, like the gold rushes of the nineteenth century but on a much larger scale, with profound social and ecological consequences for the whole region. Large parts of the Black Hills and surrounding countryside would become an industrial wasteland, with polluted air and depleted water, a land burdened with millions of tons of radioactive tailings, a "national sacrifice area." To prevent that from happening, the Black Hills Alliance formed and demanded a public debate.[4]

A large part of the Alliance's strategy was to draw attention to the unrecognized rights of Indian peoples to the land, to injustices allegedly done to them in the last century, and to suggest that rural whites as well as Indians might be victims this time around. As a third-generation white rancher asked, "If we allow these companies to destroy our land today, what will we say to our relations three generations from now?" Russell Means, speaking from Camp Yellow Thunder, called for interracial cooperation to prevent another dispossession: "It is time for the Cowboy and the Indian to join forces. Rather than continue with inane arguments over jurisdiction, ownership, and who has what with whomever, the American Indian and the new Indians should reshuffle our priorities. . . . We are [all] People of the Land. We share a common love for the Earth. That is the basis for which we have to come together. Our concerns are the same, our strategies should be shared, after all survival is what we are fighting for."[5]

Despite such talk the reality was that the races remained deeply divided in South Dakota. In large part they were (and are) divided by the old, seemingly unbridgeable conflict over land ownership. Someone has to own the Hills, after all, and in the present as in the past those who are owners seem predominately to belong to one race or the other, the reds or the whites, never to some color-free individuals. Moreover, it would appear that there are today, as always, irreconcilable differences over which culture, the European or the Indian, is superior and must dominate. Both sides have difficulty in transcending that struggle. In July 1980, for example, Russell Means called not for a common, transcultural love of the Earth in the name of survival but for a radical rejection by Indians of all contact with European and Euro-American culture, asserting the superiority of Indian moral and religious teachings. On the occasion of the Black Hills International Survival Gathering, convened on the Pine Ridge Reservation of the Lakota, and including, in addition to local Indian and white people, representatives of Greenpeace, Friends of the Earth, the American Civil Liberties Union, the Nez Perce Fishing Rights Committee, and the Union of Concerned Scientists, Means had given a stirring speech about the kind of separatism he represented. In it he rejected all forms of European thought—capitalism, Marxism, industrialism, science. "I do not believe that capitalism itself is really responsible for the situation in which American Indians have been declared a national sacrifice. No, it is the European tradition; European culture itself is responsible." "There is another way," he went on; "there is the traditional Lakota way and the ways of the other American Indian peoples. It is the way that knows that humans do not have the right to degrade Mother Earth. . . . Those who ultimately advocate and defend the realities of European culture and its industrialism are my enemies. Those who resist it, who struggle against it, are my allies, the allies of Ameriacn Indian people. And I don't give a damn what their skin color happens to be. *Caucasian* is the white term for the white race; European is an outlook I oppose."[6] Though he may not have rejected their color, he was certainly telling a large number in his audience that he despised their cultural heritage, blaming it for all the ills of the world, denying that Euro-Americans could feel any love toward the Earth, and insisting that they adopt completely the traditional Indian way of thinking.

In the deepest sense, Means's words suggested the significance of the occupation at Camp Yellow Thunder that went on over most of the decade of the 1980s. The occupation represented a repudiation of all European cultural influence, material and mental. The small dissident band of Lakota had sought to recover a vibrant Indian culture, pure and untainted by the white man. Eventually, they hoped to build a commu-

nity in the valley that would be wholly self-sufficient, relying on traditional Indian ways of getting food and energy, getting free of the European
industrial way of life. Instead of houses they would live in tents. Instead
of watching "Love Boat" on television they would tell stories around a
campfire. They would rediscover what it means to live with respect for
Mother Earth. Precisely because they were seeking a radical measure of
independence they needed a permit giving them more land and more time
than a summer crowd of Methodists would want.

But the U.S. Forest Service, and finally the American court system,
was not ready to acknowledge the legitimacy of that use of the public
lands. It was all right to mine uranium or harvest trees or even to pray
there, but it was not appropriate to enter the Black Hills in search of a
way out of the white man's America. In the "Land of Many Uses" that
was a forbidden use.

But not all of the Indians' targets were found in white society and its
alien values, its industrial economy. The contemporary life of their own
people had also become a burden and a snare. Many of the occupiers had
come from Pine Ridge Reservation, the edge of which lies an hour's drive
to the southeast. It is the second largest reservation in the country, covering some 5,000 square miles of rolling prairie and forests. Pine Ridge is
home to about 18,000 people, according to the last available federal census, a population twice as large as it was twenty years ago.[7] The median
personal income was, in 1982, slightly more than $3,000; median family
income, $7,571. This is the poorest reservation of all, which means its res-
idents are the poorest Americans of all, lower than the black poor of Mississippi, lower than the poor of the urban ghettoes. The unemployment
rate is nearly 90 percent. The rate of alcoholism is extremely high, and
Fetal Alcohol Syndrome is an increasing problem. Despite the fact that
the Bureau of Indian Affairs (BIA) spends almost $30 million a year on
the reservation, there is no alcoholic treatment center. One in five houses
lacks indoor plumbing, and many have no electricity and no heat source
but a woodburning stove.[8] Housing units constructed by the government,
plain brown stucco structures of simple design, have generally been van-
dalized; graffiti covers their walls, screens are missing, front yards are barren, dusty, filled with junk. The Indians at Camp Yellow Thunder had
come to the Hills to escape those reservation conditions as well as to protest the impending industrial invasion. One of them, a young man, told
of the peace he found in the camp: "When I was on the reservation, I did
the usual thing, got drunk. . . . We don't drink here. And we're not on the
reservation and forced to receive handouts. I feel rich here, even though I
have no money." A woman who had brought her three children to Yellow

Thunder explained, "I was afraid to let them go outside down there. There were always cars speeding past. Fights. People breaking windows. Down there the yards are made of broken bottles."[9] She too was fleeing from what the Indian world had become and would make of her children. It is the same world that the American Indian Movement had tried to draw attention to when they seized control of the hamlet at Wounded Knee, a world they blamed on the perfidy of their elected leaders as much as on the BIA and white society. But Wounded Knee now was a burned-out shell and the daily round of violence, anger, and destruction continued as before on the reservation. Obviously, some Indians had concluded, the reservation offers no future for us. We must get away from it, get into the Black Hills, where we can find a place of refuge. The only other road out of the reservation led to the city, the very center of that oppressive European culture, and taking it would mean giving up almost completely one's Indianness.[10]

Thus, saving the Black Hills from energy companies, tourism, and industrial pollution became simultaneously a means of saving the Lakota from their own pathological life on the reservation. When the encampment, carrying all the burden of all those hopes, those promises, those prodigious ambitions, was declared illegal, the occupiers and their supporters felt defeated in ways deeper than words can express. Desperately they cast about for something else to do.

In the meanwhile other Lakota had been engaged in a legal effort before the Indian Claims Commission, the federal courts, and the Congress to get back the lands taken from them in the heyday of the western frontier. The details of that effort can be told later on, but the outcome was that, on 13 June 1979, the Court of Claims, in *Sioux Nation of Indians v. the United States,* decided that in 1877 Congress had indeed illegally taken from the Lakota a large part of their property, the Black Hills, and owed them not only a payment of their original market value but interest on that money for all the intervening years. The original value of the Black Hills was fixed at $17 million, and the interest calculated at another $85 million. Congress duly appropriated that sum and placed it in an account held by the Bureau of Indian Affairs, waiting for the Lakota to claim it and acknowledge that justice had at last been done. But none of the Indians ever showed up to accept the money. On the reservations they met repeatedly to discuss the settlement, and there were many who argued they should accept and close the books on the whole matter. Always, however, there was someone in the group who would stand up and answer, "No, the Black Hills are our mother. If we accept the settlement, we sell our mother. We did not ask for the money; that was our lawyers' idea. We asked for the Black Hills. We cannot sell our mother." Silence would follow, the matter would pass beyond debate. By the end of the 1980s the uncollected money at the BIA had accumulated to the sum of $200 million, and still there was no relenting in the Lakota position.

Next step: with a charter from all the tribes, a Black Hills Steering Committee was formed to seek another outcome. The committee went to see the U.S. Senator from New Jersey, Bill Bradley, for help in Congress. In his former life as a basketball star for the New York Knicks, Bradley had conducted a sports clinic on the Pine Ridge reservation; then in Washington he had continued to take a strong interest in the Lakota's plight. The steering committee made a large proposal to him, extravagantly larger than any request to build a small, traditional community with sweat lodge and sun dance site in a little valley, so large in fact that the Forest Service, when they heard it, must have wondered whether they might lose control after all. The Lakota repeated that they did not want any permit or license to use some small part of the Black Hills; they did not want any check from Congress for lands they had lost; they simply wanted the Black Hills themselves. And they would accept nothing less.

Bradley agreed to represent them, and on 17 July 1985 he introduced a bill "to reaffirm the boundaries of the Great Sioux Reservation to convey federally held lands in the Black Hills to the Sioux Nation; to provide for the economic development, resource protection and self-determination of the Sioux Nation; to remove barriers to the free exercise of traditional Indian religion in the Black Hills; to preserve the sacred Black Hills from desecration; [and] to establish a wildlife sanctuary." The bill was referred to the Senate Indian Affairs Committee, and hearings on it were held in July 1986. It should be added that, though South Dakota's Indians generally supported the bill, not all of them did; some wanted to get the money, while others complained that Bradley's bill would give them only a small part of what was rightfully theirs.

The Bradley bill promised that the map of South Dakota would be radically redrawn, though in small print it qualified that promise considerably. All the land west of the 103rd meridian, along with an eastward-pointing spur delineated by the Belle Fourche and Cheyenne rivers, would be declared to lie inside the boundaries of a restored "Great Sioux Reservation." Within those boundaries almost all federal lands would revert to the Lakota; the exceptions would include military installations, court houses, office buildings, post offices, cemeteries, and the Mount Rushmore National Monument (the Lakota would control the tourist concession there but not the land itself or those four 60-foot-high faces of the Presidents). The entire Black Hills National Forest, established in

1897 by President Grover Cleveland, would become the Black Hills Sioux Forest. The 28,292 acres of the Wind Cave National Park, along with Jewell Cave National Monument (1,274 acres), would become the single Sioux National Park. Part of the Buffalo National Grassland would be added to the Indian estate. Congress would continue to appropriate funds to manage those lands as forests, parks, and grasslands, as though they were still in the public domain; the federal land agencies would become, legally, mere advisors to the Indians on how to spend those appropriations, assuring by their presence that the lands "remain accessible to the general public." The Lakota would have the right, however, to exclude non-Indians from areas identified as traditional religous or ceremonial sites and from any area set aside as "a wildlife and wilderness sanctuary for living things which have a special sacred relationship to the Sioux," areas to be designated as *Wamaka Og'naka Onakizin,* meaning in English, "The Sanctuary of Everything That Is." And henceforth all the lands in the Sioux Nation Black Hills would be used only "in accordance with the traditional principle of 'respect for the earth,'" a provision that suggested some criticism of previous use but was left carefully undefined in the bill, its implications for uranium prospectors, gold miners, and timber cutters unspecified and open to their lively imaginations.

Bradley's bill did firmly specify that, although all mineral and water rights pertaining to those federal lands would pass to Indian hands, no existing mining leases or timber sales would be affected by the transfer. Most important, it added, no private lands, however they had been acquired in the distant past, would be included in the transfer. Only the federal government would be asked to give up its property in order to rectify an historical injustice. All in all, the Lakota would gain 1.3 million acres, most of them actually in the Black Hills. Though larger than the state of New Jersey, that area would be only a small percentage of the newly designated reservation, covering some 7 million acres. Therefore, the "Great Sioux Reservation" would be something of a fiction, for only a small portion of what it circumscribed would actually belong to the Indians again. Finally, Bradley would give the Lakota the whole $200 million in the untapped bank account, setting it up in a permanent fund for tribal investment as compensation for the loss of the use of their lands from 1877 to the present.

All those exclusions and qualifications, all those millions in income, were not enough to convince white South Dakota to go along with the bill. However much the state's economic and political leaders had resented the federal presence in their state, grousing about the large federal holdings that were outside their jurisdiction, they were not ready to see those lands pass to the Lakota. Governor William Janklow, widely suspected of being no friend to the Indians though a very good friend to the energy companies, vehemently denounced the give-back: Did he go about insisting that land taken from his ancestors in Hungary be returned? Why couldn't the Indians follow his example and forget the past? His successor in office George Mickelson argued that the Indians were not using their existing lands wisely and giving them even more, without "further Sioux management expertise," would be futile. Governor Mickelson added that the Bradley bill would create more divisions between Indians and non-Indians in his state, for the whites feared that somehow they might be disenfranchised from hunting and fishing in the Black Hills or their agricultural water rights might be interferred with. Whites were also afraid they might find themselves subject to "unrestricted criminal jurisdiction" if they crossed onto Indian lands—an experience that many Indians in the state could speak poignantly about, after a hundred years of dealing with white police and white courts. Other politicians, Democrats and Republicans alike, lined up against the bill. Senator Larry Pressler urged the Indians to accept the settlement money only, distribute it equally among themselves, and spend it on college educations for their children—their best hope to escape reservation poverty. Representative Tim Johnson, though acknowledging that no private land would be affected, complained, "It is still a huge amount of land" that would go to the Indians and it would have "an enormous impact on the Black Hills." What kind of impact did he and others have in mind? Clearly, what most worried many South Dakota politicians and many businessmen in and out of the state was the possibility that the Lakota would be far less friendly to future economic development in the Hills vicinity than the Forest Service or the Bureau of Land Management had been; they just might say no to the corporations, agribusinessmen, and tourist promoters. They might actually begin to give sacred uses precedence over the profane. Fearing that possibility as much as intensified racial antagonism, South Dakota's politicians were unanimously opposed to Senator Bradley, and their opposition ended the bill's chance for a full-blown debate, vote, and passage. It remained stuck in committee. Though reintroduced in 1987 and 1988, Bradley was never able to bring it to the full chamber for consideration. By 1989 he had given up, at least temporarily, on getting his bill taken seriously and did not reintroduce it.[11]

Once more the Lakota had been defeated. They had refused the $200 million. They did not have the Black Hills back. And yet they would not give up the cause. In fact, it had become more crucial than ever to them; their hopes, their identity, their social cohesion had all come to rest heavily on success in this endless struggle. Acknowledging defeat might well lead to a degree of cultural despair that would be fatal to them as a people. Because of that feeling we can assume that we have not heard the last of the Lakota's claims.

Nor should we, for the issues are not really resolved. Bills can be buried—but the past cannot. The issues raised by the Bradley bill, by Camp Yellow Thunder, by the Black Hills Alliance, by the Lakota people challenge Americans to reexamine the past honestly and squarely. We can do nothing about what happened long ago in Hungary or other parts of the world, but we can do something about what has happened over the last century or so in the American West and what is still happening there today. We can ask, and because we profess to live by principle, not by mere expediency, we *must* ask: What does that past reveal about the land and its rightful ownership? Are the Lakota really the legitimate owners of the Black Hills? If so, under what law, and whose law, can they claim possession? Did the white man's courts grant them a fair hearing and a just compensation, or were there critical aspects the courts ignored? Does the religious significance of the Hills give them a claim? Have the Hills in fact been traditionally held sacred in Lakota eyes, and if so, for how long? Should white society support, on the basis of historical analysis, the Lakota cause, or should we warn them that they are indulging in an idle, nostalgic dream that can do them no good? Those are questions that cannot, and should not, be buried in a Senate committee no matter how disturbing or inconvenient the answers. Answers, however, will not be simple or obvious or easy; otherwise, the questions would have been addressed instead of being swept aside. They will require a careful sifting of the past history of the Black Hills and their various peoples.

The first and most essential question the past puts to the present is this: Does a careful reading of America's laws and treaties show that the Hills really belong to the Lakota? This is a more tangled, difficult problem than it might first appear. Ownership is often hard enough to establish within the limits of a single culture, but when one enters the cross-cultural realm all standards of judgment, all legal precedents, falter. What may appear in the eyes of whites to be a right to possess may not appear so in the eyes of the Lakota, and vice versa. After all, ownership of any property is not a right written on the Book of Nature; it is a social convention, an agreement negotiated over time, resting on a shared sense of moral legitimacy, a legitimacy that can only be established according to the particular values that any society lives by. One of the first lessons a modern law student learns is that a piece of property does not, in some absolute sense, "belong to" anybody; instead, the "owner" claims only a set of "user rights," and those rights have changed, sometimes dramatically, over time. Even within any single society at any point in time, there are conflicting definitions of those rights. Among white Americans, "first in time, first in right," is a commonly held principle: viz., whoever gets to the land first has the best and firmest right to use it. But then all through our history Americans have also believed in the principle of "first in *need*, first in right": viz., use rights belong to whoever can show the greatest material need for them. This latter principle was well expressed by President Monroe in his first annual message to Congress in 1817: "The earth was given to mankind to support the greatest number of which it is capable, and no tribe or people have a right to withhold from the wants of others more than is necessary for their own support and comfort."[12] According to this view, the aboriginal peoples of the New World had no right to hold land away from others, the incoming whites, who were as deserving as themselves and suffering from land scarcity. The natives enjoyed an overabundance, it was said; they were thinly scattered across the continent, far more so than people were in the Old World, and thus were hoarding far more property than they could really use efficiently. Driven by that logic, yet all the while respectful of the "first in time, first in right" idea, white Americans dealt with the Indians in a very complicated, and more often than not in a very circumspect, way. For the most part, they sought to purchase, through formal agreement or treaty with tribes, the land they needed for homes, farms, and industry. Through such negotiated purchase, formalized in 370 treaties, they gained control of 95 percent of the continent, creating a public domain of some two billion acres, a domain for which they paid the Indians a bargain-basement price of about $800 million, leaving (as of 1877) 140 million acres to support about 200,000 natives. In the eyes of the newcomers this was a fair, a necessary, and a quite honorable, way to redistribute the land's wealth. It was better than bloody conquest. If by conquest we mean a forcible seizure of territory, then much of North America was not really conquered by the Europeans; it was taken over through negotiation and purchase.

When the whites arrived to explore the northern plains and the Black Hills, the most obvious holders were the Lakota, and therefore by the white's own logic, they enjoyed the conventional right of prior possession which had to be respected. There were, to be sure, other Indian nations living in the vicinity, but the Lakota dominated the scene in terms of numbers, power, and extent of occupancy; and most whites felt some obligation to respect that possession. Then, as whites began to move west again after the interruption of the Civil War, they sought to cross the lands the Lakota claimed as their own—cross to the mining camps of Montana, to the northern grazing lands, to the Yellowstone. Understandably, the Lakota grew increasingly hostile to this stream of traffic traipsing through their hunting grounds, and they began to harry and attack. Major J. B. Hanson, stationed on the Missouri River, reported on the rising resentment that white travelers aroused among the native occupiers: "But a few years ago the entire Sioux nation was at peace with all whites; a white man could travel from east to west, from north to south, so far as their domain extended, and feel that he was in a land of friends and safe. Now no one ventures a mile from a post without an escort or a fleet horse and a good revolver." Hanson added his suggestion of how to defuse this rising tension, a strategy of negotiation and purchase: "It has only been where a tribe or band has been induced for a fair consideration to cede their lands to the government that anything like a reliable peace has been secured with them. ... They have been at peace because they had no country to fight for. Their land had been sold, and every year they were enjoying the income which they could not hope to do if hostile. This policy has been the best ever devised for the benefit of the Indians themselves, and, when unobstructed by the cupidity of civilized man, for the security of peace, this is my plan for effecting a final settlement of difficulties with these Indians." But in the 1850s and 1860s the Lakota and the other Sioux tribes, though ready enough to negotiate, were completely unwilling to consider selling any part of their domain. They would sign treaties but only to allow a small number of roads and military posts to be constructed in their country. That was perfectly all right with the whites, for in the early years of confrontation they were unready or unable to buy the lands of the Lakota, thus willingly accepted Lakota claims of ownership and merely asked permission to pass on by in peace.

Over a period of several months during the year 1868 a U.S. peace commission tried to negotiate an accommodation with the leaders of the different Lakota bands—leaders such as Ironshell, Swift Bear, Bald Eagle, Man Afraid of His Horses, Spotted Tail, and, last of all to show up for the negotiations, the reluctant Red Cloud, chief of the Oglalas. The Treaty of 1868, signed at Fort Laramie on the North Platte River, established for the first time in history—Indian history, white history—a clear, precise set of boundaries for the Lakota and guaranteed them against all invaders, Indian and white alike. The treaty set up a Sioux reservation that enclosed the whole western half of what would become South Dakota, from the Missouri River westward to Wyoming, from the Nebraska line north to the 46th latitude, a territory "set apart for the absolute and undisturbed use and occupation of the Indians."[13] No part of that reservation could ever be given away, sold, or traded without the written consent of at least three-fourths of the adult males. The treaty also identified as "unceded Indian territory" the northern portion of Nebraska down to the Platte River and eastern Wyoming over to the Big Horn Mountains, a place where whites could not settle or even pass through without the Indians' consent, and it allowed buffalo hunting trips down into Kansas for as long as the buffalo survived. At the very center of that vast expanse of reserved land sat the Black Hills, but there was no mention of the Hills in the treaty. In exchange for those territorial guarantees the Lakota agreed to stop attacking wagon trains, railroad crews, and cattle herds, to stop scalping and raping whites. Henceforth they would send their children to school to learn English. They would accept technical assistance in farming and blacksmithing. They would consider taking up individual family homesteads of 320 acres, patenting them as white farmers were doing and applying for regular citizenship in the United States. They would receive free plows, seeds, oxen, and for a period of thirty years after the treaty was signed, they would get free yearly clothing allotments—coats, shirts, pantaloons, hats, socks, flannel skirts, yards of calico and cotton, and a steady cash annuity. For four years after the treaty they would also draw a pound of meat and a pound of flour per day from government agents. In other words, though extracting no binding commitments, the treaty did specify that the Lakota would seriously try to make a shift from their hunting economy to a farming one, and do so very rapidly, turning almost overnight from their traditional ways, in exchange for making their borders secure. Four years later, however, when the food rations were scheduled to run out, the Lakota had almost nowhere made that shift or become self-supporting farmers. The bison had almost disappeared, the prospects of subsistence from hunting were exceedingly dim, so the federal government was more or less compelled to go on feeding the Sioux with whatever food it could scrounge up.

If the Lakota did not quite live up to expectations—and surely could not have done so in the time allotted—the whites did not carry through their promise to observe the Indian right to "absolute and undisturbed use and occupation" of their lands. Neither side honored fully their agreement. But before the story of the white failure is told, the full significance of the 1868 treaty needs to be emphasized. What the whites, in coming to terms with the Lakota, did was to accept and make part of the fundamental law of their own nation, as fundamental as the Constitution itself (treaties having that exalted status), the Lakota's claims to ownership of millions of acres of the American West. The whites created, in their own cultural terms and backed up by their own legal institutions, a set of native user rights. How, before the coming of the whites, did the Lakota acquire those acres? Quite simply, by force of arms—by naked conquest. They entered and they pushed aside whoever was there. The Crow people knew that fact and bitterly resented it; these had once been their lands, the Black Hills included, they maintained. The Cheyenne said the same. And so did the Kiowa, the Arapaho, the Mandans. All had been dwelling in the country long before the Lakota but had abruptly been shoved out, though repeatedly they tried to reenter and claim its resources, making the Lakota's tenure rather insecure and shifting. Now for the Lakota the whites offered a new, enhanced measure of security in their land tenure— at the price of their accepting the white man's ideas of law and property.

The most careful archaeological and archival studies by scholars indicate that the Lakota had their origins, like all of the Sioux family, over east in what is now Minnesota. When the French first encountered the Sioux, they were living near the headwaters of the Mississippi River in the vicinity of Mille Lacs and Lake Itasca. Possibly they hunted westward as far as the Black Hills from time to time throughout prehistory, but the available evidence suggests that they moved permanently onto the Great Plains only during the eighteenth century. In the period from 1743 to 1795 they gained control of the South Dakota portion of the Missouri Valley, forcing the Mandans farther north and other tribes farther west. For the first time they became buffalo hunters, living in tepees, raising small gardens of corn and tobacco in the river bottoms. Not until about the time of the American Revolution, the 1770s, did they become a regular presence in the Black Hills, going there frequently to cut lodge poles and hunt game.[14]

All of this should have been a rather familiar history to whites from their earliest days on the plains. They learned it from other tribes, from French explorers, and from the Lakota's own oral traditions. But the whites, out of a need to get peaceful access to the land, ignored all those competing claims and accepted the present fact of Lakota domination. In effect the whites helped set up the Lakota as the rightful owners, much as the Americans and Europeans later would set up the Jews as the legitimate possessors of Israel. In place of the moral and territorial ambiguity of the pre-white West, where land had been unfenced and undeeded, where its possession had been largely based on the principle of "might makes right," the whites introduced a modern, written, institutionalized, and highly rationalized law of possession. They applied that law to the Indians as to themselves. Then, having legitimated an Indian right and promised to protect it, they turned around and violated it.

In the summer of 1874 the U.S. Army sent its glory-seeking young colo-

nel, George Custer, with a command of nearly 1,000 soldiers and team-
sters, on a reconnaissance expedition into the Black Hills, an expedition
that was probably illegal. Ostensibly, Custer's purpose was to get a better
idea of the lay of this land that Congress had agreed to call part of the
Sioux reservation. But the practical intent of the expedition was to see
where it was that marauding bands were hiding out after attacking
whites. And, most significant, Custer wanted to discover what kind of
resources these piney mountains held in store. In his party were two private miners, scenting the possibility of gold, and the state geologist of
Minnesota, collecting rock samples. Custer himself seemed far more
interested in the agricultural potential of the Hills for growing crops and
raising livestock than he was in mineral wealth. But mainly he was out
on a lark. He managed to find an old, snaggle-tooth grizzly bear to shoot—
his first bear kill—though whether it was actually his shot that brought
down the animal or someone else's in his party was never clear. On
another day he succeeding in terrorizing a tiny encampment of Oglala
women, children, and one old man, the latter of whom was seized and tied
to an iron picket pin, his feet hobbled, until he showed them a good trail
to follow. Then near the end of July the two miners in the train discovered
gold dust while panning in the creeks near Harney Peak; whereupon Custer sent his scout to Fort Laramie with the electrifying news, "gold has
been found in several places." Immediately the news flashed from coast
to coast, and thousands of whites prepared to head for the Black Hills to
strike it rich.[15]

Obviously, many, perhaps most, white Americans saw no reason to
stay out of the Black Hills at this point, despite the solemn promises of
their government to recognize Lakota rights of use and possession. They
no more acknowledged those Lakota rights than the Lakota respected the
claims of the Crow. As the Lakota buffalo hunters had done earlier, the
white gold miners entered and took what they wanted, seeking moral justification later. In both cases there were leaders who tried to negotiate
with the invaded to reduce conflict, but their power to control their followers was limited and they were only half-willing. One key difference was
that the whites flooded into the Hills in far greater numbers than the Lakota ever did, and with far more dramatic, even catastrophic, results, for
the land and its indigenous human inhabitants.

Within two months after Custer's return to home base an advance
party of gold-seekers, including 26 men, one woman, and a boy, were on
their way from Iowa. The woman in the party, Annie Tallent, later admitted that they had been without the law, but she denied her party was
really in the wrong: "Ignoring the ethical side of the question," she wrote,

"should such treaties as tend to arrest the advance of civilization, and retard the development of the rich resources of our country, ever have been entered into?"[16] Other whites reasoned similarly, sure that they were in the right, if not on the right side of the law, and they came in to dig. By March 1876 a city of 6,000 had sprung up in the Hills, named after Custer; another town, Deadwood, numbered 10,000, while hundreds of other miners had founded little settlements like Galena, Central City, Grizzly Gulch, and Rockerville. In that same year the mines of Deadwood produced $1.5 million in gold. In nearby Lead the Homestake mine, taken over by George Hearst of San Francisco, was already yielding rich ore, and it would prove to be the richest mine ever in American history, and one of the longest lasting, yielding by the late twentieth century some $18 billion worth of gold.[17]

While the miners were coming in by horse and wagon, even by foot, determined to be masters and millionaires, the federal government was engaged in the delicate task of protecting them while trying to honor the treaty it had made. In 1875 the Secretary of the Interior appointed a commission to secure from the Lakota the rights of white citizens to enter the Black Hills to mine for gold. The chairman of the commission was Senator William B. Allison of Iowa, and its other members included a Chicago judge, a brigadier general in the Army, a missionary to the Senate, a Missouri congressman, and a St. Louis trader. They were instructed to keep in mind that they represented "these ignorant and almost helpless people," the Indians, not less than the interests of the government. They were to remind the Indians that they had become dependent on the whites for the necessities of life, that they were now living on charity costing the government over a million dollars a year, a charity that had not been promised in the Treaty of 1868 and could not continue forever. They must adapt to and become self-supporting in the white man's economy. They must accede to white demands—or they must starve. The majority of the committee decided that, rather than having to convince a full three-fourths of all the males to give up ownership, they would seek only temporary mining rights from the Lakota, though the minority emphatically insisted that "in the end it would become necessary to divest the Indians of all title to the hills."

The Lakota were likewise divided among themselves in reacting to the terms of the Allison commission. A strong majority, consisting mainly of the older chiefs, were not willing to grant any temporary mining rights, probably because they knew "temporary" might mean "forever," but they would sell—and sell for a very stiff price, $70 million.[18] A minority refused to consider any price or any concession to the whites whatsoever. It was the older men who did most of the talking. "The Black Hills are the house of gold for our Indians," declared Little Bear; "if a man owns anything, of course he wants to make something out of it to get rich on." Little Bear wanted to see that all future generations of his people would live securely, receiving food rations and annuities from the federal government forever. Spotted Tail agreed: "I want to live on the interest of my money. The amount must be so large as to support us." Spotted Bear added: "Put the money away some place at interest so we can buy live stock. That is the way the white people do." Little Wolf: "We want to be made rich too." Fast Bear: "This land that you want to buy is not a small thing. It is very valuable and therefore I am going to put a big price on it." And then Red Cloud, whose name was attached to the agency eight miles from the site where the commissioners and Indians met, and who was probably the most influential leader among the Lakota, though resented by some for being too much of an accommodationist, rose to present a very detailed list of demands:

> For seven generations to come I want our Great Father to give us Texas steers for our meat. I want the Government to issue for me hereafter, flour and coffee, and sugar and tea, and bacon, the very best kind, and cracked corn and beans, and rice and dried apples, and saleratus and tobacco, and soap and salt, and pepper, for the old people. I want a wagon, a light wagon with a span of horses, and six yoke of working cattle for my people. I want a sow and a boar, and a cow and a bull, and a sheep and a ram, and a hen and a cock, for each family. I am an Indian but you try to make a white man out of me. I want some white men's houses to be built for the Indians. I have been into white people's house, and I have seen nice black bedsteads and chairs, and I want that kind of furniture given to my people. . . . I want the Great Father to furnish me a saw-mill which I may call my own. I want a mower and a scythe for my people. Maybe you white people think that I ask too much from the Government, but I think those hills extend clear to the sky—maybe they go above the sky, and that is the reason I ask for so much. I think the Black Hills are worth more than all the wild beasts and all the tame beasts in the possession of the white people. I know it well, and you can see it plain enough that God Almighty placed those hills there for my wealth, but now you want to take them from me and make me poor, so I ask so much so that I won't be poor.

Apparently, some of their white advisors had been talking to the Lakota, telling them what was at stake; but surely the chiefs were also able to see for themselves that the economic potential of the Hills was, in the white man's eyes, enormous, and they were keen to get a price that would compensate them well into the future for the loss of their now depleted hunting grounds.[19]

The commission from the Great Father, hearing those extravagant terms but not quite believing them, expressed "serious doubts whether there was gold in the hills in sufficient quantity to make mining profitable," but they were willing "to make their proposition most liberal in order to give opportunity of testing their value." They countered by offering $6 million to buy the Hills outright or $400,000 a year to lease, with the right to mine, grow stock, or cultivate the soil, for an indeterminate period. Predictably, the Indians refused. There was no further discussion or negotiation, and no deal. The white miners would continue to be, according to American law, trespassers on the Lakota lands and the federal government was obliged by treaty to chase them out.

There was a larger question than merely getting access to the Hills, the Allison commission realized, one they were not prepared to resolve, and it was the question of "what shall be done with the Sioux people." The government counted some 35,000 of them, a few thousand still roaming the countryside but the vast majority living on the reservation, clustered around six agencies were food rations were distributed. Among them were perhaps 8,000 children, "growing up in barbarism, not 200 of whom have ever received any instruction whatever." Fed on government rations, the Indian numbers were going up rapidly. One of the commissioners, General A. G. Lawrence of Providence, Rhode Island, drew on the work of English population authority Thomas Malthus to suggest that giving the Indians free food (that pound of meat and pound of flour per day) removed all checks on their fertility; the more they were fed, the more they would increase in numbers until they became a tremendous burden on white taxpayers. The problem was, of course, one created solely by the American invaders through their deliberate slaughter of the buffalo herds, and the commission admitted as much. "But for our people the region thus taken—no matter how—would still afford them subsistence, precarious and uncertain it may be, but suited to their wants and habits. This sacrifice has brought to them destitution and beggary; to our nation wealth and power, and with these an obligation to make good to them, in some way, the loss by which we have so largely gained." Yet at the same time the commission was exasperated by the Lakota's failure to make a bigger effort to help themselves, fulfilling the terms of the treaty they had made, "a treaty which is only sacred to the Indian so far as it conforms to his whims, caprices, or interests."

In its report to Congress the commission dwelt mainly on this larger issue of the ultimate fate of the red people. "To save this race from itself, and the country from the intolerable burden of pauperism and crime which the race, if left to itself, will certainly inflict upon a score of future

States," they recommended a program of "rigid reformatory control" of the Lakota. They would give subsistence to able adults only if they worked for it. They would place all children above the age of six in school, separating the older ones from their parents, forcing them to work for their support, invoking "the power of force" to get their compliance. The commissioners would promote the system of private property among the Indians as a training ground in personal responsibility, and they would protect the individual property rights of any Indian who tried to follow the system. If possible, they would send all the Lakota hundreds of miles south to new homes in the Indian Territory (today's state of Oklahoma) "where the lands are more productive and subsistence cheaper, and where they could much more quickly and easily become self-supporting by agricultural pursuits." And the Black Hills, who would possess them? The whites would. The government should set its own fair-value price on the Hills and present it to the Lakota "as a finality, and with it they should be told that its rejection will have the effect to arrest all appropriations for their subsistence in the future, and all supplies not absolutely required by the treaty of 1868." Once again came the harsh warning: Submit or starve. There was no other choice. In the view of the commission, granting Red Cloud and his associates their list of demands, allowing them an idle life on unearned income, would work their ruin.

Congress received the commission's report but for more than a year did nothing about it. Who could altogether blame them, when the choice seemed to be between a demoralizing Indian dependency on government rations and annuities and a draconian, equally demoralizing program of removal and near-slavery? Either way the Lakota would lose their freedom, pride, and self-reliance. Certainly many in Congress and the administration of President Ulysses S. Grant were in a quandary over what to do. Not until the fateful summer of 1876 did Congress come to any decision, and then their mood was grim and vengeful. On 23 June a strong encampment of Lakota, led by Crazy Horse, Gall, and Sitting Bull, defended themselves against a completely foolhardy attack by George Custer, killing him and over 200 of his cavalry troops. On 15 August Congress declared that no federal funds could go to any hostile Indians (meaning Crazy Horse and company), that all the Lakota must leave the "unceded Indian lands" and come back to their designated reservation, and that all reservation lands lying west of the 103rd meridian (including the Black Hills) must be yielded to the government. Two weeks later another commission, headed by George Manypenny, a former Commissioner of Indian Affairs, came out to the plains to meet with the Lakota and get their peaceful acquiescence to that Congressional decision, putting an end to the fighting and an end to any right of the Indians to sell or not, as they chose.

More than any of their predecessors, the new set of commissioners expressed the utmost anguish over the line they must follow; "our cheeks," they wrote, "crimsoned with shame." Even now, more than a century later, their words burn like hot coals on the page. The war that had broken out between the U.S. Army and the Lakota, they said, was completely the fault of the whites. Custer had illegally entered Lakota lands in 1874. The gold miners had come illegally in his wake. The government had failed to keep them out—President Grant had even secretly refused to do so. The Indians had gone hungry, despite all the vaunted charity; and though in such circumstances they had been given by treaty the right to go hunt the buffalo, the army had wrongfully tried to force them back on to the reservation, and in the dead of winter. Then it had taken away their horses and weapons. Through all those outrages the Indians had checked their anger and frustration until, finally, they had done what any people, savage or civilized, would have done in defense of their homes—fought back in desperation. It was all so unnecessary, the commissioners lamented. Custer was no martyr to a just cause; the war in which he died was useless, expensive, dishonorable, and disgraceful. "Have we been uniformly unjust? We answer unhesitatingly, 'Yes.'" The final words of the commissioners' report are worth quoting at length, for they express, in the most passionate language, what eight white men—trying in the midst of so much anger to get a fair-minded, independent view, yet charged with the job of returning to Washington with a signed agreement—saw as the real, underlying moral issue encountered in the Black Hills:

It is an eternal law of the government of God that whatsoever a nation sows, that and nothing but that shall it reap. If we sow broken faith, injustice, and wrong, we shall reap in the future, as we have reaped in the past, a harvest of sorrow and blood. We are not simply dealing with a poor perishing race; we are dealing with God. We cannot afford to delay any longer fulfilling our bounden duty to those from whom we have taken that country, the possession of which has placed us in the forefront of the nations of the earth. We make it our boast that our country is the home of the oppressed of all lands. Dare we forget that there are also those whom we have made homeless, and to whom we are bound to give protection and care? We are aware that many of our people think that the only solution of the Indian problem is in their extermination. We would remind such persons that there is only One who can exterminate. There are too many graves within our borders over which the grass had hardly grown, for us to forget that God is just. The Indian is a savage, but he is also a man. He is one of the few savage men who clearly recognize the existence of a Great Spirit. He believes in the immortality of the soul. He has a passionate love for his children. He loves his country. He will gladly die for his tribe. Unless we deny all revealed religion, we must admit that he has the right to share in all the benefits of divine revelation. He is capable of civilization.... A great crisis has arisen in Indian affairs. The wrongs of the Indians are admitted by all. Thousands of the best men in the land feel keenly the nation's shame. They look to Congress for redress. Unless immediate and appropriate legislation is made for the protection and government of the Indians, they must perish. Our country must forever bear the disgrace and suffer the retribution of its wrongdoing. Our children's children will tell the sad story in hushed tones, and wonder how their fathers dared so to trample on justice and trifle with God.[20]

The commissioners did not, and perhaps could not as officers of the government, question the right of that government to take the Black Hills and other lands away from the Lakota. They admitted no violation of the 1868 treaty in that seizure, nor in the refusal to furnish food to Indians who engaged in hostilities or disobeyed federal orders. But the unmistakable import of the commission's concluding words was that, if the government now sought to punish the Indians by taking their lands, then the government must place itself under the most solemn obligation henceforth to look out for the Lakota's welfare, helping them make the transition to civilization and sharing America's blessings with them. In the view of Manypenny and his associates that obligation could best be met by moving the Lakota, as the Allison commission had recommended, to the more benign soils and climate of the Indian Territory where they could learn from the example of other Indians who had become good farmers and Christians.

Congress, however, did not follow that long-term solution when it came to pass legislation the following year. In late January William Allison introduced a bill in the Senate to ratify an "agreement" with the Sioux Nation, the Northern Arapaho, and the Cheyenne that would give the Black Hills to the federal government but not require the Indians to move south. They had themselves firmly rejected that latter idea, as did the whites living in states surrounding the Indian Territory, who were afraid of having Custer's killers relocated near them. How the Indians were to become successful farmers in an area everyone agreed was not great farming country was ignored. On 28 February legislation "ceding" the Black Hills was approved by President Grant, and the Dakota Territory (it became the two states of North and South Dakota in 1889) assumed jurisdiction over that real estate and over the miners and other white settlers living there.[21]

What kind of "agreement" had the Lakota made with the Manypenny Commission and the United States Congress? It was certainly not a formal treaty, for Congress had stopped making treaties with Indians in 1871, ending the idea, at least in Washington's eyes, that the Indians were sovereign nations or even, in the famous formula of Chief Justice John Marshall, "domestic dependent nations."[22] Congress continued to refer to the "Sioux Nation of Indians," but it would treat them more nebulously as neither a foreign nation nor as American citizens. The so-called agreement was not signed by three-fourths of all the adult males, as specified in the Treaty of Laramie; the commissioners had merely got the signatures, or marks, of many of the chiefs and headmen who represented those males. In the government's view the treaty was no longer binding, for the Lakota had been collecting rations not specified in it, had failed to carry out their responsibility to put their children in schools, and had not gotten the army's permission to wander over into Montana, into the valley of the Little Big Horn, and into Wyoming. No treaty, just an agreement. Whatever "agreeing" the chiefs did, and there is some evidence that they were confused about what was happening, they were under heavy threats to yield or go hungry.

Was the agreement obtained illegally or in some way unfairly? That is a question no one raised in the halls of Congress in 1877, but it would be seriously raised again and again in the years to come. In the early twentieth century Lakota leaders tried repeatedly to get a hearing for their view that the Hills were taken from them but met with little success. They went to their reservation agents, the Bureau of Indian Affairs, and South Dakota congressmen. They hired lawyers and appealed to the U.S. Court of Claims, but for years the Court refused to allow them or any other tribes to sue the federal government, denied the Court had any jurisdiction in such matters, or claimed it was too overburdened to take them up. When finally it did get around to a full hearing, in 1942, the Court unanimously concluded that the Black Hills had not been the subject of a "taking" in the strictly legal sense of the term. Rather, the government had acted properly as the "ward" of the Indians and had had their welfare in mind in disposing of the land to the white migrants. The Court also held that Lakota had been justly compensated for any conceivable losses through the annual expenditures Congress had made to sustain them on their reservation. In addition to the rations given from 1875 to 1877, rations worth $2,350,000, Congress had made appropriations year after year to buy the Indians food and other necessities. By 1942, according to the government, the total spent amounted to approximately $43 million. In effect, though no sale of the land had actually taken place, the Lakota had gotten what

Red Cloud and the other chiefs demanded as their price: a perpetual income for their people, though the government had always insisted that the appropriations were only a temporary measure, until the Lakota could become self-supporting. Thus, said the Court, nothing dishonorable or unjust had occurred. Case decided, case dismissed.

Fortunately for the Lakota, Congress opened a new possibility of potential redress when, in 1946, it established the Indian Claims Commission. The ICC was authorized only to make cash settlements, not return any land. In 1954 it handed down a decision to the Lakota, and it was still not the one they wanted to hear, essentially saying what the Court of Claims had already said, that there had been no illegal taking, that the loss of the Black Hills had been quite legal and fully compensated. Twenty years later, however, in 1974, the ICC suddenly changed its mind and declared that the Lakota had indeed been treated dishonorably by the government, that their rights under the Constitution had been violated. Congress, it was now admitted, had taken their lands without making any payment for them, and such a taking amounted to a violation of the Fifth Amendment.

In the Anglo-American legal tradition, a "taking" refers to the right of the sovereign, or the government, to take over private property in order to address a public need. This right of eminent domain, as it is called in the United States, began far back in the dim reaches of history, but by the time of Magna Carta (1215) its exercise had caused so much resentment that anti-monarchy reformers managed to get some restrictions imposed on it. Centuries later, when the new nation of the United States was established following a revolution against the still outrageous powers of the British monarchy, the sanctity of private property was asserted in far more radical terms. One might then have expected the right of eminent domain to disappear. It did not. It continued in force and was exercised repeatedly. The only restriction placed on the right was the Fifth Amendment to the Constitution, which reads: "Nor shall private property be taken for public use, without just compensation." For any staunch believer in the supremacy of private, individual rights, that protective clause gave only a small comfort, for it remained the practice of the courts, in America as in England, to let the government itself decide what a public use or a public good was—and, as it turned out, almost any exercise of the right of eminent domain in the name of national economic development was legitimate.[23] Worse yet, it was the government itself that had the power to decide what a just compensation should be.

When the Indian Claims Commission found for the Lakota, it did so under the belief that the Lakota were just like any other American citizens who had lost their lands to the government, or to some third party designated by the government to receive the land. Just as whites had often been forced to surrender their private property for some public purpose, for example, the building of highways, railroads, dams, parks, or court houses, so the Lakota had been forced to give up the Black Hills. Democracy required that outcome; a government that was forced to buy what it needed from whatever real estate happened to be for sale would be severely crippled in the performance of its responsibilities to look for out for the general welfare. One single, selfish, unyielding land owner could thwart the public good. The needs of all the people must take precedence over the property rights of the few. But understandably, those who were denied their rights of ownership were never happy about it. A farmer who watched a downstream mill owner construct a dam and back up the river, flooding his hay meadows, with no power to stop the destruction, with indeed the government sanctioning such destruction by the power of eminent domain, was not likely to be pleased, yet the courts had seen nothing wrong so long as the injured owner was paid a fair market value for his losses.

Now, following long-established procedures in such cases, the lands taken from the Lakota were assessed by expert appraisers, who tried to calculate what the Black Hills and their surroundings must have been worth on the market in the 1870s, before the value of the gold deposits had been firmly established. They came up with the figure of $17,553,484. It was a lot less than Red Cloud and associates had demanded in 1877, but more than three times what the government had then been willing to pay. The Lakota were owed that much money, along with annual interest at 5 percent for all the years of delayed compensation. It was by far the largest award ever made by the ICC. But now the federal government balked at the size of the award, appealed to the Court of Claims to overturn it, and received satisfaction; the Court, ignoring the ICC reasoning, declared it had already settled the matter once and for all when it had decided that annual congressional appropriations for the reservations could be counted as a kind of ongoing payment for the land, and the land was now more than adequately paid for.

Briefly, a door had seemed to open for the Lakota—before it slammed shut. Then, in 1974, another door was opened when Congress stepped in to give the Sioux assistance, amending the charter of the Indian Claims Commission to specify that "expenditures for food, rations, or provisions shall not be deemed payments" on any claims. Back to the Court of Claims for the third time came the case, and a decision was handed down on 13 June 1979. The court majority, led by Chief Judge Daniel M. Friedman, decided that there had indeed been an illegal taking (a) of Sioux land in the Black Hills and (b) of rights-of-way across other Sioux lands and that the Lakota had not yet received just compensation for those takings. They were entitled to the fair market value as determined by the ICC, plus some $85 million more in interest![24]

The administration of President Jimmy Carter was not ready to pay such a sum and appealed to the highest court in the land to have the decision overturned. On 30 June 1980, however, the Supreme Court affirmed the lower court's decision completely. Justice Harry Blackmun, writing for the court majority, concluded that Congress had never really intended that giving rations to the Indians was a form of payment for the lands they had lost. No one had ever even suggested such an interpretation until the 1950s. Instead, the rations had been given as a tacit acknowledgment that the whites had deprived the Lakota of "their chosen way of life"; they were payment for destroying a traditional means of subsistence, hunting the buffalo, and the culture that went with it. Justice William Rehnquist, on the other hand, dissented from that view, insisting that Congress had no right to reopen a case already settled long ago. He added that the Supreme Court, like Congress, was trying to rewrite history by putting all the guilt for Indian-white conflict on the whites, a view, he argued, "which is not universally shared." "There were undoubtedly greed, cupidity, and other less-than-admirable tactics employed by the Government during the Black Hills episode," Rehnquist admitted, "but the Indians did not lack their share of villainy either. It seems to me quite unfair to judge by the light of 'revisionist' historians or the mores of another era actions that were taken under pressure of time more than a century ago." Rehnquist, who would subsequently be appointed Chief Justice of the Supreme Court by President Ronald Reagan, did not persuade his colleagues.[25]

With the court decisions all out of the way, Congress then appropriated the combined sum of compensation and interest, amounting to over $100 million, and notified the Lakota that they had only to collect the money and their long, complicated, bitter struggle was over. After a little more than a full century of persistence, disappointment, rising hopes, dashed hopes, the Lakota had won their case decisively. At last they could say that they had received justice in the American legal system. Their lawyers could collect a sizable fee for their patient efforts. But then, astonishingly, the Lakota, as related earlier, decided it was not after all the money that they wanted. They wanted the Hills themselves.

To get the Black Hills themselves back, the Lakota must, in effect, recall their lawyers, throw out the whole chain of legal reasoning that had been developed in their behalf, and start on a new tack. There could not have been a taking, they must insist, legal or illegal; there could not have been any exercise of the right of eminent domain simply because the Lakota lands were not, in 1877, the private property of American citizens. And if the power to take could not have existed in the situation, then no cash compensation for such a taking could ever be appropriate. In fact, no such reinstruction of the legal staff nor any such argument has yet been made before any court. But if it were made and if there were any substance to it, then all the courts, commissions, and Congresses might have to admit that they have not really addressed the true issues, that some vital questions have not yet been asked, let alone answered, that the Lakota may have grounds enough to get their case opened once more and get their lands back.

In the first place the lawyers might argue the next time around that the Lakota were not standing before the federal government in the year 1877 as a group of American citizens. They were outsiders to the society. Though the government no longer made "treaties" with them, it continued to refer to them as the Sioux Nation—and indeed was still doing so as late as the 1980s. The Lakota, like other Indians, did not commonly become American citizens until half a century later in the 1920s. That being so, could the right of eminent domain be exercised over a people whose status was still that of a quasi-foreign nation? Could the federal government take property that did not belong to any of its citizens in order to achieve a public use benefiting some of its citizens? As a corollary, could it take lands that belonged communally to a whole "people," a tribe, not privately to individuals?

However those questions might be answered, and they have not even been formally raised so far, there is another gap in the court's reasoning that must be confronted, in Congress if not in the courts. No evidence exists that Congress, in forcing the Lakota to yield the Black Hills, understood that it was in fact exercising the right of eminent domain. No one in Washington ever mentioned that right or used it as a justification for getting the land, nor did anyone present the right to the Lakota as a governmental power that could be exercised over them. Indeed, not until the middle of the twentieth century did the notion appear that eminent domain might apply in the case. What the court and the ICC seem to have done is to find, at the urging of the Indians' lawyers and long after the fact, a proper legal cover for it; they have made a white man's law apply where and when that law did not clearly reach. In doing so, the rights of the government had had to be stretched beyond all precedents in the Anglo-American legal tradition. Perhaps after a proper reconsideration of the whole procedure Americans might decide that there was nothing wrong in it. Perhaps they might decide that the confusion inevitable in cross-cultural Indian-white legal relations excuses it. Perhaps the Lakota, who have profited immeasurably from the coming of the white man's laws, might eventually accept that procedure as necessary and beneficial to them and learn to be content with the outcome. Yet the American public ought to know the full history of the matter and think about it all very carefully: the fact that the courts first denied there had been any injustice committed, then admitted some injustice while simultaneously, and fortunately, finding its remedy—and a relatively painless one at that—a remedy that rested on a right that no one in 1877 had realized existed.

Moreover, the American public ought to understand that the right of eminent domain which has been asserted in the case of the Lakota is one of the most disputed areas of American jurisprudence. A number of legal scholars have recently complained that the right is incredibly nebulous and needs to be defined more carefully and applied with more restraint. For a long while the right was repeatedly used to allow the speedy development of the country's resources, to promote economic growth. Then, especially from the 1930s on, it was used by a more liberal, activist government to secure greater economic justice and security for the disadvantaged by the method of condemning private property in order to build grandiose public works to stimulate the economy and provide jobs. More recently, as the nation has been going through a time of environmental revolution, the doctrine of eminent domain has been frequently employed as a powerful tool to stop pollution, preserve endangered habitat, and control chaotic urbanization. Now, however, with the Lakota decision, the doctrine has become the basis for dispossessing native Americans. No wonder that Bruce Ackerman speaks of the "general incoherence of takings doctrine."[26] No wonder liberal and conservative critics alike have recommended a new look at it.

Throughout the American past it has generally been the poor, not the rich, who have been most adversely affected by this loose, flexible right of government. Poor people have been the ones standing in the way of progress and must give way. The "public good" must overrule their good. What that means is that the poor have been far less successful in getting their notions of "public use" heard and acted on than the rich. Small farmers in New England, for example, lost out to the industrialists who wanted to erect dams to power their textile mills—an obvious public good in the minds of those industrialists. Racial minorities have over and over lost out to highway builders and urban planners wielding the right of eminent domain. Now the Lakota, we are told, lost out to George Hearst and his fellow mining entrepreneurs and to all the whites flocking into their territory to find opportunity—another triumph of the public good that left the poor poorer than ever. The historical record makes it clear that the doctrine of eminent domain has not been equitably applied in the past.

What if, in the case of the Black Hills, it had been not a band of Indian hunters who were invaded by gold seekers but a President of the United States, living in idyllic splendor on his multi-million-dollar ranch? Would the U.S. Army then have managed somehow to keep the gold seekers out, or would it have allowed them to invade, settle, dig away with impunity, and then demand military and legislative protection of their "rights"? Would the Congress have decided that it was a legitimate "public use" to take the land of a President of the United States and give it to some trespassers? Of course, that is a purely counterfactual situation, with a purely hypothetical land owner, but it suggests strongly that the doctrine of eminent domain is more likely to be used to effect the dispossession of some people than others. Is that the kind of doctrine Americans believe in their hearts should be applied retroactively to the Lakota?

Ironically, the bill introduced by Senator Bill Bradley, which would return 1.3 million acres of public lands to the Lakota, would do little to change this pattern of discriminatory use of eminent domain. It would make no redress where the use of that power has been most egregiously unequal. Arguably, the national forests and parks in today's Black Hills are the only legitimate "public uses" that have emerged from the taking of 1877. On those lands anyone, Indian or white, is at least theoretically free to enter and enjoy and use; but those are precisely, and only, the lands that would be returned to the Lakota. Meanwhile, the nearby privatized property of the Homestake Mining Company and all the house lots, the business establishments, the farms and pastures in the vicinity of Rapid City, Custer, and Deadwood, all those lands that have passed into the hands of private white citizens, would be untouched and secure. The Lakota lost the largest portion of their land not to the American public seeking a public use but to a group of very individualized white men and women who have made lots of individualized dollars with that land. Can it now be plausibly maintained by the courts that those private individuals, past and present, represent a "public use" of the Hills? Can Senator Bradley really believe that his bill would cleanse the record? Only expediency, the desire of the present generation to solve a past illegality without much inconveniencing the status quo, could support such a fiction. But in the final analysis that is what the legal outcome for the Lakota, both in the courts' decisions and in Bradley's bill, must appear to be by the white man's own mode of reasoning: the triumph of belated, bumbling, timid, halting, and realistic expediency over the strictures of justice.

Try, and try again. Having repeatedly made their case as a legal argument, having made a case that ultimately failed by the only acceptable (to them) criterion of getting the land back, the Lakota attempted a second maneuver. They were completely sincere and deadly earnest in adding it, but surely they calculated that this strategy would touch the sensibilities of a nation of churchgoers where legalisms had failed. It was shaped in part by its white audience. The Hills, argued the Lakota during and after the court hearings, were more than a disputed piece of property; they were a "sacred space." The Hills are "the heart of everything that is"—they are *Wamaka Og'naka I'Cante*. As David Blue Thunder, an elder on the Rosebud reservation put it, "they are the heart of our home and the home of our heart."[27] Alienate them into white man's property, make them producers of commercial lumber, ore, and scenery, and they become profaned. Their loss in 1877 did just that and thus interfered with the Lakota's religious freedom of expression in the most vital way. Lakota religion came under a threat of extinction, and today it cannot survive unless the Hills are returned. The whites, if they persist in holding and profaning the lands, will therefore be guilty of killing the faith of a people.

In interviews with journalists and before the Senate committee considering the Bradley bill, the Lakota frequently fell back on this religious argument, like a speaker slipping into his native dialect, weary of speaking a foreign tongue. If it was a conscious strategy, it was also a cry of frustration. The plea for recision had never been for the traditional Lakota one based primarily on legal rights or economic calculus, as a corporation might sue to safeguard its patents. The Hills had an indefinable but powerful emotional appeal to them, one they had trouble translating through the medium of their white lawyers in a white courtroom. They sought to put that appeal in terms the whites might understand: the Black Hills, they explained, are to our religion what the city of Jerusalem is to you Christians and Jews, or Mecca to the Moslems—a high holy place, the highest our religion recognizes, so high that it is beyond all form of compensation.[28] No truly faithful man or woman would take money for them in the marketplace. They have an incalculable value, they cannot be sold. To try to do so would be like selling one's parents, one's God, one's very self and soul.

Religious feelings are characteristically difficult to put into words, especially the words of someone else's language. They are not rooted in cold, experimental reason, like scientific propositions, and they are never fully coherent or completely consistent, but are bundles of unsorted, and unsortable, yearnings. The heart has its reasons, wrote Blaise Pascal, that the mind knows nothing of. In advanced societies where complex written literatures exist, there are theologians who try to make logical sense out of religious intuitions, but the common people are not theologically proficient and may or may not find that logic true to their hearts. Theology is thus always a little inadequate, a little too well organized and intellectual, to explain all our tangled religious intuitions. If that is so in complex societies, how much more difficult is the situation of an unlettered people when they want others to understand. The traditional Lakota did not have any formal, written theological tradition to draw on and were all that much more inarticulate as logical analysts. Their feelings, though as valid as any Hindu's or Lutheran's, lacked a systematic examination and justification; they were embedded in an ancient, evolving folk consciousness, passed down in the form of vernacular stories their elders told the young. Today, much of what we know of traditional Lakota religion as a system of thought comes from the work of white anthropologists who cannot claim the authority, the authenticity, of an Indian equivalent of Thomas Aquinas or Jonathan Edwards, speaking from within a tradition of belief.[29] If trained anthropologists have difficulty organizing and translating the Lakota religion, then we untrained laymen must run even more risks of misunderstanding.

We have no choice but to run that risk. The fate of over a million acres of land and their ecological communities, the well-being of tens, possibly hundreds, of thousands of human beings, may rest on how Americans perceive the issues and how they react to the Lakota's religious claims. The stakes are large. They require of us all, Lakota included, as much clarity as possible, and as much frankness, even at the risk of giving offense to one another. Already, the discussion has been muddied by several kinds of unreflective reaction that we must avoid. First, for some white listeners, whatever any modern Indian says about the distant past of his people and their beliefs is automatically assumed to be so. If an eloquent man says that Indians were all "nature lovers," the auditor immediately assents. Feelings change, however, religious feelings included, and we must not assume that the feelings and the ideas in Lakota religion are the same today as they were one hundred, two hundred, or a thousand years ago. Second, too many have talked loosely about what "the Lakota believe" as though they were, and are, completely unanimous, a nation of automatons dancing to a group mind. Like whites, Indians vary in the intensity and focus of their religious feelings, and they may disagree radically among themselves on fundamental principles.

Third, the word "sacred" has often been thrown about with little thought and not much inquiry into what it really requires of us. Sacred refers to more than having warm feelings or showing love and attachment to something. As slippery as the term is, we must strive to be clear about it, specifying how it differs from other strongly felt experiences and how it differs from the profane world.

One of our best guides to the concept of the sacred, and one of the world's foremost students of comparative religion and mythology, is Mircea Eliade. In 1959 he published the English translation of his study *The Sacred and the Profane* (subtitled *The Nature of Religion*), in which he sought to explain in detail the transcultural core experience of sacredness. All societies have such experiences, though since the scientific and capitalist revolutions, large numbers of people in modern western civilization have lost them—though not all people there by any means have done so—and now dwell in a thoroughly profane world, the first group in history to live without the experience. Religion has become a twitch of irrationality for modernist man. One of Eliade's most influential predecessors, Rudolph Otto, in his book *Das Heilige* (1917), took irrationality to be the very essence of the sacred experience; it occurs, he argued, when we have been frightened out of our wits by an encounter with some mysterious, overpowering force. The sacred is terrifying. Eliade, in contrast, does not emphasize the irrationality of this experience; rather, he believes, it involves a glimpse in something "wholly other," a realm of being that lies beyond, and is far greater than, the merely human or natural. It is "numinous" experience, where the indwelling spirit or divinity of a place or natural object presents itself to the human mind. Those who put complete faith in science and are confident it tells us all we can or need to know about the objects around us, or those who can see only potential profit or loss in those objects, cannot have this experience; for them the sacredness of the world has vanished in a puff of skepticism. Eliade nonetheless asks such people to respect the sacred experience of others and to try to understand the venerable notion that it represents of how the world works.

A receptivity to the sacred requires holding a world view in which nature appears as discontinuous in time and heterogeneous in space. There are breaks, interruptions in the flow of things, points where one mode of being abruptly gives way to another and where time itself changes its rhythms. "Draw not nigh hither," says the Lord, appearing to Moses in a burning bush; "put off thy shoes from off thy feet, for the place whereon thou standest is holy ground" (Exodus 3:5). For a modern geologist that piece of land Moses walked on might appear absolutely ordinary and indistinguishable from the surrounding terrain—same rocks, same sun beating on same rocks, same radiocarbon dates showing same time of origination, all same stuff, all same history. But for Moses that particular bit of holy ground had suddenly become utterly unlike anything around it; he had come upon a momentous discontinuity in nature. He saw there, as if peering through a window, the very order of the universe laid out, and he saw its divine Creator revealed. Now the rocks appeared as distinctly different, illuminated by the bush afire; they were no longer the ordinary, everyday clutter, mere expressions of the imperfectness of quotidian life, a place where time moves on and on inexorably, where things come and go, where nature is without intrinsic form or meaning. Emerging mysteriously out of the very substance of that ordinariness, demarcated by no visible lines, identified only by the solemn voice of God, was a holy place. Time ceases to move there. One steps beyond history, beyond the fate of rocks eroding away under sun and water, and enters instantly the real world, orderly, enduring, harmonious, perfect. Eliade refers to such a moment of revelation as a hierophany: "an irruption of the sacred that results in detaching a territory from the surrounding cosmic milieu and making it qualitatively different."[30]

Any space, it would seem, no matter how drab or unexceptional, has the potential to become such a sacred window on the cosmos. Moses found his holy place in a nondescript part of the Sinai desert. Others have found theirs in a commonplace grove of trees or even along the shabby, crowded banks of a polluted river in India. But among the hierophantic places there have also been mountains and hills, some bold and awe-inspiring, some rather negligible. Mountains can seem to rise like ladders out of the mundane realm and into the holy, carrying one to a transcendental vision. In many cultures mountains have suggested an *axis mundi* around which the cosmos rotates, a vertical line connecting the two modes of being, sacred and profane. Mountains are not required for the experience of sacredness, but if near at hand they seem wonderfully cast for the role and frequently have so been used. After climbing some sacred mountain and glimpsing from its eminence the true order of the world, the religious man or woman comes down to find the whole face of lowland nature changed. Now everything, no matter how humble or familiar or routine, is seen as part of the cosmos, glowing with divinity, existing above nature and beyond time.

Eliade defines the sacred as a mode of being that contrasts with the profane. So what is the profane? In a sense, the whole of nature is sacred, and for religious man, in contrast to modernist man, nothing is absolutely profane. But for the religious most of the landscape one encounters is silent; it does not really speak to one, as God's voice spoke to Moses out of the bush, demanding worship. Without that voice, the profane world seems to lie there without meaning or order, without creative power. The profane then is the territory or object that is derivatively and inarticulately sacred. It is the place where we get our living. It offers food to whoever makes an effort to gather or farm, so it is the realm of economics and labor. As such, it offers lots of difficulties, mishaps, sickness, hunger, ordinary dangers from which one must continually defend oneself—in other words, a territory where life seems less than perfect, and our place in nature seems insecure and sometimes ill-adapted.

The profane is also the periphery of spiritual power, while the sacred space is the center of that power. Once discovered, the sacred space becomes for people a center—even *the* center—of the world, of the cosmos. And people naturally want to live as close to that center as possible, where the power and order are focused, visiting it regularly as part of their cycle of days, leaning on it as the stable foundation on which all else depends. They may even try to design their houses, tents, yurts, towns, or encampments in close imitation of the cosmos revealed at the center. They may erect special buildings, like sweat lodges or churches or temples, as a kind of surrogate of that place. Over time those special buildings may gradually displace to some extent the sacred places of the outdoors that originally inspired them. Such has largely been the outcome in western religions like Christianity, where the sacred has moved almost completely indoors and the church building itself, no matter how new or profane its construction, no matter that it may be a prestressed concrete structure fitted with the latest in Kohler plumbing and track lighting, may have been designed by an architect and put up by a team of fun-loving hard hats, becomes the only sacred center the people have. There is nothing recent in this sanctified indoors: the medieval cathedrals of Europe were holy ground as much as Moses's bit of desert and came to serve as the key window on the cosmos for their votaries; in effect they went in and shut the door on the landscape of sacralized nature. But for many North American Indians that process of wholly encapsulating the sacred in an obviously human construction did not, and even now has not, occurred, so that the great sacred places are still out there in the realm of nature, places that represent more than mere nature to the believers, but to the unbelieving eye can seem an undifferentiated part of the natural landscape. Here, answer the hierophants, if you could only see, is the Center. Here is where everything comes together and acquires order and meaning. Here is where voices speak and revelations come. To move far away from that Center or to lose access to it is to fall back into the chaos of the world, lost, confused, and alienated.[31]

All religion seems to spring from a feeling of profound nostalgia, a longing for a time when the daily world was more pure and orderly than it now appears. The religious person wants to escape the present and reenter that past existence. In Christianity such nostalgia has become, paradoxically, progressive; that is, the believer must go forward in time, following all the way to the very end through a long saga of trouble and hardship, in order to find his way back to Eden at last. The consequences of that reorientation of nostalgia from the past to the future are everywhere around us in the modern commitment to technology, economic growth, and progress. But for traditional North American Indians, lacking the idea of progress, the feeling of nostalgia was and still is focused only on the past. They are nostalgic for a paradise that existed before the beginning of time. Returning to the past is impossible in any permanent way, but glimpsing it from time to time can cleanse and rehabilitate the present. That is what one takes away from the sacred places: a renewal of life, a new beginning, starting fresh from Eden. Eliade writes about the rituals of renewal carried out in the sacred places and the memory they summoned:

> All the "sins" of the year, everything that time had soiled and worn, was annihilated in the physical sense of the world. By symbolically participating in the annihilation and re-creation of the world, man too was created anew; he was reborn, for he began a new life. With each New Year, man felt freer and purer, for he was delivered from the burden of his sins and failings. He had reintegrated the fabulous time of Creation, hence a sacred and strong time—sacred because transfigured by the presence of the gods, strong because it was the time that belonged, and belonged only, to the most gigantic creation ever accomplished, that of the universe. . . . It is easy to understand why the memory of that marvelous time haunted religious man, why he periodically sought to return to it. *In illo tempore* the gods had displayed their greatest powers. *The cosmogony is the supreme divine manifestation,* the paradigmatic act of strength, superabundance, and creativity. Religious man thirsts for the real. By every means at his disposal, he seeks to reside at the very source of primordial reality, when the world was *in statu nascendi.*[32]

In the sacred places one is taken back to that very beginning of things. Standing on holy ground, shoeless and receptive, one can glimpse the cosmos as it is and as it was at the moment of Creation. One can even, in some sense, participate in that Creation, for it goes on at every moment, the cosmos is ever renewing itself. Among many Indians, the sacred place became in their stories the actual point of Creation, where their ancestors had come crawling out of the belly of the earth into the harsh, imperfect light of day, subject henceforth to a thousand ills and misfortunes. Returning to the sacred place afforded a temporary escape from the present into that lost world of innocence—temporary but absolutely essential to bear up under the burdens of life.

Understanding more fully the relation of the sacred and the profane, we can get a better grip on what the Lakota people have been saying in recent years. And we can see what is behind their insistent demand for the Black Hills. The Indians living at Pine Ridge and other reservations have plenty of life's burdens to bear and a dire need for renewal. They (or at least many of them) tell us they are a people who once had a sacred place, more sacred than any other on the face of the earth to them, and that that place has been taken away, leaving them toiling unhappily in a present, fallen life, denying them their full identity, and robbing them of their chance for renewal. That is really why they must have the Hills back.

What are we to accept and what reject in this argument? The main issue for us, it seems clear, is not whether large numbers of the Lakota actually have a sense of the sacred, one maintained even into these secularized times—undoubtedly, they do—nor is it whether they are sincere when they talk nostalgically about the world that once was, both the world of the last century before the coming of the white man, and the world in myth-time at the point of creation—of course, they are sincere. No, the issues that want addressing, in both the Lakota and white communities, are whether in fact the Black Hills truly were a most holy place; whether they are today such a place; and whether, if they were or are such a place, that fact requires Americans, out of a decent respect for religious feelings, to return the Hills to the Lakota.

That the Black Hills have the qualifications for a holy land is obvious from Eliade's analysis: virtually any place on earth has them. The Hills were an imposing feature of the landscape, and the Lakota were an impressible people. But the historian cannot find any evidence that in the nineteenth century the Hills were in fact regarded as sacred by the Lakota. They were viewed as a valuable economic resource, furnishing food and housing material. They offered to nomadic Indian bands, as they offer vacationers today, a beautiful green respite from the summer's heat. Their thunderstorms, with dark clouds piling up on the peaks and lightning flashing across the sky, warned that dangerous spirits lived in the Hills, ready to do harm to careless folk. Likely, individuals may have gone into the mountains from time to time to pray or seek a vision—but then others went out on the open prairie to do the same. None of that, however, indicates that in the year 1877, the year they were seized by the whites, the Black Hills were understood by the Indians to be a distinctly sacred ground, set apart from the profane world in myth and ritual, to be approached only in a reverential mood.

Certainly none of the tribal leaders who met with the Allison Commission, and whose words from that meeting were recorded by the commission's secretary, referred to the Black Hills as sacred or holy. On the contrary, they spoke of them in thoroughly profane terms: they put a price tag on them, "unrealistic" though it was, and called them their "house of gold" and their property. (Recall Little Bear's words: "If a man owns anything, of course he wants to make something out of it to get rich on.") Perhaps there were Indians at the time who disliked such language, but they were silent while the leaders expanded at length on the annuity values of the Hills, like a board of directors examining their assets. A quarter-century later, in 1903, many of the same Lakota leaders were still alive, though now quite elderly and failing in memory; unsure of how they had lost the Hills but nursing a resentment, they requested a council with South Dakota's Congressman at Large, E. W. Martin. Economic conditions had become increasingly desperate for the Indians; federal rations promised under the Treaty of Laramie for a thirty-year period had come to an end five years earlier, and the people were hungry and demoralized, trying to get by on skimpy, grudging government charity. On 21 and 22 September 1903 Martin sat down at the Pine Ridge Agency with delegates from five reservations and with John R. Brennan, the U.S. Indian agent at Pine Ridge. Martin defended the government's role in acquiring the land, both under the 1877 act and the Dawes Act of 1887 (not actually applied to the Lakota until 1889).[33] According to him, the government had already given the Lakota a total of $35 million in the form of annual payments for food, education, and other needs. The Indians had no common response to that position except to express a feeling of frustration and anger. Some thought they had actually made a treaty with Washington, guaranteeing in exchange for the Hills an abundance of food and other support for seven generations—meaning, they explained, seven hundred years—so that they would never have to work again or support themselves. Others denied any cession had been made; the required three-fourths of the adult men, as stipulated in the Laramie Treaty, had not signed any cession papers. One man remembered dimly that "everybody was drinking whiskey" and making speeches, but he was sure he had insisted on the occasion that the white man could have only the mountain tops, where the gold was deposited, not the foothills, where the Indians had timber and game resources they wanted to keep. Against the Cloud argued to the congressman: "We only loaned the white people the Black Hills from one mile down [which would take one almost to sea level], but now they are full from the top to the bottom. That is why we are talking about it. We want money for it." The old, somewhat discredited leader Red Cloud was one of the most bitter. He recalled that the government had offered only $6 million for the Black Hills and that he had told them it was not enough: "It is just as a little spit out of my mouth." "You can tell the Great Father that I will lend him the top of the hill, if he is satisfied, that is what you can tell him. That is just the rocks above the pines." No one in the group seemed to realize that Congress, after the breakdown of negotiations in 1876, had unilaterally seized the Hills the following year, without waiting for any Indian signatures at all or extending any promises of endless annuities. In the eyes of the congressman and the government, the Lakota had now to get off the dole and fend for themselves. And though the old men of the tribes were certainly not going to accept that ultimatum, if they even knew how to do it, not one of them, in thirty-two pages of typed transcript, ever complained that the Hills were sacred lands and absolutely vital to their religion. What several indicated in fact was not only a willingness to sell the Hills, in 1876 and now again in 1903, but a willingness to sell the mountain peaks for mining if they could keep what to them were the more valuable lands at lower elevations. Perhaps hunger had driven them to that utterly materialistic stance, but could hunger drive out all holy memory, all reverence?[34]

Many of the same elders, who were both holy men and political spokesmen, were interviewed by the white physician who served the Pine Ridge reservation from 1886 to 1914, Dr. James R. Walker. Walker wanted to record, before they disappeared, the traditional Lakota religious beliefs. Over the years he talked to American Horse, George Sword, Bad Wound, Red Cloud, among others, and especially to Thomas Tyon, a mixed-blood who often served as his interpreter. It was Walker who provided the first full account in English of the Oglala Sioux mythology, and even now his account is one of the most valued. He got the elders to spell out their idea of the sacred, or in their own language, the concept of *wakan,* which referred to anything that was hard to understand, was mysterious, and therefore worthy of deep respect. The ultimate divine force in the world they called *Wakan Tanka,* a universal spirit comprised of many lesser spirits. "The *Wakan Tanka* have power over everything on earth," wrote Walker; "they control everything that mankind does. Mankind should please them in all things." The standard ritualistic way to do that was to offer them the aromatic smoke from tobacco, buring in a sacred redstone pipe, or from sweetgrass. In addition to pleasing the powerful universal collective spirit, the Indians tried not to give offense to many lesser, individualized spirits, the various *wakan* of the earth, mysterious forces dwelling in animals, plants, rocks, even the white man's guns and whiskey. Buffalo were particularly mysterious creatures, as were horses, wolves, bears, ferrets, foxes, and beavers. So was the dragonfly, the eagle, and certain lakes and cliffs and hills. All had a limited sacred quality that demanded respect. But nowhere in all of Walker's account of traditional Lakota religion do the Black Hills appear on the list of sacred things and places; they are never mentioned as a sacred place, or as *wakan*, in their several parts or in their whole mass. Several of his informants did talk about another, far-off place that was a prominent part of their mythology, "the Land of the Pines," and they indicated that beyond that land lay the country where "the spirits of Good Sioux go when they die." Possibly they were speaking out of some ancient memory of their former homeland farther east and perhaps too of the northern Canadian tundra region, the land at the edge of the earth. But it would seem, from his writings, that over several decades of conversation no one impressed on Walker the idea that the Black Hills was their point of origin, their sacred center, or their home after death.[35]

During the present century the most famous and revered religious figure among the Lakota has been Black Elk, an Oglala Sioux who was born on the Little Powder River in Wyoming in 1863. He was a teenager when General Custer and troops were rubbed out at the Battle of the Little Big Horn by warriors led by his cousin Crazy Horse and by Sitting Bull; and he came into adulthood during the dark years that followed, when the Lakota, in reaction to defeat and virtual imprisonment, took up the messianic gospel of the Ghost Dance, believing they were impervious to white bullets if they wore their ghost shirts—believed, that is, until they were gunned down at Wounded Knee. In 1930 Black Elk was an old man, almost blind, living near the tiny village of Manderson on the Pine Ridge reservation in a one-room log cabin with weeds growing out of the dirt roof. The white poet John G. Neihardt, interested in the Ghost Dance movement and its deeper spiritual significance, was put onto him, came out for an interview, came back again in 1944, just six years before Black Elk died. Niehardt's interviews furnished the text for *Black Elk Speaks* (first published in 1932) and *The Sixth Grandfather* (edited and published in 1984), along with Neihardt's book of epic verse, *When the Tree Flowered* (1951). If there was anyone who was authoritative on the traditional religion as well as on its modern manifestation, it was Black Elk. Nowhere in those texts, however, does he explicitly refer to the Black Hills as the sacred land of the Lakota.

When the Allison Commission came to northwestern Nebraska to powwow with the western Sioux bands, Black Elk and family were in the neighborhood. He knew well the Hills wanted by the whites, for he had gone there with his father to cut tepee poles among the lodgepole pines and to hunt deer. (His companion, Standing Bear, remembered the economic uses of that period too; he repeated to Neihardt the saying of Sitting Bull that "the Black Hills was just like a food pack and therefore the Indians should stick to it." And Standing Bear added, "I knew what he meant after thinking it over because I knew that the Black Hills were full of fish, animals, and lots of water. . . . Indians would rove around, but when they were in need of something, they could just go in there and get it.") Neihardt heard from Black Elk how the *Wasichus* [the white men] had threatened to take the Hills, whether the Lakota would lease them or not, and how it had made him sad to hear this. "It was such a good place to play" he said, "and the people were always happy in that country."

But Black Elk had more than these secondhand and dimming memories; he also had an intensely personal, unforgettable reason to cherish the Hills, for the highest mountain there, Harney Peak, had been the scene of the most powerful event in his life. In the summer of his ninth year, while his family was camped over in Montana along a tributary branch of the Little Big Horn, he heard a strange voice calling to him, the voice of the Six Grandfathers, representing the six directions of the universe, the very symbol of *Wakan Tanka.* A strange little cloud then lifted him from his parents' tepee and, after a dizzying array of moves among all the ranked spirits, beasts and gods, after riding through villages and along many unfamiliar roads on a bay horse, he was carried off eastward to the mountain. There on Harney's summit he had a vision into the very depths of the cosmos. He beheld below him "the whole hoop of the world." He saw "in a sacred manner the shapes of all things in the spirit," saw how they were connected one to another, understood the underlying, cohering order of all nature and spirit. Black Elk had been chosen by the Six Grandfathers to have this vision so that he might be able to bring his people back into the sacred hoop, into a state of harmony, back to a time when the land was all theirs and they had lived happily in a paradise of plenty. He had been given a solemn charge to lead the Lakota toward renewal. But that renewal never came. The whites continued to pour into the country and kept the Lakota confused and miserable on their reservation. Late in his life, Black Elk returned with Neihardt to Harney Peak and stood alone on the peak in his long red underwear praying to the spirits for forgiveness—terribly disappointed because he had failed his charge, the past had not returned, the Lakota had not found their way back into the sacred hoop.[36]

Harney Peak is indisputably in the Black Hills range, and indisputably it became for Black Elk "the center of the earth," though he added to Neihardt the cautionary note, "but anywhere is the center of the world."[37] Significantly, he did not maintain that the whole mountain range was in any special sense a sacred land, though he did indicate that it was a place of considerable economic and emotional importance to his people. The closest he came to making a bigger claim was a legend he related in the 1944 interview. It is the story of race around the Hills by all the different animals, divided into two opposing teams, the animals with four legs against those with wings, competing for mastery of the earth. Humans were not running in that race, but because they were enemies to the four-legged animals, killing them for meat, they were on the side of the birds. During the race the clever magpie perched on buffalo's ear, saving his energy until the finish was in sight, then flapped off and won the prize. Thus the humans won too and came to exercise domination over their four-footed rivals. Following the race, the thunder spirit told humankind that the land around which the animals had chased was "the heart of the earth. This land is a being." And he instructed them to seek it out and come live there, which eventually they did.[38] The story suggests that the Hills were a place of legend and importance, but it says nothing really about sacredness. Not until much later, indeed a couple of decades after Black Elk's death, did the Hills come to be widely designated as sacred land.

In 1970 Congress restored tiny Blue Lake to the Taos Indians of New Mexico, along with 48,000 acres of the Carson National Forest lying adjacent to the Taos Pueblo and south and southeast of Wheeler Peak. The lake, according to the Indians, was their sacred place, their church. Since it had become part of the forest reserve, which was open to grazing by non-Indians, the Taos people had lost their exclusive access to it. Like the Lakota, they had petitioned for many years to get the lake back and in 1951 had gone to the Indian Claims Commission with their pleas. The ICC took fourteen years to decide for them, recommending that Congress restore the lake and 130,000 acres surrounding it. Congress, however, cut the acreage drastically and told Taos Pueblans that they could use the lake only for traditional spirtual purposes. Then, in another case two years later, President Richard Nixon signed an executive order restoring part of Mount Adams in the state of Washington to the Yakima Indians as a sacred place. Some observers warned that these restorations would open a can of worms on the public lands; Indians everywhere would be clamoring to get something back, interfering with white uses and development. They were, in a modest way, right. Following the Taos and Yakima successes, a number of tribes began to identify sacred sites they wanted protected or returned: the Navajos pointed to Rainbow Bridge and the San Francisco Peaks in Arizona, the Cherokees to a valley to be flooded by Tellico Dam in Tennessee, the Papago to the Baboquivari Mountains in southern Arizona, the Southern Paiutes to various sites in the path of the Intermountain Power Project in Nevada and Utah, the Western Shoshones to a large part of Nevada, targeted for MX missile sites. And then of course along came the Lakota with the biggest claim of all.[39]

So far the authorities have been severely retentive with federal property, restoring it only where it had been acquired through dirty dealings over treaties or by mere executive orders, without congressional action. To claim sacred, the government says, is not enough. The quality of sacredness does not, by itself, establish a property right. Religion, it would seem in the secular world of legal America, becomes only another "interest," to be weighed against the interests of cattlemen, oilmen, electric-power men, ski-resort men. If Indians enjoy free access to their holy places on the public lands, the courts have held, then no reason exists for giving them a property right in those places. And in any event the Indians must prove not only a present religious interest in a site but also one that goes back to aboriginal times—one that is not only historic but prehistoric. Often that proof has not been easy to assemble, scattered as it is in the shadowy corners of private memory or in tattered antique stories passed down by word of mouth.[40]

In testimony on the Bradley bill, Charlotte Black Elk, secretary of the Black Hills Steering Committee and great granddaughter of Black Elk, appeared as a tribal expert on the oral history of the Lakota. She had done considerable research into the origin myths of her people, and they indicated that the Hills had been regarded for thousands of years as the place where the Lakota had first been created. After the whites stole the Hills, she went on, they sternly repressed her people's religion. In 1929 her grandfather Hollow Horn had defied the whites' threats of prison to dance the traditional sun dance. "We have documents," she said, "where people were persecuted and prosecuted for even speaking of the Black Hills."[41] Because of that repression, her people lack solid evidence that the Hills were sacred places. If there is no proof of sacredness, it is because the white man effaced it. No doubt she is right about the charge that many whites reacted hostilely when the Lakota tried to be themselves, to be "pagans" and "heathens" and to deviate from good Christian doctrine. On the other hand, she exaggerates the effectiveness and pervasiveness of that censorship and the heroics of resistance. No one threw, or even talked about throwing, the old leaders in prison in 1903 for demanding the Hills back or complaining about their compensation. No one stopped Black Elk from telling about his pagan vision on Harney Peak, though he offended his adopted Catholicism in doing so, or prevented its publication. No whites interfered with Luther Standing Bear in 1933, when he published his book *Land of the Spotted Eagle,* which speaks passionately of his love for the Hills and criticizes the sculptor Borglum who was carving the Presidents' faces on Rushmore.[42] If for nearly a full century after 1877 the Lakota left no documentary evidence that the Black Hills were their sacred place, it was not because white American society repressed them, as the Soviet Union has repressed Jews and evangelicals. More likely the evidence is not there because earlier generations did not commonly think of the Hills as holy ground. They were not exactly their equivalent of Mecca.[43]

In the midst of their latest appeals to Congress and the courts a group of Lakota brought forth an old bison robe covered with blue and red markings, the *Mar'piya Makoce Xina,* the robe of heaven and earth. According to them, it had been kept in hiding on the Cheyenne Indian River Reservation since the last century. The markings on the robe constitute maps of the Black Hills and of the sun and stars superimposed on one another, the two realms linked together like reflecting mirrors. Together, they instructed the Lakota when and where to go during the course of the year to perform important religious ceremonies: When the sun stood at a certain station in the sky, for example, they were to pack up their tepees and travel to the treeless meadow situated at the center of the Black Hills range; while at summer solstice they must be over at Devil's Tower, preparing for the sun dance. The map, it was said, established solidly the historicity of sacredness. Further research on native astronomical lore done at Sinte Gleska College in Rosebud, South Dakota, indicated that the Lakota people had designated the Black Hills the center of their spiritual universe some three thousand years ago—which means, of course, they must have been living in the area that far back, following the maps religiously, executing a carefully prescribed, hallowed pilgrimage each year through and around the Hills. If so, all the datings of white archaeologists, anthropologists, and historians must be seriously in error. Unlikely as that is, one must admit that these are more tangible evidences for a religious claim than anything offered heretofore, and as the research goes on, more and better support may materialize. However, none of it quite explains why Red Cloud, Black Elk, and other leaders of previous generations did not mention any buffalo robes, any pilgrimages, or express any desire to save their sacred places.

These strenuous efforts by traditionalist Indians to put their faith on firmer ground cannot help but remind one of Mormon and Christian fundamentalists trying to establish the facticity of their faith in the face of skepticism—marshaling scripture or archeology to prove, for instance, that Nephi actually crossed the ocean in 588 B.C. to the promised land, or that God truly brought forth the world out of darkness in the year 4004 B.C. The Lakota traditionalists hope they can find hard evidence corroborating that their people have been in the Black Hills vicinity since time immemorial, not merely since the late eighteenth century, that they had a well-established religion of the Hills, that they regularly visited the sacred places there, and that those places covered the entire region. Because the claim of sacredness remains weak, and often seems contrived for white consumption, they go on rummaging through their reminiscences and back rooms, looking for old buffalo robes, as medieval Christians ransacked for the holy shroud. They rush into court waving the latest proof aloft, as though any amount of evidence would make much of a difference to a room full of white lawyers, who never heard about ethnoastronomy or the mountain gods in law school.

What is going on among the Lakota is not so much the presentation of a legal case for sacredness as it is the awakening of a new or revitalized religion. If the Black Hills have not been certifiably sacred in the historical past, and that across their entire and vast extent, they are becoming so in the present. Indians are trying to invest every acre, every valley and slab of rock, with high numinosity, not only the scattered sites like Harney Peak, the Wind Cave, and Bear Butte, where the evidence is strongest for religious significance, not only the handful of identifiable burial sites, but the whole mountainous landscape. Insist on a belief long enough and it becomes real. And there is certainly nothing wrong with that. Nothing in the theory of religion says that a people's idea of the sacred must be handed down to them from the distant past to be any good, or that modern societies, Indian or white, cannot attach new sacred meanings to places, persons, and things, or that they cannot invent a faith rather than receive it. The Lakota are not unique in trying to create new sacred spaces. Environmentalists, to cite only one other example, seem to have done precisely that with many landscapes in North America, including the Black Hills;

from John Muir and Enos Mills on, the western mountains have drawn thousands of them, and their emotional attachments to the mountains may run as deep as those of the Lakota. That identification of sacred places by environmentalists derives from the Romantic and Transcendentalist movements of the nineteenth century, but it is gathering force and followers as modern industrial life seems to grind on to its death. The mountains have come to be places to retreat to, seek renewal in, places that can awaken our jaded, corrupted minds to the numinous order of nature, a nature that is the home of the divine. The Lakota, in their Black Hills Steering Committee and Camp Yellow Thunder occupation, are following currents of feeling similar to those flowing throughout the American nation, and on other continents too, as humankind everywhere wearies of its own inventions and yearns for a way back to the pristine wilderness. But if the impulse may be a more general one, the form it has taken among the Lakota comes out of their unique history and experience. They are drawing on emotions and issues that have been around for a long while, breathing new life into them, finding coherence of purpose and depth of meaning where it may not have existed before.[44]

For at least two hundred years, if not three thousand, this people has been traipsing across the western South Dakota landscape, and in that process they have become attached to the place by a bond that rather few whites feel about places. That attachment is for many Lakota today germinating, ripening into religious fruit. Familarity breeds affection, and affection can deepen into reverence. Add the fact that reservation life is full of troubles and the move to revitalize one's faith becomes irresistible. Adversity has sharpened those feelings into a desperate will to believe.[45]

Although we can easily sympathize with the revitalization movement going on in the Black Hills case, we nonetheless have to think carefully about the legal and equity issues involved, the precedents that may be established. Does any group that wants to practice its religion, however old or new, in the Hills deserve access, or deserve to possess them as exclusive property? What about other public lands in the West? If the Sierra Club wants to lay claim to Yosemite National Park, should we hand it over? Or what if Elizabeth Clare Prophet ("Guru Ma") and her Church Universal and Triumphant make a move on Yellowstone? An old, familiar American problem confronts us: When and how do we decide that a real human need—in this case religion—deserves being translated into property rights? How are religious, spiritual, and therapeutic needs to be weighed against other, economic ones? The Lakota say they need the Black Hills for their cultural survival, but no where on the law books is there any law, any mechanism, any office where one can file a claim to satisfy that kind of need. The economic needs, on the other hand, are well looked after. The best, or most egregious, example is the Mining Law of 1872, which declares: "All valuable mineral deposits in lands belonging to the United States, both surveyed and unsurveyed, are hereby declared to be free and open to exploration and purchase." A company that decides it "needs" those deposits has only to file a claim on any public acreage it wants, and the law gives it an *unconditional right* to prospect and mine there.[46] Similarly, someone who "needs" forage for their livestock or needs standing timber for their chain saws has a well-established, friendly system for satisfying that need on the public lands. All those users can gain property rights, however limited, for their needs. But, as we have seen in the case of Camp Yellow Thunder, religious needs are far less welcome and much less easily satisfied. The allowable acreage for that use is tiny, the term of use is severely short. Religion on the public lands comes last, if at all, in the order of favored uses. And if a people like the Lakota have big needs, if they want access to lots of sites, if they claim indeed an entire national forest and more, then they are regarded as making outrageous demands; they must not be serious.

The Lakota have followed their two major strategies of appeal, and still no lands have been restored. They lost to the legal doctrine of the power of eminent domain, and their claims to the Hills as a historically sacred place have not yet been made very convincing. On the other hand, the case of the white man for *retaining* the lands, though apparently a political success so far, has through all these appeals and decisions exposed deep flaws, which any thoughtful man or woman might cringe to contemplate. Even if the Lakota case has not persuaded whites so far, how can the whites insist that they deserve to keep the Hills? Has their ecological stewardship been exemplary? Hardly. Have they fully discharged their responsibilities to the peoples they invaded and overran? No. Do the whites need the Hills more than the Indians for economic opportunity and well-being? Of course not. Would reversion to the Lakota jeopardize the future of all peoples in the West? Most unlikely. Would recision lead to better protection for the land and its flora and fauna? In the case of the national parks, probably not. In the case of BLM and Forest Service lands, very possibly yes. The Indians have pledged themselves to manage the lands with "respect for nature," something we have not often heard from those federal land agencies. Would recision be good for the American West and the nation in other ways? Would it improve the status and pride of our minority peoples? Would it give them a greater role in decisions for the region's future? Would it increase majority awareness of their culture? Would it, in other words, benefit relations among the two races, helping the Indians without hurting the whites? The answer must surely be, it would. A deeply felt wound that has festered for a hundred years might be healed and we could get on with the task of living with one another in mutual respect. The Black Hills, or some significant portion of them, should be returned to the Lakota people.

Alaska:
The Underworld Erupts

North of the Brooks Range in Alaska, the
stegosaurian tail of the Rockies, the arctic becomes a vast treeless flat-
land running off to the horizon like a table without edges. In the short
summer the sun glares with a cold intense ferocity. Daytime temperatures
range into the 30s and 40s, sometimes soaring as high as 75 degrees, but
in the long darkness of winter they plunge to −5, −20, even −60 Faren-
heit. A few rivers trickle down the "Slope," as it is called, from the mountains to the gravelly ocean shore; the largest of them is the Colville, and
along its banks grows a brushy vegetation, a pygmy forest shorter than a
basketball team. All else is cotton grass and tundra. The mean annual
precipitation on the Slope varies from five to twenty inches; everywhere
on that dry plain, however, there are splotches of shallow ponds and lakes,
so many they are unnamed and uncounted, shifting in size and location
with the thawing and freezing of the ground. Down into the subsoil the
permafrost extends a thousand, and in some places two thousand, feet
deep. This is a hard land, make no mistake, and life survives only by the
magnitude of its tenacity. Millions of waterfowl arrive here each spring to
live among the polar and grizzly bears, the arctic foxes, the herds of caribou, the thick droning blizzards of mosquitoes. Even humans have made

it home. As early as 40,000 years ago a small number of paleolithic hunters may have crossed the nearby Bering land bridge, which must have closely resembled the arctic scene of today, and taken a first look at the North American landscape: Welcome, it said, if you don't mind the eerie quiet, the spareness, all the biting bugs. Apparently, some of those immigrants didn't mind at all and happily settled in; their descendants in the area now number 3000.[1]

In the winter of 1901 a very different group of hunters made the North Slope their destination. They were white Americans on an expedition to determine the general geological character of the region; "valuable economic results of the investigations," their leader wrote, "were to be expected."[2] The leader's name was Frank C. Schrader, and he was a scientist in the employ of the U.S. Geological Survey; with him were W. J. Peters, a topographer, and six other men. Early in February they left Skagway on the White Pass Railway, riding over to the town of Whitehorse, gateway to the feverish gold rush into the Klondike. Plenty of gold miners were still panning away in Alaska and Canada that year; the scientists were simply following a route already blazed by their enterprise. In 1895, almost four decades after the United States had purchased Alaska from Russia, the Survey had sent its first exploring parties into the territory, primarily to help the miners locate the best mineral regions. By 1900 most of the broad features of Alaska had been tentatively mapped: the important mountain ranges, the gold areas around Nome, Fairbanks, and Juneau, the Seward Peninsula, the Copper River basin penetrating into the Wrangells.[3] Still, Schrader and company had a sense of high adventure; they were going to map where no man or woman had mapped before.

The temperature when they arrived in Whitehorse was −55 F°, but it rose almost to the freezing point as they set out for the North Slope. From that point on the only transportation available in the month of February was the human foot or dog sled, and they were forced to utilize both as they started a formidable journey down the frozen Yukon River to the trading post at Bergman. They drove two sleds, using forty dogs in all counting the relief teams, mushing about 25 miles a day. Outside Whitehorse they enjoyed the dubious comforts of bush roadhouses—mere log cabins where for a lot of money one could get a rough bunk and rougher meal. Soon, though, they left those amenities behind and tried to survive on their own resources. Each night they scooped a deep hole in the snow for a fireplace and gathered fuel wood from the spruce and willow growing along the river bottoms. Evergreen boughs furnished their mattresses on the snow, and there they stretched out with their wolf robes pulled tight around them, Ursa Minor shining in their tired eyes, the aurora borealis flashing green, pink, and purple overhead. Once a day they fed the dogs a meal of rice or flour cooked with grease; the men regularly ate rice and bacon. In that whole expanse of country the only signs of game they found were moose tracks and a few ptarmigan. Arriving at Bergman, which had been set up to supply gold seekers coming inland from Nome up the Koyukuk River (the post no longer exists), they found a shipment of supplies waiting, which they gathered up, suspending further travel through the rest of the winter, packing and organizing for the real adventure that lay ahead. Then on 6 June, when the river ice broke up, they loaded their heavy canoes on a steamboat heading upriver to Bettles, the last outpost of white civilization. From there they paddled up the John to the divide, portaged over Anuktuvuk Pass (which they named), dropped their canoes into a tributary of the Colville and floated toward the delta and sea. Along that route they constantly had to wade in ice-cold water and crunch through deep unbroken snow. They shot a few caribou and fished for grayling. They saw the droppings of mountain goats but not the goats themselves. One day they came upon a native woman subsisting alone on rabbits she had caught in her traps. Down on the coast, they were met by a group of Eskimos (or, in their own language, Inupiat) who allowed them the use of their walrus-skin boats, more seaworthy craft and easier to sail than the canoes. On 3 September, after beating close and hard along the shore in the borrowed boats, Schrader's party reached Point Barrow—the face of civilization once more, though barely; there was only a mission school and trading post there in 1901. But then they were sorely disappointed to learn that their possible rides home, a U.S. Revenue Marine Service vessel or a whaling ship, had all gone south, trying to get out before the sea froze for the winter. There was nothing for Schrader and company to do but borrow again from the natives, this time taking an open whale boat and sailing west and south toward Point Hope, looking for some laggard ship. Fortunately, they came upon the steamer *Arctic* still loading fuel at the Corwin coal fields, eighty miles north of Point Hope; and it became their last hope for escaping to Nome and Seattle. In the course of that summer they had traversed 500 miles of mountains and tundra plains unknown to science, though the shortness of the season and the daily rigors of travel and sustenance had severely limited the scientific value of their work.

Schrader and Peters are significant today more for their firsthand account of early Alaskan travel than for their geological findings. But they were the first to bring scientific instruments to the North Slope, measuring and observing for their successors. Prior to their expedition, the only official knowledge whites had of the place came from the voyage of Navy Lieutenant W. C. Howard in 1866 (going east as far as Point Barrow) and the journey of J. H. Turner of the Coast and Geodetic Survey in 1890 (going inland from the coast along the U.S.-Canada border to the Porcupine River). The only mineral of economic importance Schrader's party found was gold, and that was already being mined along the upper Koyukuk by several hundred whites, the yield amounting so far to over $700,000. They saw some lead, copper, and antimony ore too, but nothing impressive. And coal, they wrote in their report, "is more or less widely distributed in northern Alaska," though not in any commercially interesting amounts. On the Colville River they picked up some lignite and used it for a camp fire; "it gave good satisfaction," Schrader noted. But there was better stuff, and more accessible, elsewhere; the Corwin mines, for instance, began operating in that same year, 1901, though aside from a few steamships stopping there to replenish their bunkers, most of the market was in Nome, where the fuel was used for domestic cooking and heating. So the Schrader exploring party confirmed the presence of coal but had no bonanza to celebrate. Of petroleum they said not a word.[4]

Russians and Americans had been coming to Alaska in search of coal since the mid-nineteenth century, though for a long while coal had been overshadowed in economic importance by other, more profitable commodities like sea otters (which the Russians called sea beavers), salmon, and gold, all ruthlessly extracted and shipped a long way off for consumption. In 1854 the Russians, under the direction of an engineer named Peter Doroshin, began digging coal at Port Graham on Kachemak Bay for marine fuel. The miners were an unwilling group of Siberian soldiers garrisoned at the site, and when the operation caught fire a few years later and burned to the ground, they must have cheered loudly. Three years after the U.S. purchase, Alaska boasted a long list of identified coal beds, with those near Cook Inlet offering the greatest promise, greater indeed than anywhere else on the Pacific Coast, deposits comparable in quality, it was said, to good Pittsburgh bituminous. However, on the famous Harriman expedition of 1899, Henry Gannett could find only an inferior grade of deposits, and none of them was being mined on a commercial scale.[5] It would be a long time before Americans realized the amazing geological truth that Alaska has some of the world's largest coal beds, amounting to perhaps five trillion tons, and that the greater portion of them lies in the far north, deep within and under the permafrost, a veritable Saudi Arabia of coal, though it is chiefly of low BTU rank—lignite, sub-bituminous, and bituminous, with little of the prized anthracite. All the gold and furs and salmon together could not, in the long run, approach the economic value of that buried treasure.

As for Alaska's oil, the geologists were even slower to fathom its possibilities. The naturalist William Dall noted oil slicks floating on the surface of a lake near Katmai Bay, opening into Cook Inlet. Gannett said nothing about seeing (or smelling) oil, nor did Schrader. One of the most fascinating early accounts of this fossil resource appeared in Ernest Leffingwell's report on the Canning River area, which lies a little over a hundred miles due east of Schrader's territory on the North Slope. Leffingwell, an affluent young adventurer, trained in geology and keen to make his scientific mark, had formed a partnership with a Norwegian, Ejnar Mikkelsen, which they called the Anglo-American Polar Expedition. In 1906 they came to explore the Beaufort Sea, making camp at Flaxman Island just off the coast. Their ship, purchased in Seattle, was a sinking ready to happen, so they tore it apart and used the timbers to build a cabin on the island, where Leffingwell lived off and on for another decade (nine summers and six winters), dwelling mostly alone, with a comfortable supply of cigars and a gramophone, and spending a lot of his father's money to produce what he claimed to be "the first accurate chart of the North Arctic coast of Alaska." Itinerant natives told him of petroleum seeps in the region, and he went out by sled and boat to investigate. He took samples that resembled axle grease and brought them back for analysis. "It is possible," he concluded, "that the formations in which these mineral fuels occur underlie part of the Canning River region, but of this there is no direct evidence. . . . Even if an oil pool were found to be in this northern region, there is serious doubt of its availability under present conditions, though it might be regarded as a part of the ultimate oil reserves that would some time be developed." How unwitting a prophet he was. Leffingwell had encamped near what would one day become the biggest oil field in North America, at Prudhoe Bay, and he was living directly over what many today would like to see become a new oil field on the coastal plain of the Arctic National Wildlife Refuge.[6] Tens of billions of barrels of petroleum, immense pools of hidden blackness, underlay those telltale seepages he found.

Oil and coal were understood well before Leffingwell's day to be hydrocarbons derived from plant and animal material deposited in enormous quantities millions of years ago. Alaska's coal came from fossilized plants, its oil from fossilized marine life on the ocean floor that got buried by sediments, preventing complete oxidation and decomposition. They represented the energy of the sun collected over long periods of time and compressed into dense, rich packages of power. To burn a chunk of coal is to reach deeply into the past and tap the force of the sun, not from a single moment's radiation but from all those millions of years of a forest's growing, getting buried in mucky bogs, being squeezed and concentrated by the pressures of the earth's crust. Tapping that fossil energy is like calling back all the protein that fed all the dinosaurs on earth for a hundred million years and gorging on it. Such a diet must produce technological giants. What neither Leffingwell nor any of his contemporaries could remotely understand was just how big the potential diet in Alaska was and just how gigantic a creature it would one day feed.

During the Schrader-Leffingwell years of frontier scientific exploration, the United States was, in its major centers of population and production, manifesting an already gargantuan appetite for the fossil fuels. As late as 1884 the country still consumed more wood than coal, but that situation changed radically over the next decade and a half. By the turn of the century America had switched overwhelmingly to a coal-based economy, with wood shrinking to a mere 20 percent of the nation's energy supply. By then America was also producing more coal than any other country in the world, surpassing even Great Britain, the country that back in the seventeenth century had invented the modern fossil-fuel-based economy, thanks to its remarkable coal deposits. The new American leader produced nearly 270 million short tons (equal to 2000 pounds each) of coal in 1899. Five years later it was producing over 352 million tons, or 36 percent of the world's total, and by 1910, 400 million tons. Great Britain remained in second place, while Germany moved into third, with about half the U.S. total. America had, in other words, grown up quickly to become the hungriest giant on earth, consuming voraciously and getting bigger all the time. Within its borders it had many lesser giants fattening on the new fuels. The leading coal producer among the states was Pennsylvania; since 1814, when mining had begun there in earnest, Pennsylvanians had dug out of their mountains over three billion tons of coal, both bituminous and anthracite. Illinois, Ohio, and West Virginia were distantly behind but were hardly negligible producers. As for petroleum, the United States produced over 63 million barrels of crude in the year 1900, worth $1.20 a barrel. That amount compared with the mere 2000 barrels produced in 1859, the year when the first oil well was drilled at Titusville, Pennsylvania. Oil would not, however, surpass coal as the chief energy source until after World War II.[7]

In terms of those national levels of fossil-fuel production and consumption, Alaska was a mote of dust in the statistical columns. In 1911 it produced a mere 116,000 tons of coal, mainly from high-grade deposits in the Bering River field and in the Matanuska Valley. Most of that output went into the fireboxes of steamers plying the coastal trade or naval vessels showing the flag around the northern Pacific. Larger markets for Alaskan coal did not exist simply because nowhere in the north, nor on the whole Pacific side of the continent, was there much heavy industry. Steel mills, manufactories, locomotive works, smelters were to be found more to the east, beyond the reach of coastal shipping. Alaska may have been the property of the foremost industrial power on earth, and the federal geologists may have been on a sharp lookout for new seams and seepages to feed that power, but Alaska was still almost completely innocent of the brute forces of industrialization. Not until that same year of 1911 did the Guggenheim interests cut a railroad from the coast to their copper mines at Kennecott, deep in the Wrangell Mountain fastness, and not until 1923 did President Warren G. Harding come to drive the climactic golden spike on the Alaskan Railroad, opening up the vast interior all the way from Seward to Fairbanks for mineral extraction and shipping.[8]

Prior to the coming of the railroads human life on the Alaskan land mass was, in energy terms, still a primitive existence. Whites like Schrader and all the gold miners, once they moved inland, had to learn how to survive in this remote, often bitterly cold environment by relying on local surface energy and the daily solar flux, much as human beings everywhere had done before the fossil-fuel era. Temporarily at least, they had to live as the native peoples had lived for tens of thousands of years and were still living in the early decades of the twentieth century. Coal and oil played almost no part in that way of life. Although some of the natives had occasionally been seen burning lignite or oil-soaked tundra in their dwellings, they had never paid much attention to the fossil fuel underfoot. How could they? For the most part that fuel was buried beyond all their knowledge and skill to recover, requiring modern geological science to discover its full extent, appreciate its potential, explain its origins, and figure out how to mine and use it. The aborigines lived without the benefit of that science and were innocent of underground mining. What they had instead was a system of energy use that depended on a sophisticated understanding of the biological order on the earth's surface. That system is now in disarray, but with the aid of anthropologists, we can reconstruct it and the mental world on which it rested, and that reconstruction can help us appreciate more fully the revolutionary changes that coal and oil have brought to Alaska in the course of this century.

The natives of the far north are a diverse set of peoples, some of them popularly known to the whites as Eskimos (Inupiats), others as Indians (Koyukons), each representing different phases of the prehistoric migration from Asia. In their traditional state, the Inupiat furnished an especially interesting case study in "primitive" energy use. How could a people, living in a habitat so scarce in resources, so limited in wood and yet so severe in climate, endure for so many thousands of years, as they had done? How big an energy supply did they need, and how did they get it? An ethnographic study by Robert Spencer, based on observations in the 1950s, provides some answers to those questions. He discovered that, before the invasion by the modern white man's economy, there were two separate, contrasting cultural groups among the Inupiat living on the arctic slope: first, the Nunamiut, "the people of the land," who dwelled inland and hunted the caribou; and second, the Teremiut, "the people of the sea," who dwelled along the coasts and subsisted on whales, seals, and walruses. Though alike in language and ethnic roots, these two peoples exploited overlapping but distinct ecological niches, and thus their energy sources were not altogether the same. They minimized competition to avoid overshooting their supplies.

The Nunamiut spent much of each year dispersed in nuclear families, drifting along the region's watercourses, roaming high into the Brooks Range in warmer seasons, then down to the plain when winter came, sleeping most of the time in skin tents mounted over a frame of willow branches. Once a year families joined together to prey on the migrating herds of caribou, chasing and driving them to their death; from the caribou carcasses they took food for themselves and their sled dogs, along with clothing and hides for shelter. Mountain sheep, foxes, wolves, wolverines, grizzlies, moose, ground squirrels, ptarmigan, brant, and eiders were also hunted, supplementing the berries, wild rhubarb, and roots they gathered. In most years they ate reasonably well, but about every six or seven years the game failed and families squeezed as best they could through "a starving time." Their main energy source, in other words, came from their own bodies feeding on the bodies of other animals harvested from the wild. But unlike their rival predators in nature they also collected non-food energy—fuel which they found growing in the upland forests, mainly willow but also some alder and dwarf birch, and piled in the form of driftwood along the river banks. The women were responsible for collecting that firewood, a heavy, time-consuming labor; a household of ten persons could burn up to fifty pounds of willows in a single day, and at that rate would soon exhaust any local supply, forcing the family to move on to new grounds. The round of Nunamiut social life was spent seeking and exchanging information from other families on where this vital fuel resource might be found more abundantly. Even then there was never enough wood, so they relied on their neighbors along the coast to provide them with a second fuel, seal oil, which they burned in stone lamps for light and heat. Regularly they met with the Teremiut in a kind of market fair to trade bundles of caribou hides, green or tanned, for that valuable supply of seal and whale oil, which they carried back inland in sealskin pokes.[9]

The coastal Eskimos who provided the oil traditionally lived in more settled villages and in sturdier wooden houses well fortified against the weather. During the months of April and May, sometimes extending into June, they went out onto the softening ice, walking along the leads opening in it, looking for bowhead whales migrating north and eastward. They too hunted collectively, seeking safety and efficiency in numbers. If a village could kill twelve or fifteen of the whales, it considered the annual hunt a solid success. In the summer they turned their harpoons on the walruses, pursuing in boats and butchering them on floating cakes of ice, the blood running back into the water; a village might harvest a hundred or more carcasses per year. Then, most dangerous of all, the men ventured onto the still, hard-frozen sea in the dead of winter, the skies dark the whole day, to spear seals coming up to breathe through the cracks and holes. All those marine animals, along with waterfowl and fish, had to provide the mainstay of the Teremiut diet (a single adult needed seven to eight pounds of meat a day, while the family's pack of dogs consumed an additional hundred or more pounds) and oil for illuminating and warming their houses. And that was all they had, all the energy that a household needed or had any reason to expect, and it came to them up a watery food chain forged from scanty sunlight, came mainly from beasts dressed thickly in parkas of blubber.[10]

Before modernity came crashing in, the Inupiat held a complicated, ambivalent outlook on this scrimpy northern world of nature and on their place in it, a complexity we may miss if we hastily seize on one idea or another as the whole of their thinking. On the one hand, the traditional Inupiat commonly took the view that the individual human can never achieve any real command over the natural course of events. As Norman Chance has written, "the Eskimo are quite aware of the tentativeness of life, the constant presence of unforeseen contingencies, and the lack of control over matters pertaining to subsistence and health." Symptomatically, their speech used "if" in cases where whites would say "when." To a degree that seems fatalistic to westerners, they inclined toward the view that nature limits human prospects severely, that they must inevitably confront hard times, that there is no pot of gold that can rescue one from all privations, and that only death is certain—only death is not an "if." One reason for such a stance may have been that there was not enough energy available to win any lasting triumph over that daily uncertainty or even to make life seem substantially more secure and predictable. On the other hand, the Inupiat looked on the daily flow of energy as an ever-renewable pattern that, with carefulness and insight, need never fail the human community completely. The fertility of the earth was irrepressible even within the Arctic Circle. What was required of humans, if that fertility was to be assured, were the qualities of hard work, self-reliance, and discipline. Instead of controlling the course of nature, the Inupiat strove to help renew it through an annual cycle of communal rituals and patterns of sharing. Nature demanded their active participation, not their passive, careless consumption. Here is Chance speaking again: "The man who works steadily at whatever task is before him, keeps his hunting and other equipment in good repair, and maintains an accurate account of the available food and other necessities of life, is not only being self-reliant; he is also exerting greater control over the world around him and thereby leaving less to fate." That outlook was more than western utilitarianism; it was a religion teaching the benevolence of the earth's spirits to provide just enough for them to survive, and it was an ethic teaching human responsibility for that cycle of renewal.[11]

Even while the rest of America was vaulting into the fossil-fuel system and the industrial way of life, the traditional Inupiat dependence on incident solar radiation, supporting a hunting and gathering existence, remained intact for a long while. The contrast between the two was profound. The Inupiat participated in the natural flow of energy without modifying it significantly. They lived on the near-at-hand ecosystem, which converted into flesh the solar energy fixed by the photosynthesis of green plants. Thus they extracted energy from their environment almost wholly to support their own bodies' metabolic processes, eating, digesting, and maintaining internal blood temperature; except for whatever their dogs added, all productive work depended on their own human muscle power. Their fundamental challenge was how to collect and store enough solar energy from the land's surface to keep their bodies fit. In contrast, the white Americans were shifting to ancient, deeply buried storehouses of energy, which freed them from almost all dependence on the surrounding surface acreage. They employed that energy to bring into their homes resources from the most distant corners of the earth, including Alaskan canned salmon, whalebone corsets, and gold watch chains. They warmed themselves in their townhouse parlors by coal they had not personally collected but had purchased from a deliveryman, who carted it about the city in a horse-drawn wagon. By far the greatest portion of the energy they consumed went to feed, not a pack of dogs, but a panoply of machines—Pullman cars to carry them swiftly across the continent, combined mower-threshers to harvest grain, dynamos to generate electricity, telephones to convey their gossip. On a per capita basis the energy that white Americans, urban and rural, could command was almost infinitely greater than that of the Inupiat and their needs far more numerous. Is it any wonder then that the two peoples did not share the same sense of place in nature? That the whites were at once less fatalistic toward the randomness of events and less concerned about performing their role in nature's cycle of renewal?[12]

Ironically, one of the dramatic, unexpected outcomes of the fossil-fuel society was that, at the same time it freed civilized people from any direct dependence on the living earth, it left them feeling incomplete. An abundance of energy produced anomie and sent many off searching for that earlier life they had lost. At once it gave them the leisure, the occupational opportunities, the easy means of transportation, and the motivation to get out of the high-energy way of life, get out as far as they could go, and to recover a more direct dependence on the earth. Schrader, Leffingwell, and their scientific associates seemed to have enjoyed immensely their chance to escape into the Alaskan wilderness, if only temporarily; they became enthusiastic travelers in time as well as in space, tourists visiting, as it were, a country of exotic energy relations. There were many others who began going north in quest of the same immediate contact with the wild: for example, the California nature writer, John Muir, who made his first trip to Alaska in 1879 on a steamer bound for Sitka, Fort Wrangell, and the misty iceberg nursery of Glacier Bay, traveling in the company of Presbyterians on a mission to the Indians. Muir came back to Alaska the next year, once more to the southeastern region. And the next year after that he came again, this time steaming in on the revenue cutter *Thomas Corwin* on a quest for a polar exploring vessel that had disappeared; they cruised along the Siberian coast, clambered over the desolate hills and cliffs of Wrangel Land, anchored off Point Barrow, before giving up and returning homeward, mission unaccomplished. Muir made a fourth voyage to Alaska in the summer of 1890, this one a return to his beloved southeast where he went sledding over the glacier named in his honor and got a bad case of snow blindness. On his fifth and final trip, he came as a member of the Harriman expedition, which was funded, organized, and luxuriously outfitted by the railway tycoon E. H. Harriman, who had the notion of making a towering contribution to science by collecting a lot of unknown facts about Alaska; in addition to Muir, there were scientists, artists, photographers, taxidermists, Harriman family members, and sundry others along, 126 in the party all told. The chief result of their much ballyhooed expedition, and that of Muir's other travels, which he fulsomely described in newspaper and book print with "wondering admiration," was to send still more tourists north. "Almost singlehandedly," writes Roderick Nash, the writings of Muir "transformed the Alaska wilderness from a liability to an asset so far as tourism was concerned." By the turn of the century there were hundreds, then thousands, of tourist-refugees coming each year, seeking the unspoiled, isolated splendor of the greatest mountains, seacoasts, and wildlife populations on the continent. Muir's own preferred strategy was to see Alaska alone, "in silence, without baggage," in order to "get into the hearts of the wilderness. All other travel is mere dust and hotels and baggages and chatter." Others, of course, insisted on bringing the hotels and chatter with them. Either way, the common means of reaching the wild north was to book a berth, as Muir repeatedly did, on a coal-burning steamer, riding out of industrial civilization with all its clanking power under one's feet.[13]

The fossil-fuel economy opened the immense frontier of Alaska to the modern world, bringing it in from its remoteness, reducing much of its scale and mystery to a shelf of travel books, packaging an experience of nostalgia, beauty, and adventure along with a measure of privation. Undoubtedly, that experience taught urbanized whites a little humility in the face of ungoverned nature, but their perceptions inevitably must be shaped by the fact that they arrived with a ticket in their hand and the smoke of burning coal in their nostrils. They could not share the full, complex Inupiat sense of passive-active engagement with the natural world, at least not after a mere few weeks of vacationing, not until they let go of industrialism altogether and set about learning to subsist permanently on the solar flux. Muir did not attempt such a complete retreat; after all, he had a family to support in California. Earlier he had chosen the life of a husband and father, with all their responsibilities, and of a fruit farmer and writer, two economic specializations that industrialism made possible. They called him back after each sojourn in the wild to a regimen of packing apples and pears in wooden crates, shipping them off in refrigerated railroad cars to city consumers, and of scribbling words and words on reams of paper, reams delivered to his study from mass-producing pulp mills, and of shipping his finished manuscripts off to urban publishers and to the same urban markets that his pears and apples fed. The Alaska of a hundred years ago was not an environment that could support either line of work. It didn't have the energy for them.

Still another famous seeker after the wilderness experience came into the north country, this time in the summer of 1920. He was a wildlife expert by the name of Olaus Murie, age thirty-one, sent out by the Bureau of Biological Survey (BBS) to survey caribou and act as game warden for the entire interior of Alaska. A foreign species, the Eurasian reindeer, had been introduced at Nome in 1892 and had multiplied rapidly; now the BBS had a reindeer "experiment lab" operating in Unalakeet and wanted to know from Murie's field studies just how easily the reindeer and caribou could be mated and what the economic prospects for their progeny might be. Hunting, Murie was also told, had to be controlled by his police authority. The territory had passed its first comprehensive game law in 1902, but it was regularly violated by Indians and Eskimos as well as whites. Murie had still another duty, shared by all the federal field biologists of his day: to collect specimens of indigenous wildlife for the Bureau. The job required a gun, heavy ammunition, a sharp skinning knife, and a tracker's stamina. The Bureau chief, E. W. Nelson, himself an old Alaskan hand, furnished the artillery and gave detailed advice on the sort of specimens needed in Washington to "complete the collection." So Murie spent a large part of his tour of duty, which lasted half a dozen years, blazing away at the animals he saw. He shot caribou to promote the hybridization studies, he shot wolves to determine whether they ate the caribou and moose, taking game away from human hunters, and he shot bears to stuff for the museums. Always on the lookout for good specimens, he shot the healthy, strong, and handsome, not the weak or sickly, animals. He hired his brother Adolph as an assistant, in part because of his superior marksmanship, though Adolph went on to become a respected authority on wolf predation. Olaus was a good enough shot himself that he took quite a toll on the grizzly population. In 1924 he wrote his superiors about one of his more interesting bear kills, this one of a mother (Tag No. 2023) who was accompanied by three yearling cubs:

> When the mother started rolling down the mountain side the cubs ran after. She gained momentum, bouncing along over rocks and little ledges. The three little fellows came galloping after, down the slope, ears forward, a look of wonder on their faces, grunting as they landed with each jump. They were following the mother pellmell over all the obstructions, but when she bounced and rolled over a steep little cliff, they checked themselves just in time and made a detour before continuing their mad rush. The old bear came to a stop on the lower slope. The little fellows approached her and sniffed a little, then became frightened and ran away some distance. Either they had caught our scent or the death of the mother had given them a feeling of terror. When we showed ourselves they fled again and disappeared behind the ridges.

The day after the kill Murie came on the cubs still sniffing aimlessly about the site of their mother's death, and he tried to take their picture, perhaps to send with appropriate caption to the office in Washington: "Baby Bears Acting Forlorn." However, he scared them off and returned with only their mother's pelt to file.[14]

Once again we see the paradoxical relation of a fossil-fuel economy to the life of a man so passionately in love with the wild, so far removed from the centers of that ecomony, a man who liked to quote in his journals the manly verses of the Yukon poet Robert Service: "The frontier, the freedom, the farness;/Oh God, how I'm stuck on it all." It is not too much to say that Murie would not have been in Alaska without the aid of the fossil fuels. No hunting society could have afforded to hire a wildlife biologist like him or allowed him to waste so much ammunition on specimens. Inextricably, he was part of a new economic organism, one that did not need him to collect food to feed the group but could use him for another kind of work altogether. He could be sent on salary to the bush, where his job would be to spend his days making careful lists of the birds and mammals he saw, managing his fellow humans' impact on those animals, and sweating over the hard labor of skinning a bear whose meat, fat, and fur no one would ever consume. In so many ways, direct and indirect, coal made that new kind of career possible. Yet all the same, and with no sense of contradiction, Murie saw himself as a runaway from the industrial life, and he would try to stay out there as long as the bureaucrats would let him.

One August day in 1920, as he was chugging toward Fairbanks on the chocolate-colored Yukon River, Murie was startled to see a skein of "aeroplanes" flying overhead, passing on either side of the boat. They had flown all the way from New York and were heading for Nome on a record-setting transcontinental flight, the first ever to pass over Alaska. The pilots called themselves the Black Wolf Squadron, and they belonged to the Army Air Service, whose sponsor was General Billy Mitchell. Below them on the steamboat Murie and his companions, a gang of gold prospectors, were all agog and abuzz. They had had a glimpse of the future of Alaska and of the coming means of its invasion, the internal combustion engine strapped to a pair of wings. In the next few years the first of Alaska's legendary bush pilots, Carl Ben Eielsen, would settle in the territory; then Noel Wien would show up from Murie's home state of Minnesota. Wien would be the first pilot to land a plane north of the Arctic Circle, dropping off two miners at Wiseman, a tiny village of whites and Eskimos, in the spring of 1925. The coal of the steamer era was giving way to gasoline, a fuel capable of powering flight, and the pace of invasion began to achieve a relentless, dizzying momentum.[15]

On 22 July 1929 Noel Wien took aboard another passenger and headed for the same Wiseman landing strip, which by now had become a regular stop. This time his passenger was young Bob Marshall, the son of a well-to-do New York City lawyer and currently a graduate student in plant physiology at Johns Hopkins University. Marshall had just arrived in Fairbanks after two long weeks of travel from the East Coast by railroad and steamer, intent on exploring a region that was still "a blank space on the map," the 15,000 square miles at the headwaters of the Koyukuk River, country that Frank Schrader had passed through a few decades earlier. Rising immediately behind Wiseman were the sharply glaciated peaks of the Brooks Range, almost none of them as yet named, at least by whites, though the natives must have known them pretty well. The mountains marked the point where the penetration of the gasoline engine ended abruptly. Into that awesome space Marshall must go afoot, hiking and fishing with a guide, a couple of pack horses, and a tent. He spent three weeks exploring the North Fork valley of the Koyukuk, passing between the two mountain sentinels that rose on opposite sides of the river and that he named the Gates of the Arctic. In fact, the student attached names all over the place—Boreal Mountain, Frigid Crags, Mount Doonerak, and so forth—before returning to his studies. Most of the mountainous north of Alaska was still, in 1929, unscaled, unregistered, and unpatented.

Marshall got back to Baltimore just in time to witness the collapse of America's industrial economy. The stock market crashed in October, and the country pitched downward into the gloom of depression, until eventually ten million people were thrown out of work. Nostalgic for his wilderness summer, Marshall had the urge and the money to escape the debacle. Soon he was back in Alaska, settled in a rustic cabin in Wiseman for the next twelve and a half months, gathering experiences for a book to be called *Arctic Village*. In addition to making further strenuous forays into the mountains, he became a much-loved member of the strange, happy little village, dancing evenings in the local roadhouse with the Eskimo girls, sitting for hours around his cast-iron stove with the old reminiscing sourdoughs. "It is 200 miles," he wrote, "to the closest pavement, the closest auto, the closest railroad, or the closest electric lights at Fairbanks. . . . Such great distances give the Koyukuk an inaccessibility reminiscent of the Nineteenth Century frontier of the West, and an isolation which lies beyond the conception of most people in the closely populated region of Twentieth Century mechanization."[16]

When he left Alaska this time, it was only to come back again and then again, making in all four journeys north, spread over the whole Depression decade. Like so many others before and after him, Marshall fell into an Inside/Outside pattern of movement: for a spell he would come "inside" Alaska, where he found a warm, friendly community of folks living nearly self-contained, safely apart from urban life; then he would return to the "Outside," the lower 48 states, to the ongoing disaster of industrial America and yet also to the society where he could pursue a professional career as a government forester and where he found an appreciative audience for his writings.

Yet the sharp distinction Marshall and many others made between the Inside and the Outside was already fast disappearing, as was the isolation of Wiseman and the Brooks Range. The twentieth century not only reached the town of Fairbanks, bringing lights, radio music, and electric refrigeration; it soon came to Marshall's wonderfully out-of-the-way village. In 1925 Wiseman got a wireless station, provided by the government. In the winter of 1929–30 a caterpillar tractor appeared to haul freight over the mountains to the town of Bettles. Marshall complained that at least four out of every six cents spent hauling that freight went "Outside for gasoline, oil, and extra parts, and is lost entirely from the coffers of the Koyukuk. It was simply another instance of a mechanical improvement which was a technological triumph but an economic injury." On 3 July 1931 still another machine arrived: a disassembled automobile which was put together under a midnight sun for the upcoming Independence Day celebration. Even when assembled, it was a piece of junk, constantly needing repair; and there were only a little over six miles of road for it to run around on, roads that were open for only four months in the year. Still, it was a bonafide automobile, a sample of the greatest invention of the age, and miraculously it was popping and exploding its pistons right there in downtown Wiseman. By 1937, that other great infernal machine, the airplane, which had brought Marshall in so many times, had also become a regular presence: 150 landings occurred that year, a plane coming in almost every other day. "As a result," the wilderness lover regretted, "Wiseman is no longer an isolated community, uniquely beyond the end of the world."[17]

To combat this noisy mechanical intrusion, which of course he himself had helped promote to a degree, Bob Marshall went back to the East Coast and threw his formidable energies into founding a new organization, the Wilderness Society, which announced itself early in 1935. Its other founders included Benton MacKaye of Massachusetts, Harvey Broome of Tennessee, Harold Anderson of Washington, D.C., Robert Sterling Yard of New York City, and Aldo Leopold of Wisconsin. Their

formal statement of organization drew on Marshall's own rhetoric and
passion all the way:

> Primitive America is vanishing with appalling rapidity. Scarcely a month
> passes in which some highway does not invade an area which since the begin-
> ning of time had known only natural modes of travel, or some last remaining
> virgin timber tract is not shattered by the construction of an irrigation project
> into an expanding and contracting mud flat; or some quiet glade hitherto dis-
> turbed only by birds and insects and wind in the trees, does not bark out the
> merits of "Crazy Water Crystals" and the mushiness of "Cocktails for Two."

While his associates in the Society had many targets for preservation,
including portions of the Smoky Mountains, the Sierras, and the Rockies,
Marshall's own special dream was to preserve in a wild state a large part
of Alaska.[18]

In 1938 he had a chance to get a hearing for that idea in a federal report
on developing the territory's resources. The people living up there, he
argued, some 59,000 of them at that point, do not need more economic
development, for their standard of living is already above the national
average. "When Alaska recreation is viewed from a national standpoint,"
he wrote, "it becomes at once obvious that its highest value lies in the
pioneer conditions yet prevailing throughout most of the territory. These
pioneer values have been largely destroyed in the continental United
States. In Alaska alone can the emotional values of the frontier be pre-
served." In particular, he urged, all the land lying north of the Yukon
River should be kept free of roads and industry. Airplanes could be permitted, and indeed were the only feasible means of mechanical convey-
ance, but no automobiles, no federal funds for roads, no leases for fossil-
fuel development. In the year after he made that recommendation, when
he was only 38 years old, Bob Marshall died of a heart attack on a train
from Washington to New York, died while riding on an instrument of the
very same industrial beast he wanted to restrain. But thanks to the money
from his sizable estate, the Wilderness Society would survive him, and
from the '30s on it would assume as one of its major goals the safeguarding
of Alaska's primitive qualities from a rampaging civilization.[19]

A lost cause? Not altogether; Marshall's favorite country would eventually become (in 1980) the Gates of the Arctic National Park and Preserve, almost eight million acres of rugged alpine landscape permanently
set aside for wilderness recreation, wildlife habitat, and subsistence
hunting. However, that was one victory set against many defeats. The
years during and after World War II would bring explosive changes to the
territory, changes that would drive the wildness right out of large areas.

Indeed, with a speed and enthusiasm unmatched anywhere else on earth, much of Alaska would be massively overrun in those years by industrial civilization and fully absorbed into and made a vital part of the modern global economy. "Seward's Folly," it had once been called, after the Secretary of State William Seward, who negotiated its original purchase: a land, some protested, for which no one would ever have any use. But in truth, as others knew from the start, there would eventually be plenty of uses for the place. It would become a home for immigrants from many states and countries, an international playground for sport hunters, a paradise of the outdoors, a vacation spot for the masses, a spoil bank of mining and dredging, and a military front line bristling with the means of instant death. In the war against Japan it would be turned into a base of operations for thousands of soldiers, many of whom would want to stay on, or return to settle, after the surrender. Then in the ensuing Cold War against the Soviet Union, Alaska would once more find itself on the leading edge of global confrontation, with radar stations, bomber squadrons, and nuclear bombs scattered across its islands and spruce forests, its tundra and gravel flats, to defend "the American way of life." As part of that continuing wartime mobilization the U.S. Army would cut a road right across British Columbia and into the Alaskan heartland, the Alcan Highway, and eventually on that road would roll trucks, jeeps, sedans, and moving vans, altogether hundreds of thousands of vehicles rolling north, bringing the American people in to look around and often to stay.[20]

In 1940 the territory's population stood at 72,500, about half of that number native, half non-native, and including 500 military personnel; that was a demographic level that had been remarkably constant since the mid-eighteenth century, though the native/non-native proportions had altered a great deal over time. In 1950, the total population had climbed above that historic plateau, reaching 129,000. One year after statehood, in 1960, the numbers had doubled to 226,000, with 33,000 counted in the military. By 1970, there were 302,000; by 1980, 402,000. Over a very brief span of time, the natives had become a small minority in their homeland, overwhelmed by the swelling tide of white in-migration.

Half of all those white people would decide to settle in the single center of Anchorage, once a mere depot on the Alaskan railroad, now transformed into the state's leading metropolis, approaching a quarter-million residents who were spread across the landscape as far as they could get and still belong to a community, still commute to work. Parking lots, freeways, gas stations, rental car agencies, motels, takeout food stands, shopping malls, traffic lights, the whole chaotic infrastructure of automobilized America, held them together. As John McPhee writes, "Almost all Americans would recognize Anchorage, because Anchorage is that part of any city where the city has burst its seams and extruded Colonel Sanders."[21]

On weekends, weary of that nervous scene, great numbers of Alaskans would leave the city streets and head en masse for the nearest salmon stream, fishing elbow to elbow whenever the reds or cohoes were running, or take to the bush to hunt sheep or moose, forming an army of riflemen big and dangerous enough to overrun an enemy nation. On an average summer day the highways out of town would fill up with their recreational vehicles, following each other like elephants linked in a circus train, huffing and puffing over the mountain passes in search of solitude. Pontooned planes, as numerous as flies at a dump, would choke the skylanes, searching out the most remote ponds for potential cabin sites, hunting lodges, or fishing camps, but crashing into one another with tragic regularity. And still more machines, more people, more desires would arrive in the state each week.

The dynamism that revolutionized Alaska came from all over America, not Alaska alone. In the span of a mere century of territorial possession, Americans turned the far north into their continental backyard. They demanded and got the ability to drive their automobiles all the way from the Caribbean Sea to the Beaufort Sea, passing right under the shadow of the Brooks Range, and to drive most of that distance on a paved road. How wild could any place really be, and for how long, with all those engines roaring to and through and around it?[22]

The postwar growth of Alaska was made possible largely by the alchemy of petroleum. From petroleum came an unprecedented mobility, dissolving all the boundaries and limits that had once confronted humans in the north. Compared with coal, petroleum was mobile even in its formative processes: a liquid squeezed out of sediments, dripping down through layers of porous limestone or sandstone, collecting into pools. When pumped from the ground, fractionated and refined into gasoline, diesel oil, aviation fuel, and other components, then poured into tanks and engines, petroleum proved wonderfully versatile, far more so than coal, and it speedily took away many of coal's markets. In 1918, the United States produced 356 million barrels of oil (each barrel containing 42 gallons); by 1948, the level was two billion barrels. The largest producers were Texas and California. Virtually all of the petroleum used to overrun and populate Alaska came, at least until the late 1970s, from those Lower 48 sources and from abroad—Sumatra, Venezuela, the Middle East. For a while, it is true, Alaska derived a tiny local supply from a sixty-acre oil field at Katalla, where the Bering River empties into the Gulf of Alaska. During its life span, from 1902 to 1933, when its refinery burned, this field produced 154,000 barrels, but that was only a trickle in the territorial gas tank. More wells would be spudded in later, many more as we will see, but the petroleum that fueled the great urban rush northward was not Alaskan in point of origin. Both the bush pilot and the Winnebago driver were energy importers. Both drew a seemingly unlimited personal mobility from the fossil past, and from the distant, deeply buried rocks of places like East Texas and Kuwait.[23]

Due to their lengthy winters and vast distances, and to their widespread mania for the outdoor camping and sporting life, Alaskans became some of the most intensive energy consumers in the world. Like other Americans, they acquired a heavy petroleum habit, a dependency that was like an addiction, but they drew more of that energy from petroleum than did other parts of the nation and world. In 1977 the average per capita consumption of petroleum in the United States was four gallons a day; in Alaska, it was seven gallons. Where the nation as a whole relied on petroleum and natural gas for 75 percent of its energy supplies, Alaska relied for 92 percent. Despite having so much coal lying under its feet, the state's population made relatively little use of it: only 6 percent of its energy supply came from coal, whereas in the United States, coal furnished 19 percent of the total.[24]

In 1978 officials of the Fairbanks North Star Borough collected some revealing facts about energy use within their borders, which enclose a 7400-square-mile area in the interior of the state, straddling the 65th latitude and which at that time counted about 54,000 people. (Alaska's boroughs, of which there are twelve, are the equivalent of counties elsewhere.) An infinitesimally small amount of the energy they used came from within the borough's borders, in the form of wood taken from the local forests. All the rest was imported, including crude oil (10.7 billion British Thermal Units worth a year), jet fuel (2.0 billion BTUs), motor gasoline (3.3 billion), coal (8.6 billion), and a miscellany of other forms and sources, ranging from propane, fuel oil, and diesel to electricity. A large part of the energy, 15.6 billion BTUs, came into the borough only to be lost in the form of heat given off to the atmosphere; for example, most of the BTUs in the coal were lost in the inefficient process of burning it for electrical generation—the heat going right up the smokestack. The biggest user of the energy that actually got delivered was the homeowner; residential use accounted for 8.9 billion BTUs, followed by government use (6.0 billion), most of that going to local military bases, and industry use (3.3 billion). The homeowner needed all that energy for heating, lighting, and driving down the avenues. He or she had to pay a substantial price for it too: electricity cost nearly twice as much per kilowatt hour in Fairbanks as elsewhere in America, and heating oil cost almost 25 percent more per gallon. In Alaska's rural areas those price differences were even more pronounced, but the locals chose to pay whatever it cost. How else could all 54,000 of them get groceries into their larders, get to work and school, run a chain saw or snowblower, read the newspaper in the long dark mornings, or stay warm in the depths of February? How else could they even remain up here, enjoying a modern American lifestyle only two hundred miles south of the Arctic Circle?[25]

Covering a far larger expanse than Fairbanks North Star is the North Slope Borough, ranging across the entire northern crown of Alaska from Point Hope to the Canadian border. In contrast to Fairbanks, its residents are largely natives, the Inupiat of old. But here too the fossil-fuel economy made deep inroads, bringing swift, radical changes to ancient ways of life. More and more the Inupiat began to live permanently in towns, making payments on houses built in the white man's style. Like the whites, they paid electrical and fuel bills to utility companies. In Point Barrow taxis appeared to cruise the streets, picking up fares going to the airport. The school boasted Apple computers, a science laboratory, and a well-heated gymnasium. The local supermarket ordered oranges from southern California, breakfast cereal from Minneapolis, bell peppers from Mexico; while a Mexican restaurant opened, dishing out tacos and enchiladas to a people whose grandparents ate mainly caribou and walrus.[26]

Today, the Inupiat still go out to hunt, and over east in places like the still rather inaccessible village of Kaktovik, they still depend on hunting to furnish more than 70 percent of their protein. They remain "subsistence hunters," which traditionally was never an occupation of poverty but of self-reliance; they were a people who provided their own food, taken from the country. A great deal of that self-reliance still exists, but it is declining for one preeminent reason: the technology of hunting has become radically unlike that of the past. The modern native hunter goes out on a motorized three-wheeler to check his fishnets along the beach. Or, armed with a high-powered rifle, he rackets over a winter tundra on a snowmobile made in a Michigan factory he has never visited. He penetrates the mountain wildernesses, the wildlife refuges, the national parks on an eight-wheeled all-terrain vehicle. Gasoline for those engines costs twice as much up here as in Fairbanks. Store-bought food costs almost twice as much too. Ammunition is likewise expensive. Subsistence hunting survives primarily because it remains, for a while, economic: it adds, in effect, several thousand dollars' worth of income to a family's living. According to anthropologists Michael Jacobson and Cynthia Wentworth,

> Overall participation in subsistence activities is greatest during spring and summer months, as this is the time of long days, mild weather, and species abundance. It is also the time when school is out and entire families can camp and hunt and fish together. The entire coast from Foggy Island to Demarcation Bay is used for summer subsistence activities. Motorboat access to inland areas by means of the rivers is normally not possible because of shallow water, but people can take their boats a few miles up the main channel of the Canning River.

Participation in the subsistence economy and the modern fossil-fuel economy, however, are more and more in conflict. Modern technology and energy do not come free. The Inupiat find they must have cash even to come together in the old ways, and that cash requires getting jobs in the white man's realm, jobs serving tourists, manning radar stations, working in the oil fields, pushing paper across a desktop. Dependence on the fossil fuels has meant dependence on the wage system, an ecological and economic spiral that has been going round and round for half a century now. The old fully subsistence economy led to sharing; whoever had food gave to those without, in the expectation that on another day the gift relationship would be reversed. Money, however, is stuff one keeps more private, hoarded in a family or personal account.[27]

The inner, cultural consequences of those material changes have been endlessly disputed, one party insisting that nothing significant has altered, that the traditions and values of the past remain unaffected by the fossil-fuel economy, another replying that the Inupiat have been totally ruined. Neither view can be conclusively proved, but the fact that substantial change has come cannot be refuted. Perhaps the soundest conclusion is Norman Chance's, made after a recent visit to a people he has observed over many decades: "The cultural life of the North Slope Inupiat has been seriously eroded."[28]

Alaska, though seeming so removed from modern history, has been a good place to stand and observe one of the greatest forces in that history, the fossil-fuel mode of production and consumption. Historians have not given that force nearly enough attention, for what it has meant both to the land and to the humans who live on the land. Energy lies at the very core of humankind's material existence, and every society is at bottom an organization for getting and using energy. In Alaska we can observe, without having to go back more than a few decades, the most profound set of changes in energy use that have ever happened to humans. No one who lived through them could have understood all that was happening as it happened, nor had a clear sense of the ultimate direction in which they were moving, nor been able to measure the pace of change. But now, looking back at it all, we can perceive more fully the broad outlines.

Within present memory in Alaska a black force began erupting out of the interior of the earth, bringing to the surface all the power of an ancient underworld. A benign power in many ways, it brought a warmer, brighter, faster, freer life to people, and a readier access to the many wonders of the Great Land, one of the most sublime landscapes on earth. But it was also a dark, destructive power, and in retrospect we are able to see more clearly just how much it destroyed, ecologically and culturally, as it oozed across the country in a viscous, volatile flood of hydrocarbons.

The Power of Blackness

One year after Frank Schrader came exploring the North Slope for the Geological Survey, in 1902, a private citizen entered Alaska looking for coal to acquire. He was an entrepreneur named Clarence Cunningham, and he prowled like a hungry bear along the teeth-numbing Bering River flowing out of glaciers, an area now part of the Chugach National Forest. Dozens of other men had been rummaging in the vicinity, digging holes and sniffing for coal seams. Cunningham, luckier than most, found a few good chunks and took them home to Seattle, where he waved them under the twitchy noses of his friends and acquaintances, men who had made some money with saw mills and mines and now wanted to invest in Alaska. Over the next few years Cunningham collected money from 33 investors and on their behalf filed claims on 5,280 acres in the Bering valley at the standard government rate of $10 per acre. Innocent ambitions to spend a little and make a lot. All the claims were on federal property, as so many other mining claims had been since the '49 gold rush to the West. That fact gave no one pause, though it should have. None of the claimants could possibly have realized how quickly he would be embroiled in bitter conflict at the highest levels of government, how notorious he would become in American history, or how eventually his case would bring down a Secretary of the Interior and his President. Their interest in the public's coal would help touch off a fierce national debate over who would control Alaska, the fossil-fuel economy in general, and the whole modern industrial apparatus. The power of coal and oil to do work is also a power held over society; who controls it controls much else besides in economic life. The Cunningham group seems to have had no grand Machiavellian strategies, no conspiratorial design to dominate the north country. They simply wanted some money out of it. But like so much else that has happened in Alaska, what began naively as a simple private hunger ended up as a titanic struggle over broad public questions. The questions appeared soon after the coal claims were filed, and they would be around for decades to come, still unresolved down to the time of the post–World War II oil boom.

Cunningham and his fellow bears were a smallish lot, but their discoveries soon attracted a large cunning monster to the feast. The Alaska Syndicate, otherwise known as the Morgan-Guggenheim trust, was ravenously hungry and looking for an opening to push its way in. At a meeting in Utah in 1907, the Syndicate offered to form a joint coal-mining corporation with the Cunningham claimants, providing capital to develop the coal in exchange for an unlimited supply over a twenty-five-year period. The Syndicate's home was far off in New York City, and like the claimants few if any of its members had ever been to Alaska. They belonged to the nation's economic elite, on the whole an avaricious lot, and already they had acquired, at long distance with hired talent, a large hold on the mineral wealth of the continent. Standing at the head of the Syndicate were the financier J. P. Morgan, of the Morgan Trust, and the mining tycoon Daniel Guggenheim, of the American Smelting and Refining Company, which had properties scattered over many western states. In Alaska the Syndicate operated a steamship line, a salmon fishery, and a copper mine, as well as a railroad to carry out the ore. By 1907 they were the biggest corporate entity in the north country. Now all they needed to make their enterprises more secure was a local supply of fuel, freeing them from high-priced Canadian sources they did not control. Given that supply, more of the wild silent beauty of Alaska might be incorporated into their private empire.[29]

Smack in the Syndicate's way stood the Department of Interior, guardian of the public lands. Since all of Alaska was federal, Interior had to approve the Cunningham claims as fair and legitimate and convey a patent to them before any coal could be dug. In earlier years that would have presented little difficulty, but in 1906 President Theodore Roosevelt had, by executive order, precipitously withdrawn from entry all known coal deposits on America's public lands, freezing their development until Congress could decide on a better policy than giving them away for a pittance. He added oil lands to the no-entry list in 1909. Roosevelt preferred a system of leasing all minerals while keeping the land under permanent federal control. So the Cunningham claimants, with the Syndicate slavering hungrily over their shoulder, tried to get an exemption from the with-drawal policy on the grounds that they had fulfilled all the requirements before the freeze went into effect.

The immediate target of the claimants' pleas was the General Land Office, whose commissioner, Richard Ballinger, had been a Republican mayor of Seattle and was well known to them as a good and true fellow. Ballinger was honest as they go, certainly not one to take bribes or line his own pockets at the public's expense, but he saw nothing amiss in the Cunningham-Morgan-Guggenheim collusion or in their application for entry. Before Roosevelt interfered, American law and tradition had long sanctioned the speedy turnover of all natural resources on the public domain to whoever got there first, and Ballinger was a scrupulous tradi-tionalist, a loyal believer in the old system; he did not support the policy of withdrawal or of leasing. Unfortunately for the applicants, however, Ballinger was in office for only twelve months, a frustrating time when his approval was stalled by underlings who suspected fraud. Once out of office, Ballinger, as it were, walked across the street to become the Cun-ningham claimants' lawyer, pleading before the same government employees he had just bossed. Then brought back into office in 1909 as nothing less than Secretary of the Interior in the new administration of President William Howard Taft, he was faced once more with approving the claims. Still he could see nothing wrong with them. Nor undoubtedly did the majority of congressmen, for despite the fact that they had made a few reforms in the public land laws to prevent grossly fraudulent entries, they held fast to the established tradition of giving away as quickly as possible all the mineral resources on the public domain—gold, silver, copper, lead, iron, coal, oil—to any private citizen who wanted them, giv-ing them at no more than token cost, giving them no matter in whose hands they eventually ended up. Many in the Congress and elsewhere in the federal government did not believe that they were morally justified or economically expert enough to do otherwise. They acquiesced in the Roo-sevelt withdrawals but generally did not like them.

Did the Syndicate finally get title to its coal? It did not. The claims were finally canceled in 1911, after a congressional investigation and national hue and cry had made their turnover politically impossible. Ironically, the coal proved to be too friable anyway to use as locomotive fuel. But that realization came later; what forestalled and defeated the claimants was the fierce protective energy of Gifford Pinchot, Chief For-ester of the United States and one of the founding figures in what became known as the conservation movement. Pinchot had followed Ballinger's moves closely in and out of office, saw them as a sell-out of the public interest, and finally concluded he had enough evidence to convict the Secretary of moral crimes and drive him from office. The evidence had been collected by a young Seattle employee of the Interior Department, Louis Glavis, who was convinced that the Cunningham claims were fraudulent (the degree of prior collusion among the claimants, he was sure, went beyond what was allowed in law). Though he had repeatedly failed to convince Ballinger of the charge, Glavis persisted, eventually including his boss in the indictment. Supported by Glavis's voluminous evidence, Pinchot launched an unsubtle campaign in the press and on the lecture circuit to get Ballinger fired. He failed in that—in fact soon found himself dismissed as an unruly presence in the administration—but he caused such a stink about the matter that finally the Secretary of the Interior, facing possible impeachment proceedings, handed in his resignation, pleading poor health. Two years later, largely because of the split the affair caused in the Republican party, President Taft was defeated for reelection and a Democrat, Woodrow Wilson, succeeded to the office. And now no one in Washington dared give up the coal lands to the claimants. There would be no feast after all; the bears must go away hungry.

The debate over just how guilty Richard Ballinger was in the Alaska coal affair has far outlasted him. Today, the consensus is that he was a man of some principle, certainly not an out-and-out criminal, and the real substance of the dispute was a disagreement over political values. The principle Ballinger upheld was that individuals ought to have an unfettered opportunity to accumulate personal wealth on the public lands. If that meant Alaska's future would be dominated by the likes of J. P. Morgan, it would be, in his view, no crime or outrage; many good citizens in Seattle would in the event come out all right too. Conservationists like Pinchot, on the other hand, vehemently rejected that principle, called it morally bankrupt, and tried by every means possible, even to the point of stretching the law, to lead the country to a new set of values regarding the use and development of natural resources. The fact that both men were finally forced out of office (Pinchot in 1910, Ballinger in 1911) suggests that neither set of values could boast having won a decisive victory.

Gifford Pinchot has been written about so many times, by so many people, including himself, and has been described so variously that the political philosophy he fought for has now become something of a muddle. Was he a patrician and elitist, looking down his long straight nose at the little scrambling frontier men on the make? Was he a democrat, fighting for the rights of the people in the face of crunching monopoly power? Or was he an apolitical technocrat who wanted to turn all national affairs over to a cadre of engineers and scientists? All those characterizations have been made and all have some truth in them, but none quite captures the core vision that powered his career as a conservationist. To clear away the muddle we need to go back and listen carefully to his own words, especially his mature self-representations, and ask what he said and what he meant. In 1947, almost four decades after he left federal office, Pinchot published his autobiography, *Breaking New Ground,* and in the last chapter, which follows hard on his retelling of the Ballinger-Pinchot conflict, he tried to put into words the key objectives of his life. He had devoted his public energies to "conservation," he wrote, the purpose of which was "the ownership, control, development, processing, distribution, and use of the natural resources for the benefit of the people." Take that sentence seriously and it should be perfectly plain that what he was espousing were the principles of natural resource socialism. Conservation for him was basically a matter of socializing all the vital resources; it did not mean saving "the ecology of the planet" or "the beauty of the landscape" or "the unspoiled wilderness." From the beginning of his public life, though more and more obviously as he went along, he advocated sweeping change in the way the country's natural resources were held as well as used. Resources on the public lands he would keep public; those dispersed into private hands he would try gradually to socialize to whatever degree and in whatever manner possible. "I believe in free enterprise," he procalimed, "freedom for the common man to think and work and rise to the limit of his ability, with due regard to the rights of others." The words were disingenuous, for the essence of the free-enterprise system, as Pinchot surely knew, was to extend private property rights over all land and resources—and Pinchot did not really believe in doing that. "The earth . . . belongs of right to all its people, and not to a minority, insignificant in numbers but tremendous in wealth and power." His unwavering conviction was that America's natural resources should be— and his words bear repeating—owned, developed, distributed, and used by and for the good of all people, not by and for an economic elite. The question of ownership was not a minor matter for him; on the contrary, it was the fundamental issue in his political philosophy.[30] A land managed efficiently by technical experts in the employ of the great corporations would not satisfy him. Had he been English, he would have been a Tory radical. Had he been German or Scandinavian, a Social Democrat. Although he was no Marxist or Bolshevist, no believer in the worker's state or the coming proleterian revolution, he most certainly was, in broad European historical terms, something of a socialist in his political leanings—but a socialist of the closet variety, eschewing any label except "progressive," never quite admitting what he was, perhaps never feeling quite free in this hostile American setting to express his leanings openly. But he could not altogether hide them, and by all traditional measures they were radical ones, beyond the views of the mainstream. Certainly that fact was understood by President Taft, who wrote unsympathetically to his daughter that Pinchot had "a Socialist tendency."[31]

Why, Pinchot must have asked himself, were private corporations successful in gathering so many of the country's resources into their hands? Why had the public, through Congress, so readily cooperated in that transfer of wealth? Simply because the corporations had convinced people that they had the technical competence to develop resources efficiently and make them yield wealth for everybody. Though widely feared for their power and lack of scruples, the corporations had established extensive credibility among Americans by their expertise. Pinchot understood that fact completely, and he decided to attack it head on. He argued relentlessly, but especially so after leaving government when he could say what he wanted, that the corporations had in truth bungled the job of building America; they had wasted resources and endangered future jobs, growth, and security. To demonstrate that waste in the case of the fossil fuels, for instance, he pointed out that "the established coal-mining practice at the present date does not take out more than one-half the coal, leaving the less easily mined or lower grade material to be made permanently inaccessible by the caving in of the abandoned workings." Only 5 percent of the coal burned on America's railways actually produced any traction power; the rest was lost through inefficiency. Natural gas was regularly allowed to escape into the air because companies had no immediate market for it. Large amounts of oil leaked into streams or "were systematically burned in order to get rid of it." What Thorstein Veblen later called "businesslike mismanagement" characterized the whole history of resource use under what was supposed to be sophisticated corporate expertise.[32]

Examples of waste and inefficiency were easy enough to find all across the land, in polluted, ravaged, abandoned mining and timbering sites where the corporations had made their money, then left. A harder task was to convince Americans that keeping the lands under federal ownership and supervision would be a considerable improvement over that corporate record. Americans may have feared the large corporations, but even more they distrusted the state in matters requiring technical, economic competence; indeed they had distrusted since the days of Andrew Jackson, distrusted through the long succession of mediocre Presidents and corrupt administrations that followed him. Pinchot had to overcome a burden of anti-state feeling that no European conservationist, socialist or not, had to confront. To be sure, Americans had always allowed that some activities could best be performed by governmental representatives—education and military defense were the most prominent—but not the exploitation of resources and the creation of national and personal wealth. There they looked to the private sector for competence, a competence, many believed, that unfettered greed would sharpen to a fine point. Somehow Pinchot and his fellow "progressives" and "conservationists" had to persuade people that the federal government could produce competent management too, a competence honed not by greed but by disinterested pride in a job well done. The Forest Service was Pinchot's best hope for demonstrating that quality; he organized it as a corps of trained men recruited from the best schools, men animated by an ideal of serving the long-run good of the country, men so tightly honest they squeaked, so zealous they glowed. The nations watched them march into the national forests in their dark green uniforms, with army-like campaign hats on their heads, whistling manfully, and it liked what it saw—in fact has liked them ever since they first appeared on the scene. Pinchot hoped to see the whole landscape filled with similar phalanxes, some of them smartly stepping off to reclaim the deserts, other to manage the rivers, still others to oversee the mining of coal and oil. If the dream was a tad militaristic, such was the case with socialist idealism all over the world. Public competence, it would seem, must always wear a uniform.

Alaska, still pristine but undergoing the first phase of an invasion, was an opportunity to realize the Pinchot vision of competent public ownership and management on a grand scale. In a 1911 article for the *Saturday Evening Post,* Pinchot put the burning question, "Who Shall Own Alaska?" His answer was not government all the way. Much of the territory might become a series of small farming communities, where lands would be put into private but safely virtuous rural hands. If people found that notion of an incipient agricultural Alaska surprising, out of synch with the place's reputation as "a land of ice and snow, glaciers and dog-teams, placer diggings, salmon canneries, undeveloped coal mines, and little else," then Americans had not yet realized how much potential was truly there. We are uninformed, Pinchot told his readers, about

> the great stretches of agricultural land ready to produce in abundance the fruits, vegetables and grains of Northern Europe; about the cattle and the reindeer pastures, vast in extent; about the great resources of timber available for use in developing the mines; and in general about the fitness of this great land—one-sixth as large as the area of all our states—to produce and support a population as hardy, as healthy, as intelligent and as valuable to the nation as the best that Scandinavia can show.[33]

Those last few words are worth particular attention, for they suggest an Alaska very different from what would eventually emerge. If Americans used their head, Pinchot was saying, Alaska might become another Sweden or Norway. The notion was not completely far-fetched; other parts of the country had aspired after European models and to some extent succeeded. California, for example, in the aftermath of the gold rush had turned from mining to cultivating a rural image of itself as western America's answer to Italy, Provence, or Spain, complete with orange trees and sunny, flourishing vineyards. Now Alaska might improve on that precedent considerably, choosing a less indolent, more progressive self-image, striving to become a Scandinavian-style democracy shining under northern lights.

The public-ownership part of Pinchot's vision focused on the timber and mineral wealth of the territory, particularly those coal fields up on the Bering River. Instead of handing them over to the Syndicate, he urged that they be kept in the public domain and carefully managed. They might be subdivided into five- or ten-acre plots to be assigned free of charge to the actual residents of Alaska to mine, as long as the miners were acting in their own behalf. All other coal should be leased to companies, not given away, under a system of strict rules and regulations with substantial royalties paid into the national treasury. The government should build its own railroad to bring the coal down to the coast (and another one to transport coal down from the Tanana and Yukon valleys), and its own wharves and storage facilities, even a fully state-owned shipping facility at Controller Bay. No Morgans or Guggenheims should be allowed to dominate that vital transportation service. In creating those projects government would show it had the competence to do a better job of supervising the fossil-fuel resource and getting it to market than any corporation or syndicate. Thus, government might keep Alaska free of the selfish, wasteful vagaries that private monopolists manifested elsewhere in the country.

Retired from federal office, Pinchot lacked any power to carry out his Alaska recommendations and could only advise from the sidelines. Due in large part to the popular influence he continued to wield, Congress passed the Alaska Coal Leasing Act in 1914. However, much to his disappointment, it also showed the strong hand of the coal interests, who would accept leasing only on their own terms. Henceforth no coal-bearing lands would be sold at any price to any private developer. Instead, the coal would be conveyed in the form of a lease, charging a royalty of two cents on every ton of coal mined. (There was the still domineering will of the interests getting their way—two cents was all but free.) A lease would last fifty years and cover no less than 2,560 acres (more influence at work). Six years later, in the Mineral Leasing Act of 1920, Congress extended the leasing-and-royalty system to cover all the coal deposits and all the oil deposits across the whole public domain, leaving only the hard-rock minerals under the old Mining Law of 1872—that is, still virtually free to any grabber at any time. When instituted, the new system for the fossil fuels proved to be only a shadow of what Pinchot had had in mind. Lessees could sign contracts noncompetitively and then never do any mining or drilling at all, while they speculated on a rise in price; and no one would ever lose a lease for inactivity. Eventually Congress would raise the limit to a munificent 46,000 acres of leases per company per state. The royalty schedules stayed persistently far below the going rate on nearby private lands. Most important for the fossil-fuel companies, the act opened up the public lands once more, after the Roosevelt freeze, to exploitation. On the other hand, the deposits now had been placed under perpetual federal ownership, potentially subject to stringent federal regulation. The new system was not socialism, or at least it was no more than nominally socialistic, but then it was not pure capitalism either, and for that Pinchot might take a measure of credit.[34]

In the 1920 leasing act the most important clause was the one dealing with oil, the coming fuel of a mobility-seeking America, not with coal, which was already becoming the fuel of the past. The immediate effect of the provision was to stimulate a spate of new public-land oil drilling in the Lower 48. Most of that drilling during the twenties occurred in such states as California and Wyoming, home to the much-publicized naval oil reserves at Elk Hills and Teapot Dome, reserves which another Secretary of Interior, Albert Fall, tried to lease to his friends at Sinclair Oil for a personal financial consideration, a dirty little deal that sent him to prison.[35] Alaska could show no comparable shenanigans because, so far, no one really knew the size of its deposits or had tried to tap them for American markets. Alaska had a little-known equivalent to Teapot Dome called Petroleum Naval Reserve Number Four ("Pet Four"), a 25-million-acre site set aside by President Harding in 1923 on the North Slope, between Icy Cape and the Colville River; but no development took place there even during the war against Japan, though the government carried out serious geological investigations from 1923 to 1926 and again from 1944 to 1953.[36] Then, after the Second World War, the Union Oil Company of California and the Ohio Oil Company, followed by Phillips Petroleum and Kerr-McGee Oil, sent wildcatters north to drill on federal property near Anchorage, on the west side of Cook Inlet (sporadic drilling had been going on there at Cold Bay since 1902), and on the Kenai Peninsula.

Still another company, Richfield, entered the scene and in 1957 made the first big strike on the peninsula at Swanson River Unit Number 1, the oil surging up from two miles deep in the ground at a rate of nine hundred barrels a day. At long last, after sitting on the remote fringes, Alaskans found themselves on the front row of national oil development—and at last they were ready to develop their own oil scandal too.

The Swanson River well was located in a two-million-acre wildlife refuge set aside in 1941 as the Kenai National Moose Range. With news of the strike, half the refuge was thrown open by the Interior Department to companies seeking leases. Hitherto all wildlife refuges had been off-limits even to exploration, so why was leasing suddenly permitted in the home of the moose? The clear answer was that the President of the United States, Dwight Eisenhower, and his Secretary of Interior, Douglas MacKay (popularly known as "Giveway MacKay"), personally wanted it that way. Most of Eisenhower's closest personal friends, his favorite golfing partners, were oil men, including W. Alton Jones, chairman of the board at Richfield Oil. Executives from oil companies spent $500,000 to renovate Eisenhower's farm at Gettysburg, Pennsylvania. They made heavy contributions to his reelection campaign in 1956, giving him $350,000 in contrast to $14,000 for his opponent, Adlai Stevenson. When Secretary MacKay resigned a few months before the election to save Eisenhower from any further embarrassment before outraged conservationists, his successor Fred Seaton became the man with the pen who actually signed the lease over to Richfield. Two years later, after an internal review of regulations forced on him by controversy, Seaton declared once more that no oil or gas leasing would be allowed in any federal wildlife refuge—except those in Alaska. Prominent men in the territory applauded the decision to open their refuges to drilling. Some of them still resented the adverse economic impact of the Roosevelt coal withdrawals and the Cunningham flap; for example, Ernest Gruening declared that due to unfortunate circumstances Alaska "has lost the coal age. It has, so far, with slight exception, lost the hydroelectric age. We do not want to lose the oil age. We do not want history to repeat itself." So the moose found themselves wandering through the stench and squalor of oil camps and blackish, smelly rigs, manned by drillers from as far away as the steamy Gulf Coast of Louisiana. The postwar oil boom was under way, and in wealth produced it would soon eclipse the gold rush of the late nineteenth century. By the end of 1957 the federal government had leased 19 million acres of Alaska for oil development.

Gathering at the Third Avenue Elks Club in Anchorage were a group of local businessmen calling themselves the Spit and Argue gang, who watched the oil play on the Kenai peninsula with some admiration and wanted to get in on the spoils. None of them was at all experienced in the petroleum business; they included Robert Atwood, publisher of the *Anchorage Times,* and Elmer Rasmusen, president of the largest bank in town. Using the classic ploy of a dummy, a man paid to front for others by getting leases in his own name and then turning them over, they began to acquire the rights to valuable federal oil deposits. The policy of the Interior Department, as noted above, was to accept oil leases noncompetitively, charging in Alaska a mere 25 cents an acre (the national standard was 50 cents). As usual in such cases, it helped immensely to have inside information or some other kind of assistance to get those noncompetitive leases. Two employees of the Bureau of Land Management, Virgil Seiser and Chester McNalley, were in charge of leasing locally, and they proved remarkably friendly to the Spit and Argue gang; so apparently was Alaska's nonvoting delegate to Congress, E. L. ("Bob") Bartlett, who secretly gave tips to them and openly pushed for more refuge drilling. Others in the Anchorage community, however, were angered at what they regarded as favoritism enjoyed by the Atwood crowd; among them was Walter Hickel, a future governor of Alaska and Secretary of the Interior, who demanded that leases be issued only after competitive bidding and that the profits go exclusively to Alaskan residents. Some of the profits certainly did do so; the Spit and Arguers, after getting their 25-cent leases, sold them to Richfield and other companies for a total sum of nearly $3 million, and then went back to their rather less lucrative pursuits of writing newspaper editorials and making bank loans.[37]

On 3 January 1959 the territory of Alaska became the 49th state in the Union. Emphatically, it was the biggest in area—378,242,560 acres—and in schoolroom geography exercises American students would superimpose its form on that of the Lower 48, their eyes widening as they took in the whole sweep from the Aleutian Islands to Mount McKinley, from the Arctic Ocean to the wet green panhandle in the south. They would trace the distance from Barrow to Ketchikan and find it as great as from Los Angeles to Kansas City. The oil companies had their maps out too, and as the Kenai–Cook Inlet fields became overleased, they let their fingers roam north to the Yukon Delta and on to Pet Four, to the North Slope, remembering all those old reports of seepages under the midnight sun. So too ran the anxious fingers of officials in the new state government, including its first governor, William Egan, who came into office with majestic, thrilling ambitions but no revenue to pay for them. Help was on the way. As a grandiose birthday present, Congress promised the state

103.5 million acres of land, a present the size of Colorado, enough land to give every resident 460 acres. No other state, on entry into the Union, had been treated so well. And certainly no foreign country, no matter how poor or underdeveloped, had received so large an aid package. Alaskans had been invited to survey the whole federal domain in the state, picking and choosing acreage like a sweepstakes winner racing through a department store, giddily filling his shopping cart with the choicest items. Not everyone, to be sure, was pushing the cart. The native population, then numbering 43,000, asked for their own separate share in the sweepstakes, safe from the state's grasp, and threatened to go to court to stop all economic development if they did not get it. So Congress eventually gave them a shopping cart too. In 1971 the Alaska Native Claims Settlement Act allowed the native villages and regional corporations to select up to 44 million acres from the public domain. Thus, the state was free to get on with its spree. Naturally, it went down the aisles looking for the richest lands first. It went after potential oil properties.[38]

The oil companies had maps and data privately ready for their own purposes, but the most promising new areas were hardly secret. Within three years of statehood seismic surveys done by federal scientists on the North Slope had indicated that at Prudhoe Bay and in the Colville River basin there were geological formations that promised to contain oil in large quantities. The state geologist urged the Egan administration to select those lands from the federal holdings, and in 1964 it did so. Then in December of that year the state offered to let leases on its new properties for exploration and drilling. Unlike the federal government, the state of Alaska insisted on competitive bidding. The companies were still interested. Two such lease sales took place, one in December and another in the following July, followed by a third in January 1967, under the new administration of Governor Hickel. Three companies won most of the leases in the Prudhoe Bay vicinity: Richfield (later merged to become Atlantic-Richfield, or ARCO) and Humble (later Exxon), which had combined their capital in a winning bid of $93.78 per acre on a 60,000-acre tract (no more 25-cent stuff); and then British Petroleum (which merged with Standard Oil of Ohio, or Sohio—you are nothing in oil if you don't have a new identity, and preferably a snappy acronym, every few years) won a bid of its own, moving off slightly to the west of the others to drill. The previous summer the British company had drilled the first exploratory well by a private outfit on the North Slope, after laboriously barging its drilling equipment down the Mackenzie River in Canada, then along the edge of the continent, setting up at Pingo Beach on the Colville. Having spent nearly $30 million to do all that, and with only eight dry holes so far to show for the effort, BP was not optimistic about striking it big, but it decided to stay in the game. It had almost 100,000 acres under lease.

In January 1968 Atlantic-Richfield made a strike but kept it quiet, trying to confirm what it had found. On 16 February company executives announced they had drilled down beneath the permafrost to a depth of nearly nine thousand feet and there had hit a zone of oil-saturated sandstone and gravel, an ancient braided river bed that had last flowed about 220 million years ago. Pictures of the drilling crew showed men wearing masks of ice over shaggy beards, looking more like frozen cavemen than modern Oklahomans, Texans, or whatever. Tough guys, in any case, a long way from home, and they had hit the jackpot. By July the *New York Times* had picked up the story, its headline in the business and financial section reading, "'68 Sourdoughs Find Bonanza in Alaska Oil." News of the bonanza kept coming down all that summer, competing for national attention with the Republican convention in Miami, where Richard Nixon was startling the delegates with his choice of Spiro G. Agnew as running mate; competing with the Democratic convention in Chicago, where Mayor Richard Daley's police were beating back antiwar protestors; competing with the body counts sent home daily from the war in Vietnam. In contrast to America's searing political trauma the North Slope must have seemed almost extraterrestrial—fascinating but unreal, as strange as the moon, even benign in a way. That reaction would have been as true of Alaskans as other Americans; they hardly knew where Prudhoe Bay was.[39]

Imagine their astonishment then when the company revealed that it had discovered the largest oil field in all of North America and one of the top twenty in the world, a field containing ten (later the estimate would mount to over twenty) billion barrels in all. With current technology they could recover almost half of those barrels.[40] The field also contained in a pocket overlying the oil an estimated thirty trillion cubic feet of natural gas. In addition, a short way west of Prudhoe another field soon materialized, Kuparuk, the second largest on the continent, with an estimated deposit of 6.4 billion barrels, of which 1.9 billion could be recovered. And there would also be Endicott field situated to the east, Lisburne lying deeper underground in a limestone formation, Niakuk about a mile offshore, the Milne Point field, Point McIntyre, West Sak, and Ugnu. Together, those fields and unnamed others on the North Slope might contain 125 billion barrels, a reservoir that would go a long way toward supplying the enormous, gnawing American energy demand. At the time of the strike the country consumed nearly fifteen million barrels of oil a day.[41]

The state of Alaska was, of course, as giddy as the oil companies with the extraordinary prospects, so far beyond anything previously discovered in its fossil-fuel history. The state would earn 12.5 percent royalties on all the oil sold. Time to do some more leasing. On 10 September 1969 the state held its fourth and biggest lease sale ever, reaping $900 million in bonus money—many times its annual state budget—yet even then it had picked out and leased only a few hundred square miles from its vast federal birthday present. Suddenly, the position of Alaska vis-à-vis the rest of the globe looked very different. As Joseph Fisher, president of Resources for the Future, told a university audience: "With the great North Slope oil discoveries added to the more modest developments around Cook Inlet, Alaska finds itself in the enviable position of being on the verge of sharing in a major way in the greatest raw material industry of the modern world. From now on Alaska will have to take a world view of its affairs and reckon with the economic, political, and social movements wherever energy sources and markets are located."[42] He might have put in a cautionary note that "sharing" in the oil industry would not mean sharing the political power that came from oil. Money might be infinitely expansible, so that Alaska could hope for a net improvement in its estate; power in the national and global political economy, however, is not. Power is a zero-sum game. Those who gain take from those who lose. The oil corporations would be the chief gainers in both wealth and power, acquiring considerable control over the north country by controlling the production of its most valuable resource. From this point on they would make most of the important decisions about the state's future economic development. The federal government had almost excused itself from the picture. The fledgling state of Alaska might have gained possession of much federal land, acquiring with it immense mineral wealth and revenues, but it would have only a minor, amateurish voice in the big decisions to come. From this point on it would have to do a lot of "reckoning" with the powers that be.

The next important decision was how to get the oil from the North Slope to those people with money and effective demand. The oil companies proceeded as though the decision were a matter for their heads and theirs alone to make. Should we pump the oil into our tanker fleet right at Prudhoe Bay and send it around the top of Canada, crunching through the winter ice in the Northwest Passage, and on to the East Coast and Europe? Or should we load it into mammoth submarines and send them cruising under the arctic ice pack? Or transport the oil overland to an ice-free port in the south? Before we can decide which route, we need to know where it is going. Who needs it? More important, who wants it and will pay the best price? Quickly the companies conferred, pooling their technical expertise and market information. The decision came down from on high: we will build a pipeline to carry the oil overland to the south. In the words of a reporter following the decision for the *Fairbanks Daily News-Miner*, "A pipeline . . . becomes a likelihood. Japan and Northern Europe appear to be our major markets for the future." America, for all its appetite, had a secure supply and the market was low, gasoline selling for a mere thirty or forty cents a gallon. Japan, on the other hand, seemed ready to pay a premium price; it had no oil of its own and depended entirely on the Middle East as supplier. Alaska was a lot closer to Japan than the Persian Gulf and seemed more reliable politically than Arab producers. Conversely, the American oil companies did not take long to realize that their wells in Alaska were as close to Tokyo as to an already well-supplied Los Angeles.

So: a pipeline, the first to reach that far north, sure to be expensive, with early estimates of construction costs running as high as $500 million. But what route should it take across the land: climb through Anuktuvuk Pass, that sublime mountain wilderness which Bob Marshall had so often hiked? Or run east of there through Atigun Pass, then south toward Fairbanks, then along the Alaska Railroad, ending on the west side of Cook Inlet where loading facilities already existed? Or should the pipeline go from Fairbanks south along the Richardson Highway through Thompson Pass and down into Valdez, the little port tucked away at the head of a fjord-like arm of Prince William Sound in an incomparably lovely setting of whales, sea lions, seals, porpoises, and sea otters encircled by cloud-swathed mountains, a town calling itself the "Switzerland of Alaska?" Or rather, into what had once been Valdez, for the town had been wiped out in the '64 earthquake by a massive tidal wave. The oil companies conferred and settled on Valdez as destination and ordered pipe from Japan. The route would cover 789 miles. They formed a consortium named Alyeska Pipeline Service Company to build and maintain the pipeline, including as members Mobil, Phillips, Amerada Hess, and Union, though ARCO, Humble, and BP remained the dominant partners, competitors in theory but not in practice. The international market beckoned, a market big enough for all of them, and their collective future seemed green with black profit.[43]

As in the case of the Cunningham coal claimants, the pipeline consortium assumed it would have a clear way opened for its enterprise. They had always had it so before. They had paid dearly for their leases and by now had invested more than a billion dollars in developing them. The state government had been friendly to them, and so was the federal government, with Richard Nixon occupying the presidency, carrying on the pro-business ideals of the Eisenhower-MacKay years, raking in large campaign contributions from the oil industry as his mentor had done, defending the companies' tax breaks through the oil depletion allowance.[44] Happier yet, the Secretary of the Interior was now none other than Walter Hickel of Alaska. So enthusiastic was he about oil development that, while governor, he had bulldozed a 400-mile road from Fairbanks to Prudhoe Bay, a violent gash right through some of the last great wild country, so that the companies could reach their drilling sites easier. So there were conservative Republicans everywhere in charge, men of the Richard Ballinger persuasion, sincere in their belief that government must not get in the way of capital but stand ready to provide a helping hand. Those party mavericks Teddy Roosevelt and Gifford Pinchot had long been dead, and so it seemed was their cause to distinguish the public interest from the private interests of entrepreneurs and corporations. All that the oil men needed from the government at this point was a right-of-way permit allowing them to take their pipeline across federal lands. Such a permit had always been readily granted in the past, and considering the strong conservativism in Juneau and Washington they expected it to sail right on through. They made application. They unloaded their pipe and began laying it out along the selected route. Then they watched in utter, naive amazement as the country exploded in political controversy.

While they had been exploring and drilling, profound changes had been going on in America's attitude toward natural resources, changes that were only beginning to show up in elections but that any competent group of planners ought to have taken seriously. If Pinchot's progressive conservation movement had long ago disapppeared, along with the issues of power he had raised, another had risen to take its place. Among its early achievements was a flurry of new laws to preserve the environment from industrial ravagers. For example, in 1969 Congress passed the National Environmental Protection Act, which stipulated that any federal agency proposing a major change in land use had to put together an analysis and assessment of its environmental effects and had to consider any alternatives that might be less destructive. That analysis was called an "environmental impact statement" (EIS). It was an astonishing, unprecedented requirement that many, even in government, had trouble accepting. When it seemed that no one in the administration had any intention to draw up such a statement for the pipeline right-of-way, three major conservation groups—the Wilderness Society, the Environmental Defense Fund, and the Friends of the Earth—went to court, naming Hickel the defendant, and they got an injunction against the right of way until an EIS was prepared. The agency charged with responsibility for preparing the statement was the Bureau of Land Management (BLM), successor to the old General Land Office of Pinchot's and Ballinger's day. The new generation of environmentalists regarded it more or less as the older conservationists had done: one of the weakest and least trustworthy agencies in government, generally inept and kowtow-ish to its lessees and permittees. When environmental leaders saw the statement the BLM prepared, a mere 200 pages long for a project that would cut Alaska right down the middle, opening up the entire north to a technological onslaught, they had their low opinion of the agency confirmed. But what the agency had done was no more, or no less, than what the President had wanted done. The Nixon government was no more ready for the new era of environmental concern than the oil companies. Stung by criticism, the Department of Interior withdrew the statement and set about preparing another, this one to be of impeccable scientific credentials and academic overkill. On 20 March 1972 they had six volumes ready, 3500 pages in all, and put it out for public comment and, they hoped, speedy acquiescence. On 11 May a new Secretary of the Interior, Rogers Morton, claiming to have read and considered the revised EIS carefully, approved the oil companies' application. Only four and a half years had transpired since the strike at Prudhoe Bay.

Though written to support the pipeline, the EIS was like the Bible in the hands of its enemies: there were plenty of verses that obscured or contradicted the intended message. Clearly the pipeline would alter the environment of Alaska more profoundly than any other single project in its history, causing ecological changes that science could hardly understand, let alone mitigate. The most trivial effect, but hardly unimportant, would be to pollute the state further with all the trash and clutter associated everywhere with the oil industry. A hint of that ugliness came from the detritus left by explorations in the Pet Four reserve: abandoned Quonset huts, rusty oil drums by the thousands, roads carved chaotically across the tundra, industrial man's garbage littering the land. For whatever mysterious reason the fossil-fuel eruption was, in every place it occurred, repulsively insulting to the earth's natural beauty. In the austere arctic one could see that insult from a long way off, and the cleansing processes would take much longer than in more temperate zones. Some sense of the immensely increased scale of that visual assault by the projected oil development came from news that the companies expected to dig up 83 million cubic yards of gravel for construction. If each of those yards were put in a box, the gravel would line up for 47,000 miles down the road. What the companies were proposing was not just unprecedented for Alaska; it was one of the largest construction projects in human history! Pipeline and fields together would occupy an area equal to some of the smaller states: the main Prudhoe Bay field would cover 350 square miles, the nearby fields another 500 square miles or so, and the pipeline 940 more, adding up to an area larger than Delaware. All the man-made structures had to be mounted on thick gravel pads so that their heat would not melt the permafrost, causing the ground to open up in muddy fissures, the structures to sink and collapse. The gravel padding must come from dredges scouring the river bottoms along the way, and a lot of aquatic life would die from the dredging. The pipeline itself would be a jumbo: four feet in diameter, insulated with an expensive metal and fiberglass jacket, the oil flowing inside at 145 degrees Fahrenheit (heated so high by the interior of the earth). In areas of permafrost, which covered more than half the distance to Valdez, it could not be buried underground, in the usual fashion, or it would melt the permafrost; therefore, it would have to be suspended many feet above the surface on strong vertical legs, raising the pipe more than twice the height of a man or woman, topped off by thermal devices to dissipate heat into the air—all of this at a sizable cost the companies had failed to foresee. Then it would stretch like a silver Chinese wall across the entire state of Alaska. How would the migrating caribou, or the elk, martens, bears, and all of the rest of the animal kingdom react to its presence? Would they learn to creep under it and carry on their lives as before, or would they change their patterns of movement, their eating and reproducing, perhaps catastrophically? Over its nearly 800 miles the pipeline would need ten pumping stations to keep the oil flowing; each of them must be a smaller version of the industrial sprawl at the fields them-selves, with pipes looping in and out, generators humming, barbed-wire fences surrounding each site for security against any saboteurs. Along the route the pipeline must make several hundred river and stream crossings, and not lose oil into any watershed or it might destroy the fisheries. It must also surmount some of the most rugged mountain slopes on the North American continent. The companies knew all that, but what they did not adequately appreciate before the EIS was that they must go through an extremely active seismic zone, and that their terminal site at Valdez, where the oil would flow into great holding tanks for transship-ment, would be sitting in the Gulf of Alaska's earthquake zone, where a quake twice as intense as the one that had destroyed San Francisco in 1906 had recently occurred and where more would occur every three to five years. So the aesthetic assault from massive industrial development was only a part of the total consequences of the project. Trash could be collected, structures might be designed more attractively, but how did the companies propose to safeguard the whole intricate web of life in the state? Did they even remotely understand it? Despite self-assured claims to expertise, they had failed completely to consider such risks until the government, under court orders secured by environmentalists, did it for them.

The most vulnerable part of the corporate project was inexplicably the least considered: shipping the oil from Valdez to global markets. The scheme involved using a fleet of 41 tankers owned by the various Alyeska consortium companies, which would make more than a thousand port calls a year to pick up the oil. The companies had no doubts about their safety and reliability. Yet by the time the revised EIS appeared, a number of ghastly tanker accidents had occurred, spilling oil into the sea in a deadly black tide: Most notable among them were the wreck of the *Torrey Canyon* in 1967, spilling thirty million gallons (about 100,000 tons), killing 40,000 to 100,000 birds off the Cornish coast, and of the *Argo Merchant* in 1976, spilling seven million gallons over the Georges Bank off New England; and then there was the blow-out of an offshore well at Santa Barbara, California, in 1969, which blackened the beaches for forty miles. The likelihood of such accidents, and the scale of their danger, was increasing with the increasing size of tankers and offshore platforms. On the horizon were supertankers capable of carrying 800,000 tons, vessels so large they required over a mile to come to a full stop and could be maneuvered only by the most sophisticated equipment and crews. But the oil spilled so dramatically, so hugely, by accident was nothing compared with the oil leaked regularly into the marine ecosystem during normal shipping operations—over a million tons a year from routine flushing of tanks at sea, dumping ballast into harbors, and the like.[45] In its first abbreviated draft the impact statement had completely ignored that aspect of the pipeline project, and William Ruckelshaus, administrator of the Environmental Protection Agency, had criticized his Interior colleagues severely for the omission. So did the Army Corps of Engineers, which complained that the statement did not (1) adequately assess the ecological consequences from the project, (2) provide sufficient data showing that the immediate development of Alaska's oil was essential to national security, or (3) estimate the cleanup costs from an oil spill at sea and determine who would bear them.[46] Now the government, covering the vulnerable flanks of the companies, scrambled to prove that the use of tankers would present no great problem.

In its final state the EIS spoke the obvious truth that it would be hard to predict how many accidental spills from tanker collisions might occur in any year, but it took an optimistic view of their potential size and damage. Coast Guard data indicated that only 0.00015 percent of all the oil transferred on the globe was spilled in the loading process, another 0.00009 percent accidentally discharged into open water. Most oil traveled safely from port to port, and so would the North Slope oil (though it was coming out of a much riskier environment than any other oil had ever done). When the fields were at maximum production, the terminal at Valdez would collect about two million gallons a day from the pipeline and then pump it down a hillside from its tank farms into tankers docking at four berths; the biggest tanker would hold 265,000 deadweight tons, or almost three times the amount of oil spilled by the *Torrey Canyon*. By calculating the amount of oil annually going out of the port, and by using those Coast Guard percentages, the statement concluded that Alyeska might spill as many as 140,000 barrels a year into the ocean, though that would be a "worst case" scenario, unlikely ever to happen because the consortium would use only the most modern tankers available, outfitted with double hulls and the finest navigation equipment, and would enjoy uncluttered sea lanes. More "normal case" projections indicated that only one collision or grounding on a reef might occur per year with the Alaska fleet. The government relayed Alyeska's own estimate that in such a collision some 40,000 to 50,000 barrels, at most, might leak out, hardly anything to worry about compared with those other disasters. "Equipment and planned procedures for Port Valdez," the statement went on, "are at the current state of the art." To be sure, that art could not be described as highly advanced anywhere; using the best cleanup equipment, only 5 percent of any spilled oil could be recovered, the rest would disperse into the ecosystem. That low recovery rate might be improved on in some parts of the earth, but not in Alaska, for reasons partly geographical, partly technological, partly economic:

> Large spills in Prince William Sound would be more difficult to contain, clean up, and restore because of the distances from sources of ships and cleanup gear and the generally limited available manpower in the region. The U.S. Coast Guard does not consider it necessary to require the terminal operator to have equipment immediately available to respond to every possible spill, but they do state that plans and arrangements should be made to provide full response equipment for the maximum possible spill within 12 hours of spillage at any point in the area. (p. 175)

So if a spill occurred at the Valdez end of the pipeline, it supposedly would be small and addressed by the best response teams money could hire, but inevitably they would have to come a long way to the scene. Therefore, in the event of an accident most of the oil would escape, and it would be acutely poisonous to all marine organisms.[47]

Spilled into the sea the hydrocarbons would act on organisms like alcohol in the human bloodstream, causing an initial state of inebriation, then a complete respiratory failure; where they did not kill, they would cause cancers and interfere with reproduction. Salmon fishermen could expect to lose fish and markets, as the spilled oil concentrated up the food chain like DDT, bound in proteins and fatty tissues all the way up to the human consumer. Economic losses to the coastal salmon fishery could amount to $400,000 a year. And the $17 million shellfish industry in Prince William Sound, which harvested a restaurateur's cornucopia of clams, oysters, and Dungeness crabs, could expect some losses too. But nowhere, the statement concluded, would the losses—at least the quantifiable marketplace ones—be so large as to outweigh all the fabulous economic benefits that North Slope oil development would bring to the state.[48]

The environmental impact statement process was never intended to resolve any cost-benefit issues or to make definitive economic assessments and judgments, but this one did. Even after substantial revision, it was a document of advocacy, demonstrating once more that the Nixon administration was, as Congressman Les Aspin grumbled, "acting as little more than a subsidiary of the oil companies."[49] By the terms of the 1969 law the government must also consider whether there were better alternatives to the proposed project. In their first version the EIS team had failed to do that, but in the revision they included a brief survey of possibilities. One of them was conspicuously absent: the option of stopping all development and of learning to live without Alaskan oil. Politically and economically, they could not look on that as a rational choice. But the government did admit that the pipeline might follow a route the oil companies had never considered: across Canada to the city of Edmonton, where it could connect with existing pipelines serving both Canadian and American consumers. In other words, there were two broad choices: a trans-Alaska pipeline (TAP), already surveyed, or a trans-Canada one (TCP), as yet unsurveyed and undetermined. The statement listed five such alternative TCP corridors, but the most promising, it indicated, were either to go up the Mackenzie River valley from the arctic coast, after crossing the Arctic National Wildlife Refuge, or to go from Fairbanks to Delta Junction, Alaska, following the Alaskan Highway and an old military pipeline route, thence past Whitehorse and on across Canada. As far as any adverse environmental impact was concerned, the statement was unequivocal; clearly the best way was to go somewhere through Canada, probably through Delta Junction, a route that would require fewer river crossings and miss all the active earthquake zones. Fish and wildlife populations would be less disturbed than by construction in pristine country. And best of all this route, like any of the Canadian ones, "would avoid the need of marine tanker shipping with its attendant oil spill threat." Did all those admitted benefits lead the Department of Interior to propose that the companies change their pipeline route? Not at all. Addressing the alternatives in less than a hundred pages out of six volumes, the statement did not really take seriously the responsibility of finding alternatives. Nor did the Department of Interior, nor anyone high up in the Nixon administration.

The non-government environmental organizations, however, which had pushed hard to have some alternatives discussed and researched, did not let those ideas lie forgotten. When Secretary Morton, a few weeks after receiving the revised EIS, approved the requested right-of-way, the environmentalists went back to the judges. This time they got a decision from the U.S. Court of Appeals invalidating Morton's permit, not on the real substance of their case, which had to do with ecological preservation, but on the grounds that the Mineral Leasing Act of 1920 specifically limited all pipeline rights-of-way to fifty feet on either side of the pipe and Morton had allowed many times that space in order for the companies to use their modern construction machinery.[50] Hardly anyone had ever observed that letter of the 1920 law, and Morton and the corporations had undoubtedly assumed they could do as they pleased too. No such luck. To their immense chagrin, they learned they must now trudge over to Congress and start the long process of getting the law changed, attending hearings, lobbying their friends, and making their case to the public. All the while that expensive pipe from Japan was lying on the ground among the spruces and lichens, rusting faster than they could treat it.

Corporate oil complained that the environmentalists were becoming obstructionists, and so they were. But obstructing whom? Were they obstructing the interests of the American people or merely that of the corporations? Naturally the corporations could see no distinction, but there was one, though in the turbulent, divided political climate of the early 1970s, no one could say for sure whether the environmentalists represented the public's interests or merely their own. Given enough say-so, they undoubtedly would have stopped all leasing and drilling for oil in the arctic. In their hearts they wanted to keep that part of Alaska unspoiled;

if pushed to choose, they would have preferred having the wilderness of Bob Marshall to the public ownership-with-development of Gifford Pinchot. Edgar Wayburn, former president of the Sierra Club, for example, pleaded to keep the whole great land of the north unspoiled, "as God made it." "I have not yet heard a careful evaluation of the immediate pressing need for this oil, yet we are acting as though we were already down to our last barrel. . . . The oil will run out—even as the gold did—whether it is fifty years from now, or sooner, or later; that resource is finite, and however much we try to do right by our oil development, the lands from which oil is removed will not again be the same. Protected wilderness, on the other hand, can remain forever as an increasingly attractive resource that will bring millions of people—and with them millions of dollars—to the state of Alaska: this is what might be called an infinite resource, perpetual money in the bank."[51] But the ideal of wilderness preservation was not one that could stop the fossil fuel juggernaut, and generally the environmentalists knew it. They understood the limits of the power of their ideas. No doubt they had acquired a political clout that the oil companies had badly misjudged, but all the same it was a limited power, the power to obstruct temporarily and force an open debate, the power to bring attention to alternative routes of development.

Through the remainder of 1972 and most of 1973 the pipeline dominated the environmentalists' national agenda. Joining forces in an Alaska Public Interest Coalition spearheaded by the Wilderness Society, they campaigned to get the enlarged right-of-way rejected and the oil brought down through Canada. They had many coastal fishermen on their side. Opposing them were the most powerful political and economic forces in the country. The Nixon-Agnew team had won a landslide reelection to the White House in the fall and were as adamant as ever that the project must go through. In Congress the leaders of the critical committees were ready to grant the enlarged right-of-way with no delay: Senator Henry M. Jackson, chairman of the Committee on Interior and Insular Affairs, and Congressman John Melcher, chairman of the Subcommittee on Public Lands of the House's Committee on Interior and Insular Affairs, both Democrats, both for oil development, though Jackson had been the principal architect of the National Environmental Protection Act. Alaska's delegates, Senators Ted Stevens and Mike Gravel and Congressman Don Young, were emphatically for TAP. And all the energy companies, among the richest corporations in America, had their numerous, well-paid lobbyists and lawyers hard at work to get their way. The major, and tensest, battleground was the Senate. There, Gravel and Stevens introduced a bill to let TAP go through, while Jackson introduced his own bill, and

Melcher submitted one to the other chamber. Hearings began in May 1973, and by August the debate was over.

Up to this point the oil companies had only a shaky case to make for their route, chosen as it had been without any real consideration of the alternatives or of the environmental risks, based solely as it was on their desire for a speedy return on their billion-dollar-plus investment and on their eagerness to reach lucrative overseas markets. Only a long tradition of deferring to their expertise had saved them from hard questions from the government. Senator Jackson, in his committee's report supporting the companies, tried to put the case on more compelling ground by arguing that the nation's vital economic interests were at stake. "There is now an obvious and growing deficiency in domestic production of crude oil and natural gas," the report maintained, "leading to a rapidly increasing dependence upon insecure Eastern Hemisphere imports." America, not merely British Petroleum, needed the oil and needed it fast. In 1973 the United States imported 36.3 percent of its petroleum from overseas, compared with 23.2 percent in 1970. The appetite for this energy resource was growing faster than domestic supplies could satisfy. In 1970 the nation's demand was 14.9 million barrels a day, and it was leaping ahead at a rate of 3 to 4 percent a year, while that same year domestic production peaked and then began to decline. Historically, the country was entering a strange new era of vulnerability, as it began to search the world over for the energy needed to gratify its desires. Other industrial societies had long been doing likewise, but Americans were not used to such dependency on foreign others and, as the report indicated, they were deeply fearful of it. They thought of themselves as self-reliant, independent, beyond the reach of the rest of the world, but they were desperate for a substance they could not live without. Alaska's oil, it was hoped, might slow that increasing dependency and put off the day of reckoning with their weakness. Answering that hope, the pipeline must go through as fast as possible, no matter what the environmental consequences.

> Regardless whether the 1969 decision of the owner companies in favor of an all-Alaska route was the wisest or the most consistent with the national interest at that time, and regardless whether the Administration's early commitment in favor of that route was made on the basis of adequate information and analysis, *the Committee determined that the Trans-Alaska pipeline is now clearly preferable, because it could be on stream two to six years earlier than a comparable overland pipeline across Canada.* (emphasis in original)[52]

In an oblique way Jackson's committee was admitting that corporate oil might not have gone to the North Slope for the welfare of the United

States, and indeed it had not. If any nation was expected to benefit from the discovery, in so far as lessening their dependence on insecure suppliers was considered, that nation was Japan. But now, in the face of the rising reform spirit of environmentalism, the committee would not propose despoiling the arctic for Japan. They claimed all the oil for the United States, even wanted to stipulate in law that the oil must be sold to Americans only, and worked themselves up to a sense of national crisis. They were more prescient than they knew, for later in that same year, after the pipeline debate was over, the oil-exporting Arab nations suddenly turned off the energy spigot in retaliation for American support of Israel; and through the winter of 1973–74 the country felt the full pain of its foreign dependency. The American position in the world no longer looked the same after that embargo, neither its power and affluence nor its independence and sovereignty. But that traumatic embargo only confirmed an insecurity that Washington professed to feel months earlier in the pipeline controversy.

Standing against Henry Jackson and his supporters and against the Nixon administration were two liberal senators, Walter Mondale of Minnesota and Birch Bayh of Indiana, and several congressmen, including Morris Udall of Arizona, John Anderson of Illinois, and John Saylor of Pennsylvania, all recognized as political spokesmen for the environmental movement. All agreed on the desirability of developing North Slope oil but wanted to explore carefully the option of going through Canada, and therefore collaborated on several bills that would delay issuance of a right-of-way until the National Academy of Sciences could make a thorough study of the Canadian routes and Washington could negotiate with Ottawa. Government, they insisted, must play its proper role in formulating policies relating to foreign commerce, the public lands, and the energy needs of the country, not merely follow the supposed expertise of the oil companies. Some, though not all of those TAP opponents, represented midwestern states, and they had a special plea to make. If the country was indeed becoming dangerously short of oil and dependent on uncertain foreign sources, that shortage was most acute in the Midwest, which was a long way from any domestic wells or refineries. Midwesterners paid some of the highest prices for energy in the Lower 48 states, yet none of the tankers shipping out of Valdez would be bringing relief to them. Instead, the oil would go to Seattle or Los Angeles, where there was already a surplus, necessitating another pipeline or two to carry that surplus inland. The truth of those arguments was verified several years later, when the *New York Times* reported that, due to an 800,000 barrel-a-day surplus projected on the West Coast by the year 1980, the Sohio company (part of BP) had applied to build a pipeline from southern California to Texas and the Gulf Coast; their best market, they now admitted, was in the Midwest, and a new southern pipeline would be a cheaper way to it than sending tankers around Cape Horn or through the Panama Canal.[53]

Support for Mondale et al. came from an academic economist, Charles Cicchetti, who did the only thorough, independent scholarly analysis of the TAP vs. TCP alternatives. After verifying that the Canadian route would indeed be ecologically superior to the all-Alaskan, he went on to discover, much to his surprise, that going through Canada would also be more economically rational. True, the TCP would be as much as 2000 miles longer, depending on the route chosen, though not if one considered any further pipelines needed from the West Coast inland. Total construction costs, however, were roughly comparable, when one added in the Valdez terminal, tanker fleet, and West Coast facilities required by TAP; "most current estimates," Cicchetti noted, "show the total difference to be less than $1 billion." Offsetting that expense would be the higher profits to be earned by bringing oil to the Midwest, which would earn the companies $3 billion more (figured at a 10 percent discount rate, or $16 billion undiscounted) over the life of the project. That the corporations would pass up such earnings required explanation. Cicchetti surmised that they were still counting on being permitted to sell North Slope oil to Japan, or to make some sort of import-for-export swap that would allow them to take their oil to high-priced overseas markets. Then too, a delay of "two to seven years" (according to Henry Jackson's committee) if they went across Canada would mean they would not make any profits nor be able to recoup their investment on drilling rigs and pipe for a while, nor would they be able to pay off loans quickly. In other words, their determination to take the more environmentally risky route was due to short-term economic accounting and a desire to show an immediate and high return on investment in their annual reports to stockholders. From their own point of view that might seem a rational weighing of options, even if it meant lower long-term profits, but by any broader, national method of accounting that determination was decidedly irrational.[54]

There was still another reason why "Big Oil," as its critics began to name it, was opposed to crossing Canadian territory to get to the best American markets. Historically the Canadian federal government had been rather less deferential to their interests than the American government. In 1959 the Canadians had established a National Energy Board, with jurisdiction over all pipelines, a power that made the companies considerably edgy. Canadians were known to be increasingly resentful of economic imperialists crossing the border from the south and buying up their resources, undermining their independence. In some of the western provinces a left-wing group, the New Democratic Party (NDP), was waxing in strength, and among their objectives was establishing public control over any and all "common carriers," from railroads to pipelines, and public ownership of the oil industry; perhaps, if they gained more power, the Canadian government might some day try to nationalize American investments. The current government in Ottawa was Liberal, the Prime Minister was Pierre Trudeau. First elected in 1968, he was forced after 1972 into an alliance with NDP to preserve his majority; though no nationalizer, he was a good deal more threatening to the private oil companies than Nixon and the conservative Republicans, who had been in executive power through most of the postwar era. In other words, there were more "socialists up there," and to send oil through their domain might be like returning to the heyday of American progressivism when Theodore Roosevelt and Gifford Pinchot fulminated against the "irresponsible trusts" and embraced the ideals of public ownership and development of natural resources.[55]

Even members of Canada's Conservative party were making hostile noises about North Slope oil. In 1971 during House of Commons debates over Alaskan oil development, a Conservative member from Prince River, Alberta, had presented a resolution opposing the TAP and tanker scheme "because of the ecological dangers . . . to the people, towns, and cities of British Columbia and the natural resources of Canada's western seas and coasts." He wanted a study of better routes and accused the Trudeau government of failing to move fast enough to work one out with the Americans. Jean Chrétien, Minister of Indian Affairs and Northern Development, replied for the government that they were, in fact, studying the entire arctic oil picture, but moving slowly, carefully, deliberately. "The United States," he declared, "first started by shipping pipe to Alaska, but here in Canada we started by undertaking research." In due course Canada would get its pipelines built, and they might be available to carry the Alaskan flow, "but not at any price. . . . [I]n developing the north we will not repeat the errors we have made in the south," where both the environment and the resident native peoples had been severely affected. "Last year," Chrétien continued, "we passed the Arctic Water Pollution Prevention Act because we were afraid that technology which could be applied in the Arctic ocean was not sufficiently advanced to assure safety." In contrast to the United States, the debate in Canada over northern fossil-fuel development centered on which political party would be the most cautious and protective, and no one wailed that getting the oil out so slowly was tantamount to national suicide.[56]

Canada had its own glittering prospects in the north, mainly in the Mackenzie River valley, which emptied into the Beaufort Sea about three hundred miles east of Prudhoe Bay. There was five times as much sedimentary rock in northern Canada as in Alaska, and only seismic surveys could indicate how much of it might bear fossil fuels; likely there was a vast wealth of natural gas, greater perhaps than petroleum, up there. In any event a pipeline, or several of them, would be needed one day to bring the energy to urban consumers. The American oil companies, with their much larger capital, might be useful in developing those resources. A pipeline corridor from Prudhoe to Mackenzie, then another one up the Mackenzie valley to the Alberta border, would at once concentrate the environmental disruption and allow an international pooling of capital and technology. Despite their cautious, skeptical stance toward American oil companies, the Canadian government was by no means hostile to the notion of striking a deal. In March 1973 the Energy Minister, Donald Macdonald, stated on nationwide television:

> If the Americans came back and said to us, "Look, we've had second thoughts on the trans-Alaska pipeline, we would like to take you up on your willingness to entertain an application about the oil line through the Mackenzie route," I think the interest of the West Coast [of Canada] would dictate that the government of Canada should enable that kind of application to go ahead.

However, his position, and that generally of the Canadian government, was consistently misrepresented to the American people by the Nixon administration. Officials falsely claimed that Trudeau insisted on majority Canadian ownership of any oil pipeline; they warned that the Canadians would restrict American use of a common pipeline to make room for themselves (though they would have no oil ready to flow from the arctic for the foreseeable future); and the White House suppressed the news that the Canadians had offered to make up any temporary shortfall caused by building along the Canadian route by increasing their exports to the United States.[57] In 1973 Canada sent 365,370,000 barrels of oil over the border, more than Saudi Arabia or Venezuela, and it was ready to sell more at a fair price.[58] The North American trade in oil was well established, so that the United States faced nothing new or untried. Yet for all the reassurances, the Canadian political climate made the oil companies nervous, and they were determined to avoid any possibility of further interference in their business, a determination they telegraphed to Washington.

What they must have been afraid of—the specter of restriction and strict regulation—became reality one year after the trans-Alaska pipeline debate. In 1974 Prime Minister Trudeau sent a commissioner to the Mackenzie valley to examine local attitudes about development, specifically the construction of a natural gas pipeline. The commissioner was Thomas R. Berger, a distinguished federal justice, and he took his responsibility quite seriously, holding hearings in 35 communities that year and into the next, listening to almost one thousand northerners representing four races, speaking seven different languages. What he heard was a little enthusiasm and a lot of anxiety and hostility, enough to give him doubts about the pace of gas and oil development. The title of his report, *Northern Frontier, Northern Homeland,* captured exactly that mixed sense of promise and threat. The promise was almost all one made to industrial society located far to the south, while the threat would come to those northern humans and nonhumans dwelling in the path of a boom. Berger feared massive declines in the fauna if development was not controlled: for example, the Porcupine caribou herd, numbering some 110,000 animals, which annually migrated to calving grounds along the coastal plain, might be severely threatened by drilling and pumping in their territory. Berger advised that companies not be permitted to build any pipelines at all from Prudhoe Bay across any of the Northern Yukon area and that the government establish large wilderness areas and wildlife sanctuaries to protect those vulnerable animal communities. But it was the native people that most concerned him, the Dene, Inuit, and Metis, who had never gotten a fair, sympathetic hearing from the government and whose land claims had still not been settled. Massive industrial development would bring an influx of white construction workers into their midst, along with alcoholism, an unraveling of the social fabric, injury to the land on which they depended for food, and the loss of their identity as a people. Their life of hunting, fishing, and trapping, a life based almost wholly on renewable resources, would give way to one based on the money economy and nonrenewable resources. They would be compelled by the disruption to accept temporary employment at unskilled wages; then, as the construction ended, they would be left unemployed and dependent on welfare. "The evidence is clear," he wrote, "the more the industrial frontier displaces the homeland in the North, the greater the incidence of social pathology will be."[59] Consequently, he recommended that even the Mackenzie valley pipeline be postponed for a period of ten years to give time for developing a more diversified economy in which natives would have more control over their lives and a brighter future. Ten whole years of delay. (In fact, there would be no pipeline through the valley as late as 1990.) The Canadian government, following such advice, would move with so much deliberation as to seem hopelessly lethargic to any go-getter

American oil crew. Berger may have been on high moral ground in his recommendations for a strictly regulated, much delayed pace of northern oil
and gas development, and the Canadian government too. But that attitude was precisely what the American oil companies deeply feared. Avoid
Canada then. Stay safely in Alaska, where the industrial frontier spirit
would dominate and rule.

The fear of falling under Canadian domination extended beyond the
oil corporations to a significant, vocal part of the American population.
For a people so determined to win markets abroad, they were crazily sus-
picious of foreigners and of any entangling trade alliances, even with so
decent a neighbor as Canada. If that nation had its own virulent nationalism, so did the United States. Never mind the fact that we boasted a
long, open, undefended border with our neighbor to the north, or that we
shared so much culturally and economically with them. Never mind that
we already depended on them for a large part of our energy resources. A
new pipeline through their territory would give them a dangerous weapon
to use against us. As a citizen of Fairbanks wrote:

> However friendly Canada now is, and however much we may hope this rela-
> tionship continues, we are placing in a foreign country a commodity vital to our
> survival as a nation. As such, this is a temptation to a power and/or a philos-
> ophy antagonistic to both our countries to act in a manner which could lead to
> open hostilities, or at least, be subversive.[60]

Canada "foreign" or "subversive"? Only to the country's paranoids. Of
course, there was no way to refute the unreason of such fears, though one
could note that Alaskan oil would all be used up long, long before any
remotely conceivable possibility of actual war between the two countries.
Or one could direct attention to the fact that shipping its oil by sea would
put America in far greater jeopardy to hostile powers than any pipeline
through Edmonton.

More sober, calculating residents of Alaska had other reasons for keeping the pipeline wholly within their borders, reasons that had to do with
jobs and state revenues. On the latter, Alaskans feared that any delay or
any rise in construction costs would affect their royalty payments, which
were figured on the market price of oil minus transportation costs.[61] The
state saw its interest inextricably tied up with that of the Alyeska consortium. Even so, as the controversy wound on and on, and no revenue
materialized, a number of state leaders began to express some resentment
of the oil leviathan. In 1971 the state established a Joint Pipeline Impact
Commission, and its chairman, a Democrat from Anchorage, Chancy
Croft, confessed that "economic conflict between the State of Alaska and

the oil industry is inevitable." He and others were aware that they were dealing with one of the most powerful groups of men in the world, enjoying "a monopoly or near-monopoly control of the product," from producing to refining to selling. More outspoken yet was the state's attorney general, John Havelock, who protested to a congressional committee that "we have been told that our proper role is to get out there and block while industry runs with the ball. Our role, the owners suggest, is simply to make things easy for them so that they can carry out their plans with the least difficulty." Everything we want to do, he went on, is in their eyes either unconstitutional or financially risky. The companies seemed to be unresponsive to state interests, protected as they were by their many tax breaks and lack of accountability, unwilling to make the state a full partner in their enterprise. "In this current period of adjustment," Havelock said, we find ourselves bargaining over who's going to wear the pants and carry the wallet."[62]

Behind that resentment was a failed history of state regulation of oil, a history that showed that it was industry actually wearing the pants and carrying the wallet. During 1972 as many as two dozen pipeline-related bills came before the state legislature, four of them becoming law, including a Right-of-Way Leasing Act, an Alaska Pipeline Commission Act (setting up a commission similar to the federal Interstate Commerce Commission), and a severance tax on oil. The first of those was the one most fiercely fought by the oil companies, though it was a comparatively mild substitute for another bill proposed by none other than the Republican governor William Egan, who had been reelected when Hickel went to Washington. Egan wanted the state to take over the entire pipeline project, to build and operate it as a public property (echoes of Pinchotism!), but the idea was, as one industry lobbyist put it, too "revolting" for words. Like the progressives of another day, Egan compromised on an adjustable leasing scheme that would peg fees at the market price of oil; naturally, the companies went to court, and they succeeded in getting an injunction against it, followed by its repeal when conservative Republicans regained the majority in the legislature. But there for a brief while Alaska's own legislature seemed on the way to acting mighty feisty, replacing, as one editor put it, "the federal hierarchy as the chief impediment to the start of pipeline construction."[63]

So far the oil industry, however initially unprepared for all the controversies, had managed to cobble together an effective defense. They had, though with some difficulty, kept the state of Alaska properly deferential, and they had recruited some of the most powerful men in Washington to their side. They had found a compelling battle cry to drown out all criticism and opposition, "Remember the energy crisis."[64] Now the companies would clinch a final victory. On 13 July 1973 the Senate took up a Mondale-Bayh amendment that would have made Congress responsible for selecting the route for transporting North Slope oil, and the Senate voted it down. On 17 July the bill proposed by Henry Jackson, giving the Secretary of Interior general discretionary power to grant rights-of-way (including one for the TAP), came to the floor for a vote. Senator Gravel introduced an amendment that would completely exempt the pipeline from the National Environmental Protection Act, the first such exemption sought in the act's four-year life span. Jackson, proud father of NEPA, opposed it, but it passed on a vote of 49 to 48. Another amendment, offered by William Hathaway of Maine, to make any company spilling oil fully liable for all damages was withdrawn under the urging of Jackson, who wanted to leave such matters to the states. Then back to Jackson's own bill. This time the vote was 49 to 49, with Senator Alan Cranston, who had abstained on the Gravel amendment, joining the Mondale nays.[65] So a tie vote, and the tension in the chamber mounted. Senators were exactly divided between those who wanted to give industry its head and those who wanted government to take command. Then the presiding officer of the Senate, Vice President Spiro Agnew, broke the tie by voting yea. It was only one of Agnew's many dramatic moments in the national spotlight, and in a few months he would resign from office, a picture of disgrace and corruption. Those voting in the majority with him were mostly the Senate's business-minded conservatives, including several members still present a decade and a half later: Lloyd Bentsen, Robert Byrd, Pete Dominici, Jesse Helms, Daniel Inouye, Sam Nunn, Ted Stevens, and several soon-to-be-retired members such as Harry Byrd, James Eastland, Sam Ervin, Barry Goldwater, and John Tower. The losing side counted among its numbers such long-term incumbents as Cranston, Joseph Biden, Robert Dole, Mark Hatfield, Teddy Kennedy, Robert Packwood, Claiborne Pell, and Robert Stafford, along with Mondale, Edmund Muskie, William Proxmire, Hubert Humphrey, and Frank Church. The final vote on the pipeline was the closest taken on a major issue in that session, and for that matter in many sessions, but it decided in a twinkling the fate of the Alaskan environment.

On 2 August the House of Representatives took up John Melcher's bill to grant a right-of-way and voted strongly for it. In the conference that followed Jackson's became the only bill, and by fall both houses had voted in favor of it once more and sent the legislation on to President Nixon, who on 16 November signed the measure to make it Public Law 93-153. In final form the act imposed liability of up to $100 million for any oil spill at sea—none for land spills—to be paid by a tax of five cents a barrel loaded on vessels at Valdez. The President was requested to determine the feasibility of acquiring energy from other sources that would make tanker shipments unnecessary and to explore the willingness of Canada to permit construction of new pipelines to carry North Slope oil across its territory, not as substitutes for TAP but as additions to it; for Henry Jackson insisted we would soon need every pipeline we could get.

Away then to the great north country of Alaska, to the land of sprawling gravel bars and muskeg, of glaciers crashing into the sea and mountain sheep skipping among the high rocks, to the land where Caterpillar tractors could be heard revving up their engines, eager for motion, where thousands of sections of pipe happily awaited the welders who would make them into a single steel ribbon, where men were flocking to look for jobs and legislators were hungry for much delayed revenue. During the winter of 1973-74 the Alyeska consortium set up construction camps north of the Yukon River, waiting for spring weather to begin the promethean task. At the peak of construction, in August 1975, over 21,000 workers were operating out of 31 construction camps along the route. They lived as hard and fast as they worked. Away then to Fairbanks and Anchorage, where the whores and pimps took their money and the bars were open all night.[66]

On 20 June 1977 the first oil entered the pipeline at Prudhoe Bay's Pump Station No. 1. It reached the Valdez terminal on 28 July and was sloshing to market aboard a tanker by 1 August. Almost immediately after that heroic opening one of the pump stations blew up, killing a man, forcing the operation to run at less than full capacity for a while. Within four years, though, the oil was flowing again at a rapid rate of 1.6 million barrels a day, and then at 2.0 million barrels. When finished and operating at capacity, the pipeline had cost $9 billion, eighteen times its earliest estimate.

By 1990 more than seven billion barrels had flowed through the long pipe, zig-zagging over mountains, burrowing under rivers, riding high through the spruce and aspen forests. Seven billion barrels may have seemed like a lot of oil, but in fact it was only enough to furnish a twelve-month supply for the United States. Spread out over more than a decade of production, that flow satisfied only a rather small portion of the nation's total demand, a little more than 10 percent. And by 1990 North Slope production had already peaked; the end of the vast arctic fields was already in sight.[67] And, most disturbing of all, America was no nearer to energy independence than before. All the early claims promising freedom from foreign suppliers proved to be empty rhetoric. At the time the pipeline won authorization, imports constituted 36.3 percent of the nation's total petroleum supply; by 1987, imports had risen to 44.4 percent. The only comeback the pipeline supporters had to their critics' complaints about dissembling was that, without the North Slope, the nation's dependence on imports would have been even greater. Had we left all the arctic oil in the ground, America would have been a full 10 percent more vulnerable to whatever demons were lurking in the world. Ten percent more at the mercy of those crazed, unreasonable, vindictive, tyrannizing Saudi and British, Nigerian and Canadian, Indonesian and Latin American producers.

Winning even that thinnish degree of energy independence required a massive industrial structure that had to be visited to be fully appreciated. Hardly any one did so, of course—it was too far north. Now and then, however, a lone Winnebago would jolt over the 300-mile Dalton highway to the oil fields, its driver stopping to admire the glistening pipe and read the billboards extolling the spectacular achievement it represented, arriving at road's end to find no restaurants, motels, or campgrounds, nor even any entry to the fields. But he or she could manage, if persistent, to glimpse the broad homely face of industrialization grinning all across the tundra landscape, as far as the eye could gaze: dozens and dozens of metal-walled well houses clustered around separation plants where the mixture of gas, hot oil, and water coming out of the ground was separated, the gas and water drawn off for reinjection into the ground (there is no natural gas pipeline to this date), the oil sent humming to the pumping station. A spaghetti tangle of pipes linking all those structures together, criss-crossing the tundra in every direction, like a massive engine turned inside out. The sparkle of permafrost melt ponds among the drab metal buildings. Immense stilt-legged, prefabricated dormitories for the work crews, housing movie theatres and cafeterias, volleyball courts and full-grown trees under glass. Dorms housing several hundred men and women workers, some white, some nonwhite, a few natives among them, all living in an automated technological cocoon, as insulated from the forces of nature as the crew of the *Starship Enterprise*. Heavy tractor-trailer rigs rumbling down the Spine Road, stirring up gray clouds of dust or snow, stopping now and then to let a caribou cross. And the caribou wandering through what had once been their home, looking as bewildered and misplaced as a family of peasants swallowed up by the encroaching metropolis.

As oil fields go, the Prudhoe Bay complex was astonishingly neat and clean. The companies knew they were on public display and that all those hypercritical environmentalists were waiting for them to make a mess. In response, they boasted a new kind of competence—"ecologically sensitive development in the arctic." They claimed the caribou would bounce back in numbers, learning to love ARCO and British Petroleum, and certainly the big gassy trucks seemed less a burden to the animals than the maddening mosquitoes that often drove them straight into the ocean. Looking ahead to the day of depletion, the companies strenuously began lobbying Congress and the public to get the nearby coastal plain of the Arctic National Wildlife Refuge opened to them, a flat, treeless stretch of 125 miles, the only part of the nation's long arctic coastline not yet open to oil leasing. During the brief summer that plain became a gathering place for millions of water birds, tens of thousands of caribou, hundreds of musk oxen and wolves. Although the Canadian government, following Thomas Berger's report, had urged that the United States protect it all as wilderness, the oil industry was vehemently opposed. Beneath the plain, said corporate executives, might lie 3.2 billion recoverable barrels of oil, though the Department of Interior admitted that the chance of finding such a field was only one in five. Let us in to drill and explore, insisted the executives, don't lock up valuable resources. The drumbeat of all-out, rapid development began anew: "America is terribly dependent on overseas supplies, our economic independence and security are once more in jeopardy, the Arctic Refuge can save us from capricious forces in the Middle East." Critics answered that the environmental cost of getting that petroleum into urban gas tanks, the endangerment of the continent's finest remaining wildlife spectacle, was far too high. Must we lay the dead hand of industrialism on this last unspoiled coast? If oil is found, they asked, will it furnish anything more than brief gulp or two? When all the deposits along the entire North Slope have been exhausted, will the United States be more or less independent of foreign producers? In 1990 nearly half the nation's supply came from abroad, and that situation would not improve no matter how much wilderness was destroyed in frenzied consumption. In *The Quiet Crisis,* former Secretary of Interior Stewart Udall wrote, "In Alaska we have a magnificent opportunity to show more respect for wilderness and wildlife values than our forebears. The wonders of the wilderness still abound there; if we spoil them, we cannot excuse their defilement with pleas of ignorance." Corporate oil responded by claiming they had now learned to show respect and that Americans could trust them completely, trust their managerial skill both to preserve nature and to deliver the oil. "After 20 years of activity on the North Slope," claimed a company brochure, "the oil industry has proven it can operate without harming the environment."[68]

The short historical record at Prudhoe Bay held a few revealing, if controversial, answers as to which side was right. The place looked neat enough, if thoroughly uninviting, but the subtle, underlying ecological realities of the place were not so reassuring. Without looking at its off-shore operations or its effects on subsistence hunting and fishing or on the health and safety problems of its workers, the oil complex had a weak environmental record, even here in this highly public showcase. First, there was more water pollution going on than the casual Winnebago or airline tourist was aware of. Over the years the companies dumped millions of gallons of used drilling muds and other wastes in 250 holding pits, many of which leaked, or they sprayed those wastes on roads and across the tundra, wastes laden with heavy metals (aluminum, cadmium, lead, and so on), hydrocarbons, and other toxic substances. In a recent two-year period almost 1000 spills of various fuels and oils had occurred, polluting the tundra ponds, diminishing the diversity and abundance of the food on which birds depended. Second, there was extensive air pollution. North Slope operations emitted as much nitrogen oxide in a year as the city of Washington, D.C., and a high amount of sulfur dioxides too; together these caused acidification of the tundra vegetation. Before any pumping began, scientists warned about the heavy fogs in the area—the phenomenon of "arctic haze"—which might pick up the oxides and then deposit them in the form of polluted droplets, as acidic as vinegar, killing the blue-green algae and the lichens on which caribou feed. The warnings had become realities. Third, there was a staggering amount of solid waste generated by the oil fields, ranging from worn-out batteries and tires to scrap metal and styrofoam. Most of it went into local landfills, some of them under investigation by the Environmental Protection Agency for toxicity. None of this should have been surprising, though it might not have been obvious even to the loyal, well-meaning stall who operated the fields; after all, no modern industrial complex spread over an area the size of Delaware could be altogether benign. Even with Big Oil's best efforts, performed for public relations or not, those impacts would be hard to avoid. Realizing that and determined to contain them, environmentalists opposed extending the industrial complex and its pollution eastward into the Arctic Refuge.[69]

But once more, the fate of Alaska's environment would be a matter for the politicians in the nation's capital to decide. The refuge was wholly federal domain, the property of every American citizen, those with cars and those without. Was the nation, through its elected representatives, still as divided, as that 1973 Senate vote suggested, between the forces of preservation and of energy development? Between a deference to private industry and a call for government responsibility? Answers to those questions would depend heavily on the people's perception of the oil companies' vaunted expertise, their competence to manage the natural resources of the nation. It was the old question that Pinchot had raised so many years ago, though by the last decade of the twentieth century the ideal of competence had evolved considerably. Now competence had come to include not only efficient, economically rational management over the long term, with a just distribution of all the benefits, but also a management demonstrating ecological sensitivity and respect for the beauty and order of nature.

Any argument in favor of the government's competence must be largely speculative, for since Pinchot's departure from office, and especially after World War II, the government had played essentially a passive, accommodating role in Alaska. On the other hand, an argument in favor of corporate oil's competence to be left in charge of northern resources had somehow to ignore a history replete with naïveté, shortsightedness, economic irrationality, ignorance, imprudent and baseless expectations, reliance on public relations more than on substance. Under that corporate stewardship Americans had ended up with the most wasteful, inefficient system of fossil-fuel use among all the industrial nations of the world, using two or even three times as much energy to produce the same dollar value as they. Because of that inefficiency they contributed far more carbon pollution to the atmosphere than any other people, carbon that was turning the earth's atmosphere into a massive greenhouse, trapping solar radiation and raising the mean temperature of the entire planet, threatening massive dislocations in agriculture, threatening indeed their own food supply. Ironically, the global warming in progress by the end of the twentieth century might one day lead to the flooding of the entire arctic coast and the whole industrial complex up there, as the polar ice caps melted and the oceans rose, lapping over the land. Put a lot of responsibility for that catastrophe, if it came, on the private fossil-fuel industry in the United States, which had long pressed for mining and consuming resources as rapidly as possible. The ultimate form of incompetence is self-destruction, and Americans had to ask themselves whether, under the leadership of private oil, they had been driving hard in precisely that direction. Whatever the answer, and whatever the alternative to the dominion of private power might be, the oil industry had created a history filled with impressive political victories but also repeated, and considerable, economic and ecological ineptitude.

Just how inept the industry could be became clear on the night of 23 March 1989, when eleven million gallons of crude oil was accidentally dumped into Prince William Sound. That little mishap would make

Alaska more than ever the center of American debates over the fossil-fuel economy.

Nature Devastated

How many slugs of vodka would it take to devastate Planet Earth? It should not be impossible to calculate. We now know how many drinks it took to send a hapless ship captain slumping to his berth, leaving in charge of an oil tanker an unlicensed mate who, bewildered and panicked, proceeded to drive it across a submerged reef, tear a hole in its hull, and spill eleven million gallons of crude oil into pristine Prince William Sound of Alaska, killing a silent multitude of sea otters, herring, salmon, marine birds, and other organisms large and small—the worst such disaster in American history.

The tanker was the *Exxon Valdez*, newest in Exxon Corporation's fleet and outfitted with the most up-to-date navigational equipment to steer its lumbering 987 feet, almost a fifth of a mile from bow to stern. Over and over it had made runs between Long Beach, California, and Valdez, Alaska, without accident. So had its many sister ships transporting North Slope oil to market; together in the first dozen years of pipeline operation they had made over 9000 trips from the terminal to the refineries, with only a few minor spills; the process had come to epitomize flawless corporate planning and technical execution. Consequently, Exxon figured, on the basis of such an unblemished record, it could do with a smaller crew; the *Valdez* had aboard a skeleton complement of twenty, roughly one crew member for every 2.6 million gallons of capacity. On the way up from California the ship carried only ballast—a hold full of scummy seawater—which it vented at the terminal. Then in less than twenty-four hours of steady pumping it was filled with oil and ready to sail out again, down the same monotonous sea lanes it had traveled so many times before. Most of the crew, under company instructions to waste no time in turnaround, stayed aboard to supervise the oil pouring into the vast, empty, compartmented interior. When loaded, the tanker drew about 55 feet fore and aft, riding low in the water like a great bladder of one-inch steel.[70]

The captain, Joseph J. Hazelwood of Huntington, New York, a man in his early forties, balding with sideburns and a beard, was one of the few who had been allowed to go ashore. During the afternnon and evening of Thursday, 23 April 1989, he had made the rounds of Valdez's shabby little cafes, taking a few drinks with friends and relaxing before it was time to go back to sea. Around 8 p.m. a taxi dropped him at the terminal, and shortly after that the *Exxon Valdez* shoved off, with Hazelwood's lunch mate, the harbor pilot, at the wheel, steering them through the Narrows with its snow- and spruce-covered granite cliffs looming on either side. Then at 11:20 the pilot turned the navigation duties over to the captain and returned to the harbor. As the vessel plowed on toward the main waters of Prince William Sound and the Gulf of Alaska, Hazelwood noted a heavy flotilla of icebergs approaching on the starboard side, icebergs calving from the nearby Columbia glacier, some of them as big as houses, glistening like blue diamonds in the sunlight but now in the midnight hour a clutter of odd, sinister shapes. The normal practice in such situations, which were not all that unusual, was to slow down and maneuver carefully ahead, or to stop completely and wait until the lane was clear. But Hazelwood made a bizarrely different decision: he abruptly turned the tanker 180 degrees to port and, putting the engines at full throttle, plunged across the shipping lanes toward Bligh Island, then set the steering system on automatic pilot, trying to outflank the ice. More reckless yet, he yielded command to his inexperienced third mate and went below to his room. Four minutes after midnight the tanker bottom struck hard against submerged Bligh Reef, all lit up with red warning lights, then ground on for another 600 feet before halting. The underwater rock had torn a long gash through the single-hulled steel skin, rupturing over half the cargo compartments, and the oil in them spewed out in a thick black vomit. Over 250,000 barrels went into the water during the next few hours. It was Good Friday—and the twenty-fifth anniversay of the deadly earthquake that had hit Alaska in 1974. This time, however, the disaster was all man-made.[71]

"One drunken sailor" was a common lament heard after the spill, but in a spirit of charity we must remember that sailors have been getting drunk since the time of the Phoenicians; it's an old weakness, one we are unlikely ever to overcome. Hazelwood was surely drunk: a blood alcohol test performed on him at 9:30 a.m. (inexplicably more than nine hours after the accident) registered 0.061 percent, well above the Coast Guard's maximum of 0.04 for sobriety. Blood alcohol is eliminated from the human body at a rate of 0.015 percent per hour, so the captain may have been well soused as the tanker was charging onto the reef. His friend the harbor pilot had gotten a whiff or two of his breath but said nothing at the time, though like almost everyone else in the business, he must have known that Hazelwood had recently lost his driver's license in New York for drunkenness and had a long record of heavy tippling, even aboard ship, in violation of all the rules. But again in a spirit of charity we ought to admit that in this case the captain may have been driven to drink by the intense speedup and heavy overtime hours imposed by a corporation trying to cut costs. Something of that forgiving attitude must have animated the minds of the Anchorage jury that tried Hazelwood months later, for they let him off on the drunken negligence charge, pointing to insufficient scientific evidence.[72]

The historian is neither judge nor jury over the personal crimes of the past but tries to step back to discover the larger forces operating a magnify a private, age-old human weakness into a social and ecological catastrophe. He looks for a cultural explanation for our mounting environmental crisis, a clarification of its causes as they operated in the prismatic waters of Alaska.

As guilty as the captain, many said, were the men who employed him and who gave so many assurances to the public that they were fully competent to handle any spill in the event that he, a mere hired hand, failed. Exxon Corporation claimed it had devised "the perfect system" of emergency response, a plan impressively set forth by experts in complete technical detail, 28 volumes thick, and installed on company shelves in its Houston headquarters with a great deal of flourishing and posturing before the media. When the disaster came, however, the plan was almost completely useless; there was no alertness, no equipment ready, no moral urgency to put it into play. The personal frailties that drove a man to overindulge were compounded by those of institutional overconfidence, stinginess, delay, and complacency that ran straight to the top of one of the largest multinationals in the world.

When first news of the grounding came to Alyeska Pipeline Service, the joint-stock company set up by seven majors in the oil industry to operate the terminal and pipeline, it too was not prepared for the disaster. Alyeska had its own contingency plan, to be sure, but hadn't read it in a long while. The plan called for surrounding any spill with a floating boom within five hours. Since oil floats on the surface of the water, drifting like a heavy, smelly blanket, the idea was to contain it inside the boom, then with a special machine skim it off the surface into a receiving vessel. But holding eleven million gallons inside a boom on the open sea, with waves rising and crashing against it, is no easy feat; the best equipment and clean-up crew could not easily keep all the glop in that tight loop. Alyeska assured that the task would be impossible by disbanding, in 1982, its special oil-spill response team. Moreover, the barge to carry the boom out to a spill was sitting in dry dock, and had been there for a long time, waiting repairs. The boom itself was buried in a warehouse, and it took an employee working several hours with a forklift to get it out and down to the dock. Obviously, Alyeska had decided that a big spill would never occur and that there were better uses for its personnel and money, decisions that were strongly supported by the majority stockholder in the consortium, British Petroleum, which had vetoed the purchase of emergency equipment. Stumbling along in the first few hours after the spill, uncertain what to do and what its own obligations were, Alyeska presented a study in organized confusion. Finally, fourteen hours after the rupture, it managed to get a boom placed around the *Exxon Valdez*. By then, though, the oil had become a slick more than ten miles long and was drifting beyond any hope of containment, spreading southwestward across the Sound, polluting several undefiled islands, and moving on toward the spectacular Kenai coast.[73]

At this point Exxon decided to assume management of the crisis and, from its New York and Houston offices, tried to devise a strategy that might succeed in the nearly futile effort of getting the stuff out of the water. They began by unloading the remaining one million barrels of oil on the wrecked tanker, fearing it might capsize and make the mess even worse, then floated the tanker off the reef and eventually towed it to repair facilities at Long Beach. Next Exxon turned to using chemical dispersants on the slick, which was quickly becoming more and more viscous in the cold water, resembling a thick chocolate mousse; the dispersants were supposed to break that mousse into millions of tiny droplets, and then the oil would wash out into the gulf and not contaminate any shorelines. Unfortunately, no dispersants were on hand in Valdez—they had been cut from the budget too—and had to be flown in from as far away as Phoenix. Then state officials insisted on a test or two to determine how effective, and how deleterious, the dispersants might be; their worry was that the dispersants might be even more toxic to marine organisms than oil. By the time dispersants were approved and ready, it was too late; the oil had spread even farther. By the fourth day, 27 March, it had traveled 37 miles from the rupture site; by the seventh day, 90 miles; by the fourteenth day, 180 miles; and by the fifty-sixth, 470 miles, as far west as the Shelikof Strait lying between the Alaska Peninsula and Kodiak Island. That last distance was as far from Bligh Reef as Nantucket Island is from North Carolina. Altogether 1,244 miles of shoreline had turned black, the oil layering six or eight inches thick in places. At that point the company could only attempt to soak it up with sorbents or blast it off with high-pressure hoses. Clearly, despite some heroic last-minute attention, Exxon had failed. In the world of finance and profit it was a mammoth power, widely regarded as one of the best-run of the oil corporations, but out here on the Sound it was nearly helpless before a spill of this magnitude, and all its clumsiness, its delays, its interminable committee meetings to decide whose responsibility the spill was, transformed that helplessness into tragedy.[74]

Prince William Sound was the home of 15,000 sea otters, one-tenth of the state's population of the furry little animals that floated innocently in the kelp beds, peering at the liquid world through dark brown eyes. The oil engulfed many of them in its smothering embrace, the fumes burning their eyeballs and nasal membranes, the thick goo matting their luxuriant fur, causing hypothermia as they lost their insulation from the cold water; while the hydrocarbons entered their digestive system as they tried to groom their fur clean, then poisoned their livers, kidneys, and lungs. How many thousands perished and sank to the bottom of the Sound was anybody's guess, but several hundred were fished out of the oil and carried off to makeshift rehabilitation centers, where people tried to wipe them clean. Ducks, loons, cormorants, and other diving birds died by the thousands. Bald and golden eagles swooped down to eat the oil-tainted carrion, along with peregrine falcons, already an endangered species, and they died too. Biologists feared that migrating whale populations would swim into the muck, as would geese and swans returning north with the spring, and that Sitka deer living on the Sound's islands would eat the polluted shore plants and sicken and die. Fisherman were frantic that their livelihood was in dire jeopardy, maybe for years to come: the herring that lay their eggs in the shallow eel grass along the shores, the salmon larvae swimming under the scum, the king crabs and shrimp. Exxon knew how to pump oil and could move tankers rapidly from port to port, but could it save all that threatened life? Sadly, no, and the animals perished on a scale unprecedented in Alaskan history. The volunteers who came rushing down to the Sound to save the wildlife collected tons and tons of carcasses, piling them on barges to be burned.

Some commentators far from the scene argued that, so long as the fishermen were adequately compensated, no great harm would be done. The loss of so many living creatures was itself nothing to fret about. A reviewer for *The Economist,* for example, declared: "Oil spills, devastating in the short term, do little lasting harm."[75] The same might be said for almost any war, airplane crash, flood, economic depression, plague, mass murder, or riot in the past. Humans recovered from them all, didn't they, so what was the use of mourning their losses? Optimistic reassurances that nothing really bad had happened could seem appallingly obtuse. Suppose one had been talking about the dropping of the atomic bomb on Hiroshima instead of the dumping of so much oil on a pristine landscape: try repeating the same words, "though devastating in the short term, it did little lasting harm." Terrifying though it was, one might argue, the Japanese recovered rapidly from the bomb; their numbers were hardly dented by the incineration of a few thousand bodies.

Eventually the country managed to get back to work and even to prosper. Toyota and Sony grew up and became rich in time. Today where there was once radioactivity the cherry trees blossom each spring, the sake flows each night. So it will soon be along Alaska's oily coast. Nature will recover. Such rosy predictions were true, though some of the damage would take decades, even a century, to heal. Nature has impressive powers of recovery from both natural and man-made disasters; otherwise, it would not have endured through all the ups and downs of a billion years of evolution. One year after the spill, a natural recovery was evident; salmon migrated as before from the Sound up the coastal streams, and sea lions could be seen raising their heads from a floating buoy to watch a ferry boat go by. By that time the casual visitor would find it difficult to locate any spilled oil. Exxon had recovered only 32,500 barrels out of 257,000, but most of the remainder had evaporated, washed out to sea, or sunk deeply into the rocks and sand along the beaches, out of sight. So what's to worry about? We can have our oil and spill it too. We can, that is, if we deny the memory of that mountain of dead birds burning on a corporate barge or those otter bodies rotting on the ocean floor.

Exxon spent over $1 billion on the so-called clean-up, most of that in the summer of 1989, before declaring the job done and going home. Critics pointed out that the much publicized expense was largely tax deductible, far less of a sacrifice for ecology than it seemed. Certainly no one in the company hierarchy suffered any real personal damage. Only Captain Hazelwood lost his job at Exxon, and even he got off easier than the wildlife that died; the judicial system seemed ready to punish him with a fine and a temporary suspension of his ship's license. Exxon's public image suffered a black eye for a while, but its stock prices remained steady and profits continued to accumulate. Compared with all the money Exxon had made from Alaskan resources, the costs of cleaning up the spill were rather small. By 1987 Exxon and the other companies had taken in $42.6 billion in profits from the pipeline and had no intention after the spill of shutting off the flow.

Most everyone living in the state had done financially well on the oil boom—and many would make money on cleaning up the spill, factors that were bound to moderate their outrage. The government in Juneau, which prior to the accident had not funded a single position for spill contingency planning, had gathered in $29 billion in royalties, taxes, and lease rents by 1987, and of that some $400 million a year had been distributed to state residents in the form of dividend checks. Disaster made those gains seem temporarily meaningless, as the state was swept by a sense of genuine grief, of unrecompensible loss, of anger. The fishermen were the maddest of all, and many vehemently told the companies to go to hell and worse. But within a few months of the spill, as soon as public feeling abated, both the oil industry and state officials, backed by strong popular approval, were joining forces once again to lobby for opening up the Arctic National Wildlife Refuge for exploration and development. Tour guides at the Valdez terminal were pointing with pride to the newly painted, well-equipped barges now standing ready at a moment's notice to sail out to a spill, even claiming credit for Alyeska's wise foresight, its "concern for the environment." Everyone, it seemed, was back in business as usual, shouting for more oil, as the long-term impact on their economic interests proved far less damaging than the impact on the coastal ecosystem.

The Alaska Oil Spill Commission, however, after completing a deliberate, careful study of the disaster, tried to remind the public and the corporations of what had gone wrong and why. Its chairman, William B. Parker, a longtime transportation bureaucrat, and the other commission members concluded very bluntly that "concern for profits in the 1980s obliterated the concern for safe operations that existed in 1977," the year the pipeline began pumping oil. In their final report, they wrote with all the controlled outrage of people who had been let down by those they had trusted:

> The system that carried 25 percent of America's domestic oil production had failed. So had the regulatory apparatus intended to make it safe. The promises that led Alaska to grant its rights-of-way and Congress to approve the Alaska pipeline . . . had been betrayed. The safeguards that were set in place in the 1970s had been allowed to slide. The vigilance over tanker traffic that was established in the early stage of pipeline flow had given way to complacency and neglect. . . . The disaster could have been prevented—not by tanker captains and crews who are, in the end, fallible human begings, but by an advanced oil transportation system designed to minimize human error. It could have been prevented if Alaskans, state and federal governments, the oil industry and the American public had insisted on stringent safeguards. It could have been prevented if the vigilance that accompanied construction of the pipeline in the 1970s had been continued in the 1980s.[76]

Strong words from sober, careful, experienced people. But even beneath that indictment there glimmered the still vibrant hope of a technologically optimistic society. It *was* possible, they were saying, to extract oil from the Slope and bring it south to Valdez without risk or mishap. It *was* possible to ship it out at the rate of a thousand tanker trips a year, despite icebergs and winter storms, dense fog and submerged reefs, and not lose a drop. With enough vigilance, the state, along with Exxon, could continue to profit from its oil and still preserve a clean, sparkling, innocent nature.

Large questions about that optimism, nonetheless, remained unaddressed in the wake of the disaster, questions that the whole history of the fossil fuels in Alaska raises, questions that go to the very core of our modern economic culture. Why was Exxon, despite all its rational planning and command of expertise, so fundamentally careless? Why have governments and corporations everywhere—in Bhopal, India; Three Mile Island, Pennsylvania; Basel, Switzerland; Chernobyl, U.S.S.R.; and so forth—behaved so irresponsibly toward the environment? And why have so many ordinary citizens living in the urban, industrial era done so much unwitting damage to the earth's fabric of life and yet been so unconcerned about it? Why has carelessness in our dealings with nature become a way of life?

Explaining the modern intensity of environmental destruction may not seem to require any new or complicated theory. There is a history of such behavior going all the way back to Australopithecine ape-man. Forests burned down because ancient hunters fell asleep by their camp fires. Farmers starved by their own depletion of soils. We humans entered the world as an often greedy, shortsighted, violent, capricious species, and ever after we have been depleting game, eroding lands, overpopulating habitats, looking for easy ways to get ahead and instead undermining our existence. Taken as individuals or as collectivities, we have never been free of ecological foibles or immune to their consequences. Though it may not flatter a contemporary executive, ensconced in an air-conditioned penthouse of chrome and glass, to think so, he has all the potential for darkness and folly that his naked, unwashed ancestors had. The debacle in Prince William Sound expressed that grim potential. It was waiting in our genes a million years ago.

All the same, the human impact on nature has changed substantially over time, so that we cannot dismiss it with the glib phrase, "Things have always been that way." In fact, things are getting worse. If we are to understand the growing seriousness of environmental problems, the causes of such disasters as occurred in Prince William Sound, there are some peculiar characteristics of modern people and their history that need confronting.

The most obvious change has been in the scale of the tools we wield. Over the last 300 years science has shown us how to construct increasingly more efficient ways to extract, ship, refine, process, and manufacture the goods and energy we consume. Fire was a potent, deadly tool for early man, but today we have dreamed up nuclear fission reactors, chlorinated hydrocarbons such as DDT, chain saws and logging mills, and a 987-foot tanker that can float over a million gallons of oil from the Alaska pipeline to southern California. Science has put into our flawed grasp a power that is unprecedented in history.

Part of the distinctiveness of modern ecological disasters lies in the fact that they involve large, complicated technologies that could not have sprung directly from any single individual's brain. They require the research, capital, and labor of many people to bring them into being, and in turn those people require an intricate degree of organization. Most of that organization in the United States has taken the shape of private, profit-seeking corporations, although like other nations, we are turning increasingly to government to develop some of the most advanced technologies, such as those of the military and of space exploration. Whatever the type or scale of organization controlling science and technology, it is bound to be driven by the same ancient human desires, the same ambitions for wealth, power, comfort, self-expression, and group aggrandizement. But the very fact that the organization is a modern one, which typically means a very big one, has changed fundamentally the context, the meaning, and the expression of the old sharp desires.

What Exxon wants these days is found nowhere near its international headquarters: black, viscous deposits of decayed marine life lying deep under the permafrost of the Arctic slope, deposits it wants to mine some 4000 direct-flight miles away from its board rooms. In other words, it wants something its officers may never have seen nor had the slightest personal relationship with, a substance that exists as purely an abstraction, one that can be translated into money. So do the consumers who buy the company's gasoline; they want an abstraction called mobility. To get that freedom to come and go at will, they have all joined as producers and consumers in exploiting a part of the earth that has no immediate presence, no visibility, no affection in their lives.

No wonder today's consumers have become so careless. They regularly assume that neither they nor their immediate friends and neighborhood will suffer from the destructive consequences of their unleashed desires. The higher they climb up the ladder of success, the greater the distance they seek between themselves and their consequences—the farther they want to live from the pollution and ugliness they have caused. Only after intense public criticism did the chairman of Exxon decide to visit the scene of the oil spill, and then it was three weeks after it happened.

If that change in scale, that distancing of people from their sources of supply in nature, were not enough, there has also occurred a major shift in our thinking about ourselves. Call it a change in self-image. Many seem to believe that in the process of becoming so clever, rich, and powerful, we have also become superior creatures all around. We are more trustworthy than our ancestors—more civilized, more rational.

That shift in self-image began in the so-called Age of Reason, which historians place in the seventeenth and eighteenth centuries. It was the point of origin for almost all the political, scientific, economic, and industrial revolutions that have created the modern world. The leading philosophers of that age began to celebrate the human mind and its wonderful potential for transforming the earth. If we can puzzle out the laws of gravity and celestial motion, they supposed, if we can create factories that spin thread, weave cloth, and turn out an abundance of everything, then we humans must surely be a very noble, special species. We are capable of the most elegant reasoning, the most astonishing technical wonders. There is nothing conceivable that we cannot do. We can even free ourselves from those primeval frailties of emotion, superstition, and vice. Potentially, therefore, we are godlike in our intellectual and moral endowment. As an American philosopher, Elihu Palmer, remarked: "The organic constitution of man induces a strong conclusion that no limits can justly be assigned to his moral and scientific improvements."[77]

The most striking implications of that new optimism about human nature appeared in the field of economics, which applied scientific analysis to the problem of creating wealth. What scientific economics discovered was that human greed informed by rationality could become miraculously productive. Heretofore, greed had been widely viewed as one of the worst human vices, requiring laws, regulations, and a general attitude of suspicion to keep it safely under control. But following the teaching of men like Adam Smith, greed came to be regarded not as raw selfishness but as the rational pursuit of self-interest—which is to say, it became a virtue. Each person was assumed to be the best judge of his or her welfare, capable of using reason to discover what that welfare entails; no one else could know it better. Let each, therefore, exercise the reason with which he or she has been endowed, seeking to maximize personal gain, and the whole society will benefit. This new moral philosophy of rationalized greed came to be seen as the most efficacious way to progress, or what we today call "growth." To promote progress and achieve growth, Smith and others of his day recommended, we should eliminate all the outmoded laws aimed at controlling selfishness, do away with most social constraints on the individual. Set free from external interference, humans will advance toward a utopia of wealth and enlightenment, securing a material abundance for each and all.

The 1980s were a period of nostalgic return to those laissez-faire principles of Adam Smith and his age, and nowhere more so than among the parties responsible for the spilling of oil off the coast of Alaska. The federal government, which had never been very critical of the oil industry, relaxed its regulation completely in that decade; for example, the requirement that tankers shipping out of Prince William Sound must have double hulls was dropped after lobbying by the oil companies, Exxon leading the effort. Had the *Exxon Valdez* had a double hull, most of the oil would not have been spilled. It did not have that hull because such a requirement would raise construction costs by 2 to 5 percent, and the owners wanted to cut costs and raise profits.[78] During the same deregulation decade the Coast Guard in Alaska began scaling back its marine traffic surveillance, replacing its radar system with a cheaper though less effective system. While President Ronald Reagan and the Congress were increasing the overall military budget by several trillion dollars, they slashed the Coast Guard's budget severely, apparently confident that the invisible hand of rational self-interest would keep all the ships prudently on course. The same spirit of deregulation, the same program of cost-cutting, and the same trust in rational greed as the ideal basis of society could be found in the state of Alaska. When 85 percent of the state's budget had been coming from oil revenues and taxes, there had been little inclination to ask unfriendly questions about the reliability of corporate self-interest. "We trusted them," said a state official after the spill. Such was the explanation heard all over Alaska as to why the spill occurred—the plaintive wail of the victimized, of the innocent bystander who feels duped and misled by sharpies. But then who really was the victim, and who was the criminal, in a culture where endless economic growth, maximum freedom of enterprise, a strong passion for fast automobiles and low taxes were the slogans that got the most votes? Did any of the actors in the spill—the tanker crew, the corporations, the bureaucrats, or the voting majority of citizens—really show themselves to be a noble species?

In the lost archaic world of the Inupiat hunters and gatherers an individual had to put up with external restraints, social and ecological, that modern Americans would find intolerable. There were rules establishing when and where hunting was permitted and how it should be done (you should humbly approach your prey and ask its permission before taking its life). There were elaborate rituals and taboos, passed down generation after generation, embedded deeply in the religious life of the tribe, that were supposed to guide the individual in securing a living. Procreation was not taken to be a private or unlimited right, but was carefully hedged about by a group-defined, group-enforced sense of environmental limits. Failure to maintain those collective checks on the wild disorder of private appetite might lead, it was feared, to destroying everybody's future. Modern societies, in contrast, have celebrated the ideal of the self-reliant, self-determined individual set free from almost all such restraints, whether those of nature or of society. We trust ourselves, far more than our ancestors did. Some of us want to extend that self-trust even farther, getting rid of almost all laws, rules, traditions, and pressures as illegitimate infringements on private rights, or at best as necessary evils to be kept to the barest minimum.

Freedom to do as one pleases, to go and come as one likes, have become, at least among the middle and upper classes, the dominant ambition. That freedom was reflected in the oily sheen on Prince William Sound and in so many other scenes of environmental deterioration, some of them sudden and dramatic like the spill, others slow and obscure like the global greenhouse effect. Will vigilance alone counterbalance that insistence on being free of all regulation? Will any technological solution, say, a new design of tankers or an advanced radar system, satisfactorily address the more profound cultural forces underlying that deterioration? The root of our predicament lies in the simple fact that, though we remain a flawed and unstable species, plagued now as in the past by a thousand weaknesses, we have insisted on both unlimited freedom and unlimited power. It would now seem clear that, if we want to stop the devastation of the earth, the growing threats to our food, water, air, and fellow creatures, we must find some way to limit both.

is conventionally referred to as the "Metropolis."[1] Hinterlands are areas that have grown less rapidly than others; consequently, they are left in a dependent or subordinate position, ruled over, or at least heavily influenced, by the Metropolis. With a few qualifications, that seems to characterize the six states of the Northern Tier. They began largely as an extension of Hill's imagination westward, and they exist now, despite many ambitions to the contrary, as a physically large but politically weak producer of staples for metropolitan consumers.

"Metropolis" refers to an entity that is more than any one city; it includes all the centers of the nation-state and of the industrial economy and of cultural innovation. Traditionally, those centers lay somewhere due east of the Northern Tier in Minneapolis, Chicago, New York, Washington, London. Over the past hundred years, however, the Metropolis has moved west, and finding it on a map has become more difficult. It has come to include many points south of the Northern Tier—Denver, Dallas, Salt Lake City, Los Angeles, San Francisco—some within the Tier itself—Boise, Seattle—and some farther west and outside the country, like Vancouver and Tokyo. Commodities move to and from all those centers, and so does capital, and so do workers and ideas.

We can also characterize the Northern Tier as a borderland. I mean that it is an area located on or near an international border, a frontier in the European sense of the word, in this case a border marked "U.S.-Canada," running more than a thousand miles from the Red River Valley to the Strait of Juan de Fuca, traversing plains, mountains, and salt water, separating (but only just, we are proud to say) two friendly neighbors, really kinfolk. In comparison to the southern borderland shared by the United States and Mexico, this northern one has gotten little attention from historians, though both have had a similar past of imperial struggles between European powers, of declarations of independence and nationality, of confrontations over sovereignty, of migration back and forth. We have no real school of northern borderlands history, no Herbert Bolton or John Francis Bannon for these parts, though a few tentative moves toward a comparative and transnational perspective have been made.[2]

Understanding the Northern Tier states as they progress into their next century will require focusing on both their hinterland and borderland status, on determining how those two characteristics may have interacted or are interacting now. To do that means learning to think about these states as an area standing not only on one end of an east-west axis but also in the middle of a north-south one. Put another way, the Northern Tier has become integrated over the past century into the larger region of the American West as it has, to a lesser extent, become more tied to its international neighbors, the western provinces of Canada, and through them to a world of affairs very different from that of, say, Louisiana or Pennsylvania.

It is the first of those points, the Northern Tier's integration within its larger region, that I want to examine in more detail. Specifically, I want to ask what, after a hundred of years of history, constitutes the underlying cultural identity of these six states, and I will argue that their identity can be found only by finding the identity of the American West as a whole— that is, by asking what is is that holds *all* these western states together. What, despite the many hinterland and borderland complications, do they have in the way of common bonds? What does it mean to live in any of them—to be a westerner?

For a long while Americans who came to live in the West, the lands reaching from the plains to the Pacific coast, were not much troubled by such questions of identity. There was little sense of need to find a special character for themselves or to be distinguished from Americans back east. They were simply, unreflectively confident that they were the best the nation had to offer, the advance guard of a rising national giant, the fist thrust boldly into a limitless wilderness. Everywhere they attached names to the landscape that spoke of an uncomplicated assurance that they were preparing the way to the nation's future: the American River, Independence Rock, Virginia City, the state of Washington, the future state of Lincoln that never materialized, the county of Jefferson, of Lewis, of Clark, of Madison, of Fremont, of Custer and Sheridan. The spirit behind that naming was at once intensely nationalistic, devoted to extending the grand entity called America, and egregiously superior, sure that the nation would be reborn in a bigger and better form as it went west.

One could get no better picture of that early devotion to expanding Americanism than by examining the Fourth of July celebrations once held religiously in the western territory. From the days of the first wagon trains down to the twentieth century, it was on that day that westerners affirmed their unequivocal loyalty to the United States of America. In the fervor of their nationalism, they tried hard to put their eastern fellows to shame. William Swain, on his way to the California gold camps, told of one such celebration on 4 July 1849, eight miles below Fort Laramie on the North Platte River. He and his companions on the trail lined up at noon and marched to the tune of "The Star Spangled Banner" toward an improvised reviewing stand, where they stood and listened to a reading of the Declaration of Independence, a patriotic address, and a rendition of "Hail Columbia." Then, in a grand banqueting hall formed by two rows of wagons and a roof of wagon covers, they sat down to gorge on their country's wealth—ham, beans, biscuits, johnny cake, apple pie, sweet cake, rice pudding, pickles, vinegar, pepper sauce and mustard, coffee, sugar, and milk. After that affirmation of American abundance, the toasting commenced, round after round after round. "The boys had raked and scraped together all the brandy they could," wrote Swain, "and they toasted, hurrayed, and drank till reason was out and brandy was in."[3] In all directions from that boisterous scene the high plains stretched silently away, utterly oblivious to their claims; but Swain and Company made them anyway, in a strident if inebriated voice: "We are Americans," they were in effect saying, "and we will make this place America, and everything we pass on our way to wherever we're going will become America too."

That was over forty years before Wyoming became a state, but it may stand for the long hold of a nationalistic sense of identity, one that was still present at statehood and is still strong at times along the North Platte River today. With William Swain, the westerner as distinctive creature did not yet exist and would not for a long time to come.

The first dissent from that uncritical nationalism and the first doubts about who they were began to appear among residents of the western states in the last decade of the nineteenth century. Particularly up and down the Great Plains and through the interior mountain valleys people began to fear that they might not, after all, be the future-dominating people they once had hoped. Instead of wresting power and wealth away from older areas and supplanting them as "America," they might become impoverished waifs, exploited, disinherited, and forgotten. We call this moment of doubt the Populist uprising, but it did not end with the defeat of the Populists in 1896. Decade by decade the doubts grew, until by the 1920s and '30s historians and other intellectuals began to take up the question of where westerners really stood in the national order. The most noted of them was Walter Prescott Webb (born in 1888), a young man from Stephens County, Texas, located in the middle of a triangle formed by Fort Worth, Abilene, and Wichita Falls. The future historian grew up with a strong sense of being far removed from the centers of American influence. "None of the books he read as a child," writes G. M. Tobin, "told him anything that would suggest that the placid routine he saw around him had any place in the wider experience of the nation as a whole; their frame of reference invariably assumed Eastern or European norms."[4] So Webb set out to write his own books and, in effect, to use history to find out who he was by finding out what his West was and how it was different from the rest of the nation. Similar motives animated Ber-

nard DeVoto of Utah, Joseph Kinsey Howard of Montana, and others in
the years between the First and Second World Wars.

The answer to that quest for identity was the notion of the West as a
colony or "plundered province." Except for California, the one golden
child in the regional family, all the western states were seen to be joined
together as victims of eastern capital, and the victimizers, men like James
J. Hill, took a roasting. This dependent condition was one that, paradoxically, only the eastern-based federal government could set right. And it
tried to do so. Stirred by a rising self-consciousness in the West, pres-
sured for recognition and aid, the federal government sent a great flood of
dollars to western states during the New Deal period; as a consequence,
in the postwar years the West began to take off into sustained economic
and demographic growth, until it was able to shift the national balance of
power considerably its way.[5]

Of course, the growth in status and redistribution of power had been
uneven. Most new residents coming into the West during the last half-
century have moved to the warmer states toward the south. Vast sections
of the region have remained rural, sparsely settled, and disadvantaged,
and they are likely to remain so in the foreseeable future. Idaho is simply
never going to become a competitor of southern California, for there will
not be not enough people in the nation to populate it; nor enough water
resources or accessible lands in Idaho to allow it. A lot of this sparsely
settled West, as William Robbins has insisted, is still being plundered.[6]
So, to be sure, are Maine, West Virginia, and Indiana; so are rural citizens
in every state, along with urban workers, women and children of all races,
various people of color, the old, the handicapped, the uneducated—anyone and everyone who is not sitting at the top of the global economy. What
is most remarkable is not the continuing fact of exploitation in many
areas, though some westerners have still to face up to that status and deal
with it; rather, the most astonishing thing is that all these postwar economic patterns have not stopped the search for identity. On the contrary,
it has become more determined and urgent than ever. Westerners may
have gone from being the avant-garde of American nationalism to being a
province plundered by eastern corporations to being an integral, sometimes dominating, sometimes subordinate part, of global capitalism. But
playing a kind of counterpoint to all those shifting relations with the outside political and economic world, there has been a steadily increasing
tendency for westerners to look within themselves and ask just what it is
that sets them apart from others.

If Webb was the first western historian to be self-consciously regional, his progeny are numerous today. There are several thousand members of the Western History Association, founded in 1961; and many more are active in state and local history societies. They are joined by a growing number of novelists and painters, along with advocates of historic preservation and the decorative arts, to form a thinking community in the region that is essential to any quest for distinctiveness. Whatever the West is, its identity is rooted in the past. It will be revealed by historians and artists examining that past and writing about it, in a spirit of sympathy but also of critical detachment. The process of forging an identity is already going on. I think it is safe to say that the imaginations of those historians and artists are no longer out there with William Swain, loudly singing "Hail Columbia" over the Wyoming plains. But then what *are* they singing? What *should* they be singing?

A few years ago, I recommended that the search for western identity come down from the wispy, mythic clouds of frontierism, where the talk has been about such abstractions as Savages and Civilization, Virgin Land and Manifest Destiny, and get its feet firmly planted on the ground—that it wedge down to the hard material reality of the region.[7] Specifically, I urged that primacy be given to agriculture and human ecology, that is, to the distinctive ways in which westerners have tried to get their livelihood from the earth. Two such ways have been widespread over the western states, setting them off from their eastern counterparts: first, an older pastoral mode of sheep and cattle ranching, and second, a later hydraulic mode of controlling water on a large scale for the purposes of irrigated farming, which has brought a more intensive use of land, close rural settlements, and densely packed urban oases. To be sure, those two ways are not wholly self-contained; both are expressions of the larger capitalist order of human and environmental relations, though they are also responses to regional conditions of climate, water supplies, and vegetation. Nor are the pastoral and hydraulic modes always mutually exclusive, commonly overlapping as they do through much of the country. Nonetheless, they have had different historical associations, different patterns of development, and, for the sake of analysis, can be usefully distinguished. Historians who want to contribute fundamentally to our understanding of western identity must, it seems to me, pursue the history of those modes of using the land. In other words, they must become informed about the ecological processes of adaptation that have gone on in this particular part of the world.

I do not mean to argue, however, that a regional identity is determined *only* by that material base. It also is the outcome of the way people *think* about each other and about the place where they live. There is, in other words, an inner cultural history, as well as an outer ecological one, that must be written about the West, and that inner history is still largely unwritten.

One of the reasons I am so enthusiastic about the work of Patricia Nelson Limerick is because she is the first scholar in a long while to pay serious attention to that inner cultural history. Her recent book, *The Legacy of Conquest*, challenges us to transcend all the details of our research and ask more broadly how people in the West have thought and felt in distinctive ways. Limerick asks us to consider what people have thought and felt about each other—what they have thought or felt, or failed to think and feel, when they looked across the racial lines. What she finds is a mental life that has gone on apart from, or even in opposition to, the external reality.

> To analyze how white Americans thought about the West, it helps to think anthropologically. One lesson of anthropology is the extraordinary power of cultural persistence; with American Indians, for instance, beliefs and values will persist even when the supporting economic and political structures have vanished. What holds for Indians holds as well for white Americans; the values they attached to westward expansion persist, in cheerful defiance of contrary evidence.[8]

We have not paid enough heed to those tenacious habits of thought, those ways of thinking that stubbornly persist even when they are inconvenient or expensive or self-destructive. The idea of racial competition and conquest is one of the most important of those habits of thought. It has survived even though the conquest has been something of a failure and racial minorities have successfully resisted the white invaders. Like cowboys riding the range in Toyota pickups, denting their ten-gallon hats against the low cabin roofs, white westerners have not learned how to accept their multiracial world as it is.

The search for regional identity becomes a little daunting when we try to follow Limerick all the way toward a multi-ethnic, anthropological perspective. We must learn, she urges, to write the cultural history of all the races and ethnicities that have struggled to find a place here, some of them arriving ten, twenty, forty thousand years ago, some only last week. If there is an identity to be found, it cannot be that of the white conquerors acting alone, superimposing their experience, their memories and beliefs, on everyone else. Above all, it is necessary to see that what has made the West distinctive is just this juxtaposition of radically unlike peoples, trying to understand one another or failing to do so: modern Asian-Americans confronting Euro-Americans confronting paleo-Asian-Americans to an extent unmatched anywhere else in the world. The history of the West has been a conversation going on in several languages at once.

Undoubtedly, Limerick is on high moral ground when she urges us to approach regional history in this way. The collective experience of whites can no longer be taken as the only important experience in the past. Granting that argument, we are nonetheless left with a predicament. Will we end up finding a truly *common* western experience, or have we instead had a past that is so ethnically diverse, so fragmented, that it defeats the search for a coherent regional identity? The hard truth, it seems to me, is that, in terms of race, there has never been much of a collective westernness. Westerners have never really lived as multi-centered creatures but rather have lived within the confines of their various ethnic groups, speaking different languages, expressing different beliefs and values, developing different identities one from another. Whites, for example, have never absorbed much of the world view of the Indians, and Indians have never absorbed fully the world view of the whites. It may be that someday a more integrated western type will emerge who will be the product of those many groups interacting over time: a westerner will have been transformed into something new by the experience of trying to penetrate all the others' points of view. But that composite westerner does not yet exist.

On still another level, Limerick teaches us a useful lesson about approaching the mental history of the West, at least when we confine our analysis to whites only: There has been a tendency here to distance one's ideals from the external world to the point of innocence and naïveté. Other historians, notably Henry Nash Smith, have pointed out the same habit of mind, though more in regard to environmental than social realities.[9] Of course, such a habit of mind is not altogether limited to the West, but there is something about this region that seems to intensify the tendency to live in one world while dreaming of or expecting another. The West is characteristically a country of daydreams and fantasies, of visions and nostalgia, where people seem constantly to want to escape from the life they have made for themselves and to enter one more satisfying to the imagination. Sometimes it is a life in the future. Sometimes it is one receding quickly into the past: a vision of a farming valley in the Rockies, for instance; of a cattle drive north from Texas; of buffalo reemerging from the earth and streaming once again across the prairie; of a boarded-up saloon where the piano still seems to be tinkling in the air. The western mind is full of such fleeting, jumbled bits of memory and romance. I believe an explanation lies in the fact that this has not been a region that grew slowly, organically out of a long, continuous past; it has been a place of rapid change, repeated dislocation, and surreal discontinuities, a place in which time has often seemed to break completely apart, leaving us with a sense not of the steady flow of experience but of vivid moments crashing along one after another. It has been a land in which the same man, as a boy, might have watched Billy the Kid ride through town on his way to a shootout and, as an oldtimer, watched a radioactive mushroom cloud rise ominously on the horizon. No wonder, then, that beliefs and dreams have often been so divorced from material reality. How could they possibly have kept pace? Things have moved too swiftly for that.

When we enter the realm of the western political imagination, the disjunction between fantasy and reality becomes especially sharp. We have not yet written a full history of the western political imagination; when we do, we will begin to appreciate just how sharp the disjunction has been and where and to what extent the westerner has diverged from the American mainstream. He or she has been eager to acquire a piece of land and to use it without any interference whatsoever from any other individual, group, or institution. It is not a desire that the West altogether invented, for it existed in the white man's mind before Lewis and Clark, even before the Constitution. We might call it the "Lockean imperative," for it was John Locke who, in the early eighteenth century, claimed that a man defines himself primarily by laboring to acquire and develop a piece of property, taking it out of a state of wildness and into one of cultivation. It is the idea that what we own is solely the result of our personal efforts and has nothing of anyone else in it. It is, furthermore, the theory that all our freedoms and rights come from the ownership of property and that a free society is one in which men have been most free to acquire and use their property as they see fit. That kind of thinking reached a peak of influence during the middle and later nineteenth century, just as the American people were crossing the great rivers to get in on the biggest real estate bonanza ever. If we accept Louis Hartz's argument that new societies take their identity from whatever ideas happen to be ascendant at the time of their founding, then the western society was shaped indelibly by this idea of private property acquisitiveness.[10] To paraphrase Hartz, westerners, unfurling the golden banner of Horatio Alger, marched into the Promised Land after the Civil War and never wanted to leave it. In the West, they hoped to acquire land and resources, exercise their entrepreneurial talents, rise to riches—and they needed no other goal, no other principle of life.

But not long after the first waves of settlement and of statehood, the region began to have another set of values foisted on it by an eastern America that had not stood still but had gone on to explore new ideas and principles. Beginning in 1891, the federal government began to withdraw lands in the West from private entry and to set them aside, in perpetuity, as a great public commons. The first such move was the Forest Reserve Act, which in a few years had permitted the withdrawal of 34 million acres of forested lands, all in the West. The idea of forming such a commons out of the public domain came primarily from a group called the American Forestry Association, whose members were mainly easterners inspired by European ideas of socialized forestry and land use. They had begun to call for a revision of the old Lockean view and to demand that the land be put under collective ownership and supervision. With the presidency of Theodore Roosevelt, that new kind of thinking expanded, and as it expanded, the federal government withdrew more and more lands from private entry and even began purchasing private lands to add to the commons. Today there are 740 million acres—one-third of the nation—under federal control. Some of those lands are forests, some parks, some grazing districts, and so forth. Overwhelmingly, they are in the western states and Alaska. Some 37 percent of the state of Montana has been taken out of the reach of Horatio Alger and John Locke, along with 65 percent of Idaho, 45 percent of California, and 73 percent of Arizona.

The implications for westerners in that course of events have been more profound than we have ever quite realized. It has put the region into a terrible ideological bind. Nowhere else on earth has the conflict between the old Lockean faith in free property as the guarantor of free men and the new faith in collective ownership as the promise of a secure society been so fiercely drawn.

It is instructive to compare this inter-regional conflict with that other, more famous one between the North and the South. The struggle between those two regions that led to the Civil War was over the question of chattel slavery: Did one group of people have the right to own another as their property? In contrast, the struggle between the West and the East has been over the question of privatization of the land: Did any set of individuals have the right to take control of all the land acquired by the nation as a whole? The South lost its struggle and, though more or less acknowledging its moral errors, has never quite forgiven the North. By now of course, the West has lost its war too; the public lands have become permanently public and they are going to remain so, more than likely remain in federal hands, for as far into the future as we can see. No sagebrush rebels have so far managed to reverse that outcome. But the wounds of defeat run deep, and resentments are never far from the surface. Many westerners are still fighting for their glorious lost cause.

The land has entered into western identity in more subtle and complicated ways than as property to be owned and fought over. In fact, it is to *all* of the influences of the land that one must finally turn to understand the innermost history of this region—not only for its dominant white majority but for all of its peoples. In a sense, westerners have long been conversing with the landscape as well as with each other, and their imaginations have been altered by that conversation beyond easy telling.

For almost everyone who has come into this country in modern times the land of the West has jolted the mind and tried the body. Very little of it has seemed designed for human ease. Even in these days of fast automobiles, the high plains are a trial of patience and a defiance to occupation. The mountains farther west are among the highest and most rugged on the planet—awesomely beautiful to contemplate but hellishly difficult to get over. And then there are the stark, hostile deserts of the interior, a landscape that even today people find hard to love, one that has often drawn the angry, the misfitted, the rejected, the alienated. Everywhere in the region there is so much space—so much amplitude of rugged rock, soil, climate, and vista—that the landscape, like the gods of old, can leave men and women feeling humbled or diminished, exhilirated or threatened.

Many of the first white comers, men like William Swain, brought with them dreams of extravagant abundance—gold waiting to be plucked from the bottoms of streams. But the almost universal reality has been that gold is an abundance that runs out fast, and then there follows an extreme privation that can be deadly. Unlike other regions, the lasting impact of encountering the western landscape has not been to encourage a sense of effortless abundance. On the contrary, this has been, in so many times and places, a land of scarcity, defying American expectations and previous experience.

Still, for all its difficult traits, the land has entered into people's identities and affections in ways that defy rational analysis or the tests of logic. Almost every western state, for example, has put some representation of the land, often a dramatic feature of its landscape or the products of its soil, on its automobile license plates. "Big Sky Country," they say, or "Land of Enchantment," or the "Grand Canyon State"; or they show a potato, a mountain skyline, a shock of wheat. Some of those icons emphatically indicate an attitude of human domination over nature, as in the case of Wyoming, where the license plate figure is of a cowboy trying to break the independent spirit of a wild horse, one of the West's favorite images of itself, repeated endlessly in the rituals of rodeo combat. Perhaps all of those license-plate badges of identification are, to some degree, similarly laden with a spirit of domination, like trophies carried home from battle, announcing to the world that an army has come to conquer and, despite the size of the foe, has succeeded. Perhaps there is also some darkly chauvinistic spirit of regionalism being revealed in those symbols, a claim that has all the belligerence and intolerance of nationalist or ethnocentric assertion elsewhere. But I think there is also something *accepting* in them—an embrace of the harshness, the grandeur, the numinous beauty of the land. More than they can quite express or know how to acknowledge, westerners have become attached to this place. They feel a part of it. They want to carry some totem of it with them wherever they travel.

You will seldom find this sense of attachment articulated in the halls of politics, for politicians, like businessmen or engineers or accountants, do not commonly deal in such matters. Writers, on the other hand, commonly do. They try to penetrate and express, through image, character, and narrative, the inner history of people; and because art requires experience, they write about the inner history of the people they know, the people they live with and among. When we turn to the art of the region's writers, we find a world of clues as to what the land means to westerners.

What I find expressed in western fictional writing is, first, a strong sense of the embeddedness of human life in the cycles and patterns of nature and, second, a fascination with the distinctive psychological content of western landscapes. White or Indian, male or female, those writers do not generally describe a human condition that is deeply, decisively cultural, bound and limited by the cumulative experience of generation following generation. Instead, they tell us about humans trying to live in places where the scale of time is so far beyond recorded history as to seem timeless. They tell us about individuals going out to make a small impact on that timelessness, often failing and disappearing, abandoning their shacks and letting them fall into disrepair, leaving their cliff dwellings empty and silent, allowing their family bones to become jumbled and lost. Even now, in writings that deal more with cities, industry, and technology, human achievement seems ephemeral in the West, the cycles of nature utterly imposing.

Outsiders as well as natives have come to that same conclusion of the futility of victory. Writer John McPhee of New Jersey, searching for the annals of a former world in Wyoming, quotes geologist David Love: "If there was one thing we learned, it was that you don't fight nature. You live with it. And you make the accommodations—because nature does not accommodate."[11]

My point is not that every westerner has actually learned that lesson of humility, for they have not. Rather, the point is that it has seemed to many observers to be *the* lesson to learn from dwelling in the West, a lesson taught by the dense abiding presence of the Cretaceous, the Permian, the Cambrian, by all the forces of rock and wind and dust, of mountain building and tearing down, of fires raging through a forest and drought searing the grasslands. This is a lesson the rest of America might come here to learn.

In the face of such natural power and persistence it seems quite illusory to insist on human domination over the earth. No contemporary writer has expressed that point better than Wallace Stegner in his famous letter on wilderness written almost thirty years ago.

> While we were demonstrating ourselves the most efficient and ruthless environment-busters in history, and slashing and burning and cutting our way through a wilderness continent, the wilderness was working on us. It remains in us as surely as Indian names remain on the land. If the abstract dream of human liberty and human dignity became, in America, something more than an abstract dream, mark it down at least partially to the fact that we were in subtle ways subdued by what we conquered.[12]

Stegner is talking about all of America in that passage, but he is talking as a westerner, one already steeped for half a century in the region, and he is looking at the American experience as a westerner is apt to do. For writers in Pittsburgh or Charleston, experience may look different. But to Stegner, as to so many western writers, the land has been and is of the first importance. It stands boldly, implacably in the foreground of experience, too wild really to tame, too old to change, too large to reduce to a mere human scale. Confronting the land, being subdued by it, westerners have found the beginnings of an identity.

Will the next hundred years produce in the western states a very different set of defining characteristics than I have discussed here, making them more like other places in the world or less so, more distinctive or less so, or distinctive in new, unexpected ways? We are often warned that the West may eventually disappear, along with all regions, into the homogenized, featureless world of the multinationals, the bureaucracies, the technocrats. On the other hand, we can see that people seem to be looking more hungrily than ever for a sense of distinctiveness and rootedness, which regions like the West can satisfy. We will have to wait a while to see which tendency wins out. In the meanwhile we have a deeper history of this place to write than any of us has yet imagined.

11 ·

A Country
Without Secrets

        I have recently been reading a book with the melancholy title *The End of Nature.** Its author, Bill McKibben, appears in his dust-jacket photo to be a young man, a fortunate resident of the splendid Adirondack Mountains of New York, an outdoorsy fellow garbed in a checked woodsman's shirt. But despite his happy setting and appearances, he is deeply worried about the global atmospheric changes that humans have set in motion. Within the next hundred years, he points out, we will double the amount of carbon dioxide in the air by burning what's left of the fossil fuels. Scientists calculate that the increased CO_2 will raise the global average temperature by three to eight degrees Fahrenheit. And that is not all: high-level ozone is depleting, the tropical forests are rapidly disappearing, every part of the earth has now come under the exploitative hand of humankind. Nature no longer exists anywhere as a separate, pristine, unmanaged entity. We have conquered nature, McKibben laments, and worse, we have utterly destroyed what we have conquered. "Nature's independence *is* its meaning; without it there is nothing but us."[1] Everything that exists on the earth has become, in some measure, a human artifact, reflecting back our own flawed human nature.

---

*This essay was originally presented in the President's Lecture Series, University of Montana, Missoula, April 1990.

Henceforth we are urged to try to be more humble, but if McKibben is right about how far things have gone, it is hard to see what good a little more humility would do.

Precisely because I too believe it is time to learn to take a more humble view of our role in the great drama of life, I am compelled to disagree with McKibben's title. If in fact we see ourselves as having succeeded in completely vanquishing nature and taking command of the planet, then we are unlikely to learn the virtue of meekness. Winners don't usually turn in their trophies.

Of course, we have much reason to worry about the ecological havoc we are causing and feel guilty about it. We have indeed become a powerful, dangerous force, not least of all dangerous to ourselves. But have we seen "the end of nature"? Is this planet now nothing but an extension of human culture? No, not at all; that is a victory we could never win. Or perhaps I should say that is a crime we are incapable of committing.

The phrase "the end of nature" reminds me of another one that was hot for a while—"the end of history." Its creator, a 38-year-old State Department official, Francis Fukuyama, maintained that with the collapse of Marxism in the Soviet Union, the United States had vanquished its only adversary and achieved a final victory. We won the Cold War of ideologies—or at least capitalism won—and the dynamic that drove modern history forward has now run out of steam. "In the post-historical period," Fukuyama declared, "there will be neither art nor philosophy, just the perpetual caretaking of the museum of human history."[2] Well, this was all rightly dismissed as solemn nonsense. Like McKibben, Fukuyama was playing a trick on us by first defining his terms in an excessively narrow, dubious way, then abolishing what he had defined. In McKibben's case the result is an excess of gloom; in Fukuyama's, an excess of national self-congratulation. In both cases the rest of us need to step back and free ourselves from the flawed definitions.

I have a personal stake in refuting these two "endisms." My calling in life is that of an environmental historian: that is, I study the interactions of people and nature over time, looking for trends, seeking the origins of contemporary problems, listening to the age-old dialogue of humans and the earth. If all nature has become culture, then there is no interaction to study. If nature is truly dead as an independent force or order, then we are making no new environmental history to write about. And if history is also dead, then I might as well start selling shoes.

Historians tend to become edgy when the air is full of high-flying abstractions or talk about an absolute "end" to anything. Examined in concrete times and places, they believe, endings always seem to be linked to beginnings and what was supposed to be over was really starting anew. Resolving one conflict laid the groundwork for the next. Before we let ourselves become too melancholy about the defeat of nature or triumphant about the victory of capitalism, we need to go out on the land itself and see what has been actually happening there as technology has encountered nature.

Everyone will have a different place to go. My own choice is the area I know best, the Great Plains of North America, the broad front door of the westward movement. This is the landscape one of its most talented native daughters, Willa Cather, once described as "a country that keeps no secrets."[3] There is nowhere on the plains to hide the truth about ourselves and nature, nothing that can block our perception of that truth if we open our eyes. So revealing and so elemental, it is a landscape that can help us get down to basic questions and get clear, forceful answers to them. Like the rest of the West, the plains were settled late by Europeans, and our (white) history there is short, easily accessible, and written in a language we can ready easily. To be sure, the Indian prehistory of the plains has more secrets from us moderns than Cather allowed—it is in fact filled with mystery. What did those who lived here before the white man's coming think about the place and what did they want to do with it? Aside from a few flint points and bones, a few remnant stories and legends, their world is hopelessly lost in the earth. Still, the modern history of the plains is naked to our eyes, and we can learn here, better than in most places, some essential truths about our changing relations with the earth.

I want you to travel with me out to a place called the Cimarron National Grassland, which lies in the extreme southwestern corner of Kansas, hundreds of miles from any metropolitan area. It was named for the Cimarron River that trickles through it. The word "grassland" suggests an immense swelling ocean of grasses, and that is in fact what one finds here: 107,000 acres covered with buffalo grass, blue grama, galleta, sideoats grama, western wheat grass, and Indian grass, all native species, along with a few exotics. There are scattered clumps of trees, shiny green thickets of cottonwood and sandbar willow along the river bottom, trees that once furnished a supply of wood and shade to travelers on the Santa Fe Trail. These days there are no bison, as there were until the latter half of the nineteenth century, but one still can see most of the animal life we associate with the wilder days of the plains, including pronghorn antelopes, coyotes, prairie dogs, redtailed hawks, and rattlesnakes. The sky is still so large it makes one feel like a mite crawling across the Astrodome floor. Underfoot the topsoil is pretty much the same old stuff it has always been, deposited by the wind during the Quaternary, darkened through a

million years of dying grasses, marked by an outcropping or two of Tri-
assic sandstone. Noting those facts, most people would agree that this
place is certainly an expression of nature. But McKibben says nature is
dead; are we, therefore, looking at an artifact of man?

The environmental historian notes that the word "national" is painted
on all the signs announcing this grassland. So he gets a grant and takes
off for the National Archives in Washington to do some research on the
origins of that word. There he finds among the papers of the Division of
Land Utilization in the Department of Agriculture that, during the years
1937 to 1943, the federal government purchased this land from destitute,
discouraged, blown-out wheat farmers and cattle ranchers. What now is
a thriving grassland was then a wasteland, part of the Dust Bowl, and
archival pictures from those years show little grass and lots of bare, desolate ground. They show too abandoned farm houses, the traces of which
now lie half-concealed in the grass—crumbling pine boards nearly black
with age, boards once brought to this place from the forests of Minnesota
to provide shelter for a rural family. Hanks of rusty barbed wire still poke
up to remind that this landscape was once fenced to manage herds and
crops.

Other records show that the Cimarron National Grassland was one of
twenty-four such land-purchase projects begun in the Dust Bowl years,
scattered over eleven western states, from Oklahoma and New Mexico
north to the Dakotas and west to Idaho and Oregon—almost four million
acres purchased in all. Then it took the Soil Conservation Service more
than a decade, and plenty of farm machinery, to get a stand of native
grasses reestablished on those acres. Eventually, when the grass was
growing sturdily again, the lands were transferred to the U.S. Forest Service, which began leasing them out to local ranchers and, in 1960, declared
them to be national grasslands, equivalent to the national forests. Today,
mixed among the antelopes, sharptailed grouse, and jackrabbits are
white-faced Herefords, a breed of beef cattle whose ancestors were domesticated in England hundreds of years ago and brought more lately to
America. The historian, in other words, finds a great deal of human invasion, human disaster, human restoration, and human purpose in the
Cimarron National Grassland.[4] Nature here has certainly been affected
by culture. Does that fact make the place a human artifact?

Before attempting to answer that question, I want to broaden it by suggesting that it has long been the ambition of western civilization to make
every part of the earth over into a thoroughly cultural landscape. Francis
Bacon, René Descartes, John Locke, Adam Smith, the Compte de Buffon,
and Karl Marx were among the multitudes who dreamed the dream of

conquest. Under their influence nature came to be seen less as a system of laws to be obeyed and more as a set of potentialities to be exploited. If the planet is now all under human management, as we are told, then their dreams have been fulfilled completely.

Americans did not invent the idea of ecological conquest, but we made it emphatically our own. We saw ourselves marching across a continent not only to dominate other human beings, in the traditional pattern of imperialism, but to subdue "the wilderness," or "the land," or "aridity"—many different abstractions, all of them our chosen adversaries. We thought our conquest would essentially be a benign, happy affair of overcoming nature with technology. With shovels and axes in our bare hands, or with bulldozers, or with nuclear power, we would make the earth yield up its infinite stores of wealth to the benefit of humanity. In that process of conquest, of course, and almost incidentally, the native peoples would have to be defeated too.

Obsessed with such abstractions, Americans often failed to appreciate the deadly side of what we were doing. Those were not exactly *people,* Sioux or Comanches, living, breathing tribes of humanity, fleeing from us or suffering by our hand; they were part of the "Nature" we were conquering. No more were those whole nations of bears, moose, beavers, aspens, and pines real beings that we were destroying. Had they been acknowledged as full-fledged beings with lively needs and interests of their own, they would not have been quite so easy for us to approach aggressively, with arms drawn. After all, Americans were, and still are, a people gathered out of grinding oppression. We have had a large capacity to emphathize with the victims of conquest. But for a long time, in taking command of the North American continent, we suppressed that capacity, thereby avoiding the moral contradictions in our situation, insisting that we were not like other oppressors and conquerors. We were not after anything so mere or mundane as profits, markets, land, house sites, or raw materials. We were fighting for an empire of the free human spirit, with liberty and justice for all. Such an empire absolutely required the driving out of all opposing ideas. Do not charge us, therefore, with slaughtering millions of bison; what we actually killed was "the primitive," of which the bison was a mere symbol. So conquest became a noble enterprise, supposedly benevolent in its destruction.

In particular, this nation has made the American West the center stage for our drama of technological conquest over nature. For a full century and more, down to approximately the decade of the 1960s, the history of the West we told was a story of fighting against Nature for the sake of grand ideals. Take away all the colorful details of Calamity Jane's love life, the gold spike joining the railroad lines at Promontory Point, the grub eaten on a thousand cattle drives, the sound of a bugle in the morning air, and what is left is a saga of competing, winning, beating, succeeding, battering down every obstacle posed by nature, gaining control over the West, all in the name of great principles. Americans were the good people—and good meant strong. Americans in the West were the best of the good and the strongest of the strong. They wore leather, even the women, and packed guns. They fought to the last man. Pick up any Zane Grey novel and the names of its characters still resonate with command: Wade Holden from *Shadow on the Trail*, the lone man Lassiter from *Riders of the Purple Sage*, Jim Cleve from *The Border Legion*. Always they ended up on top, if not in every battle, then in the last great confrontation. If the westerner sometimes did not have broad enough shoulders to fit the role, if he did not always have extraordinary physical strength, then he could conquer nature in other ways and by other agencies: by wit, reason, science, collective energy, a heart of courage, or divine authority. He could become an engineer, entrepreneur, priest, or explorer. Women could tame through the hearthside tasks of domesticity. But always, regardless of the individuals involved, the common end must be one of gaining control over the land in the name of a higher morality. No other outcome was conceivable.

The classic distillation of that traditional story of the West remains Frederick Jackson Turner's terse phrase about the frontiersman: "Little by little he transforms the wilderness."[5] For Turner, as for most of his countrymen, the single significant theme was the abstract struggle between the untamed forces of Nature on the one hand and the individual male Pioneer on the other. Only one of them could survive.

Today, perhaps for the first time in our history, we are able to look with some detachment and skepticism on that old, simplified story of "the Conquest." Many of us are actually embarrassed by any boast of going out to dominate the earth. We are less likely to hear such language these days, for it is no longer quite the fashion to gesture widely toward the horizon with promises of progress and virtue. We are a little more aware of the shortcomings of the past and vaguely sense that any talk of conquest can be both destructive and naive. So we tend to use euphemisms instead: innocuous labels like "growth" or "development" to describe what is going on. Or not quite knowing how to talk about our relation to nature any more, we change the subject—ignore nature altogether, deny it even exists, insist it's all artifact, all absorbed into our culture. The key historical fact that Americans have been a people with conquest in their eyes is downplayed without really being recanted. And the actual outcome of that conquest, for people as well as for the rest of nature, even now goes largely evaded.

Historians exist to prevent such evasions from occurring. We have the responsibility of bringing old ideas to the surface, showing how they still influence our behavior, and of asking: What did we have in mind in trying to conquer nature in the West and was that what we achieved or not? How permanent was the conquest? What did the effort do to us the conquerors?

Let's examine first the idea that we have at last conquered nature in the West. The truth is, we have not conquered the natural world in some absolute sense; we have only conquered an idea, an abstraction, that we have called Nature. McKibben finally admits as much, and the admission falls with a dull thud midway through his book. "When I say that we have ended nature," he writes, "I don't mean, obviously, that natural processes have ceased—there is still sunshine and still wind, still growth, still decay. Photosynthesis continues, as does respiration. *But we have ended the thing that has, at least in modern times, defined nature for us—its separation from human society.*"[6] The distinction is once crucial and ingenuous. If we decide to define nature as a realm completely separate from people, one that bears no trace whatsoever of human presence or action, then of course nature has ended. But then when, if ever, did it exist? Such a nature began to disappear immediately after the first hominid walked upright across the African savannah over a million years ago. Define nature McKibben's way, as a pure realm that can only exist completely apart from humans and North America ceased to be natural the day a band of wandering Asians crossed into Beringia and began hunting the hairy mammoth. Their descendants, by setting fire to the grassland, putting kernels of corn in the ground, or throwing up burial mounds, were continuing to break down the separation, and breaking it down long before the whites got here, invented the automobile, and added so much carbon dioxide to the air.

McKibben's strained, pristine idea of nature is, of course, a modern European invention. When the Europeans arrived in the New World, they thought they were encountering a nature completely separate from any human society—a state of "virginity" in their male fantasies. Instead, what they came into was a country existing apart and separate from *white* human society, not from all society; and they set about with ferocious energy to end that condition and possess the land.

Consider again that place we call the Cimarron National Grassland. Long before the Department of Agriculture came to do their work of prairie restoration, long before the wheat farmer came to plow up the sod and raise crops, nature here knew the presence of human society. True, the numbers and technology in that society were much smaller and less powerful than those of the white man. One anthropologist, Jerrold Levy, has calculated that there were approximately 10,000 native Americans living on the southern plains prior to the white invasion. That gives a population density of about one person per thirty square miles, a smaller density than that of almost any other creature there.[7] The Indians, though equipped with an intelligence no less than our own, had only a few tools and all of them were made of stone and wood. They could bring down a few bison, but could make no appreciable dent in their numbers. And when the Indians were driven out by the invaders from Europe, they left little more trace of their history than the bison they hunted. However, while they dwelled on the plains, taking their meager living from the land, they must, by the strained logic I have noted, have spelled the "end of nature."

By now we should be feeling thoroughly confused. Even out on the bare, revealing plains the substance and order of nature can seem bewilderingly complex and elusive. We are driven to the conclusion that nowhere can we find a neat simple definition of what nature is, though it is apparent that there are patterns, processes, events, and beings in the landscape that we did not invent or set in motion. We must admit that our brains can not claim credit for their existence; they are not the work of our culture. McKibben's list of "processes"—sunshine, wind, growth, and decay—are as active in the West today as they were in the beginning of time. The buffalo grass now sprouting from the soil is also a part of nature, although it may have arrived in the 1940s as seed in gunny sacks and have gotten drilled into the ground by Ford tractors. The return of the pronghorns may have owed something to human purpose, but they came on their own four feet, guided by an instinct that had evolved long before *Homo sapiens* did. In many other ways, nature has not been vanquished or even brought much under human rule. Thus, we are forced to admit that nature is something more complicated, tenacious, and subtly ordered than our languages or analyses can pin down. What we cannot easily define, we cannot really conquer.

Seen from an airplane at 30,000 feet, the Cimarron National Grassland appears to be a land under rigid, total human control. Its boundaries conform to the national land survey—the geometric grid of range and township lines that directed the entire westward movement from the Appalachian Mountains to the Pacific. But go a little higher, look at the spot from the moon, and all the man-made lines on it vanish; it appears then that the clouds and the great masses of earth and water are in control. Or come down to ground level and start walking across the terrain; even a rattlesnake can begin to look more in charge than a man. Have we really achieved total dominance over the insect order, or over weeds, or over the force of gravity, or over the soil bacteria? Mainly what we have established on the plains is a powerful but limited influence over the distribution of many of our fellow plants and animals, and we trumpet that as the conquest of nature. Yet take away that influence for a hundred years, let the plants and animals proliferate again with freedom, and it would soon be hard to find any trace of the white man's regime over most of the countryside.

We come then to a second question: How permanent has our power over nature been to date, and how long will it last into the future? Recall those mouldering pioneer homesteads in the Cimarron grassland, the roofs, floors, doors, and windows rotting into the earth, testimonals to ambitions that once flourished. They are a few of the many ghost farms on the plains. Drought and poor judgment, a lack of skills and a surfeit of greed have again and again turned agricultural settlements into ghosts. Morton County, where the Cimarron grassland is located, lost 47 percent of its residents in the dirty thirties. Despite the fact that the nation has doubled its population since that time, the ghosts have not returned to life. Indeed, more ghost farms are being made every year throughout the rural West.

What has largely kept agriculture going on the southern plains since the 1930s has been deep-well irrigation, drawing on the Ogallala aquifer, the biggest source of underground fresh water in the world—that along with federal crop subsidies and drought disaster aid. Within another thirty years western Kansas will have depleted most of its water supply; the Kansas Water Office predicts a 75 percent decline in irrigated acreage by 2020.[8] Inevitably, as that day approaches, the number of ghost farms will mount rapidly. More and more it is clear that the debacle of the thirties was not altogether an aberration; sustaining so extensive a system of crop farming in the driest part of the country, on the lands beyond the 98th meridian, has been a technological stunt that we cannot keep up indefinitely. Realizing that truth, we must reassess the entire idea of what the conquest of nature in the West has really meant. Making the land productive through agriculture was the essence of that conquest, and the farmer was long hailed as fighting in the front ranks of the battle. But if row-crop agriculture is now facing a period of retrenchment and defeat in the region, then where is the victory we were promised? It now looks more ephemeral than we ever imagined.

We can also find hundreds of ghost *towns* scattered across the West, some of them once selling merchanise to farm families, some mining minerals from the earth. Like the ghost farms, the ghost towns failed to overcome the limits of nature. Their conquest depended on having an endless abundance of rain or copper or timber or oil. I remember vividly a hike made with some undergraduate friends in 1962 up Geneva Creek, which is in the central part of the state of Colorado. All the way to the headwaters we went, to a patch of perpetual snow lying above the trees near the Continental Divide; and there we found, much to our astonishment, an entire abandoned mining town named Timberline, with cabins and tunnels and mining office virtually intact from their heyday in the early part of the century. In one of the cabins we found a man's way of life frozen in time: old *Saturday Evening Post* magazines and reading glasses, half-filled boxes of oatmeal, a coal-burning stove, bunks with blankets still in them, tools for a forge. The stream ran icily by the cabin's front door and we camped there for several days, drinking our "bourbon and ditchwater," absorbed in this museum of the past as much as in the sublimity of the landscape. Three years later we returned and found porcupines in the cabins, chewing up all the history. Another year or two passed, and some of the town came to be burned to the ground by elk hunters on a revel. Who then turns out to be the final winner in Timberline—nature or man?

The environmental historian has to conclude that, contrary to Frederick Jackson Turner, we Americans have not been triumphing over the wilderness "little by little." Such an image suggests a steady linear progression to some ultimate point called civilization. The real history we have made is rather one of cycles—rises and falls, victories and defeats, neither humans nor nature ever gaining a complete, final mastery. Only in a carefully restricted span, say, a period of a few decades or a century or two, and by carefully specified criteria, can one find more or less straight lines running one way or the other through time. The entire history of the westward movement has to date been written from a highly selective view, enabling us to tell and believe a story that ends in epic success—but the real story is not over, will never be over, and we will have lots more tragedies and failures to record as it goes on.

One linear progression we can indisputably find in modern times is an increasingly larger scale in our relations with nature. Technological and social complexity has increased substantially since the first covered wagon creaked out onto the plains. Instead of lone individuals or single families, we have become corporations and bureaucracies confronting the environment. Unquestionably, we have gained power through that collectivism and can do things that our ancestors never could have imagined,

like stripmining Montana coal and shipping it to Arkansas, burning it to
furnish electricity for microwave ovens in Little Rock. This new power
depends on very large instruments of transportation and communication
that would have been the wildest fantasies to earlier pioneers. The environmental consequences of that power are monumental, though as individuals we have considerable trouble seeing and taking responsibility for
them; they seem so remote from our lives. Unlike the Kiowas or Arapahoes of the plains, who looked the death they caused directly in the face,
we have grown less and less aware of the dying, the depleting, the destroying that our style of life demands. Paradoxically, this increasingly complicated and impersonal scale in our relations with nature has encouraged
an illusion of total victory. We have come to have a complete, childlike
confidence in our control.

Such confidence, it seems to a historian, may be quite misplaced. The
growing scale of our relations with nature may be matched by the scale of
our failures. Instead of a scattering of ghost farms and ghost towns, we
may be making our way toward a ghost civilization. Recall that dependency of modern rural life in the West on large-scale water engineering.
What future can one expect for a civilization that has come to depend
heavily on center-pivot irrigation, on massive dams like Hoover, Fort
Peck, and Grand Coulee, on thousands of miles of concrete ditches and
canals? The aquifer must dry up at some point. The reservoirs must fill
with silt and become a series of man-made waterfalls. The canals must at
some point crack apart and weeds grow in the cracks. Every large-scale
irrigation society in human history started off with the same assumptions
of permanence that we did, but by and by every one of them had to admit
defeat. The sureness of one's feeling of omnipotence has never had much
to do with reality.

History, I must emphasize, runs in cycles. The cycle of conquest is one
of the oldest, as old as Sumer or Mesopotamia. Standing on the Great
Plains forces that realization home. We must admit that the most
dependable thing humans have achieved here is impermanence.

A third question about this supposed conquest of nature has to do with
the conquerors themselves: Is conquest really a one-way process in which
power is exercised exclusively over the conquered, or does the conqueror
also get transformed? Turner, to his credit, did acknowledge that any conquest includes a process of adaptation: the wilderness masters the pioneer before the tables are turned. This is hardly a new observation about
conquests; historians have traced the ways the Normans were changed
when they invaded England and defeated the Anglo-Saxons, pointing out
that the language spoken in Britain today is not Norman French but an

amalgamation of all the tongues that once contested for primacy. So in the drive to conquer nature in the West, the white conquerors ended up adopting some of the language of the native peoples and the native environments.

Take, for instance, the matter of fencing. You cannot establish much control over the land without putting up fences. The original purpose of a fence was, as etymology suggests, "defense," that is, providing protection from marauding animals that threaten one's crops. Defensive fences go back as far as agriculture does; Indians put them up to keep game from trampling down their corn and beans. With modern Europeans fences became an offensive technology too—assertions of one's private estate against the claims of others. Defensive or offensive, the fence has always been a part of nature as much as culture. In England it might have been a grassy ditch or a hedgerow made up of native plants. In early New England the fence was commonly a stone wall. An old adage held that when a farmer bought one acre of land for plowing, he needed another acre to dump the surplus rocks; but if he piled up the rocks in the form of walls he could get two acres to use again.[9] On the plains the Russo-German farmers discovered that they could cut fences from the ledges of limestone that underlay the surface—"post rock" they called it. Others brought in the osage orange tree, which is covered with wicked thorns, to make a protective hedge around their crops, leaving a legacy of bloody scratches for their descendents trying to keep their pastures clear of the nuisance. Did those various strategies of fencing constitute a one-way conquest? Are all those fences exclusively in the kingdom of culture? Obviously not. Each of those species of fence bore the marks of their local environment.

In 1931 Walter Prescott Webb used the development of fencing on the Great Plains to show that the biophysical environment forced an adaptation on the incoming whites. Many of my colleagues find Professor Webb unconvincing these days—too simplistic, too much of an "environmental determinist," they say, and to a point I am forced to agree with them. But Webb had a few things right that modern historians need to remember. The westward movement of agriculture was at once a process of conquest *and* adaptation. To illustrate that process Webb tells the story of the invention of barbed wire, which he calls "a child of the prairies and Plains"—a prickly child, sinister in appearance, but a child of the region all the same. Though there is some disputing the facts, its parents were apparently Lucinda and Joseph Glidden of DeKalb, Illinois, a farm couple who, in 1873, were desperate to keep pigs from rooting up Mrs. Glidden's garden. Working in the kitchen and backyard with a coffee mill and grindstone, they discovered a way to weave two stands of wire around a row of barbs and thus discourage the marauders. By 1880 they had sold their invention to the manufacturing firm of Washburn and Moeb, who were turning out eighty million pounds of it a year. "The invention of barbed wire," writes Webb, "revolutionized land values and opened up to the homesteader the fertile Prairie Plains, now the most valuable agricultural land in the United States."[10] Soon the wire was stretched all over the region. Competing varieties appeared and found their salesmen; eventually they all became artifacts of the past, tacked onto display boards and deposited in museums of local history. Scholars have published contentious books and papers on the relative merits of the Ellwood Ribbon, the Lazy Plate, Burnell's Four-Point (Vicious), the Necktie, the Brotherton Barb, the Decker Spread (Modified), and the Champion or Zigzag (Obvious).[11] Here, they are saying, we have one of the leading tools of empire; or as more than one smalltown exhibit has proclaimed, we have the "wire that won the West."

Unlike the Massachusetts stone wall or Virginia rail fence, the barbed wire fence was unmistakably a product of industrial capitalism. It required the Bessemer process for making steel cheaply, complex wire-drawing equipment, massive factories for large-scale manufacture, and heavy railway cars for transport to places like southwestern Kansas, and none of those requirements seems remotely "natural." But hold on: there was *something* of western nature that got into the wire too, making it what it was. That something was aridity. Farmers were more or less compelled to buy the wire from Washburn and Moeb because they lacked the wood they wanted for fencing, and they lacked the wood, of course, because they lived in an arid or semi-arid climate. The technology of conquest therefore had to be adjusted to meet environmental exigencies. To be sure, Mr. and Mrs. Glidden might have hit upon a laser-beamed pig-zapper instead of a wire fence, and farmers might have preferred it had it been offered; the environment did not absolutely require a single solution. Still, Webb was right that the barbed wire fence was an adaptation to nature, and it made rural life in the West noticeably different than it had been in the East.

I do not mean to argue against McKibben that we have been *conquered* by nature, only that we have been *influenced* by it in a very material way— by climate, soils, water, terrain, ecosystems, light and color, the presence of animals—and that influence can be located in our technology, clothing, architecture, and landscape design. The irrigation dam is one such manifestation, though ironically an instrument of domination, and so is the western stock saddle. We may live in a world governed by the global marketplace—by what Immanuel Wallerstein calls the world economic system—but the astonishing truth is that local and regional material culture has frequently survived that conquering, homogenizing economic force, much as a Lithuanian identity has survived decades of Soviet rule. What is more, industrial capitalism has, despite its homogenizing tendencies, had to adapt now and then to the conditions in which it has found itself. You can't sell a cotton baler in Missoula or a pitchfork in Manhattan. Other environmental influences take a less material form in law, art, poetry, and social habits, making the felt experience of living in the West different from that of other places.

Environmental adaptation is, in other words, a real phenomenon that survives all our power and effort to impose ourselves on the land. We try to rule—but we also must bend. The environmental historian must look for both behaviors. To do so, he may have to overcome a lot of blindness, even a refusal to accept the reality of adaptation. Why would people refuse to accept that reality? Because it would contradict the idea running deep in American culture that the individual is, or ought to be, free of all restraint, whether it comes from genes, climate, microbes, one's own inventions, government, all forms of authority, or fate. Any form of restraint on our sovereign individuality has generally been regarded as a bondage imposed on us for dark reasons. In America, the land of the self-made man, so strong is that tradition of nonadaptive individualism that even those arguing that western settlement was essentially a collective affair, dependent on the group, still balk at the notion that nature has influenced who we are. So even do some of us environmental historians when we write about nature as though it were simply shapeless putty in human hands.

We will not wholly overcome this assumption of human autonomy without, as I have suggested, uprooting ideas going back to eighteenth-century Europe and before. But in the meanwhile we can at least try to loosen the West from some of the binding assumptions we have inherited. We can begin to try to tell its story not simply as a conquest, an imposition of an invading culture on the land, but as a process, however imperfect, of environmental adaptation.

I don't see how anyone who has spent any time on the Great Plains, studying and thinking about what has gone on here, could truly miss seeing that its history has been one of trying to meet, in Henry David Thoreau's phrase, the expectations of the land. In the first place, they must admit that environmental history is basic to the place; then, they must grant that environmental history tells a story of reciprocity and interaction rather than of culture replacing nature.

Most of that process of adaptation has been on an unconscious, unintended, often indirect level, creating a tangled web of nature, technology, and folk mentality; but there is also a story of conscious, *intentional* adaptation to tell. Now and then people did deliberately try to understand their ecological situation and developed explicit ideas about how to adjust their culture accordingly. If we look for those adaptive intentions, we might begin to see the coming of the first explorers as something more than a prelude to conquest; we might present the explorer as, in some degree, an advance man for adaptation. John Wesley Powell would be the most celebrated figure in that history, but there were dozens of others, scientists of all sorts, many of them in geology, ecology, and geography, along with agronomy, anthropology, and cultural ecology. We also have a tradition of appropriate technology in the region to write about, from windmills and solar energy to ideas about ecologically sustainable agriculture, along with a history of landscape restorations like Cimarron National Grassland. Sometimes it has been architects who have been in the forefront of cultural adaptation. Or it has been visual artists and writers. These days it is often fashionable to view all painting, building, novel writing, photo taking, indeed every human creative act, as an ordering we impose on nature—a "construct" or "design" we make out of the chaos around us. When we look at a picture or a landscape, some critics maintain, all we should see is a human hand organizing it. But some of our predecessors in the West did not understand that they were "constructing a reality." If we dismiss all their work, their designs, their creativity, as more expressions of power and conquest, we distort their purposes radically. Art can speak of the presence of the human without arguing for the annihilation of the natural.

In addition to recovering that artistic and intellectual tradition of adaptiveness, we need to pay more attention to the lives of all those anonymous people who came into the West wanting to stick, who did stick, and consider how they did it. Their stories are not to be found in the ghost settlements that thousands left nor in the booming cities where so many western historians have dwelled. Wallace Stegner writes: "If we want characteristic western towns we must look for them, paradoxically, beyond the West's prevailing urbanism, out in the boondocks where the interstates do not reach, mainline planes do not fly, and branch plants do not locate. The towns that are most western have had to strike a balance between mobility and stability, and the law of sparseness has kept them from growing too big. They are the places where the stickers stuck, and perhaps were stuck; the places where adaptation has gone furthest."[12]

Only a little of the history of those places has yet been told, perhaps because historians like me have been too interested in dramatizing the messes we have made.

Many living in Stegner's out-of-the-way places came into the West seeking wealth and opportunity but found something more satisfying. They changed their sense of who they were, becoming people of the prairies or mountains, of Wyoming's Sweetwater valley or California's Mohave Desert. When people give some of their allegiance to a place, they become more complex minds than they were before, more filled with contradictions, more unpredictable, more capable of learning. They may still persist in taking the wild risks of the uncommitted; on the other hand they may seek to discipline their desires and nurture that relationship. We have had both sorts of people in the West, as we have had elsewhere on the continent, though we have not always given those stickers and nurturers their due.

I make no claim that a history discovering the roots of environmental adaptation would, by itself, be more true than the old one of conquest, or attempted conquest. Any familiarity with the ups and downs of settlement on the plains would quickly scuttle such a notion. But we do need a better story than the one we've been telling about the West, if nothing else than to save us from gloom and excessive pessimism. We need new kinds of heroes, a new appreciation of nature's powers of recovery, and a new sense of purpose in this region—all of which means we need a new past, one with the struggle for adaptation as its main narrative, one that regards successful adaptation as a kind of heroism too.

Today, the West has become a very urban place, indeed it is the most urbanized part of the United States in terms of where most of its people live. Yet for all that, westerners may be more aware today of the significance of nature and of its role in their lives than they were fifty or a hundred years ago when they were down on the farm. So it is all over the earth. Though seemingly encapsulated in an urban cocoon, people are awakening to the whole branch, the whole great green tree, on which their cities hang. One of the surprises of our time is that people have begun to acknowledge their continuing dependency on nature wherever they live. I have to conclude from that growing awareness that many of us do not feel very much like conquerors. We are too nervous and fearful for that. If as a species we have truly conquered nature, why do we feel so insecure about the achievement?

The lessons found out here on the plains are clear and yet complex. They say that we can live without the old fantasy of a pristine, inviolate, edenic wilderness—it was, after all, never adequate to the reality of the natural world as we found it. But we could never really turn all of nature into artifact. Nor could we live without nature. For all our ingenuity, we sense that we need that independent, self-organizing, resilient biophysical world to sustain us. If nature were ever truly at an end, then we would be finished. It is not, however, and we are not.

Notes

1. Beyond the Agrarian Myth

1. Josiah Gregg, *The Commerce of the Prairies* (Lincoln: Univ. of Nebraska Press, 1926), 31.

2. Paul Horgan, *Josiah Gregg and His Vision of the Early West* (New York: Farrar, Straus, Giroux, 1972), esp. 110.

3. Ian Frazier, *Great Plains* (New York: Farrar, Straus, Giroux, 1989), 1, 209–10, 214.

4. Robert G. Athearn, *The Mythic West in Twentieth-Century America* (Lawrence: Univ. Press of Kansas, 1986), 273.

5. Henry Nash Smith, *Virgin Land: The American West as Symbol and Myth* (Cambridge: Harvard Univ. Press, 1950), 187.

6. Smith, *Virgin Land,* 187.

7. Ibid., 251.

8. Richard Hofstader, *The Progressive Historians: Turner, Beard, Parrington* (New York: Alfred A. Knopf, 1968), 103–4.

9. Ibid., 106.

10. As one of my predecessors at the University of Kansas, George Anderson, once put it, the history of the West was about growth in "banks, rails, and mails." See his essay of that title in *The Frontier Challenge: Responses to the Trans-Mississippi West,* ed. John G. Clark (Lawrence: Univ. Press of Kansas, 1971), 275–307.

11. Gerald D. Nash, *The American West Transformed: The Impact of the Second World War* (Bloomington: Indiana Univ. Press, 1985), 215–16.

2. New West, True West

1. Howard Lamar, ed., *The Reader's Encyclopedia of the American West* (New York, 1977), 710–12.

2. Frederick Merk, *History of the Westward Movement* (New York, 1978), 616–17.

3. Ray Allen Billington, *Westward Expansion: A History of the American Frontier*, 4th ed. (New York, 1974), 29, 648.

4. Turner to Merle Curti, cit., Wilbur Jacobs, "Frederick Jackson Turner," in *Turner, Bolton, and Webb: Three Historians of the American Frontier* (Seattle, 1965), 8.

5. Ibid., 9. I am aware that Turner also contributed much to our thinking about sections and regions in American history. On this subject, see Michael C. Steiner, "The Significance of Turner's Sectional Thesis," *Western Historical Quarterly* 10 (Oct. 1979), 437–66. Turner did not, however, see "the West" as a cohesive whole, fixed in place. He divided the country into eight regions: New England, the Middle States, the Southeast, the Southwest, the Middle West, the Great Plains, the Mountain States, and the Pacific Coast. (Turner, "Sections and Nation," *Yale Review* 12 (Oct. 1922), 2.)

6. Walter Prescott Webb, "The American West: Perpetual Mirage," *Harper's Magazine*, 214 (May 1957), 25. See also James Malin, "Webb and Regionalism," in *History and Ecology: Studies of the Grassland*, ed. Robert Swierenga (Lincoln, 1984), 85–104.

7. Powell used Charles Shott's "Rain Chart of the United States" to delineate the Arid Region. Shott's twenty-inch isohyet actually corresponds to the 100th meridian only in Texas and the Indian Territory (Oklahoma); then it veers slightly eastward to include all of the Dakotas and the northwestern corner of Minnesota. The western edge of the region excludes all of northern California, the Sierra Nevada, and western Oregon and Washington—following roughly the 120th meridian north of Reno. The whole embraced almost half of the United States outside Alaska. See J. W. Powell, *Report on the Lands of the Arid Region*, 45th Cong., 2nd sess., House Executive Document 73 (Washington, D.C., 1878), see map included.

8. *Historians and the American West*, ed. Michael Malone (Lincoln, 1983), 2.

9. Felix Frankfurter, cit., in Merrill Jensen, ed., *Regionalism in America* (Madison, 1951), xvi. An excellent recent essay on regionalism, with ample bibliography, is Richard Maxwell Brown's "The New Regionalism in America, 1970–1981," in William G. Robbins, Robert J. Frank, and Richard E. Ross., eds., *Regionalism and the Pacific Northwest* (Corvallis, 1983), 37–96.

10. Earl Pomeroy, "Toward a Reorientation of Western History: Continuity and Environment," *Mississippi Valley Historical Review* 41 (March 1955), 581–82. Pomeroy also rejected the claim that their environment made westerners more radical than other Americans, a point he wins hands down.

11. See Earl Pomeroy, *The Territories and the United States* (New Haven, 1966).

12. The most thoughtful student of the relation between ethnicity and region has been Frederick C. Luebke. See his "Ethnic Minority Groups in the American West," in Malone, *Historians and the American West*, 387–413; and also his "Regionalism and the Great Plains: Problems of Concept and Method," *Western Historical Quarterly* 15 (Jan. 1984), 19–38.

13. William G. Robbins, "The 'Plundered Province' Thesis and the Recent Historiography of the American West," *Pacific Historical Review* 55 (Nov. 1986), 577–97.

14. The phrase "mode of production" has its origins in Marxist scholarship, where it refers to both technology ("forces") and social or class relations. See, among other works, Barry Hindess and Paul Q. Hirst, *Pre-capitalist Modes of Production* (London, 1975), 9–12; James F. Becker, *Marxian Political Economy: An Outline* (Cambridge, 1977), 35; Aidan Foster-Carter, "The Modes of Production Controversy," *New Left Review* 107 (Jan.–Feb. 1978), 47–78. Here I use the phrase more loosely, and with revision, to indicate, first, a set of techniques adapted for the exploitation of particular environments and, second, a resulting social organization.

15. The origins of the western cattle industry have recently been traced to the Old South by geographer Terry Jordan in *Trails to Texas: Southern Roots of Western Cattle Ranching*

(Lincoln, 1981). Whatever its source, the pastoral mode became, for ecological and economic reasons, ultimately rooted in the West.

16. Gilbert Fite has reviewed some of the major titles on this subject in Malone, *Historians and the American West*, 221–24 and 230–33. What is so far missing from any of the literature on American pastoralism is any awareness that this mode has expressions all over the world, has been well studied by anthropologists, and needs some comparative and cross-disciplinary work by historians. See, for example, Walter Goldschmidt, "A General Model for Pastoral Social Systems," *Pastoral Production and Society* (Cambridge, 1979), 15–27; Brian Spooner, *The Cultural Ecology of Pastoral Nomads*, Addison-Wesley Module in Anthropology No. 45 (Reading, Mass., 1973); Z. A. Konczacki, *The Economics of Pastoralism: A Case Study of Sub-Saharan Africa* (London, 1978); and the classic study by E. E. Evans-Pritchard, *The Nuer, A Description of the Modes of Livelihood and Political Institutions of a Nilotic People* (Oxford, 1940).

17. Notable exceptions to this observation include such works as Norris Hundley, *Water and the West: The Colorado River Compact and the Politics of Water in the American West* (Berkeley, 1975); Lawrence Lee, *Reclaiming the American West: An Historiography and Guide* (Santa Barbara, 1980); William Kahrl, *Water and Power: The Conflict Over Los Angeles' Water Supply in the Owens Valley* (Berkeley, 1982); Donald J. Pisani, *From the Family Farm to Agribusiness: The Irrigation Crusade in California, 1850–1930* (Berkeley, 1984); and Robert G. Dunbar, *Forging New Rights in Western Waters* (Lincoln, 1983).

18. See, for example, Emil Haury, *The Hohokam, Desert Farmers and Craftsmen: Excavations at Snaketown, 1964–1965* (Tucson, 1976); and, for even more ancient examples, Karl Wittfogel, *Oriental Despotism: A Comparative Study of Total Power* (New Haven, 1957); Anne Bailey and Josep Llobera, eds., *The Asiatic Mode of Production* (London, 1981); Julian Steward, ed., *Irrigation Civilizations* (Washington, D.C., 1955).

19. U.S. Department of Commerce, *1978 Census of Agriculture. Vol. 4, Irrigation* (Washington, D.C., 1982), 30; Council for Agricultural Science and Technology, *Water Use in Agriculture: Now and For the Future*, Report No. 95 (Sept. 1982), 13.

20. Frederick Jackson Turner, "Contributions of the West to American Democracy," and "Pioneer Ideals," reprinted in his collected essays, *The Frontier in American History* (New York, 1920), 258–59, 278–79.

21. My own book, *Rivers of Empire: Water, Aridity, and the Growth of the American West* (New York, 1985), is an attempt to reinterpret the West as a modern hydraulic society. I discuss Steinbeck's California on pp. 213–33.

22. Webb, "The American West," 28. See also Gerald Nash, *The American West in the Twentieth Century: A Short History of an Urban Oasis* (Englewood Cliffs, 1973), 5; and Earl Pomeroy, *The Pacific Slope: A History of California, Oregon, Washington, Idaho, Utah, and Nevada* (New York, 1965).

23. For the larger dimensions of this idea see William Leiss, *The Domination of Nature* (New York, 1972); and Michael Zimmerman, "Marx and Heidegger on the Technological Domination of Nature," *Philosophy Today* 23 (1979), 99–112.

24. It might be argued that, even in the global technological society, there are and always will be regional differences—that in its triumph over nature, technology still bears the imprint of what it has conquered. But for most people the experience of living in advanced technological systems is that they lose any sense of regional uniqueness.

25. Webb, "The American West," 29, 31.

26. José Ortega y Gasset, "Arid Plains, and Arid Men," in *Invertebrate Spain*, trans. Mildred Adams (New York, 1937), 158–65.

27. Clifford Geertz, *The Interpretation of Cultures: Selected Essays* (New York, 1977), chap. 15; and Emmanuel Le Roy Ladurie, *The Peasants of Languedoc*, trans. John Day (Urbana, 1974).

3. *Cowboy Ecology*

1. The textbooks surveyed were these: *A History of the United States,* by Stephan Thernstrom, 2nd ed. (New York: Harcourt Brace Jovanovich, 1984)—½ page out of a total of 764 pages; *A People and a Nation: A History of the United States,* by Mary Beth Norton, David M. Katzman, Paul D. Escott, Howard P. Chudacoff, Thomas G. Patterson, and William M. Tuttle, Jr., 3rd ed. (Boston: Houghton Mifflin, 1990)—2½ pages out of 1,025; *The National Experience: A History of the United States,* by John M. Blum, William S. McFeely, Edmund S. Morgan, Arthur M. Schlesinger, Jr., Kenneth M. Stampp, and C. Vann Woodward, 6th ed. (New York: Harcourt Brace Jovanovich, 1985)—3 pages out of 983; *The Shaping of the American Past,* by Robert Kelley, 4th ed. (Englewood Cliffs, N.J.: Prentice Hall, 1986)—2 pages out of 872; *The United States,* by Winthrop D. Jordan, Leon F. Litwack, Richard Hofstadter, William Miller, and Daniel Aaron, 6th ed. (Englewood Cliffs, N.J.: Prentice Hall, 1987)—2 pages out of 874; *These United States: The Question of Our Past,* by Irwin Unger (Englewood Cliffs, N.J.: Prentice-Hall, 1986)—3½ pages out of 856. Even these few pages are counted generously, and in many cases they tell more about urban stockyards than life on the range.

2. Daniel Boorstin, *The Americans: The Democratic Experience* (New York: Vintage, 1973), 3–41.

3. Don D. Walker, *Clio's Cowboys: Studies in the Historiography of the Cattle Trade* (Lincoln: Univ. of Nebraska Press, 1981), 131–47. The son-in-of-law of Karl Marx, Edward Aveling, traveled to the United States with his wife Eleanor, and, despite not getting beyond Chicago, concluded: "Out in the fabled West the life of the 'free' cowboy is as much that of a slave as is the life of his Eastern brother, the Massachusetts mill-hand. And the slave-owner is in both cases the same—the capitalist." (Aveling, *An American Journey* (New York: John W. Lovell, 1887), 155.) For a discussion of the comparative freedom and well-being of ranch hands in Latin America, see Carlos M. Rama, "The Passing of the Afro-Uruguayans from Caste Society into Class Society," in *Race and Class in Latin America,* Magnus Morner, ed. (New York: Columbia Univ. Press, 1970), 28–50; and Richard W. Slatta, *Cowboys of the Americas* (New Haven: Yale Univ. Press, 1990), 93–97.

4. Walter Prescott Webb, "The American West: A Perpetual Mirage," *Harper's Magazine* 214 (May 1957): 25–31.

5. Brian Spooner, *The Cultural Ecology of Pastoral Nomads,* Module in Anthropology, No. 45 (Reading, Mass.: Addison-Wesley, 1973). The last category is unique in that the reindeer have always been a semi-wild species and their herders began as hunter-gatherers, not agriculturists. On the Scandinavian Lapps, see Tim Ingold, *Hunters, Pastoralists, and Ranchers: Reindeer Economics and Their Transformations* (Cambridge: Cambridge Univ. Press, 1980). In the other cases the key differentiating factor is average precipitation: camel pastoralism occurs in areas with less than eight inches of rainfall, while cattle pastoralism requires two or three times that amount.

6. See A. Endre Nyerges, "Pastoralists, Flocks and Vegetation: Processes of Co-Adaptation," in *Desertification and Development: Dryland Ecology in Social Perspective,* Brian Spooner and Haracharan Singh Mann, eds. (New York: Academic, 1982), 217–47. Writing in defense of the environmental impact of a modern African pastoral people are Kaj Arhem, "Two Sides of Development: Maasai Pastoralism and Wildlife Conservation in Ngorongoro, Tanzania," *Ethnos* 49 (March 1984): 186–210; and Katherine M. Homewood and W. A. Rodgers, "Pastoralism and Conservation," *Human Ecology* 12, no. 4 (1984): 431–41. The latter argue that Maasai have lived for 2000 years in their homeland without destroying either the vegetation or the competing wild herbivores. For an account of the disintegration of this culture under European invasion, see Alan H. Jacobs, "Maasai Pastoralism in Historical Perspective," in *Pastoralism in Tropical Africa,* Theodore Monod, ed. (London: Oxford, 1975), 406–25. The destructive impact of the state, the market economy, and competing agricul-

turists are major themes in John G. Galaty and Philip Carl Salzman, eds., *Change and Development in Nomadic and Pastoral Societies* (Leiden: E. J. Brill, 1981).

7. Lois Beck, "Herd Owners and Hired Shepherds: The Qashga'i of Iran," *Ethnology* 19 (July 1980): 327-51. See also Theodore Monod, "Introduction," *Pastoralism in Tropical Africa*, 1-83. On the relation of mobility to independence, see Walter Goldschmidt, "Independence as an Element in Pastoral Social Systems," *Anthropological Quarterly* 44 (July 1971): 132-42, which examines works on African and Middle Eastern cultures. Goldschmidt qualifies his generalization by insisting that pastoralists also have a strong sense of the group; their tribal identities are compatible with independent action.

8. Robert K. Burns, Jr., "The Circum-Alpine Culture Area: A Preliminary View," *Anthropological Quarterly* 36 (July 1963): 130-55.

9. A good introduction to the Andean pastoral life is Shozo Masuda, Izumi Shimada, and Craig Morris, eds., *Andean Ecology and Civilizations: An Interdisciplinary Perspective on Andean Ecological Complementarity* (Tokyo: Univ. of Tokyo Press, 1985). See also Steven Webster, "Native Pastoralism in the South Andes," *Ethnology* 12 (April 1973): 115-33.

10. The so-called "tragedy of the commons," in which self-maximizing individuals overgraze a communally managed pasture, never seems to have occurred in this case or, for that matter, in European communal agriculture generally. A good discussion of the matter is Susan Jane Buck Cox, "No Tragedy on the Commons," *Environmental Ethics* 7 (Spring 1985): 49-61. The source of the myth is Garrett Hardin, "The Tragedy of the Commons," *Science* 162 (1968): 1243-48. Under the title *Managing the Commons* (San Francisco: W. H. Freeman, 1977), Hardin and John Baden have edited a set of essays claiming—inconsistently, I believe—that the best way to prevent such tragedies is to turn to a more individualistic, free-market approach, except in the area of human fertility, which must be under a strict regime of laws and regulations.

11. Robert McC. Netting, *Balancing on an Alp: Ecological Change and Continuity in a Swiss Mountain Community* (Cambridge: Cambridge Univ. Press, 1981), 69. A parallel study, though less satisfactory in its treatment of the problem of regulation, is Sandra Ott, *The Circle of the Mountains: A Basque Shepherding Community* (Oxford: Clarendon, 1981). See also Pier Paolo Viazzo, *Upland Communities: Environment, Population and Social Structure in the Alps since the Sixteenth Century* (Cambridge: Cambridge Univ. Press, 1989), which focuses on demography.

12. Siegfried Giedion refers to this final, fatal step as "the mechanization of death." See his discussion of the meat packing industry in *Mechanization Takes Command* (New York: Norton, 1969), 209-46.

13. For a comparison of American and Argentinian ranching in their world trade patterns see Arnold Strickon, "The Euro-American Ranching Complex," in *Man, Culture, and Animals: The Role of Animals in Human Ecological Adjustments*, Anthony Leeds and Andrew P. Vayda, eds. (Washington: American Association for the Advancement of Science, 1965).

14. Granville Stuart, *Forty Years on the Frontier*, Paul Phillips, ed. (Cleveland: Arthur H. Clark, 1925), vol. II. pp. 187-88.

15. The classic account of the episode remains Ernest Staples Osgood, *The Day of the Cattleman* (Minneapolis: Univ. of Minnesota Press, 1929), chap. 7. In the seventeen western states cattle numbers increased from 7.9 million in 1870 to 21.6 million in 1886. After a sharp fall in the late 1880s, these numbers climbed back, until they abruptly fell again in the 1930s—when the federal government had to buy and slaughter one-sixth of the entire herd to keep graziers solvent and to protect pastures from overstocking.

16. A concise, earnest statement of this argument can be found in Gary D. Libecap, *Locking up the Range: Federal Land Controls and Grazing*, Pacific Institute for Public Policy Research (Cambridge, Mass.: Ballinger, 1981). Unfortunately, it is almost all neoclassical economic theory, with little historical research to root it in reality.

17. Among the many writings on this subject a good introduction is provided by John G. Francis, "Environmental Values, Intergovernmental Policies, and the Sagebrush Rebellion," in *Western Public Lands: The Management of Natural Resources in a Time of Declining Federalism,* John G. Francis and Richard Ganzel, eds. (Totowa, N.J.: Rowman & Allenheld, 1984), 29–45. In addition to Nevada, Wyoming, Utah, and Arizona passed some form of "sagebrush legislation."

18. Act of June 28, 1934, ch 865, 48 Stat. 1269, popularly known as the Taylor Grazing Act. It appears generally as 43 USCS, Section 315 *et sequitur.*

19. The Federal Land Policy and Management Act of 1976 instructed the Bureau of Land Management to take more strenuous measures to assure the long-term productivity of the public rangeland under its supervision. In 1978, the Public Rangelands Improvement Act went further to restore the deteriorated range by appropriating $365 million over the next twenty years for improved management. These laws meant that many ranchers had to cut their herd and flock sizes substantially—and the "Sagebrush Rebellion" was born. Under the subsequent administration of President Ronald Reagan the BLM gave up a great deal of its new power to the local advisory councils comprised of rancher lessees.

20. The literature on the public grazing lands is large; I have found the following titles to be the most useful overviews: Wesley Calef, *Private Grazing on Public Lands: Studies of the Local Management of the Taylor Grazing Act* (Chicago: Univ. of Chicago Press, 1960); Marion Clawson, *The Bureau of Land Management* (New York: Praeger, 1971); Philip O. Fox, *Politics and Grass* (Seattle: Univ. of Washington Press, 1960); Paul W. Gates, *History of Public Land Law Development* (Washington, D.C.: Public Land Law Review Commission, 1968); and William J. Voight, *Public Grazing Lands* (New Brunswick, N.J.: Rutgers Univ. Press, 1976).

21. The best work of this sort we have is James A. Young and B. Abbott Sparks, *Cattle in the Cold Desert* (Logan: Utah State Univ. Press, 1985). The first author is a range scientist, the second is an amateur historian. The best parts of the book are those dealing with the changing ecology of the sagebrush and bunchgrass lands of the Great Basin, while the social and economic history is full of old clichés. Near the end of the book, they briefly raise the question of whether private ownership of the entire range might have resulted in better vegetation conditions, but the book is inconclusive on that matter (see p. 233).

22. Robin W. Doughty, *Wildlife and Man in Texas: Environmental Change and Conservation* (College Station: Texas A & M Univ. Press), 154.

23. Tom McHugh, *The Time of the Buffalo* (Lincoln: Univ. of Nebraska Press, 1972), 16–17; Ernest Thompson Seton, *Life Histories of Northern Animals* (New York: Charles Scribner's Sons, 1989), vol. I, p. 292.

24. U.S. Forest Service, *An Assessment of the Forest and Range Land Situation in the United States,* Forest Resource Report No. 22, Oct. 1981, p. 168. Pronghorns are down to 2 to 3% of their original levels and the bison, of course, are down to a minuscule remnant; among big game, however, blacktailed and mule deer, numbering 3.6 million, are at approximately 100% of their level in pre-Columbian times.

25. Albert M. Day and Almer P. Nelson, "Wild Life Conservation and Control in Wyoming under the Leadership of the United States Biological Survey," pamphlet (Washington: Government Printing Office, 1928?), 1–32. The most thorough overview of predator policy is provided by Thomas R. Dunlap, *Saving America's Wildlife* (Princeton: Princeton Univ. Press, 1988), 47–61, 111–41.

26. The report was published as *The Western Range,* Senate Document 199, 74th Congress, 2d Session, Serial Number 10005 (Washington: Government Printing Office, 1936), a document that is 620 pages long.

27. In western range agronomy an animal unit indicates one cow, horse, or mule, or five sheep, goats, or swine.

28. Richard E. McArdle et al., "The White Man's Toll," *The Western Range,* pp. 81–116. Two types, the salt-desert shrub and the sagebrush-grass, were the worst depleted, with

45.6% and 36.8% of their acres respectively in a state of extreme depletion. The short grass range, so important to the cattle industry, was somewhat better off, with only 13.1% in the extreme category.

29. Ibid., 3.

30. Ibid., 7, 29–31, 484. For a defense of private stewardship see *If and When It Rains: The Stockman's View of the Range Question* (Denver: American National Livestock Association, 1938). Much of this document consists of individual rancher's experiences with changing range conditions—the folk's "wisdom" contradicting the professional's "mythology." As the title indicates, the cattlemen blamed dry weather for any range deterioration.

31. Thadis W. Box, "The American Rangelands: Their Conditions and Policy Implications for Management," in *Rangeland Policies for the Future: Proceedings of a Symposium* (Washington: Government Printing Office, 1979), 17.

32. U.S. Forest Service, *Assessment of the Forest and Range Land Situation*, 158–63.

33. Edward Abbey, "Free Speech: The Cowboy and His Cow," in *One Life at a Time, Please* (New York: Henry Holt, 1988), 15. Abbey called for a hunting season on range cattle. For other critical views see Richard N. Mack, "Invaders at Home on the Range," *Natural History* 93 (Feb. 1984): 40–47; David Sheridan, "Western Rangelands: Overgrazed and Undermanaged," *Environment* 23 (May 1981): 14–20, 37–39; *High Country News* 22 (12 March 1990), entire issue; and Comptroller General of the U.S., "Public Lands Continue to Deteriorate," Report to the Congress, 5 July 1977.

34. U.S. Forest Service, *Assessment of the Forest and Range Land Situation*, 160. Box's view gets support from the most comprehensive recent survey I know of the ecological history of the range: Farrel A. Branson, *Vegetation Changes on Western Rangelands*, Range Monograph No. 2 (Denver: Society for Range Management, 1985). Branson traces area by area, species by species, the ecological changes that have taken place since the white man appeared in the West; he concludes (p. 67) that "there was a drastic deterioration of ranges late in the last century and continuing into this century followed by some impressive improvements, especially in western rangelands in recent years."

35. Michael W. Loring and John P. Workman, "The Relationship between Land Ownership and Range Condition in Rich Country, Utah," *Journal of Range Management* 40 (July 1987): 290–93.

36. Abbey, "Free Speech," 13.

4. Hydraulic Society in California

1. The Steinbeck book was published by Viking Press in New York, April 1939, and became one of the year's best-sellers. McWilliams brought out his book, with the subtitle *The Story of Migratory Farm Labor in California*, a few months later (Boston: Little, Brown). For their reception, see McWilliams's "A Man, a Place, and a Time," *American West* 7 (May 1970): 4–8, 38–40, 62–64.

2. See, for instance, the two most recent general accounts: Cletus Daniel, *Bitter Harvest: A History of California Farmworkers, 1870–1914* (Ithaca, N.Y.: Cornell Univ. Press, 1981); and Lawrence J. Jelinek, *Harvest Empire: A History of California Agriculture* (San Francisco: Boyd and Fraser, 1980).

3. *Factories in the Field* (Santa Barbara: Peregrine Smith, 1971), 7, 48–49, 324–25.

4. Although he did not discuss the impact of California growers on the land, Steinbeck did make much of the theme in his chapters on Oklahoma and the Dust Bowl—especially chap. 11, *The Grapes of Wrath*.

5. Steward, "Introduction: The Irrigation Civilizations, a Symposium on Method and Result in Cross-Cultural Regularities," *Irrigation Civilizations: A Comparative Study* (Washington: Pan-American Union, 1953), esp. 1–5; Wittfogel, *Orientation Despotism: A Comparative Study of Total Power* (New Haven: Yale Univ. Press, 1957). See also Marvin

Harris, *Cannibals and Kings: The Origins of Cultures* (New York: Random House, 1977), chap. 13; William Mitchell, "The Hydraulic Hypothesis: A Reappraisal," *Current Anthropology* 14 (Dec. 1973): 532–34; and Theodore Downing and McGuire Gibson, eds., *Irrigation's Impact on Society* (Tucson: Univ. of Arizona Press, 1974). Arthur Maass and Raymond Anderson reject the Wittfogel thesis for California, though mainly on the basis of a narrow, distorted reading of it (*And the Desert Shall Rejoice* (Cambridge: MIT Press, 1978), 366–67.

6. Semiramis was the Greek name for Sammuramat, who ruled for five years during the minority of her son, Adad-Nirari III. See George Roux, *Ancient Iraq* (London: Allen & Unwin, 1964), 250.

7. My own thinking about the role of this idea in modern times owes much to William Leiss, *The Domination of Nature* (Boston: Beacon Press, 1974), and Max Horkheimer, *The Eclipse of Reason* (New York: Oxford Univ. Press, 1947), esp. chap. 3.

8. Michael G. Robinson, *Water for the West: The Bureau of Reclamation, 1902–1977* (Chicago: Public Works Historical Society, 1979), 108.

9. Philip L. Fradkin, *A River No More: The Colorado River and the West* (New York: Knopf, 1981), 16.

10. An excellent guide to the literature is Lawrence B. Lee's *Reclaiming the American West: An Historiography and Guide* (Santa Barbara: ABC-Clio, 1980).

11. Powell, *Report on the Lands of the Arid Region of the United States*, Wallace Stegner, ed. (Cambridge, Mass.: Harvard Univ. Press, 1962).

12. Smythe, *The Conquest of Arid America*, Lawrence B. Lee, ed. (Seattle: Univ. of Washington Press, 1969), 43.

13. Muir, *The Mountains of California* (1894; Garden City, N.Y.: Anchor, 1961), chaps. 11 and 16.

14. S. T. Harding, *Water in California* (Palo Alto, Calif.: N.P. Publications, 1960), 2–6, 79–80. Far more elaborate works were constructed by Indians at Chaco Canyon and near present-day Phoenix—see Emil Haury, *The Hohokam, Desert Farmers and Craftsmen* (Tucson: Univ. of Arizona Press, 1976).

15. U.S. Congress, House, *Report of the Board of Commissioners on the Irrigation of the San Joaquin, Tulare, and Sacramento Valleys of the State of California*, H. Ex. Doc. 290 (Washington: GPO, 1874), 25.

16. *Agricultural Lands and Waters in the San Joaquin and Tulare Valleys* (San Francisco: A. L. Bancroft, 1873), 4–7. After 1875 this canal was taken over by the Miller and Lux cattle empire.

17. *Irrigation in California—The San Joaquin and Tulare Plains* (Sacramento: Record Steambook and Job Printing House, 1873), 4.

18. Walton Bean, *California: An Interpretive History* (New York: McGraw-Hill, 1968), 271.

19. Smythe, *Conquest of Arid America*, 160.

20. No one argued this point more persistently than Elwood Mead; see, for instance, his *Irrigation Institutions* (New York: Macmillan, 1910), 23, 187.

21. E. J. Wickson, *Rural California* (New York: Macmillan, 1923), 386–89. Frank Adams, *Irrigation Districts in California* (Sacramento: California State Printing Office, 1929), gives a comprehensive history of each district. There were other forms of local water organization, for example, the mutual company, that are not discussed here.

22. Quoted in M. L. Requa and H. T. Cory, *The California Irrigation Farm Problem* (Washington: n.p., 1919), 165, 174. The early history of Imperial Valley is told in Robert G. Schonfield, "The Early Development of California's Imperial Valley," *Southern California Quarterly* 50 (Sept. 1968): 279–307; and ibid. (Dec. 1968): 395–426. The appointing of a State Engineer to oversee district financing and construction plans and to act as a liaison with New York bond markets was another inroad into local autonomy.

23. Bean, *California*, 275; Wickson, *Rural California*, 292–303. Although agricul-

tural cooperatives existed in other states, they were nowhere more successful than in California.

24. R. E. Hodges and E. J. Wickson, *Farming in California* (San Francisco: Californians Inc., 1928), 39–40. For a gloomier view, see Frank Swett, "Report of the Section on Agriculture," *Transactions of the Commonwealth Club of California* 20 (24 Nov. 1925): 345–51.

25. On labor market rationalization and control, see Daniel, *Bitter Harvest*, 101–2.

26. Frank Adams, David Morgan, and Walter Packard, "Economic Report on San Joaquin Valley Areas Being Considered for Water Supply Relief under Proposed California State Water Plan," Berkeley, California, 12 Nov. 1930, typescript, National Archives, Record Group 115, pp. 5–11. Underground water irrigation has its own unique history, though not qualifying in decisive ways the interpretation offered here.

27. Young, "Address on Central Valley Project before 19th Annual Convention of Northern California Chapter of Associated General Contractors," 18 Dec. 1937, NA, RG 115, p. 3.

28. The standard account is Robert de Roos, *The Thirsty Land: The Story of the Central Valley Project* (Palo Alto, Calif.: Stanford Univ. Press, 1948).

29. A good short, though partisan, introduction to this issue is Paul Taylor's "160-Acre Law," in *California Water*, David Seckler, ed. (Berkeley: Univ. of California Press, 1971), 251–62. See also Clayton Koppes, "Public Water, Private Land: Origins of the Acreage Limitation Controversy, 1933–1953," *Pacific Historical Review* 47 (Nov. 1978): 607–36.

30. The role of business needs in shaping federal reclamation is discussed by Lawrence B. Lee, "Environmental Implications of Governmental Reclamation in California," in *Agriculture in the Development of the Far West*, James Shideler, ed. (Washington: Agricultural History Society, 1975), 224. See also Grant McConnell, *Private Power and American Democracy* (New York: Knopf, 1966), chap. 7.

31. Thorkild Jacobsen and Robert Adams, "Salt and Silt in Ancient Mesopotamian Agriculture," *Science* 128 (21 Nov. 1958): 1254–58.

32. For examples of recent environmental problems, consult: J. E. Poland and G. H. Davis, "Land Subsidence Due to Withdrawal of Fluids," *Reviews in Engineering Geology* 2 (1969): 187–269; Charles R. Goldman, "Biological Implications of Reduced Freshwater Flows on the San Francisco-Delta Systems," in Seckler, *California Water*, 109–24; and Myron B. Holburt and Vernon E. Valentine, "Present and Future Salinity of the Colorado River," *Journal of Hydraulic Division, Proceedings of the American Society of Civil Engineers* 98 (March 1972): 503–20.

33. (New York: Harcourt Brace Jovanovich, 1967), 207.

5. Hoover Dam: A Study in Domination

1. *The Education of Henry Adams* (Boston: Houghton Mifflin, Sentry edition, 1918), 344, 380.

2. Wallace Stegner, *Beyond the Hundredth Meridian: John Wesley Powell and the Second Opening of the West* (Boston: Houghton Mifflin, 1954), part 1; and Norris Hundley, *Water and the West: The Colorado River Compact and the Politics of Water in the American West* (Berkeley: Univ. of California Press, 1975), chap. 7.

3. John Wesley Powell, "Institutions for the Arid Lands," *Century Magazine* 40 (May 1890): 16.

4. For the geological history of the river, see: E. Blackwelder, "Origin of the Colorado River," *Bulletin of the Geological Society of America* 36 (1934): 551–66; Henry James, "The Salient Geographical Factors of the Colorado River and Basin," *Annals* 135 (Jan. 1928): 97–101; Clarence Dutton, *Tertiary History of the Grand Canyon District*, U.S. Geological Survey Monograph No. 2 (Washington: Government Printing Office, 1882).

5. William Kahrl, *Water and Power: The Conflict over Los Angeles' Water Supply in the Owens Valley* (Berkeley: Univ. of California Press, 1982), 156–57; Remi Nadeu, *The Water Seekers* (Garden City, N.Y.: Doubleday, 1950).

264   Notes

6. Robert Schonfield, "The Early Development of California's Imperial Valley," *Southern California Quarterly* 50 (Sept. 1968): 297-307; (Dec.): 395-426; Helen Hosmer, "Triumph and Failure in the Imperial Valley," *The Grand Colorado*, T. H. Watkins, ed. (Palo Alto: American West Publishing, 1969), 205-21.

7. Harold Bell Wright, *The Winning of Barbara Worth* (1911; New York: Grosset & Dunlap, 1966), 145.

8. Arthur Powell Davis, quoted in Norris Hundley, "The Politics of Reclamation: California, the Federal Government and the Origins of the Boulder Canyon Act—A Second Look," *California Historical Quarterly* 52 (Winter 1973): 297.

9. Francis Crowe, quoted in T. H. Watkins, "Making an Empire to Order," *The Grand Colorado*, 172-73. See also Paul Kleinsorge, *The Boulder Canyon Project* (Stanford: Stanford Univ. Press, 1941), 185-230; Frank Waters, *The Colorado* (New York: Holt, Rinehart and Winston, 1946), 337-51; Imre Sutton, "Geographical Aspects of Construction Planning: Hoover Dam Revisited," *Journal of the West* 7 (July 1968): 301-44.

10. The story of building the project is well told in Joseph E. Stevens, *Hoover Dam: An American Adventure* (Norman: Univ. of Oklahoma Press, 1988). The Six Companies were comprised of the Utah Construction Company, Morrison-Knudsen (Crowe's employer, headquartered in Boise, Idaho), the J. F. Shea Company and Pacific Bridge (both of Portland, Oregon), MacDonald & Kahn of San Francisco, and a group known as Bechtel-Kaiser-Warren Brothers. Despite many difficulties with the workers they hired, the Six Companies completed the project in a little over two years, almost one month ahead of schedule, and made gross earnings of over $50 million. (Stevens, p. 252.)

11. For a general discussion of Horkheimer's critical philosophy, see Martin Jay, *The Dialectical Imagination* (Boston: Little, Brown, 1973).

12. Max Horkheimer, *The Eclipse of Reason* (New York: Plenum, 1974), 93.

13. Paul Barnett, *Imperial Valley: The Land of Sun and Subsidies* (Davis, Calif.: California Institute of Rural Studies, 1978), 30. See also Ernest Leonard, "The Imperial Irrigation District: Agency Behavior in a Political Environment," Ph.D. thesis, Claremont Graduate School, 1972.

14. William Warne, *The Bureau of Reclamation* (New York: Praeger, 1973), 207, 229-33.

15. Michael Straus, *Why Not Survive?* (New York: Simon and Schuster, 1955), 78.

16. J. Kip Finch, "Some Modern Wonders Named," *Civil Engineering* 25 (Nov. 1955): 33, 40.

17. Max Horkheimer and Theodor W. Adorno, *Dialectic of Enlightenment*, John Cumming, trans. (New York: Herder and Herder, 1972), ix.

18. Stevens, *Hoover Dam*, 266-67.

19. Myron Holburt and Vernon Valentine, "Present and Future Salinity of Colorado River," *Journal of Hydraulic Division, Proceedings of the American Society of Civil Engineers* 98 (March 1972): 505-7; Wesley Steiner, statement in *Salinity Control Measures on the Colorado River*, Hearings before Subcommittee on Water and Power Resources, Committee on Interior and Insular Affairs, U.S. Senate, 93 Cong., 2d sess. (Washington: Government Printing Office, 1974). Also see the international symposium on Colorado River salinity in *Natural Resources Journal* 15 (Jan. 1975); and Ralph Johnson, "Our Salty Rivers: Legal and Institutional Approaches to Salinity Management," *Land and Water Law Review* 13, No. 2 (1978): 441-64.

20. A good discussion of this issue may be found in Philip Fradkin, *A River No More: The Colorado River and the West* (New York: Alfred A. Knopf, 1981), 291-316. See also Norris Hundley, *Dividing the Waters* (Berkeley: Univ. of California Press, 1966); and Herbert Brownell and Samuel Eaton, "The Colorado River Salinity Problem with Mexico," *American Journal of International Law* 69 (April 1975); 255-71.

21. Holburt and Valentine, "Present and Future Salinity," 515.

22. Vernon Valentine, "Impacts of Colorado River Salinity," *Journal of Irrigation and*

Drainage Division, Proceedings of American Society of Civil Engineers 100 (Dec. 1974): 500–502.

23. Colorado River Board of California, *Need for Controlling Salinity of the Colorado River* (Sacramento: California Office of State Printing, 1970), 68–69, 78.

24. This conclusion is strongly suggested by Thorkild Jacobsen and Robert Adams, "Salt and Silt in Ancient Mesopotamian Agriculture," *Science* 128 (21 Nov. 1958): 1254–58.

6. Freedom and Want: The Western Paradox

1. Owen Wister, *The Virginian* (New York: Grosset & Dunlap, 1904), 502–3.

2. *The Journals of Lewis and Clark*, Bernard DeVoto, ed. (Boston: Houghton Mifflin, 1953), 14.

3. A. B. Guthrie, Jr., *The Big Sky* (New York: Time-Life, 1947), 8.

4. John (Fire) Lame Deer and Richard Erdoes, *Lame Deer, Seeker of Visions* (New York: Washington Square Press, 1972), 265.

5. Henry David Thoreau, "Walking" [1862], *Excursions*, Leo Marx, ed. (New York: Corinth, 1962), 176.

6. The experiences of both men are recounted in G. Edward White, *The Eastern Establishment and the Western Experience: The West of Frederic Remington, Theodore Roosevelt, and Owen Wister* (New Haven: Yale Univ. Press, 1968), chaps. 3, 4, 6.

7. Karl Marx, *The Grundrisse*, ed. and trans. by David McLellan (New York: Harper Torchbooks, 1971), 94.

8. Frank W. Blackmar, "The Mastery of the Desert," *North American Review* 182 (May 1906): 688.

7. Grassland Follies

1. Quoted in David A. Dary, *The Buffalo Book* (New York: Avon, 1974), 4.

2. This sentence is a paraphrase of Lewis Mumford, *The Power of the Pentagon* (New York: Harcourt, Brace, Jovanovich, Harvest ed., 1970), 393. For a discussion of the new ecological history, see my article, "Nature as Natural History: An Essay on Theory and Method," *Pacific Historical Review* 53 (Feb. 1984): 1–19.

3. Both of Webb's major works, *The Great Plains* (Boston: Ginn, 1931) and *The Great Frontier* (Boston: Houghton Mifflin, 1952), are landmark studies in the environmental impact on culture.

4. Malin, "Ecology and History," *Scientific Monthly* 70 (May 1950): 295–98.

5. A useful discussion of this problem is in John Bennett's *The Ecological Transition: Cultural Anthropology and Human Adaptation* (New York: Pergamon, 1976), esp. 162–67, 209–42.

6. Malin, "Dust Storms: Part One, 1850–1860," *Kansas Historical Quarterly* 14 (May 1946): 129–44.

7. Edwin Kessler, Dorothy Alexander, and Joseph Rarick, "Duststorms from the U.S. High Plains in Late Winter 1977—Search for Cause and Implications," *Proceedings of the Oklahoma Academy of Science* 58 (1978): 116–28.

8. Malin, "Dust Storms: Part Three, 1881–1890," *Kansas Historical Quarterly* 14 (Nov. 1946): 391–413.

9. Ibid. The distinction between pioneering and entrepreneurialism is commonly obscured in American historical writing as it is in popular mythology; indeed, they are often conflated, especially in the West, producing a "cowboy capitalism." Malin's writing is replete with the confusion.

10. See Hays, *Conservation and the Gospel of Efficiency: The Progressive Conservation Movement, 1890–1920* (Cambridge: Harvard Univ. Press, 1959).

11. See, for example, Vance Johnson, *Heaven's Tableland: The Dust Bowl Story* (New York: Farrar, Straus, 1947), chap. 12.

12. A. B. Genung, "Agriculture in the World War Period," in U.S. Department of Agriculture, *Farmers in a Changing World* (Washington, 1940), 280–84; Lloyd Jorgenson, "Agricultural Expansion into the Semiarid Lands of the West North Central States during the First World War," *Agricultural History* 23 (Jan. 1949): 30–40; *Kansas City Star,* 19 April 1935.

13. Johnson, *Heaven's Tableland,* 136–37; *Topeka Capital,* 3 Aug. 1926; *Panhandle Herald* (Guymon, Okla.), 13 Dec. 1928. See also Garry Nall, "Specialization and Expansion: Panhandle Farming in the 1920's," *Panhandle-Plains Historical Review* 47 (1974): 66–67. The largest operator of all on the Plains was located in Montana: see Hiram Dache, "Thomas B. Campbell—The Plower of the Plains," *Agricultural History* 51 (Jan. 1977): 78–91. Campbell's ambition was to be a "manufacturer of wheat"; he farmed, with House of Morgan backing, over 100,000 acres, most of it on Indian reservations.

14. Leslie Hewes, in *The Suitcase-Farming Frontier: A Study in the Historical Geography of the Central Great Plains* (Lincoln: Univ. of Nebraska Press, 1973), gives a thorough accounting of this phenomenon, and one strongly supportive of its entrepreneurial characteristics.

15. H. B. Urban, transcribed interview, 15 June 1974, Panhandle-Plains Historical Museum, Canyon, Texas; *The Dust Bowl,* U.S. Department of Agriculture, Editorial Reference Series No. 7 (Washington, D.C., 1940), 44; Clifford Hope, "Kansas in the 1930's," *Kansas Historical Quarterly* 36 (Spring 1970), 2–3; Johnson, *Heaven's Tableland,* 146.

16. A number of excellent studies of popular understanding of the Plains have been published by geographers and historians; see, for example, Brian Blouet and Merlin Lawson, eds., *Images of the Plains: The Role of Human Nature in Settlement* (Lincoln, Univ. of Nebraska Press, 1975).

17. Entrepreneurialism is essential to all forms of agricultural capitalism, whether it be potato farming in Maine or rice growing in California. But the strength of this drive may, of course, vary from time to time and place to place. Not all of American agriculture has been so unstable or risk-taking as that of the semiarid plains.

18. Frederick Luebke, "Ethnic Group Settlement on the Great Plains," *Western Historical Quarterly* 8 (Oct. 1977): 405–30.

19. One thinks, for example, of the Swedish immigrant Alexandra Bergson in Willa Cather's *O Pioneers!* (Boston: Houghton Mifflin, 1913). Though eager to acquire more and more property, Bergson responds to the land with a powerful love and yearning. "It seemed beautiful to her," writes Cather, "rich and strong and glorious. Her eyes drank in the breadth of it, until her tears blinded her" (p. 65).

20. A provocative discussion of this set of ideas is C. B. Macpherson's *The Political Theory of Possessive Individualism: Hobbes to Locke* (Oxford: Oxford Univ. Press, 1962).

21. This figure includes, in addition to ecological restoration efforts, all programs of farm price supports, rural relief, and public works expenditures.

22. Great Plains Committee, *The Future of the Great Plains,* U.S. House Document 144, 75th Congress (Washington, D.C., 1937), 63–67.

23. Malin, *The Grassland of North America: Prolegomena to Its History* (Lawrence, Kansas: privately published, 1956), 335.

24. As John Borchert has written, the flurry of federal soil and water conservation programs since the thirties has "encouraged a widespread belief that, though there will be future droughts, there need be no future dust bowl." See "The Dust Bowl in the 1970s" *Annals of the Association of American Geographers* 61 (March 1971): 13.

25. *Time* (27 June 1983): 27.

8. The Black Hills: Sacred or Profane?

1. The French gave them the name Sioux, meaning "enemies," but their own names for themselves were Nakota (eastern), Dakota (middle region), and Lakota (western), all referring to "allies."

2. My account of the occupation is based on extensive newspaper coverage in the *Argus Leader* (Sioux Falls, S.D.), the state's largest newspaper, during the years 1981 to 1988.

3. The best account of the Wounded Knee confrontation, and valuable background for this entire essay, is Peter Matthiessen's controversial book, *In the Spirit of Crazy Horse* (New York: Viking, 1983). The former governor of South Dakota, William Janklow, who felt himself libeled by the book, particularly by its allegation that he had raped an Indian girl while serving as tribal legal counsel, sued Matthiessen and forced the publisher to withdraw the book. Eventually the suit was dropped and the book reissued. Another, more hostile account of the armed confrontation is Clyde D. Dollar, "The Second Tragedy at Wounded Knee," *American West* 10 (Sept. 1973), 4-11, 58-61. The standard account of the first tragedy is Robert M. Utley, *The Last Days of the Sioux Nation* (New Haven: Yale Univ. Press, 1963).

4. I have gone through the back files of the Alliance's newspaper, *Black Hills Paha Sapa Report*. Also useful have been: Peter Matthiessen, *Indian Country* (New York: Viking, 1984), chap. 7; Rex Weyler, *Blood of the Land: The Government and Corporate War against the American Indian Movement* (New York: Everest House, 1982), chap. 1; and William Greider, "The Heart of Everything That Is," *Rolling Stone*, 7 May 1987, pp. 37-38, 40, 60, 62, 64.

5. *Black Hills Paha Sapa Report*, 3 (March/April 1982): 2.

6. Russell Means, "Fighting Words for the Future of the Earth," *Mother Jones* 5 (Dec. 1980): 30, 31.

7. There are altogether about 80,000 Sioux, and they live in eight tribes located on the same number of reservations: Oglala (Pine Ridge), Rosebud, Standing Rock, Santee, Cheyenne River, Fort Peck, Lower Brule, Crow Creek. After Pine Ridge, which counts about 20,000 inhabitants, the largest reservations in South Dakota are Rosebud, with a population of about 12,000, and Standing Rock, 8,400.

8. Department of Commerce, *1980 Census of Population*, Vol. 1, Part 43; Vol. 2, Part 2 (Washington: Government Printing Office, 1982). For a vivid description of current conditions at Pine Ridge, see Bella Stumbo, "A World Apart: Russell Means and Dennis Banks back at Wounded Knee," *Los Angeles Times Magazine* (15 June 1986): 10-21.

9. *Black Hills Paha Sapa Report* 3 (March/April 1982), 8.

10. For a provocative discussion of the relationship of the Lakota to the land today, the land of the reservation, and their ethos of place, see Frank Pommersheim, "The Reservation as Place: A South Dakota Essay," *South Dakota Law Review* 34 (1989): 246-70.

11. See the *Argus Leader*, 18 Jan. 1987, for these state political reactions. Also South Dakota Legislative Research Council, "An Analysis of 'the Bradley Bill' Proposing to Return the Black Hills to the Great Sioux Nation," Issue Memorandum 87-4, 14 May 1987, which was unfriendly to the bill.

12. James Monroe, "First Annual Message," *The Writings of James Monroe*, Stanislaus Murray Hamilton, ed. (New York: G. P. Putnam's Sons, 1902), vol. 6, p. 40.

13. For the treaty's text see *U.S. Statutes at Large*, vol. 15, pp. 635-40. A useful compilation of this and other documents is Don C. Clowser's *Dakota Indian Treaties: From Nomad to Reservation* (Deadwood, S.D.: privately published, 1974).

14. Larry J. Zimmerman, *Peoples of Prehistoric South Dakota* (Lincoln: Univ. of Nebraska Press, 1985), 127-30; and Wesley R. Hurt, *Dakota Sioux Indians* (New York: Garland, 1974), a report prepared originally for the Indian Claims Commission.

15. See Donald Jackson, *Custer's Gold: The United States Cavalry Expedition of 1874*

(New Haven: Yale Univ. Press, 1966). According to this author, Custer's expedition was "a treaty violation in spirit if not in fact" (p. 120). Also, James Calhoun, *With Custer in '74: James Calhoun's Diary of the Black Hills Expedition*, Lawrence A. Frost, ed. (Provo, Utah: Brigham Young Univ. Press, 1979); and Richard Slotkin, "'. . . & Then the Mare Will Go!' An 1875 Black Hills Scheme by Custer, Holladay, and Buford," *Journal of the West* 15 (July 1976): 60–77. Environmental change in the Black Hills from the time of Custer's expedition to the present is the theme of Donald R. Progulske's *Yellow Ore, Yellow Hair, Yellow Pine*, Bull. 616, Agricultural Experiment Station, South Dakota State University, Brookings, July 1974. Progulske and his photographer Richard H. Sewell compare the scene today with pictures taken by William H. Illingworth on the expedition; and they find a dramatic increase in pine forest cover since 1874, due mainly to the suppression of fire.

16. Annie B. Tallent, *The Black Hills; or, the Last Hunting Ground of the Dakotahs* (St. Louis: Nixon-Jones, 1988), 3.

17. The most complete account of the mining rush is Watson Parker, *Gold in the Black Hills* (Norman: Univ. of Oklahoma Press, 1966). Another useful popular account, with good illustrations, is Paul Friggens, *Gold & Grass: The Black Hills Story* (Boulder, Colo.: Pruett Publishing, 1983), part 1. See also Watson Parker, "The Majors and the Miners: The Role of the U.S. Army in the Black Hills Gold Rush," *Journal of the West* 11 (Jan. 1972): 99–113; and "Booming the Black Hills," *South Dakota History* 11 (Winter 1980): 35–52; and Howard Robert Lamar, *Dakota Territory, 1861–1889: A Study of Frontier Politics* (New Haven: Yale Univ. Press, 1956), 148–76.

18. Less than ten years earlier the federal government had paid Russia only $7.5 million for the much larger, if less accessible, territory of Alaska. And only seventy years before President Thomas Jefferson had bought France's claim to the whole Louisiana Purchase, which included the Black Hills and all the rest of the Sioux reservation, for only $14 million.

19. *Report of the Commission Appointed to Treat with the Sioux Indians for the Relinquishment of the Black Hills* (Washington: Government Printing Office, 19875), 6–9. A detailed account of the Commission appears in James C. Olson, *Red Cloud and the Sioux Problem* (Lincoln: Univ. of Nebraska Press, 1965), 201–13. See also George Hyde, *A Sioux Chronicle* (Norman: Univ. of Oklahoma Press, 1956), chap. 4.

20. Report of the Sioux Commission, *Eighth Annual Report of the Board of Indian Commissioners for the Year 1876* (Washington: Government Printing Office, 1877), appendix A, pp. 11–19.

21. For the debates over the legislation and final passage see 44th Congress, 2d sess., *Congressional Record*, vol. V, part II (Washington: Government Printing Office, 1977), 1055–58, 1615–17, 2028.

22. The Treaty of Laramie (1868) was the last one made with any Indian nation.

23. See Morton Horwitz, *The Transformation of American Law* (Cambridge, Mass.: Harvard Univ. Press, 1977), 34–40.

24. See the decision in *Cases Decided in the United States Court of Claims*, vol. 20 (Washington: Government Printing Office, 1980), 442–90. Two of the seven judges dissented.

25. *United States v. Sioux Nation of Indians* (488 U.S. 371), in *Supreme Court Reporter* (St. Paul, Minn.: West Publishing, 1982), vol. 100A, pp. 2716–52. In support of his traditionalist view of western history, Rehnquist cited a booklet, *Soldier and Brave*, written by Ray Allen Billington and published by the National Park Service in 1963, and a textbook, *The Oxford History of the American People*, written by Samuel Eliot Morison, both authors supposedly showing that there were deep "cultural differences" between Indians and whites, "which made conflict and brutal warfare inevitable." Morison, as quoted by Rehnquist in his opinion, described the Plains Indians as a people who "lived only for the day, recognized no rights of property, robbed or killed anyone if they thought they could get away with it, inflicted cruelty without a qualm, and endured torture without flinching." That this was a

racist characterization, no more true of Indians than of whites, and that in any case the general moral behavior of the Indians was not on trial, did not occur to the Justice, who ended his dissent with the Biblical injunction, "Judge not, that ye be not judged." His fellows on the bench, however, failed to see any analogy between Jesus's defense of a prostitute from a mob intent on stoning her and Rehnquist's defense of white manifest destiny.

26. Bruce A. Ackerman, *Private Property and the Constitution* (New Haven: Yale Univ. Press, 1977), 113–16. More conservative discussions of the abuse of eminent domain doctrine are Richard A. Epstein, *Takings: Private Property and the Power of Eminent Domain* (Cambridge, Mass.: Harvard Univ. Press, 1985); and Ellen Frankel Paul, *Property Rights and Eminent Domain* (New Brunswick, N.J.: Transaction, 1987).

27. Quoted in Ronald Goodman and Stanley Red Bird, "Lakota Star Knowledge and the Black Hills," in *Sioux Nation Black Hills Act, Hearing before the Select Committee on Indian Affairs, U.S. Senate, 99th Congress, 2d session* (Washington: Government Printing Office, 1986), 215.

28. An example of this analogizing is an editorial by Tim Giago in the Lakota Gazette, "Oglala Sioux and a Fight for Mecca," reprinted in his *Notes from Indian Country*, vol. I (Pierre, S.D.: State Publishing, 1984), 278–80. Giago writes: "Unable to comprehend the religious significance of the Black Hills to the Lakota people, the court seems to have decided to duck the issue by ignoring the First Amendment violation with silence."

29. The best of these are represented in William K. Powers, *Oglala Religion* (Lincoln: Univ. of Nebraska Press, 1977), and *Sacred Language: The Nature of Supernatural Discourse in Lakota* (Norman: Univ. of Oklahoma Press, 1986); and Raymond J. DeMallie and Douglas R. Parks, eds., *Sioux Indian Religion: Tradition and Innovation* (Norman: Univ. of Oklahoma Press, 1987). A still useful older study is Martha Warren Beckwith, "Mythology of the Oglala Dakota," *Journal of American Folklore* 43 (Oct.–Dec. 1930): 339–442. See also Åke Hulkrantz, *The Religion of the American Indian*, Monica Setterwall, trans. (Berkeley: Univ. of California Press, 1967).

30. Mircea Eliade, *The Sacred and the Profane: The Nature of Religion*, Willard R. Trask, trans. (New York: Harcourt, Brace, 1959), 26.

31. Vine Deloria, Jr., a Lakota and a lawyer, argues that Christians have lost any sense of the sacred in nature; their religion is grounded in time and history rather than in nature and the land. (*God Is Red* (New York: Grosset & Dunlap, 1973), esp. chap. 8.) I think he oversimplifies the Christian view. On the other hand, he shows us the potential for inconsistency among Indians when he writes, "While traditional Indians speak of a reverence for the earth, Indian reservations continue to pile up junk cars and beer cans at an alarming rate" (p. 260).

32. Ibid., 79–80.

33. On the Dawes Act and its effects in South Dakota, see Jerome A. Greene, "The Sioux Land Commission of 1889: Prelude to Wounded Knee," *South Dakota History* 1 (Winter 1970), 41–72.

34. A transcript of the meeting, simply entitled "Report of the Proceedings Held at Pine Ridge Agency," is on deposit at the South Dakota State Historical Society in Pierre.

35. James R. Walker, *Lakota Belief and Ritual*, Raymond J. DeMallie and Elaine A. Jahner, eds. (Lincoln: Univ. of Nebraska Press, 1980). See especially pages 50–54, 69, 101–2, 115, 147–74, where the concept of the holy is discussed.

36. *Black Elk Speaks: Being the Life Story of a Holy Man of the Oglala Sioux*, as told through John G. Neihardt (Flaming Arrow) (Lincoln: Univ. of Nebraska Press, 1961), chap. 3, "The Great Vision." For the return visit to Harney see *The Sixth Grandfather: Black Elk's Teachings Given to John G. Neihardt*, Raymond J. DeMallie, ed. (Lincoln: Univ. of Nebraska Press, 1984), 47–48.

37. *Black Elk Speaks*, 43 fn.

38. *The Sixth Grandfather*, 307–14. Another, fuller version of the story appears in James

LaPointe's *Legends of the Lakota* (San Francisco: Indian Historian Press, 1976), 17-19. LaPointe's book is the most complete compilation of stories connected to the Black Hills and seems to have been prepared, in part, to support the Indian claim to the region.

39. A good overview of this subject is provided by Imre Sutton, "Incident or Event? Land Restoration in the Claims Process," in *Irredeemable America: The Indians' Estate and Land Claims,* Imre Sutton, ed. (Albuquerque: Univ. of New Mexico Press, 1985), 211-32. On the Paiute's case see Richard W. Stoffle and Henry F. Dobyns, eds., *Nuvagantu: Nevada Indians Comment on the Intermountain Power Project,* Cultural Resource Monograph 7 (Reno: Bureau of Land Management, 1983). Nuvagantu is the white man's Charleston Peak, and considered a holy place for the Paiutes.

40. Laurie Ensworth, "Native American Free Exercise Rights to the Use of Public Lands," *Boston University Law Review* 63 (1983): 141-79.

41. Charlotte Black Elk, *Sioux Nation Black Hills Act,* 66.

42. Chief Standing Bear, *Land of the Spotted Eagle* (Boston: Houghton Mifflin, 1933), 43-44. "Of all our domain," he writes, "we loved, perhaps, the Black Hills the most. . . . [But] to the white man everything was valueless except the gold in the hills" (p. 44).

43. Two older Lakota men who have been leaders in declaring the Black Hills sacred are Frank Fools Crow and John (Fire) Lame Deer. On the former see Thomas E. Mails, *Fools Crow* (Garden City, N.Y.: Doubleday, 1979), chap. 20, which has many references to the Hills and to his testimony in Congress. For the latter see *Lame Deer, Seeker of Visions,* as told to Richard Erdoes (New York: Simon and Schuster, 1972), chap. 5, in which Lame Deer visits Mount Rushmore, sits on Theodore Roosevelt's head, and vents his anger at the prospect. Note that both of these books appeared in the decade of the 1970s, which I mark as the period when the "sacred Hills" theme first became prominent. See too the photo essay by Tom Charging Eagle and Ron Zeilinger, *Black Hills: Sacred Hills* (Chamberlain, S.D.: Tipi Press, 1987). In contrast to these claims, not one of the scholars, some of them Indian, some white, in the collection of essays, *Sioux Indian Religion: Tradition and Innovation,* Raymond J. DeMallie and Douglas R. Parks, eds. (Norman: Univ. of Oklahoma, 1987), refers to the Black Hills as sacred land; in fact the Hills are mentioned only once, in connection with a 1980 reservation rally.

44. The idea that the earth is the great mother-goddess for Indians has had a similar history. According to Sam Gill the idea is really one suggested to Indians by whites, who themselves tended to look on the New World as a female figure, dark and Indian; the Indians took over the idea and made it a main theme in their religion.

> By the mid 1970s and after, Native Americans' consciousness of their Indian identity was well developed. They had begun to see that their distinctiveness, their very identity as Indians, provides an alternative to the materialistic and ecologically unconscionable ways that distinguish for them Americans of European descent. Indians thus took up the theme of Mother Earth as retaliator, and saw that her exaction of retribution would surely not be directed toward them, so long as they nurtured their "Indian" identity.

See Gill, *Mother Earth: An American Story* (Chicago: Univ. of Chicago Press, 1987), 138.

45. The parallels between the sacralization of the Black Hills and the conversion to the Ghost Dance religion, centered on the messianic prophet Wovoka, which swept the Lakota in 1890, is striking. As James Mooney wrote in the aftermath of that movement: "When the race lies crushed and groaning beneath an alien yoke, how natural is the dream of a redeemer, an Arthur, who shall return from exile or awake from some long sleep to drive out the usurper and win back for his people what they have lost." James Mooney, *The Ghost-Dance Religion and the Sioux Outbreak of 1890* [1896], abridged by Anthony F. C. Wallace (Chicago: Univ. of Chicago Press, 1965), 1. See also Anthony F. C. Wallace, "Revitalization Movements," *American Anthropologist* 58 (1956): 264-81. The main difference is that today

no messianic figure has emerged to give the revitalized religion any form or leadership; the Black Hills themselves serve as the only redeemer.

46. Originally this right covered all minerals, but in 1920 the fossil fuels were excluded, leaving only the hard-rock minerals, like gold, lead, copper, or uranium, under its wide-open provisions. Under the Mineral Leasing Act of 1920 the Secretary of the Interior leases oil, gas, and coal underlying the public lands through a system of competitive bids. A good discussion of the laws appears in Carl J. Meyer and George A. Riley, *Public Domain, Private Dominion: A History of Public Mineral Policy in America* (San Francisco: Sierra Club, 1985), chap. 2.

9. Alaska: The Underworld Erupts

1. *Alaska Regional Profiles: Arctic Region*, coordinated and prepared by Lidia L. Selkregg (Juneau: State of Alaska, 1975); and John J. Koranda, "The North Slope: Its Physiography, Fauna, and Its Flora," *Alaska Geographic* I (Spring 1973), complete issue.

2. F. C. Schrader, *A Reconnaissance in Northern Alaska in 1901* (Washington: Government Printing Office, 1904), 13. For the account of their travels and advice on such undertakings see Schrader's introduction, pp. 11-17, and Peters's short addendum, pp. 18-24.

3. Morgan B. Sherwood, *Exploration of Alaska, 1865-1900* (New Haven: Yale Univ. Press, 1965), 187.

4. Schrader, *A Reconnaissance in Northern Alaska*, 98-114.

5. Frank A. Golder, "Mining in Alaska before 1867," *Washington Historical Quarterly* 7 (July 1916): 233-38; R. H. Saunders, "The Minerals Industry in Alaska," in *Mineral and Water Resources of Alaska*, U.S. Geological Survey (Washington: Government Printing Office, 1964), 13-18; William H. Dall, *Alaska and Its Resources* (1870; New York: Arno Press, 1970), 473-74; William Healey Dall, "Report on Coal and Lignite of Alaska," in *17th Annual Report of the Geological Survey, 1895-96*, Part I (Washington: Government Printing Office, 1896); Henry Gannett, "General Geography," *Harriman Alaska Series, Vol. II: History, Geography, Resources* (Washington: Smithsonian Institution, 1910), 275.

6. Ernest de K. Leffingwell, *The Canning River Region[,] Northern Alaska*, U.S. Geological Survey Professional Paper 109 (Washington: Government Printing Office, 1919), 178-79. Leffingwell found petroleum seeping from mounds of earth at Cape Simpson, southeast of Point Barrow in what is now the National Petroleum Reserve and at Angun Point, not far from his Flaxman Island camp; and he identified the Sadlerochit formation, a gray sandstone, in which much oil would one day be found. Meanwhile, his partner Mikkelson returned home by sled and steamer, then sat down to write the account of their explorations, which was published in 1909 as *Conquering the Arctic*. Lose your ship and call it conquest! That ship had a wonderfully peripatetic history: a two-masted schooner named after the partners' benefactor, the Dutchess of Bedford, she had been cobbled together in Yokohama out of the semi-tropical timbers of a wrecked Japanese war vessel, timbers that now provided shelter from the Beaufort Sea's icy winds.

7. Michael Williams, *Americans and Their Forests* (New York: Cambridge Univ. Press, 1989), 332-37; Edward W. Parker, "Coal," in *Mineral Resources of the United States, 1900* (Washington: Government Printing Office, 1901), 278-81; Parker, "Coal," *Mineral Resources of the United States, 1904* (Washington: Government Printing Office, 1905), 401-5, 438. A good account of America's transition to a high-energy society is John G. Clark, *Energy and the Federal Government: Fossil Fuel Policies, 1900-1946* (Urbana: Univ. of Illinois Press, 1987), esp. chap. 2. See also Martin V. Melosi, *Coping with Abundance: Energy and Environment in Industrial America* (Philadelphia: Temple Univ. Press, 1985).

8. Walter L. Fisher, *Alaskan Coal Problems*, Bureau of Mines Bulletin 63 (Washington: Government Printing Office, 1912). On the Kennecott copper mining complex I have profited

from the chance to read William Cronon's excellent unpublished manuscript, "Kennecott Journey: The Paths Out of Town."

9. Robert F. Spencer, *The North Alaskan Eskimo: A Study in Ecology and Society*, Bureau of American Ethnology Bulletin 171 (Washington: Government Printing Office, 1959), 132–39; Nicholas J. Gubser, *The Nunamiut Eskimos: Hunters of Caribou* (New Haven: Yale Univ. Press, 1965), 107, 240.

10. Spencer, *The North Alaskan Eskimo*, 139–45. The most thorough account of this people's engagement with their environment is Richard K. Nelson's *Hunters of the Northern Ice* (Chicago: Univ. of Chicago Press, 1969). See also Barbara Leibhardt, "Among the Bowheads: Legal and Cultural Change on Alaska's North Slope Coast to 1985," *Environmental Review* 10 (Winter 1986): 277–301. Today, and farther east around Barter Island, the natives wait until the fall return of the bowhead to go whaling and they go out in boats; see Michael J. Jacobson and Cynthia Wentworth, *Kaktovik Subsistence: Land Use Values through Time in the Arctic National Wildlife Refuge Area* (Fairbanks: U.S. Fish and Wildlife Service, 1982), 30.

11. Norman A. Chance, *The Eskimo of North Alaska* (New York: Holt, Rinehart and Winston, 1966), 71–73. Also useful are several papers in David Damas, ed., *Handbook of North American Indians*, Vol. 5 (Washington: Smithsonian Institution, 1984), especially those by Robert Spencer and Norman Chance; and Richard K. Nelson, Kathleen Nelson, and A. Ray Bane, *Tracks in the Wildland: A Portrayal of Koyukon and Nunamiut Subsistence* (Fairbanks: Univ. of Alaska Press, 1978).

12. An excellent summary of these contrasting patterns is provided by R. P. Sieferle, "The Energy System—A Basic Concept of Environmental History," in *The Silent Countdown: Essays in European Environmental History*, Peter Brimblecombe and Christian Pfister, eds. (Berlin and Heidelberg: Springer-Verlag, 1990), 9–20. See also W. B. Kemp, "The Flow of Energy in a Hunting Society," *Scientific American* 224 (1971): 55–65; R. A. Rappaport, "The Flow of Energy in an Agricultural Society," ibid., 116–33; Leslie A. White, "Energy and the Evolution of Culture," *American Anthropologist* 45 (1943): 335–56.

13. John Muir, *Travels in Alaska* (Boston: Houghton Mifflin, 1915); and *Cruise of the Corwin*, William F. Bade, ed. (Boston: Houghton Mifflin, 1917). See also William H. Goetzmann and Kay Sloan, *Looking Far North: The Harriman Expedition to Alaska, 1899* (New York: Viking, 1982); for a partial listing of the group, see pp. 207–10. The results of the expedition were collected by C. Hart Merriam in *Harriman Alaska Expedition*, 13 vols. (New York: Doubleday, Page; and Washington: Smithsonian Institution, 1901–14). Roderick Nash, "Tourism, Parks and the Wilderness Idea in the History of Alaska," *Alaska in Perspective* IV, no. 1 (1981), 6–7. For an interesting discussion of the mythic Alaska created by tourists and residents, see Stephen Haycox, "Rediscovering Alaska: Ways of Thinking about Alaska History," *Pacifica* I (Sept. 1989): 101–28.

14. Olaus Murie Papers, 1920–1946, University of Alaska Archives, Fairbanks, Box 4, Manuscript reports. See also Gregory D. Kendrick, "An Environmental Spokesman: Olaus J. Murie and a Democratic Defense of Wilderness," *Annals of Wyoming* 50 (Fall 1978): 213–302. Murie moved to Moose, Wyoming, with his bride from Fairbanks, Margaret Gillette, and in 1946 resigned, in some disgust, from the BBS's successor, the Fish and Wildlife Service. But he returned to Alaska on a visit in 1956, when he got the idea of preserving the nine-million-acre wilderness that in 1960 became the Arctic National Wildlife Range, the biggest refuge in North America. See Claus-M. Naske, "Creation of the Arctic National Wildlife Range," in *National Wildlife Refuges of Alaska: A Historical Perspective*, by David L. Spencer, Claus-M. Naske, and John Carnahan (Anchorage: Arctic Environmental Information and Data Center, 1979), 97–116. The best study of evolving wildlife and hunting policies is Morgan Sherwood, *Big Game in Alaska: A History of Wildlife and People* (New Haven: Yale Univ. Press, 1981).

15. "Report on Alaska, Yukon-Tanana Rivers," Murie Papers, Box 4. Jean Potter, *The*

Flying North (New York: Macmillan, 1947), 87. See also Stephen Haycox, "Early Aviation in Anchorage: Ambivalent Fascination with the Air Age," *Alaska History* 3 (Fall 1988): 1–20.

16. Robert Marshall, *Arctic Village* (New York: Literary Guild, 1933), 18. Marshall's outdoor adventures are described in his book, *Alaska Wilderness*, 2d ed. (Berkeley: Univ. of California, 1970). For a biographical account see James M. Glover, *A Wilderness Original: The Life of Bob Marshall* (Seattle: Mountaineers, 1986).

17. Marshall, *Arctic Village*, 132–37; Marshall, *Doonerak or Bust: A Letter to Friends about an Arctic Vacation* (n.p., 1938), 3.

18. Glover, *A Wilderness Original*, 172–82. See also Roderick Nash, *Wilderness and the American Mind*, 3d ed. (New Haven: Yale Univ. Press, 1982), 200–208.

19. Robert Marshall, "Comments on the Report on Alaska's Recreational Resources and Facilities," *Alaska—Its Resources and Development*, House Document 485, 75th Congress, 3d sess. (Washington: Government Printing Office, 1938), 213.

20. Claus-M. Naske and Herman Slotnik, *Alaska: A History of the 49th State*, 2d ed. (Norman: Univ. of Oklahoma Press, 1987), 126–27, 133–35. On the highway see the scholarly collection edited by Kenneth Coates, *The Alaska Highway: Papers of the 40th Anniversary Symposium* (Vancouver: Univ. of British Columbia Press, 1985); a contemporary, more superficial account of the project is Don Menzies, *The Alaska Highway: A Saga of the North* (Edmonton: Stuart Douglas, 1943).

21. McPhee, *Coming into the Country* (New York: Farrar, Straus and Giroux, 1977), 130.

22. One of state's leading environmentalists, and a former state wildlife official, Robert Weeden, has written about these threats in *Alaska, Promises to Keep* (Boston: Houghton Mifflin, 1978).

23. H. R. Harriman, "Alaska's Fuel Resources," *Report of Proceedings of American Mining Congress, 12th Annual Session*, Goldfield, Nevada, Sept. 27–Oct. 2, 1909 (Denver: American Mining Congress, 1909), 273–82; William Thornton Prosser, "Oil First in Solving Alaska's Fuel Problem," *Alaska-Yukon Magazine* 11 (April 1911): 3–8.

24. Kristina O'Connor, "Historic and Projected Demand for Oil and Gas in Alaska: 1972–1995," Energy Report 3-77, Department of Natural Resources, Division of Minerals and Energy Management (Juneau: State of Alaska, 1977), 4.

25. The borough study is summarized in Neil Davis, *Energy/Alaska* (Fairbanks: Univ. of Alaska Press, 1984), 12–23. According to this author, Alaskans, representing such a small portion of the American population, consumed only one-quarter of one percent of the national energy total. The per capita rate in Alaska was the equivalent of nearly one hundred barrels of oil apiece, and transportation accounted for 43% of that total (pp. 19, 23).

26. The most dismal side of modern-day Barrow is portrayed in Joe McGinniss, *Going to Extremes* (New York: Alfred A. Knopf, 1980), chap. 6.

27. For a penetrating analysis of the modern cash invasion of the native peoples living in Canada's Mackenzie Valley, see Hugh Brody, "Industrial Impact in the Canadian North," *Polar Record* 18 (1977): 333–39.

28. Jacobson and Wentworth, *Kaktovik Subsistence*, 26, 30. Norman Chance, *The Inupiat and Arctic Alaska: An Ethnography of Development* (Fort Worth: Holt, Rinehart, and Winston, 1990), 217. Also, Samuel Z. Klausner and Edward F. Foulks, *Eskimo Capitalists: Oil, Politics, and Alcohol* (Totowa, N.J.: Allanheld, Osman, 1982).

29. The most thorough account of the episode is James Penick, Jr., *Progressive Politics and Conservation: The Ballinger-Pinchot Affair* (Chicago: Univ. of Chicago Press, 1968), which tends to blame it on Pinchot's "bid to perpetuate the system of the previous administration"—with himself as the architect of domestic conservation policy. I find that interpretation a little too cynical and unsympathetic. Other useful studies are Alpheus Thomas Mason, *Bureaucracy Convicts Itself: The Ballinger-Pinchot Controversy of 1910* (New York: Viking, 1941); and Herman Slotnick, "The Ballinger-Pinchot Affair in Alaska," *Journal of*

the West 10 (April 1971): 337–47. Distinctly unhelpful is Harold C. Ickes, *Not Guilty: An Official Inquiry into the Charges Made by Glavis and Pinchot against Richard A. Ballinger, Secretary of the Interior, 1909–1911* (Washington: Government Printing Office, 1940).

30. A leading scholar of Pinchot and his followers, Samuel Hays, offers a different interpretation: their key concern, he maintains, was not resource ownership but resource use. See his *Conservation and the Gospel of Efficiency: The Progressive Conservation Movement, 1890–1920* (Cambridge, Mass.: Harvard Univ. Press, 1959), 262. I am compelled to disagree; while not rigid advocates of state ownership, and pragmatically aware of the limits of their ideals, the conservationists were definitely intent on expanding public ownership as the only sure guarantor of use.

31. Taft quoted in Pinchot, *Breaking New Ground*, 431.

32. Gifford Pinchot, *The Fight for Conservation* (1910; Seattle: Univ. of Washington Press, 1967), 6–8. Thorstein Veblen, *The Engineers and the Price System* (New York: Viking, 1921), 44.

33. Gifford Pinchot, "Who Shall Own Alaska?," *Saturday Evening Post* 184 (16 Dec. 1911): 3–4, 50–52.

34. Carl J. Mayer and George A. Riley, *Public Domain, Private Dominion* (San Francisco: Sierra Club Books, 1985), chap. 5; John Ise, *U.S. Oil Policy* (New Haven: Yale Univ. Press, 1926); Clark, *Energy and the Federal Government*, 154–55.

35. Burl Noggle, *Teapot Dome: Oil and Politics in the 1920s* (New York: Norton, 1962).

36. They drilled dozens of holes, the deepest down to 11,800 feet, and came up with estimates of up to 100 million barrels of recoverable deposits. Naske and Slotnick, *Alaska*, 243–46. K. L. VonderAhe, "The Petroleum Industry in Alaska," in *Mineral and Water Resources of Alaska*, U.S. Geological Survey, Report for Senate Committee on Interior and Insular Affairs, 88th Congress, 2d sess. (Washington: Government Printing Office, 1964), 19–25, provides a detailed summary of oil activity in the 1950s and early 1960s.

37. The Kenai leasing story has finally been told by David Postman in an eight-part series, "Inside Deal: The Untold Story of Oil in Alaska," *Anchorage Daily News*, 4–11 Feb. 1990.

38. Richard A. Cooley, *Alaska: A Challenge in Conservation* (Madison: Univ. of Wisconsin Press, 1967), chap. 2. On native response to the oil prospects see Mary Clay Berry, *The Alaska Pipeline: The Politics of Oil and Native Land Claims* (Bloomington: Indiana Univ. Press, 1975).

39. William D. Smith, "68 Sourdoughs Find Bonanza in Alaska Oil," *New York Times*, 28 July 1968. Ed Fortier, "The Driller's Mask Froze to His Face," *National Observer*, 12 Aug. 1968. See also Charles S. Jones, *From the Rio Grande to the Arctic: The Story of the Richfield Oil Corporation* (Norman: Univ. of Oklahoma Press, 1972), chap. 47. A British scholar, Peter Coates, has published *The Trans-Alaska Pipeline Controversy: Technology, Conservation, and the Frontier* (Bethlehem, Penn.: Lehigh Univ. Press, 1991), which I read in draft form.

40. The first estimates of recoverable reserves ran between five and ten billion barrels, then eventually rose to twelve to fifteen barrels. British Petroleum ended up with slightly over a 50% equity interest in the field, ARCO about 20%.

41. DeGolyer and MacNaughton, *Twentieth Century Petroleum Statistics* (Dallas: DeGolyer and MacNaughton, 1988), 63.

42. Joseph L. Fisher, "Alaska Oil in Historical Perspective," in *Change in Alaska: People, Petroleum, and Politics*, George W. Rogers, ed. (Seattle: Univ. of Alaska Press/Univ. of Washington Press, 1970), 21.

43. The companies projected a clear profit of $12 to 15 billion from a $1.8 billion investment, including leases, drilling, and pipeline costs. Arthur M. Louis, "The Escalating War for Alaskan Oil," *Fortune* (June 1972): 81.

44. The tax breaks went back a long way before Nixon. During the Kennedy and Johnson presidencies, for example, ARCO had paid not a single penny in federal income tax, though it had earned a net income of about $800 million.

45. Roger Revelle, Edward Wenk, Bostwick H. Ketchum, and Edward R. Corino, "Oceanic Oil Pollution," in *Man's Impact on Terrestrial and Oceanic Systems*, W. H. Matthews et al., eds. (Cambridge, Mass.: Massachusetts Institute of Technology, 1971), 297–318. Noel Mostert, *Supership* (New York: Alfred Knopf, 1974), 15–42; Wesley Marx, *Oilspill* (San Francisco: Sierra Club Books, 1971).

46. See Ruckelshaus's letter appended to the final draft, vol. 6, pp. A41–44. For the Corps' critique see the *Congressional Record*, 117 (10 March 1971), E1683–86. Congressman Les Aspin charged that the Pentagon had tried to suppress this embarrassing critique.

47. Senator Edmund S. Muskie opposed the pipeline, warning of "grave environmental damage to the lands the pipeline would traverse, the fishing resources of Prince William Sound and the waters of the Northern Pacific on which the oil would inevitably spill." *Congressional Record*, 117 (21 April 1971), 11307–9. See also Richard W. Schoepf, *The Trans-Alaska Pipeline and the Environment: A Bibliography* (Washington: Department of Interior, 1974).

48. Department of Interior, *Environmental Impact Statement: Proposed Trans-Alaska Pipeline* (Springfield, Va: National Technical Information Service, 1972), vol. I, pp. 159–62, 170–75; vol. IV, pp. 621–37.

49. *Congressional Record*, 117 (17 Dec. 1971), E13863–69.

50. This case, *Wilderness Society, et al. v. Secretary Morton, et al.,* was decided by the U.S. Circuit Court of Appeals for the District of Columbia on 9 February 1973, about eight months after Morton's decision to grant the right-of-way.

51. Edgar Wayburn, "A Conservationist's Concern about Arctic Development," in Rogers, *Change in Alaska*, 173, 177–78. Other representative expressions of environmental concern were George Laycock, "Kiss the North Slope Good-by," *Audubon* 72 (Sept. 1970): 68; and Harvey Manning, *Cry Crisis: Rehearsal in Alaska* (San Francisco: Friends of the Earth, 1974).

52. Senate Report No. 93-207, *United States Code Congressional and Administrative News*, 93rd Congress, 1st session, 1973, vol. 2 (St. Paul: West Publishing, 1974), 2427.

53. *New York Times*, 21 Sept. 1976, p. 1. As it turned out, Sohio built instead a pipeline across Panama, as the governor of California opposed the added hydrocarbon pollution that transshipping oil in Los Angeles would cause. See also Batelle Memorial Institute, *The West Coast Petroleum Supply and Demand System* (Richland, Wash.: Batelle Pacific Northwest Laboratories, 1978).

54. Charles J. Cichetti, *Alaskan Oil: Alternative Routes and Markets* (Baltimore: Resources for the Future/Johns Hopkins Univ. Press, 1972), chap. 6.

55. A. R. Thompson, "Policy Choices in Petroleum Leasing Legislation: Canada-Alaska Comparisons," in Rogers, *Change in Alaska*, 72–78.

56. *House of Commons Debates*, vol. 115, no. 95, 3rd session, 28th Parliament, 12 March 1971, pp. 4212, 4218–19.

57. Luther J. Carter, "Alaska Pipeline: Congress Deaf to Environmentalists," *Science* 181 (27 July 1973): 326. Walter Mondale, statement in *Rights-of-Way Across Federal Lands: Transportation of Alaska's North Slope Oil,* Hearings before the Committee on Interior and Insular Affairs, U.S. Senate, 93rd Congress, 1st sess. (Washington: Government Printing Office, 1973), Part V, pp. 33–34.

58. DeGolyer and MacNaughton, *Twentieth Century Petroleum Statistics*, 58–59.

59. Thomas R. Berger, *Northern Frontier, Northern Homeland: The Report of the Mackenzie Valley Pipeline Inquiry* (Ottawa: Minister of Supply and Services Canada, 1977), vol. I, pp. vii–xxvii. See also John Livingston, *Arctic Oil* (Toronto: Canadian Broadcasting Corporation, 1981).

60. R. C. Wilson to Governor William A. Egan, 20 March 1972, Alaska State Archives, Record Group 01, Series 81, Loc. no. 4942.

61. When the oil started flowing, the state raked in billions in royalties, enough to abol-

ish the state income tax and grant every resident of six months or more a personal check of $800 to $1000. By the 1980s over 85% of the state budget came from oil revenues.

62. State Senator Chancy Croft, "Five Billion Dollars, More or Less," talk to 23rd Science Congress, College, Alaska, 17 Aug. 1972, Alaska State Archives, RG 401, Box 1415, Croft Files, 1971–76; John E. Havelock, remarks to Joint Hearing of Senate Commerce Committee and House State Affairs Committee, 10 March 1972, Alaska State Archives, Joint Pipeline Committee Records, 1971–72, Administrative File P-2, Box 4. Most state studies of the pipeline impact were enthusiastic, and focused exclusively on the economic benefits it would bring in the way of jobs and revenues. See, for example, Arlon R. Tussig, George W. Rogers, and Victor Fischer, *Alaska Pipeline Report* (Fairbanks: Institute of Social, Economic, and Government Research, Univ. of Alaska, 1971), chap. 4. For an overview of the debate within the state see John S. Dryzek, *Conflict and Choice in Resource Management: The Case of Alaska* (Boulder, Colo.: Westview Press, 1983).

63. For a discussion of this aborted effort see Joe La Rocca, "Will State's New Oil Laws Delay Pipeline?," *Alaska Journalism Review* 1 (Dec. 1972–Jan. 1973), 1–9.

64. As Robert Engler has noted, "Wherever the [oil] industry has functioned, its concentrated economic power—the most massive of any industry in the world—has been forged into political power over the community. Law, the public bureaucracies, the political machinery, foreign policy, and public opinion have been harnessed for the private privileges and the immunity from public accountability of the international brotherhood of oil merchants. Formidable perimeters of defense manned by public relations specialists, lawyers, lobbyists, and obsequious politicians and editors keep the spotlight away from the penetrating powers of oil. Instead the focus is placed on the mystique of petroleum technology, corporate benevolence, and the possibility for an amenable public to be cut in on 'something for nothing.'" In Rogers, *Change in Alaska*, 14. See also Engler, *The Politics of Oil: A Study of Private Power and Democratic Decisions* (Chicago: Univ. of Chicago Press, 1961). For another critical view see John Hanrahan and Peter Gruenstein, *Lost Frontier: The Marketing of Alaska* (New York: W. W. Norton, 1977).

65. Technically, the key vote was on a motion to table a motion to reconsider the Jackson bill. See the *Congressional Record,* 119 (17 July 1973), pp. 24316–17.

66. Stan Cohen, *The Great Alaska Pipeline* (Missoula: Pictorial Histories Publishing, 1988), is an admiring, heroicizing account of the construction phase. A somewhat better account is James P. Roscow, *800 Miles to Valdez: The Building of the Alaska Pipeline* (Englewood Cliffs, N.J.: Prentice-Hall, 1977).

67. Alaska's oil revenues peaked much earlier, in 1979, and were in decline by 1981, as the price of oil began to go down from its high point of the OPEC oil-price revolution of the 1970s. According to Arlon Tussig, without that fortuitous revolution, Prudhoe Bay oil would have been nearly worthless. See Tussig, "Alaska's Petroleum-Based Economy," *Alaskan Resources Development: Issues of the 1980s*, Thomas A. Morehouse, ed. (Boulder: Westview Press, 1984), 58–59. But the 1990s saw another spurt upward, due to Middle East politics, one that might bring a temporary upturn in state revenues. But for the long term Prudhoe Bay must offer a rapidly diminishing source of financial hope.

68. Stewart L. Udall, *The Quiet Crisis* (New York: Avon Books, 1963), 193–94. See also T. H. Watkins, *Vanishing Arctic: Alaska's National Wildlife Refuge* (New York: Aperture/ Wilderness Society, 1988), 65–80. Dianne Dumanoski, "The Last Great American Wilderness," *Boston Globe Magazine* (9 July 1989): 16, 39–48, 56–57. ARCO Alaska, "On Top of ANWR," pamphlet, August 1989.

69. Studies of these problems include: Lisa Speer and Sue Libenson, *Oil in the Arctic: The Environmental Record of Oil Development on Alaska's North Slope* (Washington: Natural Resources Defense Council, 1988); Edmund Schofield and Wayne L. Hamilton, "Probable Damage to Tundra Biota through Sulphur Dioxide Destruction of Lichens," *Biological Conservation* 2 (July 1970): 278–80; Ecosystems Impacts Resource Group, National Research Council, *Energy and the Fate of Ecosystems,* Supporting Paper No. 8 (Washing-

ton: National Academy Press, 1980). For a more general assessment of the ecological threat see F. R. Englehardt, ed., *Petroleum Effects in the Arctic Environment* (London: Elsevier Applied Sciences, 1985).

70. The most comprehensive account of the spill is Art Davison, *In the Wake of the Exxon Valdez: The Devastating Impact of the Alaska Oil Spill* (San Francisco: Sierra Club Books, 1990). I have drawn on Davison's work for many details, along with state and national newspapers, and the impressive document, *Spill: The Wreck of the Exxon Valdez: Final Report of the Alaska Oil Spill Commission* (Juneau: State of Alaska, 1990), in five volumes. See also Page Spencer, *White Silk & Black Tar: A Journal of the Alaska Oil Spill* (Minneapolis: Bergamot Books, 1990), and Brian O'Donohue, *Black Tides: The Alaska Oil Spill* (Anchorage: Alaska Natural History Association, 1989).

71. Though the largest spill in American experience, this was not the largest in the world. The tanker *Amoco Cadiz* dumped 68 million gallons on the coast of Brittany in 1978, and the offshore well Ixtoc I in the Gulf of Mexico, when it blew out the following year, spewed out 140 million gallons of crude.

72. "Captain of Tanker Had Been Drinking, Blood Tests Show," *New York Times*, 31 March 1989.

73. "How the Oil Spilled and Spread: Delay and Confusion Off Alaska," *New York Times*, 16 April 1989.

74. Exxon tried to blame its failures on the government's slowness to allow the use of dispersants, and that charge has Davison's qualified support; he suggests that the environmental damage done might have been lessened by anywhere from 9 to 50% had dispersants been available and had they been used immediately. Davison, p. 123.

75. *The Economist*, 19 May 1990, p. 100. For the effects on wildlife see Malcolm W. Browne, "In Once-Pristine Sound, Wildlife Reels under Oil's Impact," *New York Times*, 4 April 1989; *ibid.*, 9 April; *ibid.*, 25 April. See also Jenifer M. Baker, Robert B. Clark, and Paul F. Kingston, "Environmental Recovery in Prince William Sound and the Gulf of Alaska," Institute of Offshore Engineering, Heriot-Watt University, Edinburgh, Scotland, June 1990.

76. *Spill: The Wreck of the Exxon Valdez: Implications for Safe Marine Transportation*, Report of the Alaska Oil Spill Commission, Executive Summary, January 1990, foreword.

77. Elihu Palmer, *Principles of Nature* (1801), quoted in *American Ideas*, Gerald N. Grob and Robert N. Beck, eds. (Glencoe, Ill.: Free Press, 1963), vol. I, p. 140.

78. Both the Alaska Oil Spill Commission and the National Transportation Safety Board made this point, and Congress seemed, in 1990, ready to require double hulls in the future. For debate on this matter see the *New York Times*, 15 May 1989.

10. Grounds for Identity

1. The concept owes much to political economist Harold Innis. See, for example, his *The Fur Trade in Canada: An Introduction to Canadian Economic History* (New Haven, Conn.: Yale Univ. Press, 1930); and *The Cod Fisheries: The History of an International Economy* (New Haven, Conn.: Yale Univ. Press, 1946). A good recent introduction is L. D. McCann, "Heartland and Hinterland: A Framework for Regional Analysis," in *Heartland and Hinterland: A Geography of Canada*, L. D. McCann, ed. (Scarborough, Ontario: Prentice-Hall Canada, 1982), 2–35. See also J. M. S. Careless, "Frontierism, Metropolitanism, and Canadian History," *Canadian Historical Review* 33 (March 1954); 1–21.

2. Robin Fisher, "Duff and George Go West: A Tale of Two Frontiers," *Canadian Historical Review* 68 (Dec. 1987): 501–28; David H. Breen, "The Turner Thesis and the Canadian West: A Closer Look at the Ranching Frontier," in *Essays on Western History*, Lewis H. Thomas, ed. (Edmonton: Univ. of Alberta Press, 1976); Doug Owram, *Promise of Eden: The Canadian Expansionist Movement and the Idea of the West, 1856–1900* (Toronto: Univ. of Toronto Press, 1980).

3. J. S. Holliday, *The World Rushed In: The California Gold Rush Experience* (New York: Simon and Schuster, 1981), 167.

4. G. M. Tobin, "Landscape, Region, and the Writing of History: Walter Prescott Webb in the 1920s," *American Studies International* 16 (Summer 1978): 10.

5. I have made this point in terms of federal development of water resources in my book, *Rivers of Empire: Water, Aridity, and the Growth of the American West* (New York: Pantheon, 1985). Gerald D. Nash argues that it was military investment during World War II that was decisive; see his *The American West Transformed: The Impact of the Second World War* (Bloomington: Indiana Univ. Press, 1985), chap. 2.

6. William Robbins, "The 'Plundered Province' Thesis and the Recent Historiography of the American West," *Pacific Historical Review* 55 (Nov. 1986): 577–98.

7. See Chapter 2.

8. Patricia Nelson Limerick, *The Legacy of Conquest: The Unbroken Past of the American West* (New York: W. W. Norton, 1987), 35–36.

9. Henry Nash Smith, *Virgin Land: The American West as Symbol and Myth* (Cambridge, Mass.: Harvard Univ. Press, 1950).

10. Louis Hartz, *The Liberal Tradition in America* (New York: Harcourt, Brace & World, 1955), esp. chaps. 1 and 8. The latter chapter describes the evolution of liberal thought during the post–Civil War years, when the main influx of settlers came to the West and began to form its institutions and define its cultural norms.

11. John McPhee, *Rising from the Plains* (New York: Farrar, Straus, Giroux, 1986), 104.

12. Wallace Stegner, "Coda: Wilderness Letter," in *The Sound of Mountain Water* (Lincoln: Univ. of Nebraska Press, 1980), 147–48.

11. A Country Without Secrets

1. Bill McKibben, *The End of Nature* (New York: Random House, 1989), 58.

2. Francis Fukuyama, "The End of History," *The National Interest*, no. 16 (Summer 1989): 3–18.

3. Willa Cather, "Nebraska: The End of the First Cycle," *The Nation* 117 (5 Sept. 1923): 238.

4. The story of the national grasslands can be found in R. Douglas Hurt, "The National Grasslands: Origin and Development in the Dust Bowl," *Agricultural History* 59 (April 1985): 246–59; "National Grasslands Established," *Journal of Forestry* 58 (Aug. 1960): 679; and H. H. Wooten, *The Land Utilization Program, 1934 to 1964*, U.S. Department of Agriculture, Agricultural Economic Report No. 85 (Washington: Government Printing Office, n.d.).

5. Frederick Jackson Turner, "The Significance of the Frontier in American History," *Frontier and Section: Selected Essays of FJT* (Englewood Cliffs: Prentice-Hall, 1961), 39.

6. McKibben, *The End of Nature*, 64.

7. Jerrold E. Levy, "Ecology of the South Plains," *Patterns of Land Utilization and Other Papers: Symposium*, Viola E. Garfield, ed., Proceedings of the American Ethnological Society (Seattle: Univ. of Washington Press, 1961), 18–23. Levy calculates that, from at least 1836 to the reservation period, there were 1800 Kiowa and Kiowa-Apaches, 3500 Cheyennes, and 2500 Arapahoes, along with smaller numbers of Comanches, Wichitas, and Tonkawas. He adds: "Even using the minimum buffalo population, the maximum human population, the maximum consumption, and assuming the most wasteful butchering techniques, and the slaughter of females exclusively, the effect upon the herds was probably minimal" (p. 22). However, recent historians and anthropologists have argued that we have much understated the devastating impact of European diseases on North America's aboriginal populations, and if so, that fact might cause us to revise Levy's numbers upwards for the pre-1836 populations.

8. Kansas Water Office, *Ogallala Aquifer Study in Kansas: Summary* (Topeka: Kansas Water Office, 1982), 3.

9. Rowland C. Robinson, "New England Fences," *Scribner's Monthly* (Feb. 1880): 502-11.

10. Walter Prescott Webb, *The Great Plains* (Boston: Ginn and Company, 1931), 317.

11. Henry D. and Frances T. McCallum, *The Wire That Fenced the West* (Norman: Univ. of Oklahoma Press, 1965), chap. 19.

12. Wallace Stegner, *The American West as Living Space* (Ann Arbor: Univ. of Michigan Press, 1987), 25.

Index